BEER
AND
CIRCUS

MURRAY SPERBER

BEER

AND

CIRCUS

★ HOW BIG-TIME

COLLEGE SPORTS

IS CRIPPLING

UNDERGRADUATE

EDUCATION

HENRY HOLT AND COMPANY ★ NEW YORK

Henry Holt and Company, LLC
Publishers since 1866
115 West 18th Street
New York, New York 10011

Henry Holt® is a registered trademark
of Henry Holt and Company, LLC.
Published in Canada by Fitzhenry & Whiteside Ltd.,
195 Allstate Parkway, Markham, Ontario L3R 4T8.

Library of Congress Cataloging-in-Publication Data

Sperber, Murray.
    Beer and Circus : how big-time college sports is crippling
undergraduate education / by Murray Sperber.—1st ed.
    p.   cm.
    Includes bibliographical references and index.
    ISBN 0-8050-3864-7 (hb)
    1. College sports—United States—History. 2. College sports—
Economic aspects—United States. 3. College sports—Moral and
ethical aspects—United States. 4. Universities and
colleges—United States—Administration. I. Title.

GV351.S63   2000
796.04'3'0973—dc21

                                                              00-037021

Henry Holt books are available for special promotions
and premiums. For details contact: Director, Special Markets.

First Edition 2000

Designed by Victoria Hartman

Printed in the United States of America

10   9   8   7   6   5   4   3   2   1

For my mother,

GLADYS EPSTEIN SPERBER,

1912–1976,

who introduced me to reading and writing

and, most important, critical thought

CONTENTS

PREFACE

College students constitute the most neglected, least understood element of the American academic community. . . . Understanding [them] requires something of a gigantic effort if we are to overcome the unrecognized bias of American academic tradition. That tradition acknowledges the rise and fall of [college] presidents, professors, courses of study, and endowments. As for students, however, they flow rather aimlessly in and out of our picture.

—Frederick Rudolph, preeminent historian of
American higher education

Rudolph's comments, though totally relevant today, were written over thirty years ago in an essay on the history of student life. During the 1990s, as the controversies on "political correctness" and "multicultural curriculum" swirled about, and I mainly faced a rising tide of undergraduate illiteracy in college English courses, I often remembered Rudolph's call to study student life. The 1990s controversies, so prominent in the national media, seemed irrelevant to the writing and reading problems of my students at Indiana University, Bloomington, and to the undergraduates whom I encountered at similar institutions.

Allan Bloom denounced the educational trend he termed *The Closing of the American Mind,* but he taught at the University of Chicago and did not know the legions of undergraduates whose minds had never opened. Dinesh D'Souza condemned what he considered *Illiberal Education* at Ivy League schools, but he never asked a classroom of state university students for a definition of liberalism, then waited as only one or two hands hesitantly raised. Those authors, as well as the multitude of other writers decrying the state of American higher education, follow the tradition depicted by Frederick Rudolph: they place the presidents, the faculty, or the courses at the center of American universities and colleges, and they consign student life to the periphery. Most of all, the critics fight the curriculum wars, and they ignore the undergraduate cultures outside the classroom—where the vast majority of students spend most of their time and energies, mainly oblivious to the curriculum.

Because the critics described a university so contrary to what I have experienced in my years in American higher education, I decided to study undergraduate life. Having spent all of my student and faculty career at large public universities, I also worried about what I perceived as the decline of undergraduate education at these schools. My undergraduate experiences at Purdue University in the late 1950s and early 1960s had transformed me, convincing me to pursue an academic career. When, after graduate school at the University of California, Berkeley, I returned to the state of Indiana as a faculty member at Indiana University, Bloomington, I faced undergraduates from the teacher's side of the classroom, and I continue to do so after almost three decades at IU. In surveying my academic journey, I am struck by the fact that, as a first-year student at Purdue, I took freshmen English in a class of fifteen students, taught by a full faculty member; whereas at Indiana, I now teach freshmen English in classes of 150 students each, and I cannot begin to help students acquire the reading and writing skills offered to me and my Purdue classmates. (Both Purdue and Indiana are typical, large public universities, very representative of similar institutions across the country.)

At Purdue and most other schools in the 1950s and 1960s, honors programs for undergraduates did not exist. Universities treated all students equally, and full faculty members conducted most classes. Many undergraduates ignored these educational opportunities, but they were available to every student who wanted them. However, in doing the research for this book, I discovered that the rise of honors programs at many schools in the 1980s and 1990s frequently signaled the abandonment of general undergraduate education at these institutions, the closing of opportunities for the vast majority of students.

The 1999 *U.S. News & World Report* college issue described "an honors education" at large state schools, contrasting the small honors classes "taught by professors rather than by teaching assistants—in many instances, by the most accomplished [faculty] on campus," versus the huge lecture halls and the indifferent instruction supplied to most undergraduates at these schools. For example, "honors freshman at [the University of] Maryland take Math 141-H, a calculus course taught in classes of about 20 students" as opposed to the "non-honors version, Math-141, taught to a few hundred students at a time," often by teaching assistants from foreign countries, with shaky command of English. A late-1990s report funded by the Carnegie Foundation summed up the situation: The ordinary "baccalaureate students who are not in the running for any kind of [honors] distinction may get little or no attention" from the school.

At many of these universities, administrators as well as students proclaim: "You get out of this place whatever you put into it"; in other words, those nonhonors students who work very hard, who aggressively find good teachers and courses, can obtain a decent education here; on the other hand, those undergraduates who "go along with the flow" will not learn very much, if anything, at this institution.

This argument reminds me of scenes in the old Disney wildlife movie *Happy Valley*, which showed salmon returning to their annual spawning grounds, hurling themselves against waterfalls to reach the calm headwaters of the mountain streams high above. Only a small number of salmon succeeded. Similarly, at most large public universities today, some determined and hardworking nonhonors students manage to obtain good educations, reaching the pools of high-level literacy and numeracy. But often these students achieve this goal despite their university and the flow against them.

Within this context, honors programs and colleges are small hatcheries, set apart from general undergraduate education. A nationally published college guidebook notes, for example, that the honors program at the University of New Mexico "offers special seminars that emphasize reading, discussion, and writing," whereas regular undergraduate education at UNM often consists of "monster [sized] courses" where, by definition, because of the lack of contact with a teacher, students cannot easily improve such basic skills as writing and reading. UNM students "complain about class sizes, which can be as big as five hundred students in introductory courses," but they are quickly distracted by their beloved "Howling Lobos," the school's college sports teams. The guidebook also indicates that the party scene at UNM is excellent.

The University of New Mexico is merely one of a legion of schools in this situation. Considering the democratic ideals in the charters of public universities, the commitments of these institutions to the taxpayers of their states, as well as the large amount of money that they take from students and their families, it is unconscionable that these universities place the vast majority of their undergraduates in a kind of Darwinian wild where only a minority thrive.

★   ★   ★

We certainly can't give our students a quality degree—not with class size growing geometrically and our 30-to-1 faculty/student ratio—but at least we can encourage students to have fun, and root for our teams while they're here. . . .

Football Saturdays are great here and so are winter basketball nights. In our Admissions Office literature, we've stopped saying that we provide a good education—our lawyers warned us that we could get sued for misrepresentation—but we sure promote our college sports teams.

—An administrator at a Sunbelt university

This school is a *Big-time U: a large public research university with high-profile football and/or men's basketball teams playing at the highest NCAA levels.* This institution is typical of many universities that have stopped trying to give their students a meaningful undergraduate education, but, because student tuition dollars are a major and dependable source of income, they attempt to provide their students with something in return for their money. An Admissions Office brochure for this Big-time U noted that students receive "a wonderful lifestyle experience here"—the text accompanied by photos of student fans cheering at football and basketball games. A junior at this university phrased it more succinctly: "This place is a four-year party—one long tailgater—with an $18,000 annual cover charge."

Few critics of higher education examine undergraduate student life, and none consider the impact of big-time college sports upon undergraduates. Because, for many years, I have studied and written about intercollegiate athletics, its history and its current problems, I have long wondered about its relationship to student life and undergraduate education—after all, intercollegiate athletics originated in nineteenth-century student life, and undergraduates have always been among its most ardent supporters. In the mid 1990s, I set out to research this topic, mainly through questionnaires and interviews at various schools, primarily but not exclusively those sponsoring big-time college sports programs. (In 1998, I also placed my questionnaire on the World Wide Web.)

The results of over nineteen hundred survey responses and almost one hundred interviews revealed a powerful synergy between big-time college sports and contemporary student life. I concluded that many universities, because of their emphasis on their research and graduate programs, and because of their inability to provide quality undergraduate education to most of their students, spend increasing amounts of money on their athletic departments, and use big-time college sports—commercial entertainment around which many undergraduates organize their hyperactive social lives—to keep their students happy and distracted and the tuition dollars rolling in. University administrators deny that they employ this strategy, but their denials do not change the reality: at many Big-time U's, *beer-and-circus—the party scene connected to big-time college sports events*—replaces meaningful undergraduate education. Many students enjoy and willingly participate in beer-and-circus, but their assent does not alleviate the problem; indeed, it compounds it, making solutions more difficult.

In this book, I explain the origins of beer-and-circus, its current manifestations, particularly the epidemic of student binge drinking, and I offer a plan to remedy it. However, it is essential to place beer-and-circus within the context of contemporary American society, and to inquire into the social costs of the neglect of general undergraduate education.

★   ★   ★

An entire academic field—outcomes and assessments—attempts to measure student learning at various educational levels. Some of the findings for college graduates are astounding, and depressing:

> In the area of qualitative skills, 56.3 percent of American-born four-year college graduates are unable consistently to perform simple tasks, such as calculating the change from $3 after buying a 60-cent bowl of soup and a $1.95 sandwich. Tasks such as these should not be insuperable for people [with college degrees].
> —From *An American Imperative:*
> *Higher Expectations for Higher Education*
> by the Wingspread Group

The National Adult Literacy Survey (NALS) administered face-to-face interviews with over twenty-six thousand Americans, and discovered such items as the high percentage of college graduates who could not compute a simple amount of change, as well as an even higher percentage who could not read and understand a simple set of directions.

When the U.S. Department of Education examined the transcripts of thousands of college graduates, the majority from public universities, including many big-time college sports schools, it discovered one reason for the low level of numeracy and literacy. Almost 40 percent of these grads had no college credits in English or American literature; almost 31 percent had never taken a college course in mathematics; 26 percent had no courses in history or political science; and 58 percent had no university exposure to a foreign language.

Other exit surveys and tests of graduates produce similar results—low literacy and numeracy rates. The main conclusion is that many colleges and universities, rather than acknowledge their failure to educate a majority of their undergraduates, pass them through to meaningless degrees. At one level, this is consumer fraud; at another, because state and federal money is involved, it is a public scandal.

Apparently some students have a mordant sense of humor about their lack of education. In the rest rooms of bars near some Big-time U's, above toilet paper dispensers, graffiti often proclaims, "BACHELOR DEGREES FROM THIS SCHOOL: TAKE ONE."

The problems in American undergraduate education transcend big-time college sports; in fact, they go beyond colleges and universities to the country's secondary school system and its failure to prepare large numbers of its graduates for higher education. The solutions to this dilemma are not simple. However, rather than write another diatribe about "the whole mess," I prefer to focus on an overlooked and important aspect of the problem: the connections between beer-and-circus at Big-time U's and the neglect of general undergraduate education at these schools. Considering that these universities contain almost 40 percent of all undergraduates in America, I do not believe that I have overly narrowed the scope of this book. In addition, because many schools wish to join the big-time college sports ranks, the problems discussed here are not shrinking but growing.

★   ★   ★

A Note on the Term Beer-and-Circus

In ancient Rome, the poet Juvenal used the phrase *bread and circuses* to describe the political strategy of a number of corrupt Roman emperors. To keep the populace happy and to distract them from foreign and domestic policy failures, these emperors provided cheap daily bread and frequent circuses—mainly gladiatorial contests and other riveting games. According to Juvenal, the strategy worked: because of the bread and circuses, the people showed no interest in politics.

During the twentieth century, many writers called big-time college sports a "circus," and, ten years ago, I began the preface of my book *College*

Sports Inc.: The Athletic Department vs. the University with a quote from A. Bartlett Giammetti, former president of Yale University and former commissioner of major league baseball: "What was allowed to become a circus—college sports—threatens to become the means by which the public believes the entire enterprise [higher education] is a sideshow."

In 1991, on a fall football weekend, while driving past a student apartment complex next to Indiana University's stadium, and seeing crowds of undergraduates gathered around beer kegs on lawns, I thought of the term *beer-and-circus*. Since that time, I have not found a better phrase to describe the party scene connected to big-time intercollegiate athletic events and its effect upon many undergraduates at large, public research universities.

★   ★   ★

A Note on the Questionnaire Used for This Book

Throughout the book, I discuss the results of a questionnaire that I devised to probe the impact of big-time college sports upon undergraduate students. The survey contained thirteen multiple-choice questions and four questions requesting written answers, as well as an open-ended P.S. section at the end ("If you wish to comment further on any aspect of intercollegiate athletics and student life prompted by this questionnaire, please place your comments below"). I am not a social scientist, and I make no claims about my quantitative results being "accurate to within three or four percentage points." In addition, because of the mixed nature of my polling method—I distributed the questionnaire in undergraduate classes at various schools, in public places on many campuses, and I put it on the World Wide Web—the results should be regarded as anecdotal, not scientific, evidence. When I handed out the questionnaire, I asked students not to put their names on it. When I put the survey on the web, I protected the anonymity of the respondents by using a public server (HoosierNet) that does not maintain log files; as a result, a completed form came to me with no identity codes and with no return address for the sender.

In tabulating the results, I found the written comments to be as valuable as the quantitative ones. Not only did students write comments in response to the questions requesting written answers, but often they put notes next to the multiple-choice questions, and they wrote, sometimes at length, in the open-ended P.S. section at the end of the survey. In the book, I quote extensively from these written comments, and I hope that the reader learns as much about contemporary college life from them as I did.

Of the 1,906 students who filled out the questionnaire, 1,071 were male and 835 were female. This does not reflect the gender ratio in American higher education: the imbalance occurred when many more males responded to the web survey than did females, probably because undergraduate men are more interested in college sports than are women. Of the total respondents, 1,312 attended NCAA Division I schools, and 581 were students at NCAA Division III institutions. These divisions constitute the standard separation between big-time intercollegiate athletics (almost all members of Division I give athletic scholarships), and low-pressure, low-profile college sports (no Division III school grants athletic scholarships). In addition, the number of respondents at Division II and NAIA (National Association of Intercollegiate Athletics) institutions was negligible (13), but because these schools give athletic scholarships, I placed these responses into the Division I group.

The poll does not account for the millions of students at junior colleges (JUCOs) throughout the country nor the large number of undergraduates at schools, particularly urban ones, that do not field intercollegiate athletic teams. However, because these institutions are so far from the world of the NCAA, I believe that including their students in the survey would distort the results. (JUCO colleges do provide athletes for NCAA schools, and this phenomenon is discussed on pages 236–41).

I undertook the survey, in part, because social scientists have done almost no polling on undergraduate attitudes about big-time college sports and its connection to the student party scene. In the end, I hope that my work prompts social scientists to undertake research on these topics, and to produce much larger and more authoritative surveys than mine on these issues crucial to the future of American higher education.

★   ★   ★

A Final Personal Note

In the introduction to this book and throughout the text, I discuss the various university subcultures, particularly the collegiate and academic ones. I also mention that individual students sometimes move from one subculture to another during their undergraduate years. In fact, I did this at Purdue University: I started within the collegiate subculture, even becoming president of my fraternity and vice president of the Inter-Fraternity Council, but, as a senior, thanks to a number of excellent professors, I became engaged in academics and went on to graduate school and university teaching.

My journey was somewhat unusual in two ways. Most faculty members spend their entire university careers in the academic subculture: as fresh-men, they gravitate to it, and they remain there for the rest of their under-graduate, graduate, and professorial years. Secondly, as a late-blooming academic, I was fortunate to attend a large public university like Purdue when it, and peer institutions, could accommodate me and similar students. The contemporary Big-time U is much less responsive to late bloomers than was its predecessor; moreover, after years in the hard terrain of huge lecture classes, it is difficult for a student to flourish academically.

I also believe that my undergraduate experience gives me a unique per-spective on, and empathy for, students within the collegiate subculture. Because most academics at Big-time U's have known only their own sub-culture, they have minimal interest in, and some antipathy for, the world in which a majority of their undergraduates live. As a result, they rarely study it and almost never write about it.

Personal reasons prompted me to write this book—both my experiences as an undergraduate and as a teacher of undergraduates—and I hope that the reader shares my anger about the current state of general education at large, public research universities, and agrees with my suggestions for re-form.

Ten years ago, a commentator wrote about my book *College Sports Inc.*: "This thorough investigation identifies the time bomb planted within Amer-ican higher education and offers a plan for defusing it." At the time, and for that book, I considered the statement somewhat exaggerated. However, I stand by it for *Beer and Circus: How Big-time College Sports Is Crippling Undergraduate Education.*

ACKNOWLEDGMENTS

Many people helped me with this book. Foremost were my friend and agent John Wright, and my sympathetic editors, David Sobel, and his assistant, Anne Geiger. John has helped me with every one of my college sports books, and his timely intervention during the writing of this one saved the entire project, turning a horse close to being scratched into one able to hold the rail and go the distance. Now that the book is completed, I look forward to spending many pleasant hours with John at the track, and accepting his advice on subjects other than writing. (Thanks also to Terry Golway for insisting that I listen to John.)

David Sobel inherited this book when its original editor left Henry Holt and Company. Not only did David treat this "orphaned" work as one of his own book "children," but he provided excellent advice throughout the project. He also remained calm when the author was much less so, and his reassuring e-mails and baritone presence on the telephone soothed very jangled nerves. In another life, he would make an outstanding athletic coach, able to size up his players and intuit what will produce the best effort from each.

Anne Geiger did a marvelous job of line editing the manuscript. She possesses the key quality of a superb line editor: rather than try to impose her ideas of style and argument on an author, she gets inside a writer's prose and subject, and offers astute suggestions on how to improve the manuscript. Considering that the subject of this book was far from her natural interests, her accomplishment was remarkable.

In addition, a word of thanks to Bill Strachan, former editor in chief at Henry Holt and Company, and now president of Columbia University

Press. He made possible my previous books on college sports, and also accepted this one for publication. He believed in the project from the first time he heard about it, and, as a former swimmer at Carleton College, he enlightened me about the world of Division III intercollegiate athletics.

I am also very grateful to the many persons whom I interviewed for this book. First on the list is the late Edward "Moose" Krause, longtime athletic director at the University of Notre Dame. I was fortunate to speak with Mr. Krause before his death, and I am pleased to use some of his comments in this text. (I must also thank my friend and fellow author John Kryk for sharing the transcripts of his interviews with Mr. Krause with me.)

More than one hundred other interviewees helped me with this project. Whether they spoke on or off the record, they were invariably generous with their time and observations. I was able to fit only a small fraction of their words and names into the final text, but they all greatly contributed to my knowledge of student life and college sports, and I thank them. I owe a special debt to the officials of Emory University, where I spent a week during April 1999: among others, President William M. Chace; lecturer in English JoAn Chace; Admissions Director Dan Walls; Athletic Director Chuck Gordon; and the sports editor of the student newspaper, Reid Epstein. Although, in the end, I used only a few of their statements in the text, they provided ample evidence that the Division III model is the best one for intercollegiate athletics, and they will see their point of view reflected in many comments in this work.

Similarly, I wish to thank a number of faculty and staff members of the University of Iowa for making my visits to that school so pleasant. At the top of the list are Steve Weiting, Judy Polumbaum, John Soloski, and Bonnie Slatton. Many other faculty and staff members of other institutions helped me with my work in many different ways, most notably: Aaron Baker at Arizona State University; Howard Bray of the Knight Center at the University of Maryland, College Park; Andy Geiger at Ohio State University; Lynette Carpenter at Ohio Wesleyan University; Alfredo Gonzalez at Hope College; Joe Ricapito at Louisiana State University; Joanne and Chris Eustis, formerly at Virginia Tech; Frank Cioffi at Central Washington University; Mike Oriard at Oregon State University; Hugo Witemeyer at the University of New Mexico; Tom Haskell at Rice University; Gerry Brookes at the University of Nebraska, Lincoln; Howard Schein at the University of Illinois, Champaign-Urbana; John Hess at Ithaca College; Ann Shapiro at Cornell University; Bill Fischer at the University of Buffalo; Richard Purple at the University of Minnesota (Twin Cities); Joe Roberson at the University of Michigan, Ann Arbor; Todd Crosset at the University of Massachusetts (Amherst); and Jeff Fry at Ball State University. In addition, there were many faculty members and administrators at other schools—I visited more than forty NCAA Division I-A institutions—who aided me greatly but who wished to remain anonymous; I have honored their requests, but I do want to thank them in print for their valuable aid.

At the University of Notre Dame, where I did research for my previous two books and also this one, I am forever indebted to head archivist Wendy Clauson Schlereth; Charles Lamb, in charge of the archives' graphics collection; and associate archivists Peter Lysy and Wm. Kevin Cawley. I must also thank University of Notre Dame vice president Richard W. Conklin; and university staff members George Rugg, Dennis Brown, Sharon Sumpter, and Bob Thomson.

Special thanks also go to my colleagues in the National Alliance for College Athletics Reform for supporting my work on college sports over the years, listening to my ideas, and arguing so vociferously with me. I have learned more from them about this topic than from any other faculty group in America. Heading this list are Jon Ericson, Allen Sack, Ellen Staurowsky, William Dowling III, Linda Bensel-Meyers, Ed Lawry, Rob Benford, and Andrew Zimbalist. I look forward to working with them in the future, and I hope that NAFCAR can make a difference in the reform of intercollegiate athletics.

At my own school—Indiana University, Bloomington—many persons helped me with this project: in the main library, Ann Bristow, head of the reference department, and her assistant Dave Frasier; also thanks to other members of the reference staff, Mary Buechley, Mark Day, Anne Graham, Jeff Grau, Jian Liu, and Frank Quinn, as well as graduate assistants Steve Duecker, Merlyne Howell, Brian Smith, and Joe Tennis. In addition, I must thank Christine Brancolini and Colleen Talty of the IU library's media/reserve services, who have aided me in so many ways over the years, including on this project.

In the English department of Indiana University, I received assistance from many people, most notably the chair, Ken Johnston, and staff members Reba Amerson, Susan Osborne, June Hacker, Linda Goodwin, and Will Murphy, as well as faculty members Don Gray, Susan Gubar, Charles Forker, Roger Mitchell, Lew Miller, Jim Naremore, David Nordloh, and Albert Wertheim. In other IU departments and the administration, David Pace, Dave Nord, Tim Long, Ken Gros Louis, and Steve Sanders were especially helpful. Special thanks go to the Teaching Resources Center at IUB: Director Joan Middendorf and her able past and present assistants, Alan Kalisch, Jen Bauers, and Kathy Gehr, helped me in many ways with my teaching and with this book.

In addition, I must thank all of the Indiana University undergraduate students with whom I have shared classrooms over the years. I learned more from them about college life and college sports than from any other single source. At this point, after almost three decades of teaching at IU, I have encountered close to five thousand undergraduates in my classes, and I remember the majority of them very clearly and with affection.

I also owe a special debt to the 1,906 students across the country who filled in my questionnaire for this book. They will see their opinions and statements throughout the text, and, without their assistance, this book would be far less informative.

I must also thank all of the readers who wrote to me after reading my previous works or various magazine articles. In an Internet age, I very much enjoy receiving e-mail from them, and I urge them to write to me with their comments about this book. My e-mail address is: sperber@indiana.edu; my home page is: http://php.indiana.edu/~sperber.

At my publisher Henry Holt and Company, many people helped with this book and my previous ones, and I appreciate the time and effort they extended on my behalf. Special thanks go to marketing director Maggie Richards, publicity director Elizabeth Shreve, her former assistant Robin Bacon, and current assistant, Heather Fain; copyeditor Nora Reichard; and production editor David Koral. At the *Princeton Review* college guidebook, I must thank editors Paul Cohen and Julie Mandelbaum for their help.

Finally, I am forever indebted to my wife, Aneta, for her love, strength, and good advice; in addition, she put my questionnaire on the web, and without this assistance, the project would have suffered greatly. I also must thank my daughter Gigi, and former foster daughters Jayme and Logan, for their patience and understanding, as well as their willingness to sit with me during late-night dinners, and early-morning breakfasts.

Lastly, I acknowledge my eternal debt to my late son, Oliver, who was so inspiring in life and whose memory has kept me company during the long hours in the library, and in front of the computer. Ollie taught me the difference between the trivial and the important, and how sports should be fun and play. To treat sports with deadly seriousness is to ruin them, and to profane the reality of life and death.

BEER

AND

CIRCUS

INTRODUCTION

This "introduction" provides definitions of the four major student subcultures that have long existed in American higher education: the collegiate, the academic, the vocational, and the rebel. An early-1960s study by sociologists Burton Clark and Martin Trow outlined the main characteristics of these subcultures and noted that "an individual student may well participate in several of the subcultures available on his [or her] campus, though in most cases one will embody his [or her] dominant orientation."

Almost forty years later, although more students than ever before participate in several campus subcultures, and sometimes move from one dominant one to another, Clark and Trow's description of the subcultures—with major emendations and additions—still apply to undergraduate life in America. However, as they stressed and it is important to repeat: These "are types of subcultures and not types of students," and stereotyping undergraduates serves no purpose; in fact, it obscures the study of them.

Past college student life is prologue to the present, and the past reveals the depth and continuity of the undergraduate subcultures. The past also provides the key to understanding contemporary beer-and-circus. Therefore, this introduction adds necessary historical material to the basic definitions.

★ ★ ★

Collegiate Culture
The collegiate culture [is] a world of football, fraternities and sororities, dates, drinking, and campus fun. A good deal of student life on

many campuses revolves around this culture. . . . Teachers and
courses and grades are in this picture but somewhat dimly and in the
background. The fraternities have to make their grade-point-average,
[other collegiate] students have to hit the books periodically if they
are to get their diplomas, some gestures have to be made to the adult
world of courses and grades which provides the justification for the
collegiate round . . . the busy round of social activities. . . .

It [the collegiate culture] is, however, indifferent and resistant to
serious demands from the faculty for an involvement with ideas and
issues.

—Burton Clark and Martin Trow, sociologists

The undergraduates who participate in this subculture are usually
termed *collegians* or *collegiates*. The subculture began in the eighteenth
century when the sons of the rich came to college for four years of pleasure
and social contacts. They considered academic work an intrusion on their
fun, and they were content to pass their courses with a "gentleman's C"
grade. As higher education expanded in the nineteenth century, many sons
and some daughters of the middle class entered universities, and the new
collegians started the fraternity and sorority system, as well as the first
intercollegiate athletic teams. The collegiate subculture remained antiedu-
cational, and this characteristic continued into and through the twentieth
century, with student social activities, particularly the campus party scene,
taking precedence over academic endeavors.

From their founding in the nineteenth century, college fraternities became bastions of the collegiate subculture and its mores. Adopting Greek
letter names and elaborate ceremonies (in imitation of the Masonic order),
Greeks used high-minded rhetoric to justify their traditions and customs,
but, then as now, their main purpose was fellowship and partying. In the
first half of the twentieth century, they so dictated the terms of student life
that the Gamma Delta Iota movement began.

Some undergraduates, either not invited to join a fraternity or sorority
or unable to afford the expenses of Greek life, remained independent and
lived in university dormitories or off-campus rooming houses. But these
students wanted to participate in the collegiate subculture—particularly its
partying and support of intercollegiate athletics—and they banded together, calling themselves Gamma Delta Iotas (God Damn Independents),
turning their housing units into versions of Greek houses. As their name
indicates, the GDIs took pride in not being Greek, but they so imitated the
originals that they canceled the meaning of the term *independent*. Most

important, they extended the boundaries of the collegiate subculture to include large numbers of non-Greek undergraduates.

In the second half of the twentieth century, the size and influence of the collegiate subculture varied from school to school and from decade to decade. In the 1950s, particularly at state universities, the collegiate subculture was large and powerful (the movie *Animal House* attempts to portray Greek life in this era), but, in the politically turbulent 1960s, the subculture shrank, even at Big-time U's. In subsequent decades, the collegiate population increased considerably, and, at the beginning of the twenty-first century, at some public universities with residential campuses, a large percentage of undergraduates belong to Greek organizations, or live in highly collegiate dorms, or in off-campus mini-versions of Greek houses. On the other hand, at many urban schools and small private colleges, the collegiate subculture has never been an important factor in student life and shows no signs of becoming one. No matter what its size or influence at an individual institution, this subculture has always retained its antiacademic bias and formed the core of the campus and off-campus party scene.

★ ★ ★

Academic Culture
Present on every college campus, although dominant on some and marginal on others, is the [undergraduate student] subculture of serious academic effort. The essence of this system of values is its identification with the intellectual concerns of the serious faculty members. These students . . . work hard, get the best grades, and let the world of ideas and knowledge reach them.
—Burton Clark and Martin Trow, sociologists

At the beginning of American higher education, the first teachers were ministers, and the first students were the sons of the rich—except for a small number of clergymen's sons and some young men hoping to join that profession. These latter students refused to participate in the fun and games of the collegiate subculture; moreover, unlike the collegians, they did not regard the minister teachers with hostility—quite the opposite, they considered them role models, and they emulated their seriousness. The ministers responded by paying special attention to this small group of students, rewarding some, upon graduation, with academic positions, and helping others acquire church pulpits. In this way, the ministers perpetuated themselves and their vocations. Similarly, in the nineteenth century, when colleges evolved into universities, and minister teachers gave way to professional faculty members, these men and women also chose their successors—the minority of students with academic ambitions—and this tradition continues to this day.

From the eighteenth century on, the collegians scorned their academically inclined classmates, regarding them with suspicion and as fair game for pranks and insults. One historian of American higher education terms the serious undergraduates *the outsiders:* on many campuses they were, and still are, outside the mainstream of student life—the collegiate subculture.

Unlike the collegians who mainly exist in a world of immediate gratification, the outsiders practice deferred gratification. They accept the curriculum and the discipline imposed by the faculty because they believe that, after four years, they will enter graduate or professional school and have a professional, often an academic, career. As a result, they are the undergraduates who do all the reading assignments, who turn in their papers on time, who prepare for exams and perform excellently on them, and who attend the professor's office hours.

In the nineteenth century, the collegians called serious students, among other derogatory names, "grubs," "polers," "bootlicks," and "toadies." In the twentieth century, the jibes persisted, only the terms changed: "grinds," "geeks," "dweebs," as well as expressions referencing the more overt sexuality of the age, "brown-noses," "ass-lickers," and "throats." Academic students have always tried to ignore the insults, and have continued to raise their hands in class. Outside of class, the young academics sought one anothers' company, often living together in on- and off-campus housing units. If a university contained a sizable number of serious students, they created their own subculture within the larger undergraduate world; however, if only a few attended the school, they usually became isolated and lonely.

As Clark and Trow indicated, the academic subculture is "present on every college campus, although dominant on some and marginal on others." Today, at some private colleges and universities, a large percentage of undergraduates belong to it; such institutions as the University of Chicago and Brandeis University send a large percentage of their students on to graduate and professional schools. However, at many public universities, academically inclined students constitute a single digit minority, and this translates into a very low percentage of the school's graduates going on for advanced degrees.

Some men and women who began their university careers within the academic ethos of a private institution end up teaching at Big-time U's with huge collegiate subcultures and small academic ones. As a result, these faculty members have minimal understanding of, and sympathy for, the majority of their undergraduate students. In addition, even those professors who attended public universities as undergraduates, because usually they belonged to the academic subculture and disliked the collegiate one, often exhibit an animus toward the collegians in their classrooms. They were outsiders as undergraduates, and they remain outsiders as professors.

★　　★　　★

Vocational culture

For [vocational students], there is simply not enough time or money to support the extensive play of the collegiate culture. To these students, many of them married, most of them working anywhere from twenty to forty hours a week, college is largely off-the-job training, an organization of courses and credits leading to a diploma and a better job than they could otherwise command. . . . But, like participants in the collegiate culture, these students are also resistant to intellectual demands on them beyond what is required to pass the courses. To many of these hard-driven students, ideas and scholarship are as much a luxury and distraction as are sports and fraternities.

—Burton Clark and Martin Trow, sociologists

Vocational students have long existed in American higher education (today, they constitute over half of all college students). Traditionally, vocationals were characterized as students "working their way through college," and they neither participated in collegiate life nor, unlike academic students, attracted special attention from the faculty.

The first wave of vocational students entered American higher education at the beginning of the twentieth century. Often the children of recent immigrants, they mainly attended urban colleges and universities, and usually lived at home, lacking the money or inclination to reside in a dormitory or a Greek house.

Unlike collegians at residential schools, vocationals did not regard college as a "fun interval" between adolescence and adulthood; for vocationals, attending university was another job, similar to their part-time or full-time occupations. As a result, most vocational students lacked the time and energy to intellectually engage their schoolwork, and they considered their classes as obstacle courses with hurdles to be jumped as efficiently as possible.

Vocationals were more conscientious students than the collegians—the casual "gentleman's C" was alien to them—but they tended to do their homework quickly and often achieved what was called the "plebian C." Most of all, they wanted their C's to add up to a college degree. However, unlike the collegians, who viewed a sheepskin as an excellent trophy of the good times at Ol' Siwash, or the academic students, who considered a diploma as proof of attaining a high level of knowledge and culture, the vocationals saw a degree as an entrance fee into the middle class.

After World War II, an enormous wave of vocational students permanently changed America's colleges and universities. As a result of the legislation popularly known as the GI Bill, more than a million ex-service personnel entered higher education, many of whom were the first persons in their families to attend college. The vets regarded going to college as a job, and often took "extra loads" of courses to finish as quickly as possible.

To accommodate these students, and to gain their government-paid tuition dollars, many private colleges, small and sleepy domains of class privilege before the war, transformed themselves into large, bustling, and democratic facilities; public universities grew exponentially, also expanding their clientele from the children of the middle class to multiclass and multiage students; and municipal schools benefited greatly, their long-standing vocational orientation fitting the vets well.

In the post–WWII period, the undergraduate population on most campuses doubled or tripled from prewar levels, and the number of college graduates increased accordingly. In 1939–40, around two hundred thousand Americans received college degrees; ten years later, the first graduating class that included WWII vets pushed the degree total to close to five hundred thousand, and, in the 1950s, the total continued to grow as increasing numbers of nonvets entered higher education. The GIs, who pioneered so much of modern consumer America in the 1950s, including the necessity of owning a car and a house, turned a college degree into a required consumer product, mandatory for all classes of Americans. Henceforth, for a person to succeed in the United States, he or she needed a college diploma.

America's colleges and universities welcomed this new public attitude—it helped reposition them from their historic place on the periphery of American society to the center of postwar commerce and prosperity. Once a college degree became an indispensable consumer item, it guaranteed schools a large and continuous stream of students. It also convinced legislators and taxpayers to support higher education with much more public money than ever before.

Previous to 1945, in the entire history of American higher education, change had occurred at a relatively slow pace. At the end of WWII, higher education entered a phone booth as mild-mannered Clark Kent and came out as Superman, bursting with muscles and money, ready to take on the world. The postwar university soon became, in the words of the president of the fastest-growing school in the country, the University of California, "a multiversity," enrolling many more students than previously. Yet, the traditional student subcultures continued, the vocational one competing for pride of place on some campuses with the collegiate and academic ones.

Not all undergraduates liked this configuration, and, in the 1950s, the rebel subculture, long in existence but marginal at almost every school, began to grow in numbers and importance. Then, in the 1960s—to the bewilderment and distaste of the majority of Americans—the rebels became the largest student group at many institutions, permanently influencing the future of higher education and American society.

★   ★   ★

Rebel Culture

Some kind of self-consciously nonconformist [rebel] exists in many of the best small liberal arts colleges and among the undergraduates in the leading universities. These students are often deeply involved with ideas, both the ideas they encounter in their classrooms and those that are current in the wider society of adult art, literature, and politics. . . .

The distinctive quality of this student style is a rather aggressive nonconformism, a critical detachment from the college they attend and from its faculty.

—Burton Clark and Martin Trow, sociologists

The goal of rebel students in all eras has been self-development, finding their own way through the maze of higher education and into the complexity of adult society. As part of their search for identity, rebel students exhibit a selective studiousness. Unlike the collegians and vocationals, they are not anti-intellectual. When rebel students enjoy a college course, they do the required work in it and much more, usually attaining a top grade; however, when they dislike a course's content, they dismiss it as irrelevant to their personal interests, and often disappear from class, accepting a low grade, even an F. Rebels differ from academic students who pursue an A in every class, whether they like the material or not, and who always try to please their faculty parents.

Rebel students often do not relate to their professors, even in the courses in which they work hard. Rebels see their "nonconformist" values in conflict with "straight" academic ones, and, as Clark and Trow indicate, "To a much greater degree than their academically oriented classmates, these students use off-campus groups and currents of thought as points of reference . . . in their strategy of independence and criticism" of university and all other authorities. The connection of rebel students to vital parts of the wider culture, notably the political and artistic avant-gardes, occurred throughout the twentieth century and became this subculture's most important contribution to higher education.

More than any other group of undergraduates, the rebels helped destroy the real and imaginary walls that, historically, had detached colleges and universities from their surrounding communities (the concept of a university as an "ivory tower"). The rebels also led the fight against the artificial *in loco parentis* (in place of parents) rules that enabled schools to confine their students to campus housing and to restrict their off-campus movements. Equally significant, the rebels created viable off-campus areas for themselves and other undergraduates.

From the 1950s on, after their college days ended, either through graduation or, more often, after dropping out, some rebels remained near their schools and established the prototypes of the off-campus districts that now border almost every college and university in America. In the 1950s, enclaves of ex-student rebels lived near the University of California at Berkeley, Harvard, the universities of Chicago, Michigan, Wisconsin, and a few other schools. They started alternative bookstores, coffee houses, and other establishments, transforming the off-campus streets into areas that accommodated political and cultural dissidents as well as members of the university community. These off-campus sections also became magnets for rebels in the region who had no affiliation with the school but wanted to live in a congenial place.

The rebels and their off-campus areas flourished in the 1960s, and, during this period of political protest and lifestyle experimentation, more undergraduates belonged to the rebel subculture than at any other time in the history of higher education. At some schools, the rebels formed a majority of the student body and, in alliance with off-campus rebels, led large demonstrations in favor of civil rights and against the war in Vietnam, and they also started communes and other housing experiments.

But, as the protests of the 1960s waned, so did the number of rebel students. Today, they comprise a small minority at most colleges and universities. Rebels continue to search for personal identity, and some participate in current political protests while others welcome the newest manifestations of avant-garde art and music. Undergraduates in other subcultures watch and sometimes join them, and, even though the rebel subculture may never again attain its 1960s size and importance, rebel students will always have a place in higher education.

★　★　★

In surveying the long history of America's colleges and universities, the persistence and continuity of the student subcultures amazes the observer. The world outside the university changes radically, but the preoccupations of undergraduates remain remarkably similar. In their early-1960s study of student subcultures, Clark and Trow noted that, above all, rebel students "pursue an identity"; collegians "pursue fun"; academic students seek "knowledge"; and vocationals fix on "a diploma."

At the beginning of the twenty-first century, the necessity of university certification—a diploma—is more important than ever before for almost all students. Nevertheless, the vocationals remain the undergraduates most preoccupied with this credential, and the rebels the least concerned. The academics need to receive a diploma—preferably one "with honors"—on their way to advanced degrees; and the collegians consider it a "large ticket" consumer item, a purchase akin to an expensive automobile, but something that should not obstruct college fun and beer-and-circus.

PART ONE

THE RISE OF
BEER-AND-CIRCUS

1

ANIMAL HOUSE

The 1960s marked a low point for the collegiate subculture on American campuses; numerous fraternities and sororities downsized or closed their doors as some of their members, and many incoming students, joined the rebel subculture. But scores of Greek organizations, particularly at large public universities, survived the 1960s and, during the following decade, wanted to attract a new generation of college students. The popular film *Animal House* proved crucial to the recruiting campaign of the collegiate subculture.

★   ★   ★

Animal House is to me the story of a fraternity house full of friends. They don't have much in common, just drinking beer and drinking some more beer, but isn't that enough? . . . [People] underrate the importance of *Animal House*. The movie came out during my freshmen year in college when I joined a fraternity. Of course I can barely remember the three years that followed. It is more than a movie, it is a social statement, a commentary on a generation.
—Kyle, an *Animal House* fan on the World Wide Web

Animal House is one of the most remarkable movies in Hollywood history. Costing only $2.3 million to make—and turned down by most studios before Universal reluctantly backed it—the film grossed $141 million domestically, and earned many more millions abroad and in video sales. Most film reviewers disliked the movie, but the public embraced it, legions of young people returning to see it again and again. An important element in the 1978 film's success was its setting—not the post Vietnam present but the pre-Vietnam past. The filmmakers consciously placed *Animal House* in the early 1960s, attempting to exploit the nostalgia for the simpler pre-Vietnam era—as George Lucas had done in his popular 1970s film about youth culture, *American Graffiti*—but with a collegiate twist.

The main writer on *Animal House* explained: "We wanted to blow away that *Graffiti* sentimentality," and show that "people in college were *bad* then, because it was fun, people were into being sick," vomiting from over-drinking, and also playing "sick" jokes. Thus, *Animal House* connected to the old collegiate tradition in student life, but, contrary to the filmmakers' intentions, the movie reflected the late 1970s as much as the early 1960s. Such characters and scenes as the pot-smoking professor (played by Donald Sutherland) in bed with one of his students would not have made sense to early-1960s undergraduates, but received applause from late-1970s colle-gians—they saw the character as representing the few "hip profs" on fac-ulties at this time.

Most of all, *Animal House* confirmed the validity of collegiate life in the 1970s and helped reinvigorate it. The *Chicago Sun-Times* speculated that "*Animal House* may be the Woodstock of 1978. All over the country stu-dents are waiting in long lines to see it. . . . The question is: Will life imitate art? The answer is: Don't be surprised." Some observers had noticed that, after the rebel 1960s, "gradually during the 1970s college life revved up again. Essentially some collegians—wanting more, but not understanding how to create it—reverted to the old standbys of college life: the Greek system, organized athletics, pranks."

Each generation of college students tries to distinguish itself from its predecessors, if only in differences of clothing styles, slang, and musical tastes. After Watergate and the end of the Vietnam War, many 1970s un-dergraduates rejected the political activism of the previous student gener-ation and, in a failure of imagination, turned back to collegiate life.

Nationwide membership in fraternities doubled from about one hundred thousand in 1970 to two hundred thousand in 1980, and doubled again to almost four hundred thousand by 1990. Similarly, sorority membership, usually about half of the fraternity numbers on most campuses, increased even more rapidly during these decades, reaching almost 250,000 in 1990. In addition, many fraternity and sorority chapters that were on life support at the beginning of the 1970s were thriving by 1980, building additions on their houses and sponsoring new chapters at other schools. During the next decade, the number of new Greek chapters exceeded one thousand nationwide. Most university officials encouraged this expansion, viewing Greek organizations as benign and their members as easier to control than the 1960s rebels had been (as various Greek-inspired riots later demonstrated, this calculation proved incorrect).

In the mid 1980s, a nationally published guidebook for prospective college students, offering "the inside scoop" about social life on campuses around the country, charted the resurgence of Greek life. For example, at the University of Miami, "since 1980, fraternities have expanded by 30 percent" a year, and they have extended the traditional collegiate subculture to include nonresidential students: "Commuters are joining up, too, since otherwise their tenure at school would be very much like going to a nine-to-five job." Then, in a comment that would have pleased the Chicagoans who wrote *Animal House*, the guidebook asked, "What university now has the biggest Greek system in the United States? Let's hear it for the UNIVERSITY OF ILLINOIS! How about fifty-five fraternities! Twenty-five sororities!" Huge houses, all full, and with members consuming amazing amounts of alcohol. Soon after the film's release, a University of Illinois fraternity man exclaimed, "Oh brother! The movie *Animal House* is NOT strictly nostalgia. Last year when a member got pinned [pre-engaged], we got superloaded and took him to a farm and handcuffed him inside a pen with a bull. The farmer called the cops and they uncuffed him, but it was pretty funny."

University dormitories also became highly collegiate in the 1970s and 1980s; because most schools abandoned *in loco parentis* regulations early in the 1970s, collegiate life ruled in many residence halls, particularly at large public universities. Stereo systems blasted rock music, and raucous partying occurred during many nights, not just on weekends. One higher education writer reported that dormitories "are often so noisy that they fail to serve even their most elementary function" as sleeping places; moreover, "the noise and chaos that surrounds" students becomes intolerable for some, especially those few trying to study in their rooms. Indeed, many schools conceded this point when they established "quiet floors" in their residence halls, i.e., a small number of dormitory floors set aside for students who wanted to live and sleep in a tranquil environment. University personnel monitored these areas to ensure quiet, and they moved disruptive residents to regular dorms. However, the implication of "quiet floors" was highly negative: schools were admitting that the vast majority of the floors in their residence halls—all those locations not designated as "quiet"— were far too loud and often zoolike. Residents and visitors constantly confirmed this reality.

The collegiate culture thrived in the dorms. Rutgers anthropologist Michael Moffat lived in and studied the resident halls at his school, and noted that in the 1970s, "the single most popular event [was] the floor party . . . with beer kegs and highly potent punch and other liquor in the lounges" of the floor. Significantly, fraternity and sorority members often attended these parties, and reciprocated with open invitation events of their own, frequently setting up kegs of beer on the front lawns of their Greek units. A Penn State alum remembered his campus in the 1970s as awash in booze, openly consumed on university grounds and everywhere else: "It was one of the reasons the place became known as Happy Valley."

Helping increase beer consumption on college campuses in this period was the campaign by major brewers to push their product to student consumers. The companies, as well as their local distributors, hired undergraduates as "campus reps" to set up booths and hand out free cups of their product at college sports events and other occasions. In addition, the famous Anheuser-Busch Clydesdale horses entertained football crowds, and the Bud Light Daredevils, an acrobatic squad, performed during college basketball games. The brewers also supplied huge inflatable plastic beer cans of their brands as signs at party sites, serving as beacons for all students to follow to the "suds."

Therefore, when *Animal House* appeared in 1978, many undergraduates in America were well prepared—or, to use the slang of the time, "well oiled"—to watch and enjoy it, the film sanctioning their present behavior and also providing ideas for future antics. As one fan of the movie exclaimed, "At the Delta house anything goes: you wanna throw shit out the window? Okay. You wanna crush a bunch of beer cans on your forehead, and pour honey mustard all over your chest? Go right ahead."

In addition, the main character, brilliantly played by John Belushi, became a folk hero to many collegiates of this generation. One fan rhapsodized, "Bluto is the man. He's the kind of guy who slugs back entire fifths of whiskey, then proclaims, 'I needed that.' The kind of guy who puts a cream-filled Snowball into his mouth, puffs up his cheeks and spits it out, and then says, 'I'm a zit—get it?' " At one point, the villain of the film, the old-fashioned authoritarian dean, tells Flounder, a young fraternity member, "Fat, drunk, and stupid is no way to go through life, son." But Bluto, and millions of other collegians with him, responded, "IT SURE IS."

One film reviewer commented that "*Animal House* will confirm every parent's worst fears—that they are paying $5,000 each year to send their sons and daughters on a vacation called 'college.' " Parental worries and college costs escalated, as did nationwide imitations of *Animal House* behavior, into the 1980s. Then, a reaction occurred: groups like Mothers Against Drunk Driving (M.A.D.D.) lobbied against excessive drinking, and against allowing legal purchase and consumption of alcohol to begin at age eighteen; as a result, in 1984, the U.S. Congress passed legislation that pushed states to mandate twenty-one as the minimum drinking age, and, by 1987, every state had complied. But these laws, even though they obligated schools to curtail open drinking on their property, did not end the *Animal House* era on college campuses.

The law of unintended consequences enveloped the twenty-one-minimum-age legislation: like Prohibition in the 1920s, the new regulations failed to reduce student drinking. For underage students the laws added an interesting element to ordinary boozing—a lively hide-and-seek game with the authorities. In addition, the legislation helped increase enrollment in Greek organizations at an even greater rate than previously, and it also prompted large numbers of students to move into off-campus apartments and houses. One researcher reported that as "colleges cracked down on alcohol in the dorms, many Greek houses became underage drinking clubs. [Also] fraternity and sorority membership opened to more campus types." Numerous Greek houses, after their near-death experiences in the late 1960s, were happy to add as many new members as possible, including some vocationals and even some students with obvious rebel tendencies—as long as the neophytes were willing to pay for their share of the booze and participate in the drinking rituals.

Because Greek living units overflowed with beer and members in this period, many of the upperclassmen moved off campus. In addition, as universities terminated open drinking in their residence halls, many collegians went directly from the dorms to off-campus housing. In the article "Beer and Loafing [at Indiana University]: A Fifth-Year Senior Reflects on Years of Madness," Robert J. Warren described the party scene at his apartment house in the late 1980s: "We lined the edges of the balcony and took turns pumping beer from the keg. . . . We were keg vultures, refusing to leave her side." However, sometimes a member of the group would fall or jump off the balcony and seriously hurt him- or herself. But that was part of the revelry: "Chris plummeted . . . and met the concrete porch below [with] his face. He jumped up with a satisfied screech, blood pouring between his eyes and around his nose. An Indian with natural war paint." Of course, not every drunk falling off a balcony bounded back up—nationwide, seven "loaded" students died this way during spring semester

1986—but risk and bizarre behavior have always been an essential part of collegiate life, totally sanctioned by scenes in *Animal House* and its many knock-offs.

★   ★   ★

In the film, the scene that begins the Deltas' final, riskiest, and most hilarious prank starts when they learn that the dean of students has expelled them from campus. One of the members groans, "War's over, man, Wormer dropped the big one." To this, Bluto replies:

> Over? Did you say 'over'? Nothing is over until we decide it is! Was it over when the Germans bombed Pearl Harbor? Hell no!
>
> OTTER [a fraternity brother]: Germans?
>
> BOON [another fraternity brother]: Forget it, he's rolling.
>
> BLUTO: And it ain't over now. 'Cause when the goin' gets tough [*thinks hard*], the tough get goin'!

The Deltas loved Bluto's ignorance, and collegiate audiences enjoyed the film's profoundly anti-academic stance. The few scenes that occurred inside a classroom depicted the students as totally bored and indifferent to education. An *Animal House* fan explained that the movie proves "college is not about studying and growing up. In the Deltas' eyes, this is their last chance to have fun with their lives." Similarly, in a poll of college student attitudes begun in the late 1980s, to the question—"After you graduate from and/or leave your university, what do you think you will remember most vividly about your time here?"—very few respondents mentioned courses, professors, or anything connected to the academic functions of their school. Almost all the answers centered on extracurricular experiences: having fun at memorable parties and at college sports events, participating in great pranks, and friendships with peers.

Anthropologist Michael Moffat observed the anti-academic ethos at his school, and commented:

> Imagine, for instance, that you were an undergraduate who had been reading a sonnet by the poet Shelley for a classroom assignment, and that it had really swept you away. Unless you enjoyed being a figure of fun, you would not have dared to articulate your feelings for the poem with any honesty in the average peer group talk in the average dorm lounge [or any other average college housing unit].

However, if you were an academically inclined undergraduate and living in an honors college or off-campus with a group of your academic friends, you would probably discuss your enjoyment of Shelley and other intellectual or emotional discoveries. Moreover, you would live almost as far outside the student mainstream at your school as your faculty mentors did. You and your professors could discuss Shelley and other topics with understanding and feeling, but none of you could broach such subjects with the average student at your university. Moffat pinpointed this distance when he stated that "almost all of" his fellow professors at Rutgers "would have been confused and uncomfortable in the average dorm talk session, and none of them would have had any inkling of how to go about locating a good party on the College Avenue Campus." Possibly the academic undergraduates at his school would know how to find "a good party"—however, probably they would not attend it for fear of being mocked or even assaulted by drunken collegians.

During the 1970s and 1980s, the old ritual of faculty bringing their undergraduate sons and daughters into the academic profession continued—the present university outsiders selected the future outsiders. In 1980, a sociologist noted that "a disproportionate percentage of academics . . . come from that small fraction" of undergraduates "taught by faculty members with a desire . . . to introduce students into what an earlier era would have termed the 'mysteries' of their craft." Not only did these "mysteries" include the wizardry of research, but also the mastery of the arcane jargon of various fields and disciplines.

Significantly, although the barriers between most student subcultures began to drop in this era, the one separating academic undergraduates and other groups only lowered slightly. Few academic students participated in the collegiate subculture of time-consuming social rituals, long periods of partying, and fervent support of college sports teams. Indeed, many academic students, like their faculty models, still defined themselves in opposition to this subculture (this began to change for academically inclined students in the 1990s, see p. 104).

In the 1970s and 1980s, the lack of interest in college sports not only separated academics from the mainstream of university life at many schools, but also from an important component of popular culture outside the university. As the electronic media ratcheted up the coverage of all sports, especially intercollegiate athletics, more students embraced their college teams than previously, and more members of the general public became college sports fans. Nevertheless, a majority of academics remained indifferent to the fun and games, usually spending basketball nights and football afternoons doing course work (if students) or research (if faculty). However, the cultural division over athletics had major consequences for higher education when college sports controversies and scandals occurred.

The people within universities who were supposedly in charge of intercollegiate athletics—the college presidents—usually came out of academic backgrounds and, as a result, knew little about college sports. In the 1970s and 1980s, when various university presidents tried to exert control over "power coaches" or corrupt athletic departments, deplorable incidents often happened. Because these episodes took place so frequently and had such negative effects upon schools—and this phenomenon continues to the present day—it seems appropriate to begin the next chapter with a discussion of a famous 1980s incident, and also probe its core cause, the gulf between the academic and collegiate subcultures.

2

COLLEGE SPORTS
WINNERS AND LOSERS

Winning has always been important in college sports, one historian of higher education noting, "The games had to be won. Americans lacked a psychology for failure." The 1970s began with a U.S. president in office who regularly quoted the maxim, "Winning isn't everything, it's the only thing." In that decade and the following one, the college sports obsession with victory often undermined the educational objectives of university administrators, as well as the health and welfare of the workers in the college sports industry, the multitude of vocational student-athletes.

★   ★   ★

The State of Indiana has a love affair with basketball, and Bob Knight, IU's coach, was a legend long before I arrived [in 1987 to become president of Indiana University]. In my first year I learned an essential lesson: Intercollegiate athletics can be an all-consuming diversion from the academic goals of a university president. . . .

How would an Ivy League type, who came from the East Coast and wore bow ties, react to basketball as the Hoosier lifeblood? Many asked that question.

—Thomas Ehrlich, former president of Indiana University

In this memoir, Ehrlich maintained that he understood college basketball before he arrived in Indiana, but, considering his academic background, his claim is dubious, and subsequent events revealed his ignorance about the game. During the first year of Ehrlich's presidency, Bob Knight appeared on a national television program on the topic of job stress; Knight was asked by Connie Chung how he handled the intense pressure involved in coaching a big-time college basketball team. He compared the pressure to rape, noting that "if rape is inevitable, relax and enjoy it." That a high-profile public figure could make such a remark in 1988 mainly revealed the isolated, macho world in which Knight lived, his obliviousness to the women's movement of the previous decades and to the feelings of most Americans on the subject of rape. But Knight had recently won his third NCAA men's basketball championship and had become the emperor of Indiana, living in his high castle.

Predictably, many IU faculty members protested to Knight's boss, the IU president, about the coach's remark. Ehrlich issued a mild statement mainly indicating that Knight's views did not represent the views of Indiana University. This enraged the megalomaniacal coach, and he threatened to leave IU and accept an offer from the University of New Mexico, which was at the time looking for a new coach. As Ehrlich wrote, "The matter was on the front page of every paper in the state" of Indiana, and precipitated a huge public debate concerning the pros and cons of keeping Bob Knight at IU. In the end, Ehrlich backed down, apologized to Knight, helped convince the coach to stay at IU, and, in so doing, blighted his presidency. (In his memoir, Ehrlich avoids the negative parts of the story, blandly commenting, "Knight stayed at IU and the crisis passed.")

Forever after this incident, a majority of IU faculty viewed Ehrlich as weak and ineffectual, and they would not cooperate with his policy initiatives. In addition, constantly reminding the faculty of Ehrlich's capitulation to the basketball coach were newspaper photos, as well as TV shots, of the president sitting in the IU section at every home game, wearing a silly cream and crimson suit (IU's colors) and cheering his lungs out for the "Hurrying Hoosiers." Ehrlich hung on for six more years, and then terminated his failed presidency, which had been moribund from the day he revealed who possessed actual power at Indiana University: the coach, not the president.

Would Ehrlich have acted differently if he had not been mired in the academic culture and had known something about college basketball or, at the minimum, had consulted with someone who did? Probably so. Ehrlich could have called Knight's bluff; he could have summoned the coach to his office and said, "Bob, I think that you will love it in 'The Pit' [the nickname for the University of New Mexico arena]. Bob, you will particularly love recruiting for the Lobos [by all accounts, Knight hates recruiting]. Bob, you will have the pick of all those blue chip players who come out of New Mexico high schools [almost none do; New Mexico is not Indiana where, in the 1980s, Knight "gathered" rather than recruited]. And Bob, what you will particularly like is going into the L.A. ghetto as all Lobo coaches have to do, and taking what remains after UCLA and other Pac-10 schools get the cream of the crop, and also after Tark the Shark gets his guys for UNLV. Bob, you will love the prospects that are left, the most academically and socially marginal players around. They are exactly the kind of athletes who respond to your yelling and your regimented style. Take the Lobo job, Bob, it's perfect for you."

But knowing nothing about college basketball, Ehrlich never made this speech. Instead he trusted his academic training to help him survive the situation. It didn't. A faculty member who provided a back channel for Ehrlich and Knight remarked on the enormous distance between the president's world and the coach's, and how "Ehrlich spoke of Knight as if he were a member of a different social class from himself . . . whose behavior was bound to be different from his own." However, to be fair to Ehrlich, probably his presidency was doomed before he ever set foot in the state of Indiana. Not only was he an outsider by birth and background, but, as an academic, he was an outsider within his own highly collegiate university. He never understood the majority culture at IU, and after he alienated his natural allies—the faculty, his fellow academics—the game was over.

In analyzing the Ehrlich-Knight confrontation, two higher education writers commented that it "reinforced a basic research finding: When a president deals with college sports, three things can happen, and two of them are bad." The only good outcome is if the president's university has a winning team in a high-profile sport; then the CEO can ride the wave of victory and good feeling, garnering lots of student, alumni, and fan support. Bad things happen if the president has a nasty public confrontation with a prominent coach, or an athletic director, or an athlete (for example, a quarterback flunking out of school); a confrontation will set off a firestorm of negative comments from fans on- and off-campus, as occurred in the Ehrlich-Knight encounter. Worst things occur when a scandal envelops a university athletic department, particularly one involving popular coaches or players; then the media arrive on campus, and soon the headlines blare such news as, SECRET SLUSH FUND FOR BIG-TIME U ATHLETES. The president, as the person in charge of the university, must investigate, try to clean up the mess, assure the various university constituencies that such scandals will never occur again . . . ad infinitum.

★ ★ ★

Rarely does a day pass when the daily newspaper doesn't contain some story of recruiting or ethical violation in some athletic department in some grove of academe.
—Ira Berkow, *New York Times* columnist

Berkow offered his comments after surveying the long river of college sports scandals during the 1970s and 1980s. Like all steady flows, the river contained some prodigious pieces of flotsam and jetsam. Berkow cited the case of Dexter Manley, the NFL All-Pro end who admitted that he had entered Oklahoma State University in 1977 unable to read or write, played there for four years, and left still "illiterate." Other commentators highlighted the early-1980s scandal at the University of New Mexico, where, for a number of years, the basketball coach arranged for players to receive academic credit for extension and summer school courses that they never took (the Lobos coach wanted to ensure the playing eligibility of the academically marginal athletes that President Ehrlich should have reminded Bob Knight about). And by the late 1980s, with the river flowing faster, a book about corruption in the Southern Methodist University football program summed up the situation with its title, *A Payroll to Meet*. (The polluted river rolled on through the 1990s, with illegal pay scandals at many schools, including Texas Tech and Michigan State, and the decade ended with academic messes in the athletic departments of the University of Minnesota and the University of Tennessee.)

During all these years, the NCAA possessed police powers but patrolled the river in canoes, not speedboats. "Consequently," as one sports authority wrote, "close observers of the college sports scene, including coaches and athletes, estimated that only a small fraction of the total violations resulted in punishment by the NCAA." Some observers maintained that the NCAA did not really want to clean up intercollegiate athletics; instead, mainly for PR reasons, it pulled out the especially putrid programs but let most other offenders float along.

Supplying the players with academic and financial favors while in school constituted two major areas of dishonesty, but enticing them to enroll—the recruiting process—produced another large cesspool. In 1988, an authoritative preseason football guide divided cheating in Division I-A recruiting into three categories and sets of percentages: (A) 15 to 20 percent of all programs made illegal offers of cash and/or goods to recruits; (B) 65 percent assured an athlete's "social comfort and/or academic success if he signs"; (C) 15 to 20 percent "occasionally bend a rule" to sign a player. Therefore, all schools cheated in one way or another. If 100 percent was the total in football, then basketball, with many shady coaches and hungry players, easily reached that number and, if it had been possible, would have surpassed it. The recruiting scandals continued through the 1990s, involving such "usual suspects" as Louisiana State and Louisville, and "new kids" Southeast Missouri State and Weber State.

Another important area of athletic department deception, one almost unknown to the public but familiar to university administrators, was fiscal. Throughout the 1970s and 1980s, cases of athletic directors and coaches committing fraud emerged, but more systemic and outrageous were the overspending practices of almost all athletic departments. During these years, even as college sports revenues increased significantly, expenses rose faster, generating huge amounts of red ink. According to the NCAA's own financial reports, the vast majority of its members lost money on their college sports programs, often millions of dollars a year; however, because the NCAA allowed athletic departments to engage in "creative accounting," outside experts calculated the real losses as at least three times higher than the reported figures. Moreover, universities had to cover these annual deficits with funds that could have gone to academic departments, student scholarships, or other educational objectives.

Athletic department mismanagement, lavish spending, and waste caused most of the annual losses, but university officials, including presidents, were extremely reluctant to assert control over athletic department finances. Nasty and debilitating confrontations with ADs (athletic directors) and coaches—the people benefiting most from the overspending—constituted the first "bad thing" that happened "when a president deals with college sports." As a result, when the 1990s economic boom pumped even more dollars into athletic department coffers, the annual deficits continued to increase (see pages 219–29).

Coaches and ADs profited from this system, but how did the athletes fare? Tales of corrupt jocks filled the media from the 1970s to the end of the century and beyond, but the NCAA and other sponsors of intercollegiate athletics always argued that the media focused too much on jocks on the take and ignored the multitude of honest athletes who, without attention, played their sports and went to class. The NCAA and member schools have long called these undergraduates "student-athletes."

Isiah Thomas, a college and NBA star in the 1980s, and now a pro basketball executive, commented:

When you go to college, you're not a student-athlete but an athlete-student. Your main purpose is not to be an Einstein but a ballplayer, to generate some money, put people in the stands. Eight or ten hours of your day are filled with basketball, football. The rest of your time you've got to motivate yourself to make sure you get something back.

The situation that Thomas described resulted from a key event in the history of intercollegiate athletics, one that transformed the majority of student-athletes into athlete-students: in 1973, the NCAA changed athletic scholarships from guaranteed four-year awards to one-year renewable grants. From their inception, the four-year deals had ensured some institutional commitment to an athlete's education; whether the player became an all-American, a benchwarmer, or never suited up due to injury, he or she could continue in college on scholarship. But coaches despised the four-year grants—from their viewpoint, it wasted far too many scholarship slots on athletes "who didn't work out"—who didn't help the team win—and the coaches pressured the NCAA into changing all athletic scholarships to one-year awards, renewed or canceled every July 1. After the rule came on line, at most NCAA schools, coaches made the annual decisions on their players, generally renewing or cutting on the basis of athletic ability.

The one-year grants gave coaches enormous power over their athletes, and, throughout the 1970s and 1980s, as college sports became more popular and the rewards of winning ever more lucrative, particularly for coaches, in the form of enhanced contracts and endorsements, their demands on their athletes escalated. In previous eras, every college sport had an off-season during which some athletes caught up on their studies, and others just relaxed and recuperated. However, in the 1970s and 1980s, as weight-training and other conditioning methods became an essential part of athletics, the off-season disappeared from the college sports calendar. Then, in-season leisure time for athletes became briefer, to the point where, in the early 1990s, observers noted that because college athletes "can expect to spend . . . 50 hours or more each week in their sport, coaches generally expect the hours required for team-related tasks [meetings, videotape viewing, etc.] . . . to be taken from leisure time, which they often consider a low priority."

For many generations, the lives of college athletes in big-time programs had resembled those of regular vocational students. In the 1970s and 1980s, when many other students edged out of their "dominant subcultures," most athletes withdrew further into their vocational mode, to the point where even the proponents of intercollegiate athletics worried about the intense daily pressure placed upon the jocks. In 1991, a nationally published guidebook for college athletes and their parents began chapter one with:

> The label of student-athlete says it all. A college student who is also an athlete is asked to live two roles and be two people in one. No other college students are identified in this hyphenated way—no others are pulled in two completely different directions. No other students are asked to be one person for half the day and someone else the other half.

Without realizing it, authors Stephen K. Figler and Howard E. Figler placed student-athletes in the traditional vocational category. However, contrary to their assertion, many other students "are pulled in two completely different directions," and endure split lives—all those men and women who work at full-time jobs and also attend college full-time, as well as all those who are parents and must divide their lives among family, school, and job obligations. (By the early 1990s, vocational students comprised over 50 percent of the national undergraduate population, but, ironically, demographers excluded student-athletes from that pool; the demographers, not recognizing that athletic scholarships were payments-in-kind for full-time sports jobs, counted athletes as regular students.)

The Figlers, even if they never used the term *vocational,* expressed the athletes' dilemma in the same way that university counselors described the lives of stressed-out vocational students: instead of the full-time job or family, "The team demands so much of your time that you cannot perform . . . in courses that you want or need for your future." In addition, the outside pressure constricts your daily life, and narrows your college experience; for athletes this occurs because "coaches arrange aspects of your life (such as meals, housing, [etc.] . . .) so that you will interact primarily with other athletes, and thus be more completely under the control of the coaching staff."

Similar to highly stressed vocationals, intercollegiate athletes tended to remain within their own group, directed by their coaches' extreme emphasis on sports and frequent neglect of everything else, including academics. Coaches phrased their priorities more positively, usually invoking the word *commitment*, as in demanding an athlete's *commitment to the program.*

The Figlers explained "commitment" in a section titled, "Winning versus Your [Athletes's] Welfare: Coaches feel that the time commitment they demand of athletes is necessary in order to have a winning team." Yet, these writers never discussed the benefits to coaches in high-profile sports who win consistently: annual incomes that in 1991 averaged $300,000 (and today average closer to $600,000, with an increasing number of coaches topping $1 million annually). Winning coaches receive among the highest salaries at their universities, but their supplementary earnings— endorsements of sneakers and other products, lucrative summer camps, public-speaking engagements, et cetera—generate an even larger proportion of their annual incomes. All aspects of their jobs depend on winning; for example, no trade association ever paid a losing coach $20,000 to speak at its convention.

Fred Akers, a NCAA Division I-A head football coach from the 1970s to the early 1990s explained the process: "The more you win, the bigger the bucks. But you can never win enough—I won at UT [University of Texas at Austin] but got fired for not winning more." Akers then went to Purdue, but had some losing seasons there and was fired again. He commented: "I was out of step. Most coaches believe that the best way to win is to put their players in the most intense training possible. Keep at 'em from dawn to dusk and into the night. I never did that, I didn't feel it was fair to my guys, I wanted them to go to class and have time to study. But I'm not in college coaching anymore."

Nevertheless, college athletes are not entirely the victims of obsessed coaches; the jocks have long participated in their fates. If they possess the talent to win an athletic scholarship, they enter university hoping to star at the college level and then move up to the professionals. As a result, many college athletes regard their university years primarily as minor league training for the pros and secondarily as an opportunity for an education. That only a small percentage of collegiate athletes ever achieve their pro sports dream is irrelevant to its power over them and its role in shaping their lives at school, especially their willingness to devote so many hours a day to athletics.

In 1991, the NCAA instituted a rule that provided a basic test of the athletes' and the coaches' commitment to their sports, as well as the NCAA's commitment to reform. Under pressure from the critics of college sports, including such members of Congress as Bill Bradley and Tom McMillen (authentic student-athletes in their college days), the NCAA moved to control the excessive number of hours that intercollegiate athletes spent in their sports and, by implication, not in their studies. The association passed a rule limiting "a student-athletes's participation" in his or her sport "to a maximum of four hours per day and twenty hours per week." The NCAA hailed the rule as one of the most important pieces of legislation in its history, and even some critics were impressed.

Unfortunately, the rule contained an immense loophole: the NCAA defined the four daily/twenty weekly hours as "mandatory time" required by coaches; however, the rule allowed athletes to spend as many hours per week as they wanted in "voluntary" sports activities, for example, informal practices, weight-training, conditioning, et cetera. Even the NCAA's PR director admitted that "under the new rules, athletes can practice more than twenty hours a week. One hundred hours a week if they want, if it's *voluntary.*"

Immediately, the line between mandatory and voluntary blurred. The coaches kept time sheets on the hours that they required their players to be on the practice field or court—and the totals never exceeded four daily or twenty weekly. But the coaches also *encouraged* their athletes to *volunteer* to do all the other activities related to sports success. During the first year of the rule, Jerry Eaves, an assistant basketball coach at Howard University, admitted that in his and other sports the athletes "are still doing everything that takes up the same amount of time" as before; "they're still running" the same training distances, "they're still doing maximum physical conditioning," and also "they're playing" so-called pickup games to supplement official practices.

Many athletes also regarded the four-and-twenty–hour rule as a sham, and they felt that voluntary/mandatory merged into one time unit. A Division I men's volleyball player remarked that, beyond the mandatory hours in afternoon practices, the other functions are voluntary, "but it's not like you don't have to show up if you don't want to. We work out as much or even longer now than we did before the rule. . . . Also each of us wants playing time and needs to keep ahead of everyone else. We know that the coaches totally monitor who is doing the voluntary work. Guess which players the coaches put in the starting lineup?"

The NCAA four-and-twenty–hour rule continued through the 1990s, obeyed so little that in the fall of 1999, *USA Today* published a routine item on USC football player R. Jay Soward, in his team's doghouse because he "was a no-show at workouts that officially were voluntary but were attended by nearly every player on the team." Soward's absence "didn't sit well with Trojans coach Paul Hackett," and resulted in people "in the program questioning his [Soward's] work ethic and commitment." Apparently, no one told USC that they were supposed to pretend to obey the NCAA rule, not openly discuss their flaunting of it with a reporter on a national newspaper.

But from its inception, with the inclusion of the "voluntary" loophole, the four-and-twenty–hour rule was never a serious reform, and mainly revealed the hypocrisy of the NCAA, as well as its bureaucratic impulse—coaches rightly complain about the burdensome time sheets that they must fill out for the NCAA, serving no "real world" purpose whatsoever.

Yet, in a symbolic sense, the four-and-twenty–hour rule captures the essence of the modern NCAA: its PR pretense of guarding the welfare of student-athletes, versus the reality of its high-powered promotion of a billion-dollar-a-year college sports business, and its lack of concern for the workers in that industry. Joe Abunasser, a former NCAA Division I assistant basketball coach, commented: "The irony of the entire organization [the NCAA] is that its proclaimed intention is to regulate and reform college athletics, when in reality it is the cause of the corruption."

Propelling the NCAA's corruption is the almighty dollar. From a wealthy organization in the 1970s and 1980s, the association, thanks to television's insatiable appetite for college sports programming, moved into the billionaire range in the 1990s. As a result, the NCAA became an essential part of sports media programming, with the total revenue from college football and basketball games exceeding that of the richest professional leagues in the world.

3

THE NCAA, THE TUBE,
AND THE FANS

In the 1970s and 1980s, big-time athletic departments became franchises in College Sports Inc., a huge commercial entertainment enterprise with operating methods and objectives frequently opposed to the educational missions of the host universities. Feeding the growth was the increased revenue from the television networks for the rights to broadcast college sports events, notably the NCAA's men's basketball tournament. During this period, an athletic director at a small Ohio college defined the motivation of the men directing big-time intercollegiate athletics: "There are three definitions. . . . Greed, greed, and greed."

★ ★ ★

> At one time, coaches and ADs openly ran the NCAA, now they have to pretend that their [schools'] presidents are involved in the association's decision making. But if you look at who is making the real decisions, from the Executive Director on down, you will find men and women who come out of college coaching and AD positions. They shape the thinking of the NCAA and probably always will shape it—for them, it's the present and future of the coaching and AD professions, the jobs of their close friends, that's at stake.
> —William Atchley, former president of Clemson
> University, and of the University of the Pacific

One of the most pernicious myths about the NCAA is that the association represents the will of its member colleges and universities, and that it tries to keep intercollegiate athletics in line with its members' educational objectives. In fact, as President Atchley and other critics of the NCAA have argued, the NCAA functions mainly as a trade association for coaches and athletic directors, implementing their wishes regardless of whether these are in the best interests of the member schools, or the multitude of athletes engaged in intercollegiate athletics. Coaches and ADs changed the basic rules on athletic scholarships, and no amount of pressure by university presidents or anyone else has ever returned the grants to guaranteed four-year deals or, as the American Council on Education has advocated, "need based only" scholarships, removing control from the coaches and giving it to the university's Financial Aid Office. Similarly, even though congressional pressure and the desire for positive PR forced the NCAA into the four-and-twenty–hour regulation, the coaches and ADs immediately subverted it with the "voluntary" loophole.

Basic to the NCAA's growth and power, particularly in the 1970s and 1980s, was its empire-building, its rules that forced schools into enlarging their college sports programs and facilities whether they could afford to expand them or not. On the local level, athletic directors and coaches benefited most from the NCAA's expansion mandates—more teams and bigger facilities enhanced their own jobs and their mini-empires. For example, in the early 1980s, the NCAA required many schools, if they wanted to remain in Division I-A football, to increase the size of their stadiums. When six of ten members of the Mid-America Conference failed to comply with the new stadium regulations, the NCAA threatened to exclude them from I-A football. This forced these institutions to undertake costly construction projects; for Mid-America Conference universities, football has always been a red-ink proposition, but never more so than after obeying NCAA expansion rules. (Of course, schools can always leave big-time college football and basketball, and some have over the years. However, ADs and coaches know how to pressure presidents and other administrators contemplating "dropping out" into reconsidering, and, as occurred in the MAC, most schools swallow hard and pay the NCAA price.)

In the 1970s and 1980s, the NCAA, despite losing its monopoly over college football telecasts, continued to dominate the sport through its power to dictate the structure of football programs, including the numbers of assistant coaches and players, as well as the rules on recruiting and athletic scholarships. In addition, the NCAA regulated bowl games and their payouts to participating schools; in this area, it encouraged the bowls, as well as individual athletic departments across the country, to seek corporate sponsorships. In the early 1980s, the Tangerine Bowl became the Florida Citrus Bowl, and soon the John Hancock Sun Bowl appeared, and even the venerable Sugar Bowl became the hard-to-remember USF&G

Sugar Bowl (now the Nokia Sugar Bowl). Meanwhile, local athletic departments sold their scoreboards, the backs of their tickets, and all other available spaces to whoever was willing to pay the going rate. By the end of the century, only the Rose Bowl refused a corporate name, although it enlisted various corporate sponsors, and almost every athletic department had multiple business tie-ins for its football program. However, all of the corporate dollars and increased bowl game payouts did not translate into black ink for most college football programs, and, ironically, many bowl game participants lost money on their postseason trips (see pages 222–24).

From the 1970s on, NCAA football costs outpaced revenue, and, even when some schools reconfigured their conference memberships and schedules to capture more TV dollars, they could not change the economic reality. An ESPN executive remarked, "The bottom line is money. College football has become a very big business, just like IBM and General Motors. As expenses increase, they [athletic departments] have to find a way to pay the bills. And getting more television money from football is one way to do that." But it never turned out to be enough money.

Fortunately for the NCAA, although college football was a "mature business" in the final decades of the century, college basketball exploded, most notably the association's annual Division I men's basketball tournament. Yet, even though March Madness revenue went from the million-dollar to the billion-dollar range in ten years, it failed to alter the amazing economics of college sports: most schools continued to lose money on their intercollegiate athletics programs. Nevertheless, the infusion of March Madness dollars, along with the money from football, fundamentally changed college sports, moving them ever closer to corporate professional sports and transforming their role in college life. Driving this transformation was the NCAA.

> The Michigan State–Indiana State [final game in the 1979 NCAA men's basketball tournament] was different because it changed the face of the sport at two levels, ushering in an era of prosperity for the NCAA and the NBA. When Larry [Bird] met Magic [Johnson], it brought people to their television sets in record numbers. The 24.1 rating and the 38 share for that game remain the highest for a college basketball telecast. It was the sporting equivalent of Neil Armstrong's setting foot on the moon.
>
> —J. A. Adande, *Los Angeles Times* sportswriter

The NCAA created the Division I men's basketball tournament in the late 1930s, but, during the next four decades, the association failed to generate national interest in the event. Even when the great UCLA teams of the 1960s won consecutive championships, the NCAA could arrange national telecasts only for final round games, sometimes even accepting Saturday afternoon time slots for the title contest. During the 1970s, the association kept trying to sell more tournament games to a major television network and gradually made progress, although the TV payouts remained low. Similarly, before 1976, no major network broadcast a regular-season game of the week, and finally, when one did, it paid a very low rights fee. In the 1970s, only fans who lived in basketball-crazy states like Indiana and North Carolina could see a number of college games per week, mainly thanks to local and regional stations.

The 1978–79 college basketball season changed everything, taking the sport from its twenty-mile-per-hour national popularity to over seventy miles per hour. The superb play and star power of Larry Bird, the rural white kid at obscure Indiana State University in Terre Haute, and the equally great play and wattage of Ervin "Magic" Johnson, the urban black athlete at Big Ten powerhouse Michigan State, became a season-long media drama, culminating in their big game against each other—the final of the 1979 NCAA men's basketball tournament. The NCAA entered the tournament still at twenty miles per hours—it scheduled the final round in a fifteen-thousand-seat arena on the University of Utah campus—but it exited ready to capitalize on the phenomenal TV ratings for the Bird-Magic matchup.

After that game, the NCAA sold the TV rights for future tournaments for much larger fees than ever before, and, as important, the association made a special "side deal" with a cable TV network that began operations in the summer of 1979—ESPN. The sports channel agreed to televise all the tournament games that the major network broadcaster, CBS-TV, did not pick up. In addition, ESPN arranged to telecast hundreds of regular season games; this increased the fan base for college teams from local and regional followings to national ones, and multiplied the audience for the March tournament. Conferences like the Big East soon became ESPN favorites, and their basketball programs moved from relative obscurity to national prominence, the TV exposure crucial to their coaches' recruiting efforts and improving won-loss records.

From this synergy with television came the NCAA's major money machine, March Madness. The Division I men's basketball tournament, before 1979 an interesting competition for regional audiences, became one of America's premiere annual sporting events, rivaling major league baseball's playoffs and World Series, and aiming at the NFL playoffs and the Super

Bowl. By the mid-1980s, the NCAA received $32 million a year from CBS-TV to televise the tournament (the network concentrated on final regional games and final-round contests), and a few million from ESPN, still doing every game not carried by CBS. However, in 1986, CBS doubled the annual payout and agreed to broadcast many more games, including some early-round contests in prime time. Then, in 1989, CBS stunned the television industry by buying the next seven years of the tourney for $1 billion dollars, and demanding all games, thus ending ESPN's coverage. (In 1994, the NCAA and CBS renegotiated the fee to $1.7 billion for all tourney games until 2002, and, in 1999, they renegotiated again, upping the fee to almost $6 billion through 2013.)

In addition to the TV revenue, from the mid-1980s on, the NCAA earned millions in ticket sales by moving the Final Four round to huge domed stadiums. In fact, the association passed a rule that required a thirty-thousand-seat or larger facility for all Final Fours, thus turning a small-sized court game into a circus event. Basketball aficionados protested, legendary UCLA coach John Wooden commenting that "domes are not a good place to play basketball," but he acknowledged that NCAA "decisions of this sort are made because of money."

Also in the mid-1980s, the NCAA increased the entry field to sixty-four teams, generating more tourney games and more entrants with mediocre season records. Jerry Tarkanian, the coach of strong UNLV teams during this period, remarked, "I think the tournament should be a reward for teams, and I'm opposed to a team that wins only 50 percent of its league games getting into the tournament."

For all of the money streaming into the NCAA from March Madness, a surprisingly small percentage continued on to the schools participating in the tournament, and even less flowed directly to other members of the association. In the 1990s, 25 percent of the revenue went to the participants and their conferences, with some first-round losers failing to cover their traveling expenses. Most of the money stayed in the NCAA, much of it for the association's gargantuan "administrative services" budget and payroll. The NCAA also spent millions on "public affairs," a.k.a. publicity and promotion, including all those halftime TV spots to convince viewers that only authentic student-athletes played big-time college sports, young men and women so devoted to their studies and their sports that they should never be sullied by any of the money that they generated for the NCAA.

Therefore, who benefited from the tremendous surge in college basketball popularity after 1979? Obviously, the NCAA made out wonderfully;

however, member schools, including many of the perennial basketball pow-erhouses, never managed to staunch the annual flow of red ink in their athletic department finances. On the other hand, any coach with a team in the tournament field could request a raise and a contract extension, and if his squad reached the Final Four, he could generate hundreds of thousands of dollars in additional personal income. Moreover, winning the tourna-ment placed him in the $1 million annual range for the rest of his coaching career. (Similarly, the increasingly popular Women's Division I basketball tournament lost money for participating schools but aided the careers and bank balances of coaches with successful teams.)

Do the athletes benefit from March Madness? Most players, particularly those intent on pro careers, love the TV exposure during the tourney, but few make any pretense about keeping up their schoolwork during the many weeks of the tourney. Longtime college basketball reporter Rick Bozich commented, "Put a kid on the road to the NCAA Finals, and the road will take many twists. . . . Few of the twists will include a pit stop in the class-room." Football players involved in bowl games—also NCAA approved events—have similar problems, especially acute for them because practices for their bowl game often begin during their school's final exam period.

Unlike the athletes, many regular students of schools in the NCAA men's basketball tournament claim to benefit in all possible ways and see no downside to March Madness. In a poll of college student attitudes begun in the 1980s, to the question—"After you graduate from and/or leave your university, what do you think you will remember most vividly about your time here?"—students at universities whose men's basketball teams reached the Final Four during their undergraduate years often mentioned that event as one of their most vivid college memories, particularly if they took a "road trip" to the site of the Final Four. Frequently they did not obtain tickets to the games—the domed stadiums were sold out—but milling around outside the arena provided them with sufficient pleasure. Most of all, by wearing their school's paraphernalia and being identified as students from that university, they achieved what some termed "a per-sonal victory."

In the history of American colleges and universities, intercollegiate ath-letics had always been important to students in the collegiate subculture, but, in the 1980s, with the introduction of wall-to-wall media coverage of college sports, many collegians began to define their university careers in terms of the success or failure of their schools' teams, particularly the high-profile football or basketball squads. This marked a new phenomenon in higher education, one that subsequently became central to student life.

* * *

In a 1980s experiment, Dr. Robert Cialdini, professor of psychology at Arizona State University, discovered that

> After the home team wins a football game on Saturday, . . . university students at seven major NCAA schools systematically chose to wear apparel to class on Monday that announced their school affiliation. They wore sweatshirts, t-shirts and team jackets with insignias and emblems that designated them as part of the university in far greater numbers after the team won than after it lost. The larger the victory margin, the stronger the tendency to show off.

In previous eras, public exhibitions of student pride in a winning team usually occurred at pep rallies, games, and postgame celebrations, and did not extend to clothing choices during the school week. But the 1980s expansion of SportsWorld to fit the cable-ready universe transformed all sports, including intercollegiate athletics, into a primary and constant part of every fan's existence. In terms of university life, one student noted, "College culture today [1990] is a direct extension of sex, alcohol, and rock 'n' roll. Now, college sports, thanks to TV, has enlarged the holy trio to four, and most students like that."

At this time, another campus observer, Allen Bogan, used the term *fandemonium* to describe the growing "obsession with sports teams and star athletes," with college sports fans exhibiting a particularly virulent form of the "disease." Bogan based his comments on the work of psychology professor Edward Hirt, and the *Miller Lite Report on American Attitudes Toward Sports*.

In the early 1980s, the Miller Brewing Company commissioned, in its words, "The most comprehensive sports study ever conducted." Miller compared its inquiry to the Carnegie Report of 1929—except, unlike the Carnegie Foundation, the brewery did not want to reform intercollegiate athletics: it sought to understand the fans better and, in so doing, create more effective ways to sell them its beer. The results of the *Miller Lite Report* and other market studies convinced the brewery to increase its already huge sponsorship of TV sports programming, and to amplify its popular Miller Lite commercials featuring famous athletes.

The *Miller Lite Report* also provided useful information on the evolution of "fandemonium." One key question asked: "When your favorite team or athlete wins, do you feel something *important* has been accomplished?" Most respondents who identified themselves as "sports fans" and, significantly, most who did not, answered affirmatively—over 90 percent of the former, and over 80 percent of the latter. Thus, even many nonfans assented to the increasing cultural importance of athletics and chose teams to follow at a distance; this paralleled the growing importance of college sports to many noncollegiate students, particularly vocationals.

Similarly, when asked, "When your favorite team or athlete wins, how often do you feel [that] you've gained a *personal* victory," only a minority of fans and nonfans answered "rarely" or "never." The importance of victory and the personal connection to it—even though fans and nonfans have almost zero input into building and running teams—was confirmed by the responses to, "When your favorite team or athlete loses . . . do you feel *depressed?*" Sixty-six percent of the fans answered yes. And when asked—"When your favorite team or athlete loses . . . do you feel *as if you suffered a personal loss?*"—38 percent of the fans replied affirmatively. Again, this response illustrates the imagined personal bond that many people have with their favorite team or athlete, and it prompts cries of "Get a life." Miller would prefer calls of "Get a Lite," and, a generation later, probably many more people would answer affirmatively to these "personal attachment" questions, and also feel that they possessed a full life with beer and sports.

The main difference between the early 1980s and now is summed up in four letters—ESPN. The twenty-four-hour all-sports cable network began as a small operation in late 1979 and exploded in the 1980s, allowing fans to spend every waking hour within SportsWorld. Never before in sports history was this possible.

ESPN first attracted widespread attention through its college basketball telecasts, not only with March Madness games and events but also with its regular-season coverage of the sport. For its college b-ball programming, it concocted *Big Monday, Super Tuesday, Championship Week,* et cetera, and it hired such superenthusiastic announcers as Dick Vitale to provide commentary on the games. A college student in the early 1990s explained, "ESPN generates a level of energy and intensity that is really fun for college basketball fans. I love all the hours that I can watch games from around the country, and how ESPN cuts from a great moment in one game to another in another game." ESPN both fed and validated this fan's obsession, and also—as its increasing ratings demonstrated—it generated new fans and caught the attention of nonfans.

ESPN also changed the sport of college basketball in various ways, one of the most telling and innovative was Midnight Madness. In the 1970s, when the NCAA ruled that coaches could begin basketball practices on a certain day in October, Lefty Driesell at Maryland decided to begin at midnight of the designated day "to get an edge, start [as] early" as possible; a few years later, Driesell invited Terrapin fans to watch the early start, and several other coaches imitated the "midnight open practice." In the early 1980s, ESPN—always having to fill twenty-four hours of airtime with some sort of sports programming—began televising some of the early A.M. practices, hyping them as Midnight Madness. Soon, many coaches joined in, offering ever gaudier shows in the hopes of being on the ESPN Midnight Madness telecast. Thus, instead of the traditional quiet afternoon practice to begin the long season, Midnight Madness took hold—almost every school in Division I now does it—and the new breed of college fan reciprocated, turning the occasions into huge raucous parties.

With its Midnight Madness programs, ESPN also transformed a sports nonevent into must-see TV for many fans and even nonfans. ESPN extended this concept when it mutated casual athletic endeavors like skateboarding into elaborate sports competitions like the X Games. ESPN became the master magician at turning noncompetitive sports and nonevents—for example, the NCAA's bureaucratic selection of teams and first-round games for its annual men's basketball tournament—into required viewing, particularly on college campuses.

In a late-1980s survey of how college students spent their time, the researchers discovered that, on average, undergraduates watched 9.2 hours of TV per week. Many women followed daytime television soap operas and their evening equivalents, but men preferred sports, both the telecasts of games and, increasingly, ESPN's daily program *SportsCenter*. An early-1990s researcher noted that in all-male college housing units, particularly off-campus ones:

> Dinner is frequently eaten in front of the TV in order to watch the 6:30 P.M. edition. For the 10:30 P.M. edition, many males group in front of the large TV screens in the Student Union building or their fraternity houses or dorms to watch. Another large contingent watches in the various sports bars [in college towns]. In addition, many choose to view the program at 2:30 A.M. because they have missed the earlier editions or because, as they explain, they "cannot get enough of it."

A large part of *SportsCenter*'s appeal was (and is) the language of the studio announcers, a combination of traditional sentimentality and hip skepticism. Both forms of sports reporting continued very old styles—the upbeat "Gee Whiz" approach and the skeptical "Aw Nuts" attitude, but ESPN's innovation, borrowed from such sportswriters as Dan Jenkins, placed the sentimental and the skeptical side by side. When longtime *SportsCenter* anchorman Chris Berman showed a clip of a home run, he often intoned, "Back-back-back . . . ," consciously paying homage to old-time broadcaster Red Barber's call of a famous drive by Joe DiMaggio in the 1947 World Series. Then Berman would mock a player by giving him a comic nickname, e.g, outfielder Mel "Kids in the" Hall; and Berman's partner, Keith Olberman, would show a clip of Hall dropping an easy fly ball, and groan a nasty, "Guh!" For long football runs resulting in touchdowns, announcer Larry Beil would yell, "Run, Forrest, run!," evoking scenes from one of the most sentimental movies of the 1990s, *Forrest Gump*. But when showing an injured player on the sidelines during practice, announcer Dan Patrick sometimes commented, "He's listed as day-to-day, but then again, aren't we all."

For TV viewers, the perfect mind-set for watching *SportsCenter*, particularly when seeing clips from college sports events and knowing all about the corruption in intercollegiate athletics, was (and is) the equivalent of what George Orwell defined in *1984* as "doublethink": the ability to believe contradictory ideas simultaneously, for example, acknowledging the dysfunction of college sports while fervently following its teams and games. College students were (and are) especially prone to doublethink: encountering intercollegiate athletics firsthand, they often relate inside stories about the jocks on their campus receiving special financial and academic deals, but when those jocks take the court or field, they cheer madly for them, particularly if the team is winning.

A nationally published guide, *How to College in the 1990s*, perfectly caught the student doublethink attitude toward college sports, as well as its connections to beer-and-circus, and the importance of winning:

> Come game time, all this [college sports corruption] seems trivial. When you're chugging your eighth beer and passing your buddy's girlfriend up the stadium rows while your football team clobbers its archrival, or [you're] vacationing in New Orleans while your team plays in the NCAA basketball championships, you couldn't care less if the star player got an F in Remedial English 1. You're happy, you're partying, and he helped you get to that state of mind.

When ESPN started a print magazine in the 1990s, it focused on college-age readers, and it filled each edition with doublethink (as well as numerous ads for beer and liquor products). In an issue with a syrupy article on a University of Tulsa basketball recruit who had been home-schooled before entering college, *ESPN The Magazine* also published a feature comparing "Halloween vs. Midnight Madness," asking, "Two rituals that ease fall into winter, but which best fulfills its promise? Tykes hopped up on sugar. Undergrads polluted on grain alcohol. Let's see how they stack up." The magazine formatted the piece as a gambling chart (many college students bet on sports events, and ESPN caters to their habit, see pages 208 and 213–14). Among the entries were:

Category	Halloween	Midnight Madness	Advantage
Roots	Pagan	Drunken	Halloween
Hidden Danger	Razor blades in apples	Harricks on the Rhode Island payroll [Corrupt father-son college coaches]	Halloween
Chaperones	Always a good idea for little kids	Always a good idea for Prop 48 kids [Academically disqualified recruits]	Halloween
Unfortunate Potential Side-Effects	Diabetes	Point-shaving	Halloween
Last Chance	To be a unicorn	To see sophomores before they turn pro	Halloween

The negativity and cynicism about intercollegiate athletics in this feature would have startled earlier generations of college sports rooters, yet current fans cheer as loudly for their teams as their predecessors did, mainly illustrating the power of doublethink.

In the final decades of the twentieth century, however, not all college sports fans moved to doublethink: indeed, this attitude marked a generational divide among college sports enthusiasts, younger fans adopting it much more readily than their elders. College students and young alumni accepted corruption as the norm while embracing their favorite teams and athletes, but older fans, particularly those over fifty, tended to believe in the NCAA's student-athlete ideal as portrayed in the association's halftime TV clips (younger fans remarked that these promos occurred at a time when most viewers were not watching TV but opening refrigerators or flushing toilets).

Marketing surveys charted the generational split. In the early 1990s, one study reported that "fans aged 18–31 are much more tolerant . . . than their elders" about off-the-field problems, including "the commercialization in sports." For example, a majority of all older fans believed that "beers shouldn't be allowed as sponsors" of sports events, whereas almost two-thirds of young fans had no problem with brewery or even cigarette sponsorship (also opposed by older fans). In the twenty-first century, surveys would probably reveal a greater spread in the numbers, with youthful indifference and cynicism increasing every year.

The split between doublethink and single-minded fans also varied somewhat from region to region and from school to school. Regardless of their age, many supporters of athletic programs that openly cheated and got caught justified the dishonesty with the "everyone does it" line; this attitude never prevented these fans from treating their corrupt coaches and athletes as traditional sports heroes, especially if they won. Doublethink prevailed in such conferences as the SEC, Big East, and Pac-10; on the other hand, universities adhering more closely to the NCAA rules kept and attracted fans of all ages who believed in the student-athlete ideals and wanted their schools to observe them, e.g., Penn State, with Joe Paterno (JoPa) heading its football program. (ESPN often treated JoPa reverently, but in 1997, in a radio ad campaign promoting its college football coverage, two announcers mocked Paterno's nonconference "easy schedules," predicting that West Chester State of Pennsylvania would play next year in Happy Valley!)

Just as doublethink evolved out of earlier, more unified attitudes about college sports, beer-and-circus also connected to various traditions, especially the collegiate fun and games surrounding intercollegiate athletics. Indeed, without such rich collegiate ground to plow, well fertilized by the *Animal House* mentality of the 1980s, companies like Miller Brewing could not have so easily instituted corporate beer-and-circus. The next chapter examines this phenomenon.

4

CORPORATE
BEER-AND-CIRCUS

From the founding of intercollegiate athletics in the nineteenth century, drinking often accompanied college sports events, particularly football games. As sociologists Clark and Trow indicated, this revelry formed an important part of the collegiate subculture. However, contrary to *Animal House*, in the pre–Vietnam War era depicted in the film, collegians mainly partied on the weekends and rarely consumed the massive quantities of alcohol downed by Bluto and his fellow Deltas.

In the 1980s, beer-and-circus escalated, in large part because of marketing strategies by the major brewing companies. The college guidebooks for prospective students paralleled this escalation when they began to emphasize the collegiate subculture on university campuses, and to downplay the educational aspects of a school. The guidebooks often provided detailed descriptions of life as a college sports fan at a particular university, and tied this to the party scene.

★   ★   ★

If the prospect of cheering the Razorbacks at football games with chants of "Ooh-Pig-Sooey" doesn't send anticipatory shivers up and down your spine, don't even consider attending [the University of Arkansas]. This custom is known as "calling the hogs," and if you can't do it with conviction then you probably don't belong here.

"I'm a true Razorback fan!" gushes a junior. The sentiment is heartfelt and practically inbred. Arkansas students grow up as Razorback fans and can't wait to go to college and call the hogs in person. "My family loves the Razorbacks passionately," a student

confided. To love the university—and [its] students surely do—is to
love sports and spirit rallies and calling the hogs.
              —*Lisa Birnbach's New & Improved College Book*

Of all mass market college guidebooks in the 1980s and early 1990s,
Lisa Birnbach aimed hers most directly at prospective college students, informing them in detail about extracurricular life and the "social scene" at
different schools. She mentioned the educational aspects of universities—
but mainly in such categories as "Most Popular 'Blow-Off' Courses," and
numerical student ratings of the quality of education at their institutions:
at the University of Arkansas, students rated "overall academic excellence"
as 6.5 (out of 10), and "overall interest in learning" exhibited by students
as 5.75. (In contrast, the next school in her book, Cal Tech, received student ratings of 10 and 9.6 in these categories but, predictably, low ratings
for "leisure opportunities" and social life. Birnbach's ratings, although not
scientific, did indicate the way students in her extensive polling regarded
different aspects of their universities.)

Of much greater interest to her readers than the academic ratings were
such observations as: "long known as a party school," at the University of
Arkansas, "liquor flows fast and steady on and off campus, and despite a
state ordinance against underage drinking, no one lacks for opportunities
to imbibe." Birnbach frequently interspersed her commentary with quotes
from students: an Arkansas undergrad stated, " 'Many people [here] party
and party often,' " and another claimed, " 'The worst thing about the
school is sometimes there are too many parties,' " and it's hard to choose
which ones to attend. Birnbach's guidebook also discussed the role of
Greek organizations on each campus. At Arkansas, about 20 percent of
undergraduates belonged to them, but "they infiltrate everything," setting
a collegiate tone for the university.

Obviously, college sports, partying, and Greek organizations had existed
for many generations at the University of Arkansas before Lisa Birnbach
visited the campus; however, the main difference between the old fun and
games and the 1980s rise of beer-and-circus was the corporate nature of
the latter. In this decade, national brewers greatly increased their advertising in the campus newspaper, the *Arkansas Traveler*, and in the local/
regional paper, the *Northwest Arkansas Times*, as did local beer distributors and liquor stores. Additionally, the local outlets, aided by the national
brands, promoted their products much more aggressively than ever before
with a plethora of marketing gimmicks, including below-cost specials and
paraphernalia giveaways. Moreover, the University of Arkansas, also be-

coming more corporate, sanctioned beer-and-circus in various ways, e.g., allowing its alumni association and athletic department to escalate such alcohol-drenched events as the tailgate barbecues and parties before and after football games and, with the rise in the rankings of the Razorback basketball team, before and after b-ball contests.

The Arkansas administration also tried to link the school with the national sports media, encouraging its athletic department to court the national networks in every possible way, for example, agreeing to start contests at whatever hour they requested, no matter how inconvenient to students and other fans. The school also ended its historic association with the Southwest Conference and moved to the SEC, mainly for the increased TV coverage and payouts (throughout this period, the athletic department consistently lost money).

However, to be fair to the University of Arkansas, in the 1980s its students were not the only marketing target of the beer and liquor companies, but merely part of an immense and extremely well-funded national campaign (see below). Also its administrators and athletic department personnel were not alone in chasing TV dollars, nor singular in switching conferences.

For the Razorbacks, departing the Southwest Conference (which eventually folded) meant ending such historic annual games as the contest against the University of Texas at Austin. Older Arkansas fans hated this move—the game was approaching its centenary—but the younger generation considered the SEC and the increased national TV coverage "cool," and then everyone drank more beer and called more hogs. Finally, in this period and afterward, like many schools, the University of Arkansas claimed to be trying to improve its academic standing. But it spent much more proportionally on its research and graduate school facilities than it did on general undergraduate education.

The rise of corporate universities and corporate beer-and-circus in the 1980s was not confined to large public institutions like the University of Arkansas. Other schools, including some private ones in other parts of the country and at other places on the economic scale, underwent similar transitions. But all of these schools possessed a number of the same characteristics: they had large and influential collegiate subcultures, flourishing intercollegiate athletic departments, well-earned reputations as party schools, and administrators who emphasized research and graduate programs over undergraduate education ones. The University of Southern California provided a good example of this phenomenon, and also illustrated the influence of the national media on student attitudes, as opposed to campus and local media in college towns like Fayetteville, Arkansas.

> Indisputably a sports school, or to put it less politely, a "jock" school, USC can (and does) boast that it has won more NCAA team championships . . . and produced more Olympic athletes than any other university. . . . So pronounced is the emphasis on athletics that students have sneered that they attend "a football team with a classroom tucked in the bottom of it."
> —*Lisa Birnbach's New & Improved College Book*

Like the University of Arkansas, the academic aspects of USC did not impress Lisa Birnbach and her investigators. Her guidebook stated: " 'You can slide by here in the easiest classes like at a junior college,' students have said. But for more serious students—and people swear they do exist [here]—USC does have extensive options." The highly selective USC Film School was supposed to be one option, although the "Most Popular Mic' Course" on campus was Exploring Culture Through Film (for each school, Birnbach inserted the local slang term for an easy course, here—appropriate, considering its movie origins—"Mic" for "Mickey Mouse").

Equally revealing about USC were such comments as, "If you're looking for a party, you can always find one, [including] Monday through Thursday," and one of the best party weekends of the year occurs when "three to four thousand [USC] students fly or drive to San Francisco" for the USC at Berkeley or the USC at Stanford football game (these take place in alternate years). Birnbach also noted that "Greeks are the dominant social force on campus and represent 22 percent of the undergraduate student body."

In the history of collegiate life, USC has long played a central role, serving as the inspiration for, as well as the site of, many Hollywood films depicting carefree collegians and the excitement of college sports. In the 1980s, the school also provided the location, and some of its students worked as extras, for a number of beer commercials for national brands. In addition, several of the marketing agencies that held brewery and liquor accounts tested their campaign ideas on USC students. Posters of Budweiser's Spuds Mackenzie, the most popular "party animal" of the decade, hung on walls of housing units at USC long before they arrived in Fayetteville, Arkansas.

*   *   *

In the last 10 years [1979 to 1989] as the campaign to protect young people from the perils of alcohol abuse has intensified, so has the alcoholic beverage industry's efforts to hawk its wares to a youthful market. The nation's beer, wine, and liquor producers spent more than $1.3 billion in 1987 to advertise their products. Beer advertising alone—totaling $847 million—has more than doubled since 1980 with the push for a younger drinking audience.

—Diane Alters, *Boston Globe* reporter

In comprehensive market surveys in the 1980s, beer, wine, and liquor companies determined that 10 percent of the U.S. population bought almost 60 percent of their products, and that the largest segment of purchasers were young men. Moreover, demographers indicated that, with baby boomers aging and drinking less, the alcoholic beverage industry faced a shrinking market. As a result, as one industry expert stated, in the 1980s the national companies saw "themselves in a life-and-death battle to maintain strong sales," and felt much more threatened by demographic trends than by M.A.D.D. and other antialcohol groups.

The industry's marketing research also ascertained that males between the ages of eighteen and twenty-four not only represented a huge percentage of current profits but also promised future sales. During their college-age years, drinkers developed brand loyalty and tended to stay with their favorites for many years. Thus, alcohol producers decided to spend a disproportionate amount of their advertising budgets on campaigns aimed at college-age drinkers and, more specifically, sports fans. *The goal was to turn the major characteristic of college sports fans—personal loyalty to their teams—into a similar allegiance to their favorite alcohol brands.*

Miller Beer began the 1980s with a highly successful campaign featuring famous athletes arguing about whether they loved Miller Lite because it "tastes great" or was "less filling." Even though the athletes were past their college and professional playing days, the ads appealed to college students, so much so that some of the retired jocks became campus celebrities. In 1985, the students at Michigan State University invited one of the Miller Lite athletes, Bubba Smith (an outstanding Spartan lineman in the 1960s, and then a NFL All-Star) to be Grand Marshall in the school's Homecoming Parade. Smith was upset by what occurred: "I thought everyone was very fired up" with school spirit as the parade went down the street. "All of a sudden, one side of the street started yelling, 'Tastes great,' and the other side would answer, 'Less filling.' It just totally freaked me out. Then when I went to the bonfire [pep rally], they [the students] were just completely drunk out of their heads." As a result, Smith refused to do any more Miller Lite commercials. Bubba Smith's stand against excessive campus drinking was unusual; Miller offered no comment on Smith's resignation and simply hired another well-known athlete to replace him.

Miller started the 1980s as the second-largest brewer in the United States, and, with its jock celebrity ads, it began closing the gap on college campuses between its Miller Lite brand and its main competitor, Anheuser-Busch's Bud Light. However, an advertising agency with the Bud Light account conceived of Spuds Mackenzie, and subsequently Bud more than kept its lead.

Make Way for Spuds Mackenzie

The dog, dubbed The Original Party Animal by his employer, Bud Light beer, was introduced to national television during the fourth quarter of this year's Super Bowl. . . . Since that commercial, his popularity has soared nationally and spawned a growth industry of T-shirts and other Spuds paraphernalia. Posters of the Ayatollah Partyollah, in which he often appears surrounded by beautiful young women, are now the best-selling pin-ups in the country.

—Beth Ann Krier, *Los Angeles Times* reporter

Many observers, including Ms. Krier, described Spuds as resembling John Belushi, and Spuds's title as "The Original Party Animal" clearly referenced that actor's famous movie role in *Animal House*. In addition, Spuds's name echoed a popular term for beer, suds; and MacKenzie repeated the name of a successful 1980s comedy team—the MacKenzie brothers, two Canadians who loved drinking beer.

Spuds's commercial at the 1987 Super Bowl was merely his national debut; in fact, he had first appeared in 1983 in test market ads in Chicago and Los Angeles aimed at college beer drinkers, mainly those at Northwestern University, USC, and UCLA. Spuds tested wonderfully, and his fame spread, one writer noting that "he quickly became a cult figure on college campuses," with posters of him—given out for free by nearby liquor stores—soon plastered on student bedroom walls.

Despite his odd shape and size, Spuds loved sports, and many commercials featured him engaged in athletic activities. Bud Light aired the ads before and during college sports events and, in 1988, in conjunction with the Winter and Summer Olympics. Spuds also made live appearances at various athletic events, including college football and basketball games, and minor league baseball contests. Most of all, Spuds sold tons of beer for his employer, Anheuser-Busch, keeping Bud Light ahead of its rivals, Miller Lite and Coors Light.

Part of Spuds's success resulted from the fact that women liked him almost as much as men did. One researcher commented that Spuds's "crossover appeal [was] unusual for beer ads . . . but not unwelcome" because brewers had discovered that, in the 1980s, females, particularly college women, had started to consume much more beer than ever before. Women found Spuds "cute, cuddly, adorable, fun to watch," and thus he became the perfect beer marketer, so much so that Budweiser produced thirty-foot inflatable replicas of Spuds for college sports games and campus events, and also licensed his image to T-shirt, toy, and other manufacturers. After the 1987 Super Bowl ad, Spuds became a national craze and, inevitably, drew criticism from M.A.D.D. and officials like Surgeon General C. Everett Koop.

Spuds was attacked at congressional hearings, and Miller Beer tried to counter Spuds with parody ads featuring clay figure animals announcing, "Three out of four party animals prefer the taste of Miller Lite." Coors Light, always more conservative than its competitors, countered Spuds with such campaigns as a 1990 "Special Edition Coors Light Beer Can, Commemorating the University of Nebraska Cornhuskers' Championship Football Season." Then, in the early 1990s, Budweiser decided to retire Spuds gracefully, a vice president of brand management for Anheuser-Busch commenting, "We've always prided ourselves on getting out of an [advertising] idea before people are tired of it."

Undoubtedly Americans, particularly college students, would have experienced "Spuds MacKenzie fatigue," but they never became bored with the party atmosphere that he represented. One expert, analyzing the breweries' marketing strategy, explained: "Advertising doesn't create cultural trends, it capitalizes on them. The brewers didn't dream up" collegiate drinking, "but because of the money invested" in advertising aimed at students, the brewers try to "shape what comes out. They can encourage and shape the trends in their interest. *The underlying message [of their college campaigns] is that it's naturally part of college life to drink*" (emphasis added).

Just as demographics drove the advertising campaigns of the alcoholic beverage industry, it motivated colleges and universities to accept beer-

and-circus. After the last of the baby boomers passed through higher education in the 1970s, the number of college students dropped precipitously—from over 3 million in 1978 to less than 2.5 million in 1993—causing panic in Admissions Offices and administration buildings and, according to the *New York Times*, creating "a favorite indoor sport among educational pundits . . . predicting how many private colleges will be folding because of the declining number of 18 year olds in the population."

In a period when most institutions of higher education had many more places in their undergraduate classes than students to fill them, and schools desperately needed to increase the flow of tuition dollars, they marketed themselves in every way possible, many emphasizing their big-time college sports programs and party atmosphere, usually depicted as "collegiate good times." This marketing game plan succeeded, and, as a result, it continues in a mutated form in the twenty-first century.

5

ADMISSIONS OFFICE SCAMS

In the 1980s, some higher education officials began to discuss "the student as customer," referring to applicants as well as undergraduates. Pleasing this customer, soon termed a "consumer," became paramount at many schools. Colleges and universities needed to fill their classrooms and dorms—overbuilt to accommodate the baby boomers of the 1960s and 1970s—and, as a result, except for the most prestigious schools in the country, the demographic crunch of the 1980s and early 1990s transformed admissions from a selection process to a sales campaign, often involving clever scams.

★   ★   ★

Colleges [and universities] . . . are business enterprises competing for a limited clientele: the students. They know that competition for students [especially those able to pay full tuition] is intense; that is why they pump so much money into the production of videos, brochures, viewbooks, catalogs, and all the other promotional material that becomes a blizzard of hard-to-distinguish hype. . . .

In fact, very few of this country's colleges and universities are selective. *More than 80 percent of our institutions of higher education admit virtually all their applicants* (emphasis added).
—*Peterson's Guide to College Admissions*, 1991 edition

Many college-bound students and their parents ignored the reality described by *Peterson's Guide* and fixated on the competition to "get into" the small number of truly choosy schools. They failed to examine the actual acceptance rates of most universities, easily obtained in the national guidebooks; for example, the annual college editions of *U.S. News* printed tables revealing the rate for every school, including the hundreds who admitted between 90 and 100 percent of their applicants. Many applicants fell into the admissions trap set by a majority of institutions, including famous public universities: phony selectivity. Schools pretended to be choosy—in reality, they accepted almost everyone. One admissions official acknowledged that his university and most others never actually looked at applicants' SAT/ACT results, but said, "If we didn't ask for the scores, we would be regarded in the marketplace as having very low prestige."

(From the mid-1990s on, when the children of the baby boomers began entering college, enrollment numbers improved, but de facto "open admissions" continued. Because higher education's appetite for undergraduate tuition dollars is insatiable, most schools, including some with reputations for selectivity, still admit a large majority of their applicants: for example in 2000, Wisconsin at Madison—73 percent, Georgia Tech—75 percent, Texas A & M—86 percent, Purdue—87 percent; and hundreds of other colleges and universities accept over 90 percent, such as Auburn, Bowling Green, and on through the alphabet.)

Peterson's Guide to College Admissions has long discussed the direct marketing tools that schools use, and it has advised readers on how to interpret Admissions Office literature, e.g., "One of the quickest ways to determine the flavor of student life at a particular college is by studying the student activities. . . . Do descriptions of athletic events outweigh those of other extracurricular activities?" Also, how do the brochures depict the "marching band, homecoming," and other collegiate events? In other words, if you seek a beer-and-circus school—or wish to avoid one—this is how to do it. Moreover, high school seniors should ask themselves, "Do you want an academically demanding college program, or would you prefer a school where you can get respectable grades without knocking yourself out," and have lots of time for collegiate life?

In addition to direct mailings to potential students, from the 1980s on, Admissions Offices sent out recruiters "to beat the bushes" for applicants, visiting countless high schools, and also manning booths at college fairs in all parts of the country. At these events, usually at least one hundred and sometimes many hundreds of colleges and universities set up booths, and recruiters handed out as much promotional material on their schools as potential applicants could carry home. In addition, the sales people, resembling college athletic coaches on the prowl, buttonholed prospects and gave them their best spiels. One university, in a *New York Times* Want Ad seeking Admissions Office recruiters, listed "ability to close" a deal with a prospect as an essential qualification. (In the late 1990s, schools supplemented these marketing strategies with elaborate sites on the World Wide Web, including virtual tours of their campuses.)

The demographic and economic crisis in higher education not only affected average institutions, but also famous universities like the University of Southern California. In September 1990, the *Los Angeles Times* headlined, "USC FRESHMEN ENROLLMENT STARTS SEMESTER DOWN 18%," continuing the downward trend of previous years. Southern Cal's response was to hire more "admissions executives" and increase "recruiting in the Midwest, Pacific Northwest, Texas, and Florida." Recruiters coordinated their campaigns to coincide with USC's football appearances in various regions, and, in their mailings, the Admissions Office emphasized the national fame of the Trojans and the school's "festive" (party) atmosphere.

Some colleges and universities, even prestigious ones, tried to solve their admissions problems by going much deeper into their applicant pools than ever before, pulling out students with far lower SAT/ACT scores than their previous norms. Other institutions, particularly those with shallow applicant pools and de facto open admissions, had to use more imaginative—and frequently unscrupulous—devices to generate applications and enrollment. Some schools played "let's make a deal" with applicants, offering such financial "come-ons" as reduced tuition bills if the student enrolled at their institution. But, as the *New York Times* pointed out, these schools often used "bait and switch" tricks, extending generous packages for the freshmen year but then greatly reducing the aid for subsequent years, particularly for "those students who have made the most successful transition to college—and are thus less inclined to transfer." (For a detailed discussion of the financial pressures on colleges, and the rise in tuition costs, see chapter 9.)

In the hunt for applicants, universities with prominent college sports programs felt that they had an advantage over schools with mediocre or no NCAA Division I teams. The Admissions Offices of Big-time U's could arrange "fun weekends" for potential students, including free football or basketball tickets to home games as part of the package. These institutions believed that they could clinch the application-and-enrollment deal if they could "get the buyer inside the store," i.e., onto campus. They had discovered, according to a Carnegie Foundation report, that "the appearance of the campus is, by far, the most influential characteristic during campus visits," and, if a school appeared highly collegiate, featuring a big-time college sports program and party scene, this "look" persuaded many touring high school seniors to apply. Big-time U's sponsored collegiate activities for visitors, and, at a time of financial crisis in higher education, many schools spent millions on their grounds and the exteriors of buildings, and almost nothing on the insides of those structures—neglecting classrooms in deplorable physical condition and also ignoring deteriorating undergraduate education programs.

In a sense, many schools created Potemkin Villages and, like the historical precedent, never showed visitors the hollow interiors. The Carnegie investigators described a typical campus tour and its emphasis on collegiate life:

> During this tour, prospective students and their parents learned about festive occasions, but not who teaches undergraduate classes. They visited the student union and the dorms, not the library. The winning football record was discussed, but no mention was made of academic honors. Visitors heard about "keg parties," not about concerts and lectures. One had the distinct impression that the campus was a place with abundant social life. Education was ignored.

On the questionnaire for this book, many students responded positively to the queries, "How important a factor in your decision to attend your university was the fame of the school's intercollegiate athletic teams?" and ". . . the fame of the school's party scene connected to its college sports events?" In the results, because only a few percentage points separated the responses to both questions, the totals were combined, revealing that at NCAA Division I schools, 56 percent of males considered these factors "very important" or "moderately important"; 31 percent, "neither important or unimportant"; and 13 percent "moderately unimportant" or "very unimportant." Females at these schools responded much less enthusiastically: 26 percent positively, 38 percent neutrally, and 36 percent negatively. Some respondents added in the P.S. section of the questionnaire such comments as, "I always dreamed of wearing purple and gold in college [Louisiana State's colors], and majoring in tailgating. I'm glad I fulfilled my dream."

Undergraduates at Division III institutions—schools that do not give athletic scholarships—recorded numbers that almost reversed the Division

I males. Few students at these institutions considered the fame of their schools' college sports teams and the accompanying party scene important in their college choice; some even wrote sarcastic comments about the questions in the P.S. box. A woman at Emory University in Atlanta remarked, "What kind of dumb-ass chooses their college on the basis of its sports teams and boozing? Does anyone actually say yes to these questions?"

In the last decade, in their college choice, many students at the University of Oregon have responded affirmatively to these questions, selecting this university, in part, on the basis of the Ducks' high rankings in the Pacific-10 football and basketball standings, and the school's high rating on various "Party School" lists, including the *Princeton Review*'s. How Oregon achieved these distinctions, and also solved its admissions problem, is a story worth exploring in detail.

★   ★   ★

[Intercollegiate] athletics are extremely popular at the University of Oregon . . . games [also] draw large numbers of cheering spectators for the great tailgate parties. The marching band divides up into sections and plays school fight songs for the often inebriated revelers.
—The *Insider's Guide to the Colleges*, compiled by
Yale [University] Daily News staffers, 1997 edition

During the 1980s and early 1990s demographic crisis in higher education, some universities so successfully marketed their college sports/beer-and-circus scenes that they bucked the trend and held or increased their enrollments. The University of Oregon, the film location of *Animal House*, performed the latter feat, ironically altering its campus reality to fit the Hollywood view of it.

The longtime PR director of the university conceded that when the movie was made in Eugene in the 1970s, the school "wasn't like that, really." At that time, the University of Oregon was regarded as a haven for health and environmentally conscious students, also known as "joggers and tree-huggers" (the school and the town provided one of the first jogging paths in America, and the Oregon track program produced many famous runners as well as Phil Knight, founder of Nike Shoes, which has its headquarters in Eugene). Additionally, the Oregon Ducks' football and basketball teams rested comfortably near or at the bottom of the Pac-10 Conference, ignored by most undergraduates. A small Greek contingent existed, but it barely resembled the Deltas of *Animal House*.

Then, in the 1980s, the university administration tried to upgrade the intercollegiate athletics program, and, by the end of the decade, the Ducks made it to their first bowl game in a quarter of a century (the Independence Bowl). A few years later, they won the Pac-10 and played in the Rose Bowl. Accompanying the rise of the Ducks was the revitalization of fraternities and sororities, as well as collegiate dorms, and a drinking scene that imitated *Animal House*. In her early 1990s guidebooks, Lisa Birnbach described "two distinct groups" of undergraduates at Oregon, almost equal in size: "liberal vegetarians and beer-drinking Greek types," with the latter ending their "annual rush events" by consuming large amounts of booze during the "ritual of watching *Animal House*."

In its admissions literature, the school now proudly referred to its *Animal House* connections and to its big-time college sports programs; throughout the 1980s, its enrollment held steady, then it began to rise in the early 1990s. Oregon's success was particularly noteworthy because of the university's dire financial situation in this period. Beyond the student demographics and federal cutbacks to higher education, the state of Oregon drastically reduced its funding from over 50 percent of the school's budget at the beginning of the 1980s to less than 15 percent a decade later. However, the Oregon president, Myles Brand, had a plan: he surveyed the even worse condition of higher education in neighboring California—caused by draconian cuts in state spending there—and he ordered an aggressive recruitment campaign of California high school seniors, with an emphasis on Oregon's new collegiate image (showing supreme confidence in his plan, Brand also convinced his board of trustees to double out-of-state tuition to increase the anticipated flow of dollars).

As part of his strategy, Brand continued to upgrade the athletic department; again, he faced greater difficulties than the presidents of most other universities. Intercollegiate athletics at Oregon ran ever larger deficits in the 1980s, and the state legislature refused to help the school cover the losses—in fact, some politicians wanted the university to drop out of the Pac-10 and play college sports at a less expensive level. But Brand saw Pac-10 membership as essential to "recruiting . . . students," and he tenaciously fought the proposal to deemphasize. He also raised money for the Ducks from various sources, an Oregon faculty member noting that the president "can work the alums at a football game as well as anybody."

Thus Brand's "repositioned" University of Oregon was more "student friendly" and offered a more collegiate atmosphere than the deteriorating California public colleges and universities. Soon, Brand's plan paid dividends: increasing numbers of entering freshmen came from out of state, the majority from California suburbia, and they willingly paid the high out-of-state tuition fees. Then, during the year after Oregon appeared in the Rose Bowl, applications jumped another 20 percent, out-of-state applicants comprising the largest percentage of the new cohort.

The Oregon admissions saga was somewhat unusual—part of its success connected to a financial crisis in a nearby state with a huge population—but this university was also typical of schools that found Enrollment Valhalla in the 1980s and 1990s by emphasizing beer-and-circus. In fact, Oregon's 20 percent increase in applicants after its major bowl appearance was part of a national phenomenon, known to admissions directors as the "Flutie Factor," strengthening the link between the athletic department and the Admissions Office. (The next chapter discusses this in detail.)

In the mid-1990s, when the "baby boomlet" (the children of the baby boomers) entered higher education, enrollment numbers improved, but at many Big-time U's, the lessons learned during the down period of the previous fifteen years—market the hell out of college sports and the festivities surrounding it—were ingrained and continued into the twenty-first century.

6

THE FLUTIE FACTOR

From the mid-1980s on, many admissions officers have prayed for the "Flutie Factor" to hit their schools, and many university administrators have invoked it to justify their excessive spending on college sports. The phenomenon has become so central to the link between intercollegiate athletics and student life, and created so much mythology, that it merits full examination.

★   ★   ★

Suddenly, with television's saturation coverage of collegiate sports, small schools could gain national reputations. . . . The applications for admission to Boston College rose 25 percent in the year following Doug Flutie's exploits as quarterback. Athletics success on the small screen would mean increased enrollments.
—Mary Burgan, executive secretary of the American Association of University Professors (AAUP)

For college sports fans, particularly the new ESPN generation, Doug Flutie's last-second "Hail Mary" pass in a nationally televised Thanksgiving weekend game, enabling Boston College to beat heavily favored Miami, was one of the most memorable moments of sports theater during the 1980s. Flutie also won the Heisman Trophy that year (1984) and, according to media commentators, put his school "on the map," especially for younger sports fans. A surprising result of Flutie's triumph, never previously seen in American higher education, was that applications for admission to BC spurted upward during 1985–86; hence the term "Flutie Factor" for application jumps sparked by nationally televised college sports victories. (Subsequently, when BC's football fortunes declined, so did applications, yet they remained higher than before the "Hail Mary" touchdown.)

Nevertheless, in all of the commentary on the Flutie Factor, writers have overlooked a concurrent factor at Boston College and most other schools experiencing the Flutie phenomenon—an increase in the party atmosphere at the school. BC, historically a quiet Jesuit institution in suburban Boston enrolling many local students, became a "hot school" in the mid-1980s for numerous high school seniors throughout New England and beyond—partly because of its new college sports fame, but also because of its expanding party scene. And a key element in BC's beer-and-circus appeal was geographic location: in the 1980s, Boston became a "hot college town," popular for its many bars, including the prototype of the Cheers pub in the hit TV series, and a magnet for huge numbers of college students as well as a site of on-going revelry, escalating on the weekends.

In the wake of the Flutie years at BC, Lisa Birnbach reported that some students there "unhesitatingly call BC a 'party' school, and say that, in fact, the worst thing about the place is that 'school is almost second to drinking, etc.'. . . [In addition, students] make full use of the Boston nightlife." Other publications offered somewhat similar portraits of BC, also emphasizing the Boston locale and the college sports connection; the *Insider's Guide to the Colleges*, compiled by *Yale [University] Daily News* staffers, began a mid-1990s description of the school with, "As the game-winning field-goal sailed through the uprights in Boston College's historic 1993 upset of top-ranked Notre Dame, BC was instantly vaulted into the national spotlight." Again, a sports triumph on national TV caused another surge of applications; but, a few years later, when BC football players were involved in an ugly gambling scandal, the media attention damaged the school's reputation, also earning it the ESPN nickname, "Notre Dame's Evil Twin." Applications to Boston College dipped and then, for the next few years, remained on a plateau, matching the football team's ordinary record.

However, for doublethink fans, notably the college applicants among them, winning and media attention seem to transcend all else, including scandals. As a result, schools like Boston College continue to pursue victory in college sports, pumping millions of dollars into their intercollegiate athletics programs; in addition, like BC, they willingly cover large athletic department deficits, all in the hopes of having a future Flutie moment.

★   ★   ★

In the 1990s, university administrators began to discard the term "Flutie Factor" in favor of "mission-driven athletics"; in other words, no matter how much money the athletic department loses, no matter how much bad publicity the coaches and jocks generate with misconduct and scandals, a school should promote its big-time college sports program as an essential element of its "mission." Of course, this "mission" has little to do with education and everything to do with keeping enrollment high and tuition dollars flowing. The saddest part of this formulation is that its premise— many applicants seek schools with high-profile college sports programs and flourishing party scenes—seems correct. And the most amazing part of the situation—a triumph of media images over reason—is that many high school seniors confuse winning in sports with academic quality.

In the late 1980s, Carnegie Foundation investigators discovered through extensive polling that large numbers of high school students, "apparently impressed by 'The [College] Game of the Week' " and other televised college sports events, "say that an outstanding athletic team means that a college will have an 'above average' academic program." This explains one element of the Flutie Factor—sometimes high school seniors with SAT/ACT scores above a school's regular applicant average are in the Flutie cohort— and it also prompts Admissions Offices to fill their literature with images of college sports events and of happy students cheering for their teams, and to hope that their teams win.

Subsequent polling of enrolled students at Division I schools revealed that to the question—"When applying to colleges for admission, how well informed were you about the intercollegiate football and/or men's basketball teams of the schools to which you applied?"—88 percent of males and 51 percent of females answered positively ("very well informed" or "moderately well informed"). However, to the question—"When applying to colleges for admission, how well informed were you about the undergraduate education programs of the schools to which you applied?"—among Division I respondents, only 39 percent of males and 42 percent of females answered affirmatively.

Predictably, the responses from students at Division III institutions were very different: they showed much less prior knowledge of their schools' sports teams and much more of undergraduate education programs.

Because common sense, as well as consumer awareness, dictates that applicants to colleges and universities should inform themselves fully about undergraduate education, the responses to the question on this topic from Division I students, and particularly the cohort at Big-time U's (Division I-A universities) are distressing—but not surprising. How could these applicants find out about the quality of education at these institutions? Invariably, Admissions Offices gloss over general undergraduate education in their literature, instead supplying endless photos of small groups of students sitting in seminar rooms or on grassy lawns with a professor (lawns, because of the high ambient noise level and distractions from passersby, are rarely conducive to teaching or learning).

The responses to the question about knowledge of football and men's basketball squads are also predictable. Not only do Admissions Offices feature these teams in their material, but, more important, the media pours out constant information about them, the volume increasing enormously as ESPN and other all-sports outlets expand. In addition, the media often focuses on the party elements surrounding college sports events, including TV shots of drunken students with painted bodies, holding up their index fingers to signify, "We're Number One!"

Admissions Offices are more subtle about beer-and-circus, using photos of the festivities surrounding college sports events but, in deference to M.A.D.D. and for fear of scaring parents, never showing alcohol being consumed. However, high school seniors know how to interpret the pictures of parking lots full of tailgaters and pre- and postgame student gatherings, particularly after hearing about the campus beer-and-circus scene from friends attending the school and after making on-campus visits. Therefore, the results to the survey question on the importance of the fame-of-team-and-party-scene in college selection were predictable.

Beyond the quantitative results of the poll, individual responses to the P.S. request—"If you wish to comment further on any aspect of intercollegiate athletics and student life prompted by this questionnaire, please place your comments below"—were revealing. A typical comment came from a sophomore at Syracuse:

> In high school, I found myself applying to colleges based on how their sports teams performed. Among my choices were Syracuse, Arizona, Seton Hall, and Indiana. These were all schools with big-time basketball programs. I wanted to win a basketball national championship while in college and what better place to go than Syracuse, especially because I love to celebrate b-ball victories.

A striking element of this response—and found in quite a number of others—was the student's identification with the team, "I wanted to win" a title. Syracuse never won an NCAA men's basketball championship during this student's undergraduate years, but, if it had, only coach Jim Boeheim, his assistants, and the players could use the first-person pronoun to describe their goal and victory.

In earlier periods, and to some extent in the present era, many college applicants chose schools mainly for geographic reasons—they wanted to remain near their homes, or they sought a warm climate, et cetera. But in an age of national TV, increasing numbers of high school seniors, particularly those seeking to participate in a collegiate subculture, apply to schools with winning sports programs.

An admissions official at a university that experienced the Flutie Factor after appearing in a Rose Bowl game commented, "It seems funny to say that sports validates an institution for a student [who is applying to college] . . . but students want to go to a school that people are talking about. It may be subliminal but it is real." Subliminal for some applicants, but clear and articulated by many others.

Nonetheless, what occurs in the Admissions Offices of schools pursuing college sports victory and fame but falling far short? In the final decades of the twentieth century, the two-edged sword of sports media attention not only swings back at universities with athletic department scandals, but also at those with teams that lose too much. Because sports fans, particularly college-age ones, are increasingly obsessed with winning and attaching themselves to winning teams, their contempt for losers also grows. In a cynical age, doublethink fans shrug off scandals involving their favorite teams far more quickly than they do defeats—for these partisans, cheating is not the worst thing, losing is. Therefore, when the media labels the teams of certain schools as "losers," an anti–Flutie Factor probably occurs, with applications dropping below their regular average (no Admissions Office would respond to questions on this formulation, but common sense suggests the drop). In this case, "mission-driven athletics" could drive a university into an unforeseen cul-de-sac.

The media is central to the anti–Flutie Factor, but it never examines it. However, a detailed study of a university currently experiencing this phenomenon reveals important and relevant information, particularly useful to schools contemplating a move into big-time college sports.

★   ★   ★

Bests and Worsts [in College Football]
Worst team: [University of] Buffalo in its first major college season.
—Steve Weiberg and Jack Carey, *USA Today* reporters

The University of Buffalo got blown out Saturday. Again. And after a demoralizing 41–20 loss to Mid-American sad-sack Kent [State University, longtime owner of the worst losing streak in big-time college football]. It's a good bet UB will have to wait until the 21st century before getting the first win of its new Division I-A era. . . .

"I can't change the perception [of us as losers], I can't change how people react," said Bulls coach Craig Cirbius.

—Mike Harrington, *Buffalo News* reporter

Of course, this coach and the university officials above him at Buffalo could have changed "the way people react" and the loser tag; instead of moving the school into NCAA Division I-A big-time college sports in the 1990s, they could have remained in a lower group or, even more appropriately, returned to nonathletic scholarship Division III where Buffalo resided in the 1980s. UB administrators could have also improved and promoted the educational parts of their institution instead of spending a fortune on big-time intercollegiate athletics. According to one UB professor, these days [spring 2000], "faculty ask, why not take the dollars out of the football team and put them into the academic side?"

In the 1960s and 1970s, the State University of New York at Buffalo, emphasizing its graduate and research programs, attained membership in the prestigious Association of American Universities (AAU). In college sports, Buffalo could have joined the low-key Division III University Athletic Conference, and played such academically important schools as nearby Rochester, Carnegie-Mellon, Case Western Reserve, and New York University. Instead, Buffalo administrators, and an eager athletic department, decided to take the school to the top college sports level, no matter what the financial cost or the appropriateness to the educational mission of the institution.

University president William Greiner explained, "You do [big-time] athletics because . . . it is certainly a major contribution to the total quality of student life and the visibility of your institution." "Quality of student life" is often a code word for student partying in conjunction with college sports events, and the Buffalo athletic director suggested as much when he commented, "Not having big-time college athletics at Buffalo meant there was a quality of life element that was missing here" for our students. Also missing at Buffalo during the 1980s and into the 1990s were the usual number of undergraduates—the demographic drop in college enrollment effected UB, as did deep budget cuts by the State of New York. In addition, unlike schools able to recruit a sizable cohort of out-of-state students, Buffalo could not break into double digits in this endeavor. Hence the administrative belief that big-time college sports would solve the university's enrollment problems, and, with a winning team, the Flutie Factor would occur. Applications, including from out of state, had increased at the University of Massachusetts (Amherst campus) in the early and mid 1990s after the Minutemen had excellent runs in the NCAA men's basketball tourney; why couldn't that happen at SUNY-Buffalo? The school was changing its name to the University of Buffalo, why not transform its image?

"Every school wants to believe they will be the one to make it big" in college sports, explains NYU president Jay Oliva, but they mainly end up wasting huge amounts of money on the effort—funds that could be spent on academics. Newcomers also "believe that they can avoid the scandals that have marred Division I-A athletics," as well as the accompanying bad publicity. But again, according to Oliva and other experts, the best-case scenario almost never happens; for example, UMass endured messy sports scandals during its basketball rise, as well as a negative beer-and-circus reputation as "ZooMass." Nevertheless, although Buffalo has so far avoided major scandals (minor ones have occurred), it has generated a new kind of adverse publicity—the loser tag. (In addition to its winless football team, its basketball squad went 1–17 and 3–15 in its first years in Division I conference play.)

Moreover, true to newcomer form, Buffalo has racked up major financial losses. It joined the Mid-America Conference (MAC) and had to upgrade its intercollegiate athletic facilities to NCAA Division I-A standards at a multimillion-dollar cost. It also had to increase its athletic department's annual budget to the $10 million range (as opposed to the $3 million average in Division III), and school officials acknowledge that the sea of red ink will expand during the first decade of the twenty-first century. In a small-city sports market featuring the popular NFL Bills and NHL Sabres, and with almost no college sports tradition, marketing the collegiate Bulls is a "hard sell." A local sportswriter noted: "Fans accustomed to seeing the [Miami] Dolphins won't be too thrilled about Kent State, Toledo, and Central Michigan [of the MAC]. The [UB] team will have to win big to draw. . . . Over the next few years, he [the head football coach] has to get the program to a high competitive level or risk embarrassing himself before disappointing home crowds."

Why did UB embark upon this risky venture? The university president provided part of the answer when he discussed his hopes of moving his intercollegiate athletics program from the MAC to the Big East, and then to the Big Ten, his school's "peers in research, teaching, and service." However, if his teams cannot win in the low-wattage MAC, how can they compete in higher-powered conferences? Only someone like this university president, an academic with apparently no knowledge of college sports recruiting, could believe that a new Division I-A team in Buffalo could suddenly snatch blue chip recruits away from Syracuse and Penn State—the dominant football powers in the region—or from Notre Dame, Michigan, and other national programs who regularly pluck high school All-Americans from the area. UB, at the bottom of the football recruiting food chain, can only scavenge the scraps that remain after the majors, as well as many lesser but well-established programs, obtain their fill. The University of Buffalo Bulls seem fated to recruit badly and lose an enormous number of football games.

However, the athletic director suggested another reason for Buffalo's "mission-driven athletics" when he signed on to his president's ambition to join a major athletic group like the Big Ten: "A big conference isn't going to reach down to some undergraduate teaching institution and say, 'We want you to be with us.' " But "we fit the profile" of Big-time U's, and, like them, Buffalo does not emphasize undergraduate education. Therefore, big-time college sports—and, by implication, beer-and-circus— would make "a huge difference on campus. The students and faculty don't know what they're missing."

According to *The Princeton Review*'s 1999 and 2000 ratings of colleges and universities, UB undergraduates are definitely missing their professors. In the category, "Professors make themselves scarce," Buffalo came first in the entire United States both years. It also topped all other schools in "Professors [who] suck all life from materials" both years; and third (2000) and fourth (1999) in "Least happy students." Another directory, the Yale *Insider's Guide to the Colleges*, 1999 and 2000 editions, explained one source of undergraduate discontent at Buffalo: the enormous lecture classes and the fact that "professors don't usually know students' names or answer many questions in the larger classes." One UB student commented, "There are many classes where I haven't come within 20 feet of my professor." Predictably, Buffalo also ranked high in the *Princeton Review* category, "Class discussions rare (1999), and in a new category for 2000, "Teaching assistants teach too many upper-level courses."

Within this context—the school's neglect of general undergraduate education—Buffalo's move to big-time college sports makes sense. UB's situation is typical of many universities: because they cannot provide their undergraduates with an adequate education, but they need their tuition dollars, they hope to improve "the quality of student life" on their campus, in other words, bring on the beer-and-circus.

At Buffalo, because of the losing teams, the move to big-time college sports has failed up to now; nonetheless, at many schools with successful teams, beer-and-circus rules, and the student happiness level rises. Buffalo is using a paradigm that has succeeded elsewhere but, because of the demography of college sports recruiting, probably will never work for this school. Indeed, with consistently losing teams, UB might generate an anti-Flutie effect, an image as a "loser school" with declining enrollments. UB professor William Fischer worries that this "negative halo effect," along with a decade of state funding cutbacks, will further "degrade" his school.

In contrast, Florida State University has achieved an almost permanent Flutie Factor. With fertile southern high school football fields to harvest, the Seminoles are always near or at the top of the national football polls, as well as the "party school" lists (it held its high ranking in the *Princeton Review*'s "Party school" list throughout the 1990s). But FSU also rates very low in quality of undergraduate education. In addition, as a university with research ambitions, Florida State officials have poured millions into its research and graduate programs. This school is the current national champion in college football, and a prime example of an institution that provides its students with beer-and-circus and not much undergraduate education. If a beer-and-circus poll existed, FSU would be the national champ.

The next section of the book details the neglect of undergraduate education and the entrenchment of beer-and-circus. To understand this phenomenon, one must first examine the finances of higher education in the final decades of the twentieth century, and the inability of university leaders to confront the new economic reality, while at the same time pursuing research prestige for their institutions. With this framework in place, the role of beer-and-circus in the contemporary research university becomes clear.

PART TWO

COLLEGE LITE:
LESS
EDUCATIONALLY
FILLING

7

SHAFT THE
UNDERGRADUATES

In an influential early-1960s book *The Uses of the University*, Clark Kerr, the president of the University of California system, contrasted the established research university, for example, Harvard, Yale, and his campus at Berkeley, with newer schools striving for research prestige. He noted that "the mark of a university 'on the make' is a mad scramble for football stars and professorial luminaries. The former do little studying and the latter little teaching, and so they form a neat combination of muscle and intellect" that keeps the faculty and the collegiate students happy. In addition, the administrators who create this conjunction between football and faculty stars do well: they bring fame and fortune to their schools and enhance their jobs.

Kerr described the beginnings of a phenomenon that, because of the turmoil in higher education from the mid-1960s to the early 1970s, was temporarily put on hold. But his vision of universities "on the make" and their use of intercollegiate athletics as campus and public entertainment started to come true in the mid-1970s. He also foresaw an "inevitable" side-effect: "a superior [research] faculty results in an inferior concern for undergraduate teaching."

This section of *Beer and Circus* focuses on this phenomenon: universities striving for research fame, neglecting undergraduate education, and promoting their college sports franchises.

★   ★   ★

Table 1 lists the universities in the 1906 ranking, matched against the order of the top 15 in 1982. These listings demonstrate that a reputation once attained usually keeps on drawing faculty members and resources that sustain the reputation. . . .

Over the nearly 80 years from 1906 to 1982, only three institutions dropped out from those ranked as the top 15—but in each case not very much . . . and only three were added.

—Clark Kerr, University of California president emeritus

Clark Kerr went from the University of California to head the Carnegie Foundation for the Advancement of Teaching and, in 1991, he published an important article comparing the rankings of the top fifteen research universities in 1906 with those in 1982. Considering the momentous changes in higher education during that time span, his findings were unexpected but, after analysis, were entirely logical: the rich arrived first and stayed on top, and no matter what the rest did, they could never overtake these institutions. In 1906, the early period of university research and graduate schools, Ivy League universities dominated the top-fifteen list, and almost eighty years later, they continued to prevail. Similarly, the first private, non-Ivies that emphasized research and graduate education—Johns Hopkins, Chicago, MIT, and Stanford—were still in the top fifteen, as were the first public universities that embraced research and PhD programs—Berkeley, Michigan, and Wisconsin. Predictably, at the beginning of the twenty-first century, almost all of these schools remain in the top echelon, with only Duke and Cal Tech now consistently joining them.

Kerr titled his article, "The New Race to Be Harvard or Berkeley or Stanford," and he began, "All 2,400 non-specialized institutions of higher learning in the United States aspire to higher things. These aspirations are particularly intense among the approximately 200 research and other doctorate-granting universities." He then demonstrated that this race was a fool's errand for almost all participants. Additionally, it had negative side-effects for all schools, including the winners: the emphasis on research devalued undergraduate education, and "the regrettably low status of teaching in higher education provides faculty members less reward from that activity than they expect to gain from heightened research" work.

In his article, Kerr also discussed the phenomenon of "Upward Drift": those universities, whether they could afford the cost or not, that relentlessly added graduate and doctoral programs in order to compete in the research prestige race. Moreover, administrators of Upward Drift schools chose this course of action during a time of economic difficulties for higher education: in the 1970s and 1980s, with the end of the baby boom, tuition revenue dropped; also, state legislators and taxpayers, disillusioned with most public agencies, drastically cut funding to higher education; and inflation squeezed every school's financial resources. But Upward Drift continued.

With diminished revenue, most schools had to make choices. Only the richest universities could afford to maintain high-powered graduate schools and quality undergraduate education programs. Some small private colleges that had started graduate programs during flush times cut them, concentrating their resources on undergraduate education. Upward Drift universities made the opposite choice: they put scarce dollars into their graduate schools and neglected undergraduate education. A 1990s study explained that the pursuit of research fame and prestige were the "potent drivers of institutional direction and decision-making" at Upward Drift U's. The study also indicated that these schools continued this policy in the 1990s, despite "much talk on campuses about downsizing and concentrating on the core business of undergraduate teaching."

In 1973, Clark Kerr created a classification system for higher education that also provided a way to measure Upward Drift. His top category, "Research Universities I," consisted of those institutions granting at least fifty PhD's per year, giving a "high priority to research," and meeting various other criteria. The established research universities dominated the group, but, in the next two decades, a number of schools joined them. Significantly, almost all of the new members of Research Universities I also belonged to NCAA Division I, for example, Arizona State, Florida State, Kansas, Kentucky, Louisiana State, Nebraska, Temple, UConn, UMass, Virginia Tech, and West Virginia. However, even though these schools frequently had top-twenty college sports teams, none of them ever broke into the top *fifty* on the standard rankings of national universities. But all of these universities changed the nature of their institutions: as the authors of the Upward Drift study indicated, "Despite pressures to emphasize the role of undergraduate education, ambitious institutions" were and are "beguiled by the promise of prestige associated with doctorate-level education." These universities spent, and continue to spend, enormous sums of money on their graduate departments, and much less proportionally on undergraduate teaching.

Upward Drift also involved schools moving up to "Research Universities II" (fewer doctoral programs than in RU-I, but still committed to graduate education). Among the new arrivals in II were Houston, Mississippi, Ohio U, Rhode Island, South Carolina, Texas Tech, and Wyoming—all members of NCAA Division I but, predictably, trailing their wealthier siblings in that field as well. Upward Drift continued in the lower categories—Doctorate-granting Universities I and II (smaller graduate programs and fewer PhD's per year)—and included many schools near the bottom of NCAA Division I trying to climb the research and athletic polls. Again, none of these universities ever made the top-fifty rankings of national universities, but they all chose to participate in the research game—even though, before the 1970s, some were liberal arts colleges doing a good job of educating undergraduates.

The universities sitting on top of the research polls throughout the twentieth century have always dictated the rules of the game. The result, according to one critic, "is a monolithic status system that pervades all of higher education, a system which places an inappropriate value on so-called 'pure' research and on the national reputation for the person [the professor] and the institution that this research can bring." Since the 1970s, the administrators of almost all universities have endorsed this "monolithic status system"—whether suitable to their particular campus or not—believing that research prestige was the way to attract attention to their institution and to improve its standing in the academic world.

For an Upward Drift school to move higher in the prestige polls, it has to pass a more established research institution. But higher-ranked schools are not standing still or drifting downward; in fact, they work hard to improve their positions in the polls. For example, the University of Illinois at Champaign-Urbana, with very tight budgets throughout the 1980s and 1990s, continued to pour millions into its graduate programs and to neglect its undergraduate ones. An editor of the University of Illinois student newspaper described the state of her campus in the late 1980s: "It's clear that all the money is going to research. It seems so blatant when you see the run-down English [and other classroom] buildings and the fancy new research buildings. The U of I is really a research park that allows undergraduates to hang around as long as they don't get in the way."

★   ★   ★

At Rutgers University we have spent the past fifteen years [from the mid-1970s through the 1980s] successfully competing both for talented junior faculty [researchers] and for world-class scholars by promising them minimal teaching schedules. I know of junior colleagues who have been on the faculty roster for two years and have scarcely seen the inside of a classroom.

—Benjamin Barber, Rutgers professor

Schools try to ascend the academic polls by accumulating faculty who possess or will achieve research fame. Rutgers, the main public university in New Jersey, provides an example of a university "on the make" for research prestige. In the 1970s and 1980s, it aggressively tried to move up in the academic research world (it also entered big-time college sports at this time), but, for all of its efforts, as well as some success in faculty hiring, it never managed to break into the top-fifty rankings of national universities in the *U.S. News* poll (or the top twenty in the sports polls). Moreover, as Rutgers anthropologist Michael Moffat documented in a 1980s book, general undergraduate education at the school was abysmal and deteriorating.

Professor Barber also related an anecdote about an "Ivy League university, disturbed by the disrepute into which teaching had fallen, [that] recently offered its faculty a teaching prize. The reward? A course off the following year!" Amazingly, other schools offered similar bonuses as part of their teaching awards. These stories, as well as the Rutgers tale, spotlighted the faculty's role in the deterioration of undergraduate education during the era of Upward Drift.

Trained in the old and the new graduate programs, most professors come from the ranks of academically inclined undergraduates, and exhibit the traditional professorial distaste for teaching large numbers of collegiates and vocationals. Only the faculty's academic "children" and some rebels were worthy of their time—but not too much of it. In a 1980s study, the Carnegie Foundation determined that at research universities, only 9 percent of the faculty spent more than eleven hours a week teaching undergraduates, whereas 65 percent logged less than ten hours a week in this endeavor, and 26 percent spent zero hours on undergraduate teaching (two decades later, there is even less classroom contact between faculty and undergraduates, particularly between faculty and nonhonors students).

Yet, the Carnegie investigators found that faculty members were busy with their research, a majority devoting more than twenty hours a week to it, and many over forty hours per week. Professors sometimes criticized their school's "publish-or-perish" syndrome, but they participated in it, usually quite willingly. Their language revealed their priorities: faculty referred to their "teaching loads," as if pedagogy were a burden—at a time when most research universities established two-courses-per-semester as the standard teaching assignment for a faculty member, that is to say, six hours per week in class (however, at least one-third of all professors managed to spend fewer hours in a classroom, sometimes none at all). Faculty also talked about "research opportunities"—those bright, shiny projects and grants to live and die for. Moreover, when professors discussed their "own work," they never meant their teaching, only their research.

In America, because money measures the value of work, universities send clear signals with their pay scales. Before the 1970s, a few star professors received more money and perks than their colleagues; however, most faculty salaries were uniformly low but equitable, with years in rank as the main criteria. Upward Drift and the tight financial budgets of the 1970s and 1980s created a new pay scale: universities generously rewarded all professors who furthered the institution's research goals, and they gave the rest of the faculty—no matter how excellent their teaching—minimal raises. Similarly, they rewarded "productive faculty," a.k.a. researchers, with such perks as personal research accounts, extended paid leaves to do research, and fewer, if any, undergraduate courses. Only faculty who became full-time administrators continued to climb the salary ladder, but not with the same speed as the outstanding researchers.

In addition, in promotion and tenure decisions, universities emphasized research achievements and potential to a greater extent than previously; if a candidate was an ordinary researcher but an outstanding teacher, his or her chances for promotion and tenure were slim to none. The research imperative drove the reward system, but American business culture, notably its obsession with quantitative measurements and numbers, influenced the process. University administrators and committees could count a faculty member's publications; however, they could not evaluate teaching in any numerical way (even quantitative student evaluations were and are unreliable because of instructor manipulation and student subjectivity). Most important, research built a faculty member's reputation outside the institution and reflected back upon the school, enhancing its reputation; whereas the fame of even a superb undergraduate teacher rarely extended beyond campus boundaries and made almost no impact on the national ranking of the university.

Faculty members at research universities have long divided their loyalties between their professional disciplines (their academic fields, societies, meetings, and colleagues throughout the world) and their home universities. In the 1960s, sociologist Burton Clark described those professors immersed in the world of their disciplines as "cosmopolitans," and faculty mainly involved in their teaching and other duties on their particular campuses as "locals." Before the 1970s, most universities had a healthy percentage of "locals"; by the 1980s, when the Carnegie Foundation measured the percentage of locals versus cosmopolitans, it discovered that at research universities, only 21 percent of the faculty felt that their school was "very important" to them, whereas 79 percent considered their professional discipline as "very important," the center of their academic lives. (A generation later, the percentage of "locals" probably has dropped to single digits at many institutions, with the Internet enabling cosmopolitans to remain based at, but permanently apart from, their schools.)

The decline in faculty loyalty to their home institutions also reflected universities' decrease in loyalty to them, particularly the failure of schools to reward their "locals," usually their best undergraduate teachers, with salary increases and promotions. The signal, especially to young faculty, was unequivocal: to gain rewards from a university, be a "cosmopolitan" researcher. And well-traveled "cosmopolitans" began to consider the university as "a place to hang one's hat" until they accepted a better offer from another institution.

In the 1970s and 1980s, as Upward Drift schools tried to lure researchers away from other institutions, and cosmopolitans responded willingly, often initiating contact and soliciting "outside offers," the market overheated, frequently rewarding researchers with amazing deals. This situation further degraded the worth of undergraduate instruction—teaching talent had no value in a market driven solely by research fame. In the late 1980s, a number of analysts concluded that "American academe may be moving toward a single faculty reward structure, a system designed to maximize published scholarship and to minimize the time and effort faculty spend on instruction" of undergraduates.

At the beginning of the twenty-first century that single structure is in place, and despite all the lip service that universities now pay to a "commitment to undergraduate education," most have established a faculty reward system that relentlessly denigrates undergraduate teaching. In addition, most faculty members are only peripherally involved in undergraduate education. In the 1970s and 1980s, as a way of pleasing research faculty and increasing their research productivity, universities turned over the teaching of many undergraduate courses to lowly paid part-time instructors, as well as to even more poorly paid graduate students. Again, the "monolithic status system" and Upward Drift drove the process.

★　★　★

In my four years at Michigan State, I have had exactly four classes with under twenty-five students and a real professor in charge. All the rest of my courses have been jumbo lectures with hundreds of students, and a professor miles away, or classes with TAs [graduate-student teaching assistants], or not regular faculty, people who come in off the street and teach a course or two. Very few of the TAs or these part-timers know squat about how to teach, some of them don't even know anything about their subjects.

—A Michigan State senior woman in a 1995 interview

In the 1970s and 1980s, the new and expanded PhD programs at Upward Drift U's and the diminishing number of tenure-track faculty positions due to economic conditions created a glut of young PhD holders unable to obtain permanent faculty jobs and willing to work as part-time instructors for low wages. In addition, because doctoral programs maintained their full complement of graduate students, these men and women provided their schools with another source of inexpensive labor. An economist who studied this phenomenon stated that the part-timers and TAs are "like any part-time employees that McDonald's would hire—cheap labor that colleges and universities are relying on to save money." *Exploiting* seems a more accurate term than *relying on*; furthermore, the money saved often went into salary raises for research faculty, as well as contingency funds to match outside offers made to "cosmopolitan" professors.

This situation accelerated the decline of undergraduate education. *Time* magazine reported on the part-timers in 1987—it termed them "Academia's New Gypsies"—and noted that, nationally, 30 percent of humanities faculty were now part-timers. Other surveys in this period placed the number of part-timers in the sciences and many other academic areas in the 20-to-30 percentile range. Gypsies (also called Nomads) did the bulk of undergraduate teaching at many universities: nationally, by the late 1980s, they taught almost 40 percent of all undergraduate courses, and at some schools as much as 70 percent.

In addition to the part-timers, graduate students did a large amount of undergraduate teaching. Not only did grad assistants aid professors with the latters' undergraduate classes—usually teaching sections of the course, grading almost all the essays and exams, meeting students in conferences, and so forth—but grad students also conducted courses completely on their own, so many that these accounted for close to 25 percent of all undergraduate classes taught annually in the late 1980s.

With the part-timers conducting 40 percent of the classes at an average research university, and the grad students 25 percent, then the regular faculty must have taught 35 percent. Not really: if those courses with grad assistants carrying the teaching ball for faculty were subtracted from the professors' total, often only 25 percent of all undergraduate classes were under the sole control of tenure-track faculty. Predictably, in exit interviews at public universities in this period, recent graduates frequently noted that they had only taken a few classes during their student careers taught solely by full-time faculty, but, in many cases, they could not "remember the profs' names." (By the end of the century, the distance between tenure-track faculty and regular undergraduate students had grown even wider than previously, with more part-timers and grad assistants in charge of undergraduate classes than ever before.)

What is wrong with part-timers and grad students teaching undergraduates? For part-timers, the tenuous circumstances of their employment frequently negates whatever positives they bring to the classroom. Part-timers generally toil under oppressive conditions: they have minimal job security and prospects; they teach a course or two at one school, a course or two at another, and sometimes courses at a third or even a fourth university during a semester, and they spend much of their time traveling to and from various institutions—in California, they are called Freeway Fliers. For their labor, they receive short-term (usually one-semester or one-year), or per-course contracts (about $2,500 per course), and zero benefits. When they arrive on a campus, generally they do not have an office or a regular place to meet students in conferences. They try to be polite to undergraduates, but rarely do they have the time or energy to establish meaningful teacher-student relationships. Four, five, or six courses a semester—with normal preparations, as well as stacks of papers and exams to grade—grinds down the best-intentioned undergraduate teacher in the world. It is not a formula for producing quality undergraduate education.

Graduate students share many of the part-timers' difficulties—short-term contracts, and long hours at low pay—but many universities compound the teaching problems of grad students by failing to prepare them for their classroom assignments in a systematic or effective way (the main preparation for part-timers are the semesters of trial-and-error as grad student teachers). Because university teaching has long been a poor cousin to research, formal teacher training has rarely existed; graduate students spend years acquiring research skills and little time learning how to teach. Indeed, their main pedagogical model is the graduate course, and, sometimes, when teaching an undergraduate class for the first time, many grad students make the fatal error of trying to conduct the class as a mini-graduate course, even using PhD research material, much to the confusion or boredom of the undergraduates present.

In addition, many grad students, when thrown into a class full of students from the collegiate, vocational, and rebel subcultures, remember their recent undergraduate days and their dislike of these undergraduates. As academically inclined students, they had defined themselves in opposition to students in other subcultures; now, as instructors, they are supposed to be nice to them and to understand their spotty class attendance and frequent apathy toward academic work. Some graduate students climb over these obstacles and become good teachers; others allow their insecurities and inexperience to sabotage their teaching efforts, and they watch in frustration as students mentally and physically depart their courses.

All teachers take student indifference and/or hostility personally; sometimes undergraduates so wound beginning instructors that the latter never recover. On the other hand, successful, experienced teachers place negative student attitudes within an institutional context, and understand the difficulties of breaking through the subculture walls surrounding most undergraduates. These teachers try to work with the undergraduate reality, and do not take student attitudes personally.

Therefore, the main difference between part-timers and grad-student instructors is experience: the former have enough to survive to fight another semester; the latter either learn from their mistakes and improve, or they give up, or sometimes they go on to become outstanding researchers but bad teachers as regular faculty members.

A 1999 study charted higher education's ever-growing reliance on, and exploitation of, part-timers: nationally, the percentage of part-timers on university faculties had reached 40 percent. And when grad student teaching was factored in, they and the Gypsies conducted more classes than ever before—at some schools, almost 75 percent of all credit hours taken by undergraduates. Yet a majority of Americans believe that experienced professors teach most university classes. As one writer observed: "The general public, which pays most of the bills" for universities through taxes and/or tuition for their children, "sees teaching undergraduates as the primary mission of higher education, and perhaps the only important one." Moreover, the public does not understand the research bias of Big-time U's, nor does it have much sympathy for it. Nor should it.

8

THE GREAT RESEARCHER =
GREAT TEACHER MYTH

In the late 1980s, in reaction to growing criticism about the research imperative of large, public universities and their neglect of undergraduate teaching, some university presidents and administrators promulgated the myth that great researchers are also great teachers. They hoped that this myth would make the problems in their general undergraduate education programs disappear.

★   ★   ★

Great Teachers and Teaching . . .
Teaching and research are too often polarized—at least by those outside the university. . . . It turns out time and again that those we honor for excellence in teaching are the same faculty we honor for excellence in research.
—Thomas Ehrlich, former president of Indiana University

Myth: The good teachers are good researchers . . .
The available empirical evidence calls the "good-researcher = good-teacher" argument sharply into question . . . scholarly productivity and instructional effectiveness have less than 2 percent . . . in common. That means that about 98 percent of the variability in measures of instructional effectiveness is due to something *other* than research productivity or accomplishment.
—Patrick T. Terenzini and Ernest T. Pascarella,
education professors

To promote the myth, many schools established annual teaching awards to reward their best undergraduate teachers, and, lo and behold, at the head of the line were the institution's most prominent researchers. Local media covered the award ceremonies but rarely inquired into how the school arrived at its decision to honor this particular professor. Too often, no criteria, other than wanting to promote the "great researcher = great teacher" myth, existed. In some cases, the award was also an attempt to stroke the already huge ego of a star researcher, or to show a professor with an "outside offer" that the school cherished her/him in yet another way. And sometimes the award included the famous "course off" prize.

Terenzini and Pascarella examined the myth closely, concluding that its proponents invariably "argue by anecdote" and cite that small cohort of "extraordinary" faculty on every campus who manage to be good researchers and good teachers. Lew Miller, a professor at President Ehrlich's university, admitted: "I envy and admire such colleagues, those rare few who," in addition to full research schedules, "insist on a full schedule of [undergraduate] courses and who continue to put in long hours grading papers and meeting individually with their students. But I do not for an instant believe that there are enough of these extraordinary people to staff" whole departments, never mind large universities.

This criticism pinpointed the flaw in the "great researcher = great teacher" fable: teaching is labor intensive, and to do an adequate job—not even a good or first-class one—requires many hours per week, at least thirty for minimum results, and closer to forty or fifty to approach excellence. But research work is also labor intensive: whether in the sciences or the humanities, the researcher must spend at least thirty hours a week staying abreast of his or her field, preparing research materials, as well as writing time-consuming grant proposals, conducting research, and writing it up. Then there are meetings to attend, colleagues and assistants to talk with, and so forth; and, in the present age, added to traditional duties, e-mail to answer, Internet sites to monitor, and so forth. Thirty hours a week is a baseline for research activity, but most faculty spend many more hours per week in this endeavor, particularly during the frequent "crunch times" when papers, articles, and books are due.

That some faculty members can actually find enough time in a week to teach well and to maintain their research at a high level, and even do some service, mainly proves that in any large sample of humans, a few will accomplish extraordinary feats. Finally, the "great researcher = great teacher" myth resides alongside the "great athlete = great student" one: yes, Bill Bradley was an outstanding basketball player and a Rhodes Scholar, and yes, every year, some Division I athletes attain perfect grades in difficult majors—but they are a tiny minority of the more than one hundred thousand athletes playing big-time college sports annually, about the same small percentage as great researchers/great teachers. Intercollegiate athletes, working forty, fifty, or more hours a week in their sports jobs, have the same problem as research professors—lack of time and energy for undergraduate education.

Professors Terenzini and Pascarella went beyond the anecdotes about great professors/great teachers, and they examined every serious study on the relationship between "scholarly productivity and instructional effectiveness." They also plowed through the vast literature on the latter topic— the elements that produce effective teaching and those that do not. Their conclusion, cited above and published in 1994, should have driven a stake through the "good researcher = good teacher" myth, but it did not. (Note that they use the word *good*, not *great* as Ehrlich and others did; nevertheless, their weaker version did not come close to reaching their lowered bar.)

The myth endures in the twenty-first century because it serves large, public universities so well: officials can continue to hire, promote, award tenure, and give high salaries to researchers because previous university presidents and administrators have equated outstanding research with outstanding teaching; don't all those teaching award winners, commemorated with plaques on a wall in a prominent place on campus, prove the equation? On this issue, circular reasoning triumphs, illustrated by the awards and the on-going rationale (phrased here by Ehrlich): "*I underscore that students benefit immensely from having as role models faculty members whose energy in the classroom derives from their continual learning [and productivity] in research and scholarship.*"

This argument, much beloved by university administrators, is wrong on every count. Only a minority of undergraduate classes are taught—often badly or indifferently—by research professors; hence, these faculty members are infrequent and negative role models. And when these professors conduct an undergraduate course, they rarely teach their research because the latter is too technical or abstruse for undergraduates.

More importantly, as Terenzini and Pascarella show, effective teaching has almost nothing to do with "scholarly productivity or accomplishment." A University of Michigan study illustrated the actual attitudes of many researchers toward undergraduate education with the comments of a science professor at that school: he "noted that the nature of his discipline is such that he cannot teach his research to undergraduates, and he concluded, 'Every minute I spend in an undergraduate classroom is costing me money and prestige.' "

Paul Strohm, a longtime critic of university hypocrisy and cant, remarked that, despite the reality, administrators love the "good researcher = good teacher" equation, and they will never give it up because "it solves the problem of conflict between research and teaching by denying its existence." In addition, the myth not only helps administrators preserve the status quo at their schools, but it also creates a situation where, according to Terenzini and Pascarella, "the research on effective teaching methods will continue to be ignored," and undergraduate education will continue to decline.

★ ★ ★

Another higher education myth that Terenzini and Pascarella debunked was: "Traditional methods of instruction provide proven, effective ways of teaching undergraduate students." They focused primarily on lecturing—the main teaching form for faculty at large, public universities—and its failure to meet the educational needs of most undergraduates. One of the studies they examined was the 1980s report of the Carnegie Foundation on undergraduate education; in it, Carnegie investigators described a typical lecture class:

> At a freshman psychology lecture we attended, 300 students were still finding seats when the professor started talking. "Today," he said into a microphone, "we will continue our discussion of *learning*." He might as well have been addressing a crowd in a Greyhound bus terminal. Like commuters marking time until their next departure, students in this class alternately read the newspaper, flipped through a paperback novel, or propped their feet on the chairs ahead of them, staring into space.

The irony of this professor's students not appearing to learn anything from a lecture on "learning" apparently escaped this faculty member.

Lecturing has long been the pedagogical workhorse of higher education. Before the twentieth century, when textbooks were expensive and scarce, lectures were an efficient way to convey information to a large number of students—as long as they took adequate notes. Lecturing also mirrored more authoritarian, paternalistic societies: the supposedly omniscient, older male stood in front of the young students, all knowledge flowing from him to them. Then industrialism seemed to confirm the wisdom of the lecture system, particularly the placing of workers/students in neat rows, and the checkpoints/tests during the production process. Except, by all accounts, most undergraduates did not learn much in their lecture classes.

In the twentieth century, the lecture format continued, achieving limited success with undergraduates—the academically inclined and some vocationals took good notes and performed well on exams—and greater success with graduate and professional school students. This elite and carefully selected group demonstrated that lectures worked well in special circumstances: students needed to bring a high degree of personal motivation to the lecture course (they were determined to become doctors, lawyers, professors, etc.); in addition, they needed to master a large amount of material as quickly and efficiently as possible to pass difficult examinations (a good lecturer provided a pathway through mountains of information); and they possessed the analytic abilities to comprehend and take notes on the lectures, as well as the studying and library skills to complement the lectures with outside work (most graduate and professional school students started to acquire these skills as undergraduates, and built on them). These ambitious and atypical students made their lecture courses as active a learning experience as possible—whereas lectures rendered most undergraduates passive, if not inert. Thus, the exceptional minority provided university officials with the higher education rationale for a method imposed upon the vast majority of students throughout the twentieth century.

Yet, early in the century, some educators questioned the lecture method, pointing out that not only did most undergraduates learn little in large lecture halls, but generally they failed to master course material in small classes when the professor stood in front of them and lectured. Into the folklore of college life came such jokes as: "During a lecture, information passes from the instructor's notebook to the student's notebook without going through either head." Nonetheless, lecturing continued as the standard teaching method in higher education, in part due to faculty tradition and familiarity, but also because the alternatives to lecturing—student-centered learning in discussion and collaborative groups—were difficult for faculty to envision and, if attempted, required a large investment of professorial time and energy. Alternative methods also demanded a major attitude shift for faculty: they had to yield some of their supposed omnipotence and omniscience in the classroom and actually listen to students—not easy tasks in an era when a majority of professors regarded most undergraduates with contempt, and also wielded their authority as shields against the "uncultured masses."

In the first half of the century, some small, liberal arts colleges like St. John's in Annapolis, Maryland, insisted that their faculty avoid lecturing and teach mainly in the Socratic manner (Q-and-A dialogue between the instructor and students). Unlike the predictability of the lecture method, courses at these colleges demonstrated the creative messiness of student involvement in the classroom, as well as its apparent effectiveness—more than the graduates of traditional schools, alumni of progressive colleges attributed their subsequent success to their "special undergraduate education." In the 1960s, during protests at research universities, rebel students regularly invoked such educational models as St. John's; however, the rebels failed to break the faculty's commitment to lecturing.

In the 1960s, custom and attitude prevented the professoriate from abandoning the lecture method; in the 1970s and 1980s, in addition to the traditional reasons, other powerful factors—especially Upward Drift and cost efficiency—allowed lecturing to flourish. As a result, universities place the lecture class at the center of general undergraduate education, ensuring its continuing ineffectiveness in the twenty-first century.

As university budgets tightened, administrators realized that the way to lower the course load for research faculty, and still gain maximum dollars from their teaching, was to assign a professor one huge lecture class per year. The math was simple: according to standard accounting practices within higher education, universities calculated that, based on faculty salary, it cost them "$15,000 or more per class taught by a full-time professor"; therefore, if students paid $250 a credit hour, thus $750 a course, three hundred undergraduates in a class generated $225,000, and the university started this lecture course $210,000 ahead. After factoring in other expenses, say, $10,000 to pay five teaching assistants ($2,000 each) for their work in the course, and about $2,500 for the maintenance and utilities on the lecture hall and section rooms, and $2,500 for various miscellaneous and hidden costs, the bottom line for New Siwash was $195,000 profit.

But what were the numbers when a professor taught a class of twenty undergraduates? Tuition dollars totaled $15,000, a teaching assistant wasn't necessary, and upkeep and miscellaneous expenses dropped to about $1,500 on the smaller room. But because this course, like the lecture, was taught by a full-time professor, it still cost "$15,000 or more." The bottom line on the faculty member's twenty-student class: New Siwash lost $1,500! But why not give this class to a part-timer and pay that person $2,500 for the course? The new bottom line: the school made $11,000. Hence the administrative decision to encourage Professor Mumble to do his lecture course every year and drop other undergraduate courses from his schedule, giving them instead to part-timers and grad students. Multiply Mumble by tens of thousands of professors across America, and the result was an expansion in the number and size of lecture courses from the 1970s to the present, and no growth in small undergraduate classes—as well as a shift from faculty to part-timers and grad students in charge of many of the small classes.

In its 1980s study of undergraduate education, the Carnegie Foundation declared that a large percentage of undergraduate "students at research universities report that 'most' or 'all' of their classes have more than one hundred students enrolled" in them. A Rutgers professor noted that at his school, "classes of three hundred and four hundred were quite common," and only a minority of "students had even one class, out of the four to six they were carrying [per semester], with twenty-five or fewer students in it." The University of Illinois at Champaign-Urbana was a typical Big Ten offender: U of I featured a panoply of huge lecture courses, often enrolling five hundred students or more, sometimes even exceeding one thousand. One Illinois political science professor taught an introductory course that enrolled almost twelve hundred and, during alternating years, he did a lecture course with six hundred students—he called the latter his "lounge act."

Some students saw lecturers in the same terms as this political scientist, but they rounded out the portrait. An undergrad at Ohio State remarked:

> A good prof in a lecture course is an entertainer—very far away and not a person to speak to one-on-one. A bad prof is a prison guard—definitely not a person to speak to one-on-one. Can you believe that I had a prof [last year] who took daily attendance by making us always sit in the same seat, and having his grad assistants walk up the aisles with the seating charts, marking off the absent students? And he was the world's worst lecturer. Talk about a captive audience. I know what the hostages in Beirut felt like.

The *Chicago Tribune* reported that at many research universities, "Students find themselves in lecture halls seating 1,200. . . . Many undergraduates leave college without having had a one-on-one conversation with a professor." Not surprisingly, the combination of huge lecture halls, undergraduate anonymity, and bad teaching produced a stream of negative student comments. A University of Illinois junior condemned his mechanical engineering professor because the latter "faced the blackboard the entire time," almost never taking student questions, apparently contemptuous of the undergraduates. An aggressive Indiana University senior remarked:

> Every semester here I have encountered a professor who uses an overhead projector and writes continuously on it for the whole class, every class. No questions allowed, no eye contact made. I always feel compelled to ask these profs why they do not simply hand out all the notes they're going to write on the overhead at the beginning of the semester, and just let the students show up for the tests? Not one of these instructors has ever answered this question. They just walk away from me.

(In the twenty-first century, some lecturers use computer projectors, furiously typing their notes to appear on the overhead screens. Technology advances; the lecture method remains as stagnant as ever.)

Sometimes these sarcastic and astute reviews of faculty lecturing appeared in student course evaluations—if the school's scantron form also provided space for written comments. Anne Matthews, a writer on higher education, quoted a sample of student remarks that she found: "Never let this man near students again; his hobby is general condescension." "Eurobore." "Cancels lots of classes." Matthews commented that "some reviews are deliberately mean, some pan performance and ignore content, some are heartfelt and perceptive notes tossed over a very high wall." Many undergraduates realized that their university screwed them over in lecture courses. Nevertheless, students failed to understand that, to quote Matthews:

> Few campus adults in power take [student] course comments seriously. Who cares what the students say? The greatest of all campus secrets is passing time. Wait them out. They leave eventually. We stay. [Faculty always say] *You can't allow students to dictate in the classroom. No one is going to tell me what I can or can't do in my own courses* (original emphasis).

Matthews tracked student reactions from the late 1980s into the 1990s, but, at the beginning of the twenty-first century, the complaints about the lecture system continue. In a random, cross-country survey of a recent edition of *The Insider's Guide to the Colleges* (compiled and edited by the staff of the *Yale Daily News*), the reader finds that at SUNY-Buffalo, "Most required lecture classes for first-year students have enrollments as large as

200 to 500," and many students "just kind of sit through them, gazing off into space." At Michigan State University, one undergraduate noted that the huge size of lecture classes makes it "impossible for the professor to give anything but multiple choice tests, the professor and TAs would never have enough time to grade five hundred essays.' " At the University of Colorado at Boulder, "Class size averages two hundred to five hundred for introductory" courses and many other ones. And at Washington State University, "Introductory classes, especially those that meet the core requirements, can enroll as many as five hundred students, and the norm in the other introductory courses is one hundred to two hundred." To be fair to these schools—all Upward Drift research universities and members of NCAA Division I-A—undergraduates at similar institutions make the same complaints. In fact, the most astonishing note in this litany is the proclivity of universities to burden their least academically capable students—freshmen and sophomores—with the largest and meanest lecture courses.

★   ★   ★

> In contrast to the passive roles students are encouraged to play in lecture/discussion classes, individualized and collaborative teaching approaches require active student involvement and participation in the teaching-learning process. Such methods encourage students to take greater responsibility for their own learning; they learn from one another as well as the instructor. The research literature indicates active learning produces greater gains in academic content [acquisition] and skills.
> —Patrick T. Terenzini and Ernest T. Pascarella,
> education professors.

Significantly, these experts contrast "lecture/discussion classes" with "active learning" situations; they and others discovered that not only did professors lecture undergraduates in huge halls, but that graduate assistants continued to lecture them in so-called "discussion sections"—small subsets of lecture classes with about twenty-five students. The effect upon undergraduates was almost the same in both situations—passivity, lack of responsiveness, and frequent failure to comprehend the material. One study found "lecturing to be the mode of instruction of 89 percent of the physical scientists and mathematicians, 81 percent of the social scientists, and 61 percent of the humanities faculty." Another study calculated that the number of questions from students per classroom hour in discussion sections and lecture halls averaged 3.3, moreover, most of the queries were "procedural" (for example, Is the final exam in this room?), and did "not really get at the substance" of the course. Even good students with good questions complained about the lecture format, particularly its rigid structure; one undergraduate commented, "Lectures frustrate me because they whiz along, and when a prof brings up an interesting point, he never stops to allow students to delve into it and to really think about it."

This student cried out for an "individualized instructional approach," and Terenzini and Pascarella stress that "Long trails of research suggest that . . . [these] approaches are consistently more effective in enhancing subject-matter learning than are the more traditional" techniques like lecturing. The student-centered methods "emphasize small, modularized units of content, [and] student mastery of one unit before moving on to the next"; whereas the premise of every lecture is that "all students learn at the same rate . . . learn in the same way, and through the same set of activities"—listening to the lecturer, taking notes, and taking multiple-choice tests and exams en masse.

A vast and growing body of scholarship supports the nonlecture position, one expert on "Interactive Methods" summing up the findings: "While students may sit passively in a lecture class, they are forced to assume active roles" in nonlecture situations. However, a key to the success of alternative methods is "frequent feedback to students on their progress" in a course, not simply with numerical grades on scantron tests, but through lengthy conferences with the instructor during which the teacher carefully goes over the student's work in the course. The phrase *individualized instructional approaches* means exactly that, and strikes fear into faculty who want to spend minimal time with undergraduates, as well as administrators who want to keep their universities as research-oriented and cost-efficient as possible. If a class of twenty students taught by a professor loses money, imagine the cost of a class of ten students working with a faculty member and doing individual and collaborative projects; one in which, in addition to class time, the ten students meet one-on-one with that professor in semester-long tutorials? The actual dollar loss is high, but the time spent by the professor goes from about five hours a week to at least twenty.

Beyond the amount of faculty time and energy involved in nonlecture teaching, most professors will not accept "individualized instructional approaches" because they reject their basic premise: faculty can learn from all of their students; therefore, listening to each at length is a worthwhile endeavor. Every faculty member in America mouths the cliché about "how much I learn from my students," but when questioned about this, most professors respond with about as much clarity and detail as their lecture course students exhibit when confronted by an obscure exam question. In fact, in surveys of faculty opinion, professors at research universities continually complain about the "attitudes" of average undergraduates, particularly their passivity in class, their absence of intellectual curiosity, their lack of questions, and their reluctance to do the course readings and discuss them. Of course, almost all faculty contact with average undergraduates occurs in lecture classes, so these criticisms are self-fulfilling—lecturing produces student passivity, absence of intellectual curiosity, and so on. Finally, professors rebuking students for not being engaged by lectures is an exercise in blaming the victim.

The average undergraduate understands the situation better than most doctorate-holding professors; a University of Texas (Austin) junior commented, "The reason for the lack of student interest in most classes at my school is the fact that profs fail to engage their brains during lectures. They seem so bored, and they're always in a hurry to leave as soon as the class ends. We know that faculty are concerned about their research, and not in teaching us, and so, like the profs, we go essentially 'brain-dead' during class."

Ernest Boyer summed up the situation in *College: The Undergraduate Experience in America*:

> If faculty and students do not see themselves as having important business to do together, prospects for effective learning are diminished. If students view teachers as distant and their material as irrelevant, what could be a time of exciting exploration is reduced to a series of uninspired routines.

Fortunately, some excellent small universities and colleges still exist, and faculty there usually provide their students with individual attention and a multitude of active learning situations. At these schools, students often see faculty outside of the classroom and office hours, an almost unheard of occurrence at most research universities—indeed, at the latter, with students constantly "cutting" class, and very few going to faculty office hours, many undergraduates rarely see their professors at all. This reality is the final refutation of the myth that "great researchers = great teachers."

9

NEW SIWASH IN RED INK

As the quality of undergraduate education declined in the final decades of the twentieth century, the price of tuition increased dramatically. Universities claimed that their costs had grown enormously and that they had to pass on these expenses to their "customers," their students. The public, particularly parents of undergraduates, complained, but they could not discover the real reasons for the increases. And the media mainly focused on the price tag for a year at various famous schools, rarely investigating the causes or the situation at large, public research universities.

For most schools, the source of their financial problems were the drastic cuts in public and private funding to higher education during the final three decades of the twentieth century. By the late 1990s, some experts began to use dramatic metaphors to describe the situation, including the sinking of the *Titanic*:

> All in all, our actions [in higher education] are akin to a boat hitting an iceberg and the captain announcing that his highest priority, as the boat sinks, is saving the crew. The next priority is avoiding any inconvenience by continuing all activities—the midnight buffet, the bingo game, the shuffleboard tournament. The third priority is repairing the boat. And the fourth and final one, should time permit, is saving the passengers.
>
> —Arthur Levine,
> president of Teachers College
> at Columbia University

Dr. Levine's metaphor implied that while American higher education sank, college presidents mainly wanted to save the crew—the faculty and staff. Presidents also continued all university auxiliary activities, including big-time intercollegiate athletics and the accompanying party scene; moreover, these officials not only failed to repair their schools but showed little concern for the soon-to-be-drowned passengers/students.

Dr. Levine defined the iceberg as the sharply reduced funding and public support for American colleges and universities. He argued that through much of the twentieth century, higher education had been a "growth industry," generously supported by all levels of government and the public, but during the 1980s higher education became a "mature industry," with major expansion no longer possible. The economic prosperity of the late 1990s did not alter this situation; however, universities ignored this reality, instead squandering their resources in a cutthroat competition for research prestige, money, and undergraduate enrollment. And when students matriculated, schools gave them fun "activities" instead of meaningful educations.

Some critics compared higher education to corporate America, noting that many industries had downsized in the 1990s and, in lean-and-mean modes, prepared for the twenty-first century. But not higher education: university spending had continually outpaced revenue in the final decades of the century, also rising faster than the rate of inflation and the consumer price index. Then, when the stock market shot up and university endowment funds grew with it, this new source of money barely dented the escalating costs. The balance sheets of many universities mirrored those of their big-time athletic departments: no matter how many dollars came in, expenses exceeded income, resulting in year-end scrambles to balance the books. (Some research universities did downsize some departments, but invariably they moved the savings into other divisions. Moreover, the one unit that never shrank, and indeed grew faster and fatter than all other areas of the university, and lost greater sums of money every year, was the athletic department.)

The major cost for universities was the pursuit of research prestige. A U.S. government report noted that "research expenses at public colleges [and universities] increased 157% between 1981 and 1995," most of it for salary raises for star professors and lesser research luminaries, as well as for equipment and other amenities to help academic departments try to move upward in the national rankings. Another huge and expanding cost was "bureaucratic bloat": from the mid-1970s to the mid-1990s, the number of nonresearch and nonteaching administrators and staff rose by 83 percent nationally and, at many schools, by well over 100 percent.

Administrators fueled "bureaucratic bloat" by employing more assistants, secretaries, receptionists, et cetera, and by encouraging academic departments to do the same—often to relieve research professors of contact with undergraduates. In addition, administrators allocated millions of dollars for buildings and grounds, in part to attract students to their schools (see page 56), and also to keep them happy while on campus. George Mason University in Fairfax, Virginia, made a typical move by constructing a new $30 million student center, containing a state-of-the-art movie theater and food court. This school and many others also poured millions into their intercollegiate athletic facilities, but much less proportionally into undergraduate classrooms and libraries.

Increasing expenses put college presidents and their assistants on fundraising hamster wheels, engrossed in a never-ending search for dollars, primarily from the private sector. This obstructed long-range planning and attention to systemic problems, particularly undergraduate education. A former university official explained, "These days, all levels of university leadership are expected to devote . . . [up] to 50 percent of their time to fund-raising."

Traditionally, presidents and administrators of public colleges and universities gained the most amount of money for their schools from state legislatures and, to accomplish that task, they merged fund-raising with lobbying. In this endeavor, in the last decades of the twentieth century, they failed to avoid the iceberg that Arthur Levine described, and watched while state appropriations to their institutions plummeted.

> States now typically supply much less than half the funding [for their public colleges and universities] and, in 1995, state funding had dropped to 11 percent of the budget of the University of California. . . . A joke that circulates among [public] university presidents goes like this, "We've gone from being state-supported to state-assisted to state-located."
>
> —Nancy J. Brucker, higher education consultant

Historically, public universities lived up to their names—the University of Illinois, the University of Michigan, and all other State U's were founded and supported by the people of their states, and, up to the 1970s, legislatures funded a large percentage of the financial needs of state schools, usually 75 percent or more. Then, taxpayer disenchantment with all government operations, especially universities, as well as difficult economic times, slashed state contributions to higher education across the country, down to the twenty-percentile-or-lower range in many regions.

The boom times of the 1990s did not reverse this trend; in addition, in 1999, an important report on this topic predicted that "state spending on higher education will probably take a turn for the worse" in the first decades of the twenty-first century. The report also suggested that public colleges and universities would continue to compensate for meager state appropriations by extracting the missing and desperately needed dollars from their only dependable source of income—their undergraduate students.

In the 1970s, when state legislatures first started cutting their funding for higher education, university administrators, searching for new revenue, decided that because tuition rates were generally low, schools could raise the price on this item and thus cover their budgetary shortfalls. As the tuition increases accelerated through the 1980s and beyond—the U.S. General Accounting Office noted that from 1980 to 1995, the tuition fees of four-year public universities jumped *234 percent*—students and their families felt more than a monetary pinch; in fact, "the portion of household income needed to pay for college nearly doubled." Adding to the average student's financial dilemma, the Reagan and Bush administrations severely cut federal loan programs subsidizing tuition for many undergraduates: thus, while tuition costs rose, federal money shrank, forcing many students to borrow privately and to assume massive debts.

Paralleling the tuition increases at public universities were even more dramatic ones at private institutions, particularly in the Ivy League and at other prestigious private colleges. These schools noticed the success of public institutions in raising tuition, and they decided to follow and then trump them. For example, tuition at Penn went from $3,790 in 1976 to $24,230 in 1999; other Ivies and sub-Ivies had similar leaps, caused in part by increasing costs but even more by what economists term the *Chivas Regal Effect*—the consumerist belief that price equals quality.

In the 1980s, Ivy League administrators discovered that many Americans believed that the higher the tuition price, the better the education product, and so the Ivies began to raise tuition at an extraordinary pace. Helping them sustain these increases was their selectivity in admissions, convincing many consumers that hard-to-obtain places in freshmen classes were another sign of quality undergraduate education. Often the Ivies delivered an excellent product, but, more important, they produced a "halo effect," consumers believing that many other schools with escalating prices, including

some public ones, also offered first-class undergraduate education programs.

When experts studied this phenomenon, they quickly concluded that
tuition was rising faster than educational quality. In fact, as the Carnegie
Foundation and others proved in the 1980s and 1990s, general undergraduate education at some private schools and at most large, public research
universities was usually mediocre and sometimes wretched. However, the
media buried this reality under countless stories on the difficulties of "getting into" Harvard and other Ivies, as well as the necessity of high SAT/
ACT scores for admission—the latter topic was also hyped by the ubiquitous advertising of companies selling SAT/ACT tutorial programs.

From the 1990s on, as a result of the media misfocus and the desire for
a Chivas Regal education, many college-bound students and their parents
ignored the actual acceptance rates of most universities. They should have
read the annual guidebooks carefully: those publications punctured the selectivity myth, revealing that the vast majority of America's colleges and
universities rarely rejected applicants. *U.S. News* even listed the hundreds
of schools who accepted over 90 percent of their applicants. That's nine-
plus out of ten students who send in application forms! One wonders what
disqualified an applicant to these schools? Perhaps the lack of a pulse.

Yet, despite a market heavily weighted in favor of student buyers, tuition
prices continued to rise, and the quality of undergraduate education sank.

★   ★   ★

Robert Rosenzweig, president of the Association of American Universities, an association of 58 major research universities, put it very
bluntly when he charged: "For too long, universities, led by the best
of them, dealt with their neglect of undergraduate education by as-
serting that simply being in the presence of faculty working at the
frontiers of their fields was beneficial to students. That sometimes
seems to mean little more than being in the same city with them."

Compounding the neglect to which Rosenzweig refers is the unhappy truth that while students were being shortchanged in the classroom, they were shelling out more tuition dollars at the bursar's
window.

—*U.S. News & World Report* college issue for 1990

Ten years later, the neglect of undergraduate education has become, at
many research universities, the abandonment of undergraduate education.
The recent Boyer Commission report, *Reinventing Undergraduate Educa-*

tion: A Blueprint for America's Research Universities (funded by the Carnegie Foundation), called for a total overhaul of the current system and a major commitment by research universities to educating their undergraduates. The report also contained a large number of specific proposals—indeed, if implemented, undergraduate education at these universities would equal the product now provided by small colleges like Swarthmore. However, to achieve this result, large, public research universities would not only have to obtain and spend enormous sums of money on general undergraduate education, but also transform their internal culture. Therefore, even if the money miraculously appeared, the likelihood of these schools changing their value systems and privileging undergraduate education is extremely remote.

One writer on this topic explained that the primary value for administrators and faculty at research universities is *"prestige maximization,* a dedication to the goal of *institutional excellence"* (emphasis added), as gauged by the fame of the school's research programs and professors: "Being at the top of the heap is the quintessential *positional good"* for these institutions, yet the top "is limited by its very nature to a few winners—but all can aspire." However, "one of the by-products" for every school in this competition is the "declining state of [their] undergraduate education" programs.

Even *U.S. News,* generally an advocate for "the student consumer," acknowledged the difficulty of emphasizing undergraduate education at large, public research institutions. The magazine's 1999 college issue discussed such "reforms" as "making faculty teach more and research less," but admitted that these changes "would involve big trade-offs. Research can bring a college public notice and improve its reputation, which can boost enrollment and donations, which in turn can boost academic standing and help the [school's] bottom line."

Moreover, the intractability of the research-equals-prestige equation is confirmed by *U.S. News's* criteria for rating universities. The magazine gives *"greatest weight* . . . to [academic] reputation because a diploma from a distinguished college so clearly helps graduates get good jobs or gain admission to top graduate schools." The magazine arrives at numerical rankings on "academic reputation" by asking presidents and other administrators of research universities to evaluate peer institutions on this item. Predictably, these voters value research prestige—not the quality of undergraduate education—most highly. For example, in the 2000 edition, on *U.S. News's* five-point scale, they rate the University of Wisconsin at Madison, famous for outstanding graduate programs and also for huge lecture classes and beer-and-circus, at 4.3; and Clarkson University, lacking major research facilities but renowned for faculty attention to undergraduates, at 2.6.

A key word in *U.S. News*'s explanation is *diploma*—significantly, they use it and not *education*. The magazine implies that the label is of primary importance, that because it says Chivas Regal or Big-time U Baccalaureate, the Scotch whiskey is superb and the person holding the degree well educated. Clearly, this is not true. A California higher education expert commented, "I see students graduating who cannot write a business letter, balance a ledger, or use a computer to do so. I see other students graduating from the same colleges with the same degrees" who perform academic tasks at a high level and "are clearly very well prepared" for future jobs and advanced schooling (similarly, some graduates of Clarkson are better trained than some Wisconsin grads in the same fields).

For large, public research universities, labeling replaces learning, and, unfortunately, many students participate in this game by entering college with a single goal in mind—to obtain a diploma as easily as possible. One experienced teacher complained that for too many students, "It turns out that *having been* to college is thought to be the important" thing, not "acquiring knowledge" while there. This attitude connects to the historic disdain of collegiate and vocational students for academics and intellectual achievement but, ironically, Big-time U's promote this point of view by trumpeting the label value of their degrees and downplaying their general education programs. According to the recent Boyer Commission Report, when Big-time U's treat "undergraduate programs as sideshows to the main event" (research), students receive very clear signals about their marginal place within the academic parts of the institution.

"This school treats the average student [undergraduate] like shit," said a senior at Ohio State University. "And so we blow off our classes and party on High Street. *Go Bucks*. I've had a great four years of partying and following the Bucks, but an awful four years of course work." Whether this student offered a reason for his devotion to beer-and-circus at OSU, or a personal rationalization for the time and energy he spent on it is impossible to say. The synergy between the neglect of general undergraduate education and beer-and-circus is so profound that it is impossible to separate cause and effect. But the resulting reality dominates many campuses today.

10

STUDENT MIX
AND MATCH

Students at large, public research universities respond to their schools' emphasis on research and indifference to general undergraduate education in predictable, unpredictable, and sometimes unscrupulous ways. However, they always filter their reactions through the true center of their college lives, the subcultures to which they belong. This chapter examines the current state of the traditional subcultures—collegiate, academic, vocational, and rebel—and how these shape contemporary student attitudes toward the education, or the lack of it, that they receive at Big-time U's.

★   ★   ★

In their essay, Clark and Trow look at four student subcultures. Currently at Indiana University [April 1998], their divisions remain somewhat accurate. But I also feel students today may easily belong to one group but have lots to do with another subculture simultaneously.

Because I have to work my way through school with several part-time jobs at once, I basically identify with the vocational subculture. But I have done my fair share of partying and socializing (collegiate), and have lots of collegiate friends. I'm also a huge Hoosiers fan (collegiate). But I know many students who belong to only one subculture and to me that is the waste of a wonderful learning experience.
—A female Indiana University undergraduate

This woman's comments, typical of the majority of student responses to a question about the Clark and Trow categories, indicated the current state of traditional undergraduate subcultures. In the last generation, the barriers separating the subcultures continuously lowered, permitting many students to live within one subculture but to incorporate elements of others into their daily lives. In addition, although some undergraduates still remained within one dominant subculture for their entire college careers, an increasing number moved from one to another. Indeed, during the 1990s, some students made dramatic four-year odysseys from mainly collegiate as freshmen, rebellious as sophomores, vocational as juniors (when full awareness of the cost of their college educations dawned on them), and even academic as seniors (finally engaged by course content, able to take small classes in their majors, and considering attending graduate school, although usually unprepared to do so).

The main motivation for belonging to one subculture, moving to another, and incorporating elements of another into one's life has always been attachment to peers. Beyond financial circumstances, far beyond parental wishes, and even further beyond any influence exerted by university officials, undergraduates behave in certain ways and also change their behavior because of their peers. Alexander Astin, in the most extensive polling of student attitudes ever done, commented (his emphasis): *"The student's peer group is the single most potent source of influence on growth and development during the undergraduate years,"* and *"Students' values, beliefs, and aspirations tend to change in the direction of the dominant values, beliefs, and aspirations of the peer group."*

Those students who begin their university careers as collegiates usually have friends from their hometowns already in a campus sorority, fraternity, or dorm, or they quickly make friends with students on the same collegiate wavelength. If, after a year or two, some of these collegiates rebel against this subculture, they tend to do it with friends in the same housing unit, and they move into off-campus housing together. Then, if financial circumstances force them to obtain jobs to pay escalating college costs, often they work for the same employer. Finally, if they become academic, usually they form on-going study groups and hang out with their academic peers.

In addition, cutting across the migrations from group to group are the frequent incorporation of elements from other subcultures into the dominant one. In the 1980s and early 1990s, as college expenses increased, many students, including collegiates, had to obtain part-time jobs and adopt some vocational values to remain in school. Then, because universities kept raising the price of tuition and other fees, student vocationalism continued in better economic times. An Indiana University male senior explained this point of view (various observers quote analogous comments from undergraduates in all parts of the United States):

I think Clark and Trow's definition of collegiate is dated in its assumption that collegiates do not have to worry about money or do not care about grades. I and some of my fraternity brothers have to work at part-time jobs and also have large student loans to pay off. Also this change in collegiate attitudes is brought on, not by a resurgence [surge?] of genuine academic interest, but by a job market that often demands course work beyond a four-year degree. Many of us might go on for MBAs.

In other respects, the collegiate definition is still true. I love my football weekends, b-ball nights, activities with sororities, fraternity dances, and general partying. Most of all, I appreciate my fraternity brothers and the lifetime friendships I've made with them.

Less typical but far from idiosyncratic were the undergraduates who incorporated elements of the rebel subculture into the collegiate one. Helped by the accessibility and merchandising of the national rebel culture, particularly its music, a male sophomore wrote in 1995:

I am a collegiate/rebel who lives in a house on Second Street with some of my pledge class buddies from the fraternity. But we also constantly listen to the Grateful Dead and are deep into the culture surrounding the band and even join the Deadhead tour whenever possible. However, we still belong to our fraternity and go to functions there. We also love basketball and football and have season tickets for both. Our favorite bar is a totally Greek hangout, but we do our drugs at our house.

When Clark and Trow conducted their research in the 1950s, they would have never encountered this response: collegiate/rebels! Even in the 1960s on some campuses, fights occurred between Greeks and rebels. However, by the 1980s and subsequently, collegiates could easily participate in aspects of rebel culture, primarily the music and the drugs, incorporating them into their leisure activities.

Another cross-subcultural group, in part necessitated by rising tuition and other college costs, were academics who became vocational to help pay for their college educations. Some academic/vocationals existed during the first three-quarters of the twentieth century, but the modern era greatly increased their number. A male discussed his journey:

I am a history major with an almost perfect GPA. I also work twenty hours a week in a mind-numbing job at 7–11. However, I was recently accepted for graduate school at Berkeley and I know that I will do well there. I also hope to obtain a Teaching Assistantship there to help solve my financial problems, and to integrate working for money into my life.

This student then added a P.S. that illustrated his time with yet another student subculture:

I should mention that I dropped out of college for a semester and lived in Mexico because my girlfriend, and my best friend, and his girlfriend (all really smart people and top students) convinced me to do it with them. That was our rebel phase. What a waste, financially and intellectually. Also I missed a whole Big Ten basketball season.

The story of the Mexican sojourn illustrates how peer groups affect even academic students, the subculture most in tune with parental and professorial demands. To a much greater extent, peer pressure influences collegiates, resulting in unwritten dress and speech codes, and a high degree of conformity. Similarly, many observers have noted the ironic conformity of rebels, also often adhering to dress and speech codes, as well as peer pressure to be cool or hip. And in a final twist of contemporary consumer culture, national clothing companies merchandise the rebel look, and, as an authentic female rebel student complained:

There are all too many sorority girls on this campus wearing flannels and getting tattoos and piercings because this is the prevalent [rebel] image offered by MTV and other media. This trendy conformist non-conformism dismays those of us who truly wish to pull away from the mainstream in order to acquire an individual perspective.

Similarly, many fraternity men insert earrings and other body jewelry and don appropriate rebel clothes for weekend "raves" and "clubbing," only to return to the "catalog" collegiate look (Abercrombie & Fitch, Tommy Hilfiger, et cetera) during the week.

Finally, some members of one group of vocational students—intercollegiate athletes—have adopted a number of the traditional customs of the collegiate subculture, notably initiation and drinking ceremonies. Throughout the 1990s, alcohol-related incidents involving college athletes occurred, as did some nasty hazing episodes. The increasing isolation of athletes from the general student population, and their sense of their teams as elite units, often prompted the hazing of new members. Ironically, team initiations escalated at a time when fraternity and sorority hazing declined somewhat, and campus administrators had great difficulty in curtailing the athletes' activities.

At the core of the problem for university officials is their escalation of big-time college sports. From the first contact between an athlete and a school, the jock knows that he or she is special and is treated much better than ordinary student applicants—among other perks, the university usually pays for the visit. This treatment continues when the athlete enrolls, and it extends through his or her time at the institution. Even though the jock, working in a sport for thirty, forty, or more hours per week, definitely earns her or his athletic scholarship, the sense of specialness and immunity from ordinary rules never departs; in fact, when combined with anger over excessive work demands, the result can be antisocial, even criminal behavior. Many intercollegiate athletes pay a high personal price for being big-time college sports entertainers. But their schools promote, and large numbers of regular undergraduates love, the beer-and-circus that the jocks provide.

★   ★   ★

Party, Party, Party [at Louisiana State University]
Nearly every [student] organization on campus hosts parties throughout the year. . . . [For football weekends] all of the campus streets are closed to accommodate the massive number of people tailgating, drinking, and partying. . . . Such frenetic activity and enthusiasm extend to all aspects of student life at LSU, and often preclude more serious activities like studying.

What is a typical [student] weekend schedule? Friday—drink, fall asleep in someone's bathtub; Saturday—leave bathtub, watch the game, drink; Sunday—drink lightly.
—*The Insider's Guide to the Colleges*, 2000 edition

One of the few campus activities at Big-time U's that unite undergraduates from different subcultures are college sports events, even prompting some uniformity of dress on "game days" and "game nights." On football Saturdays at Louisiana State, most students dress in the school colors of purple and gold. At Ohio State University before football games, a majority of students wear scarlet and gray to support their beloved Buckeyes, and many participate in such rituals as buying a slice of cake from the "Cake Lady" outside Ohio Stadium. Similarly, as many Indiana University undergraduates mentioned, whatever their "home subculture," they were Hoosier fans.

One expects collegiates to fervently support intercollegiate athletics but, at the beginning of the twenty-first century, as the electronic media increasingly emphasizes sports, many vocational students have also become fans, listening to or watching the broadcasts of their universities' teams while at work or commuting. Similarly, because sports have become so central to American culture, some academic students feel compelled to follow their schools' teams or be tagged "total losers," a fate worse than normal scholarly "nerdiness." Only hard-core rebel students adamantly hold out, such as the female rebel who complained about sorority girls and also "dissed" college sports. However, more casual rebels like the IU Grateful Dead fans enjoy intercollegiate athletics.

In the questionnaire for this book, students revealed how much time they spent during the average school week viewing live sports events, watching or listening to sports broadcasts on TV, radio, or on the Internet. The results indicated the major importance of athletics to contemporary collegians, particularly males: only 16 percent of men spent less than five hours per week in sports fan activities; 56 percent logged between six and fifteen hours; 19 percent, sixteen to twenty-five hours; and 9 percent, more than twenty-five. On the other hand, 71 percent of women spent less than five hours per week on this pastime; 26 percent, between six and fifteen hours; and 3 percent logged more than ten.

As always, totals varied according to type of school: male respondents at NCAA Division III schools, mainly liberal arts colleges, recorded times similar to the national women's averages, and 38 percent of the women at these colleges spent zero hours per week as sports fans. However, at NCAA Division I schools, the totals for both men and women exceeded the national averages, and, most striking, a significant percentage of male students (32 percent) spent more hours per week as sports fans than they did "studying and doing course assignments." One respondent explained in a P.S.: "Me and my housemates really attend Bristol University, not Ohio U, but we party here in Athens." (Bristol University is part of an ESPN advertising campaign depicting the network as a university, and its announcers as professors teaching the only worthwhile subject in America—sports in all its combinations and permutations.)

For student sports fans, part of the attraction of ESPN, particularly ESPN2 and the network's websites, are the constant updates of scores of games in progress and final results. This information feeds the sports fan's appetite and also helps student gamblers who have "money down" on various games. The latter group, mainly males at beer-and-circus schools, consume many hours per week following their bets, and this undoubtedly boosted the totals on the question on sports spectatorship. (See chapter 17 for a full discussion of sports gambling on campus.)

Few professors at large, public research universities would express shock or dismay to learn that many of their male undergraduates watch more hours of sports per week than they study. However, even fewer of these faculty members could name their students' favorite daily TV sports program (*SportsCenter*) or identify Dan Patrick or Linda Cohn (*SportsCenter* announcers).

★   ★   ★

Many [university] teachers live entirely in the tiny, incestuous, self-enclosed world of academia, and haven't the faintest idea what goes on outside of it [even on their own campuses].

Many college teachers have a very limited frame of reference. They can tell you on what day of the week the Treaty of Utrecht was signed, or the name of Jonathan Swift's maid, but they will have no idea who Oprah Winfrey or Danielle Steel or Bo Jackson is.

Solution: . . . Pity the poor isolated soul.

—Scott Edelstein, author of a nationally
published freshman handbook

Some academics would point out—if they could identify Bo Jackson—that sports heroes come and go, and that popular culture is ephemeral and not worth following. Whether one agrees or disagrees with this argument, Edelstein's comments indicate the huge gulf between academic culture and undergraduate life, never wider than on the topic of sports, especially intercollegiate athletics. Pollster Lou Harris ascertained that a large majority of faculty have little or no interest in college sports; moreover, they tend to disparage their colleagues who do, including those professors who serve on Faculty Intercollegiate Athletics Boards (or Committees), often terming them "jock-sniffers." In Harris's poll, faculty gave board members a 77 percent negative rating; whereas only 11 percent marked positive, and 12 percent had no opinion.

Harris's results, combined with the surveys for this book, also suggest a generation gap on the college sports issue between many faculty members and a growing number of their professional "children," academically inclined undergraduates. Nevertheless, the latter maintain very positive views of the faculty, whereas Scott Edelstein articulated a more typical undergraduate attitude, "Pity the poor isolated soul."

Actually, this jibe is generous compared to some of the derogatory remarks, often well deserved, that nonacademic undergraduates hurl at professors. In interviews for this book and in P.S. notes on the questionnaire, contemporary students—whether they belonged to the collegiate, vocational, or rebel subcultures—generally expressed negative or indifferent feelings toward the faculty, often regarding professors as beings from an alien world. The recent Boyer Commission study also noticed this phenomenon, commenting, "At many universities, research faculty and undergraduate students do not expect to interact with each other," and these expectations are usually fulfilled.

Undergraduates often illustrate the "two solitudes" at Big-time U's with vivid anecdotes. In a story that students throughout the country could repeat, an Indiana University junior told his school newspaper:

> I had the good fortune to be among the many hundreds of people honored at the [university's] Founder's Day celebration. . . . I marveled that the place seemed to be packed completely full, including the balcony, with proud parents and friends—except for this one big hole up front, in the section reserved for faculty. . . .
>
> There were only about twenty or thirty or so faculty representatives there . . . [of] the more than one thousand faculty members here in Bloomington. [At the time, there were 1,539 IUB full-time faculty members.]
>
> —William Tam

At most research universities, faculty attendance at graduation and other school ceremonies is appalling low, and dropping, mainly because research professors feel little attachment to their institutions and even less to the average undergraduate within them. In addition, some faculty do not attend because they regard these ceremonies as empty "PR shows," mounted by administrators to sustain the pretense that general undergraduate education is important.

A humorous but no less telling example of the distance between undergraduates and the faculty appeared in a cartoon in the University of Michigan student newspaper. U Magazine, a monthly insert in hundreds of college papers, subsequently reprinted it, confirming its meaning to undergraduates at other schools. The first panel shows a young student exulting,

"The thing that excites me about college is the professors. The leading minds of the world are at my disposal. I can talk face to face with them and deeply benefit from their knowledge."

In the next panel, the student exclaims,

"Here comes my history professor, now."

In the final panel, the student shouts,

"Professor Holmes."

The faculty member, never breaking stride or glancing around, mutters,

"E-mail me."

The Michigan cartoon puts a contemporary spin on the traditional hostility between regular undergraduates and the faculty; it also refutes one of the main propaganda lies of Big-time U's—the presence of famous faculty on campus improves general undergraduate education.

Finally, however, the *U Magazine* cartoon and William Tam's description belong in the anecdotal evidence file. Much more authoritative information on the ocean between the faculty and undergraduates at research universities comes from the annual *Princeton Review* surveys based on interviews with almost sixty thousand undergraduates at more than three hundred schools. In addition, these results reveal the shorter distance between professors and students at institutions emphasizing undergraduate education.

★   ★   ★

The [*Princeton Review*] rankings are based directly upon what students on each campus tell us about their college [in their responses to our questionnaire surveys]. . . . Once the surveys have been completed and the responses stored in our database, each college is given a grade-point-average (GPA) for its students' answers to each individual multiple-response question.

It is these GPAs that enable us to compare student opinions from college to college, and to gauge which aspects of the complete experience at each college rate highest and lowest according to the institution's own students. [The GPAs also generate the top-twenty lists in various categories.]

—*The Princeton Review*

The *Princeton* surveys do not specifically explore the different student subcultures at schools; nonetheless, their results often indicate which subculture dominates undergraduate life at a particular institution. Many universities in the top twenty of the "Jock schools" category finish high on the "Students pack the stadiums" and "Party schools" lists, signifying institutions with strong collegiate subcultures. In fact, the *Princeton Review* explains its criteria for the "Party schools" ranking as "Based on a combination of survey questions on the use of alcohol and drugs, hours of study each day, and the popularity of the Greek system."

The "Party schools" list for 2000 resembles the polls of top NCAA football and basketball teams. *Princeton*'s first five are Florida State, University of Florida, Michigan State University, Seton Hall University, and University of Mississippi, trailed by such traditional sports powers as Alabama, Georgia, and Arkansas, as well as such college sports hopefuls as Washington State and Ohio University in Athens. High on the "Party school" list in previous years—and almost certain to reappear in future—were Arizona, Auburn, Colorado, Kansas, Louisiana State, Miami (Florida), Ohio State, Oregon, Syracuse, Texas (Austin), Tulane, West Virginia, and Wisconsin (Madison).

Similarly, in the late 1990s and 2000, schools with strong rebel subcultures turn up on the "Most politically active," "Students most nostalgic for George McGovern," and "Students ignore God on a regular basis" lists (Wesleyan, Simon's Rock College of Bard, and College of the Atlantic rated very high in these categories), and these colleges and similar ones (particularly Reed, Bennington, and Marlboro) appeared on *Princeton*'s "Alternative Lifestyle" lists: "Gay community accepted," "Birkenstock-wearing, tree-hugging, clove-smoking vegetarians," and "Aesthete schools."

Colleges with a strong academic ethos also cluster on various *Princeton* lists (see below). Only the vocational subculture is less visible, in part because so many undergraduates belonging to other subcultures also hold part-time jobs and vocational attitudes, thus merging this subculture into others, particularly on residential campuses. Nonetheless, one list—"Least happy students"—contained a majority of schools with large numbers of traditional vocational students, that is, those also working full-time jobs or supporting families. In the late 1990s and 2000, most institutions in this category were urban—for example, Temple, Loyola of Chicago, Hofstra,

Queens College (CUNY), Hunter College (CUNY)—and, undoubtedly, the hectic, overcommitted, and often unhappy lives of large numbers of their vocational students contributed to these schools' high ranking in this category. The University of Buffalo also finished very high on this list in the late 1990s and 2000, probably in part because of its sizable contingent of vocational students, as well as its academic problems (see pages 65–68).

After the "Least happy students" category, turning to the schools on *Princeton*'s "Best overall academic experience for undergraduates" is a more pleasant experience. Rice University has frequently made the top ten on this list, including in 2000. According to the *Princeton Review*:

> Rice has a varied and challenging academic program without some of the intense competition that often accompanies such stature. . . . Getting the classes you want is easy for freshmen and seniors alike. . . . [Most classes are small and] "You can take a test in the morning and then eat lunch with the professor afterwards," explains a junior majoring in biology.

In the "Best overall academic experience for undergraduates" category, the predictable candidates appear—Swarthmore, Amherst, Williams, and other schools providing a quality undergraduate education. In this category in every *Princeton Review* edition in the 1990s and for 2000, only one institution played in NCAA Division I-A, Rice University—the exception that proves the "Best overall academic" rule. Rice made the list every year, but, with only twenty-six hundred undergraduates, it is the smallest institution in I-A, and its athletes are much less vocational than at other I-A schools. Predictably, its football and basketball teams frequently lose, and they never receive much media or fan attention. (Long ago, when Rice was a less academic institution, the Owls were a power in the old Southwest football conference; as a result, Rice entered NCAA Division I-A when that grouping began and never bothered to drop out afterward.)

In addition to low-key intercollegiate athletics, Rice neither permits fraternities and sororities nor encourages a non-Greek collegiate scene. Instead of placing students in huge, soulless dorms like Big-time U's frequently do, it houses them in human-sized "Colleges," patterned after the Oxbridge model, with a faculty member and his or her family living in an apartment in each College. In these ways, the school consciously stunts the growth of the collegiate subculture.

As important, Rice promotes the academic subculture by emphasizing undergraduate education, hiring faculty committed to that endeavor, and enabling them to teach small classes. This system closes the gap between professors and undergraduates, and prompts Rice students to rate their "academic experience" as "outstanding." (Crucial to Rice's success is its large endowment, much of it from Texas oil money. Nevertheless, the school uses its money wisely and resists the temptation to squander it in an attempt to become a big-time research university with a panoply of graduate programs and TAs, drifting upward and away from undergraduate education.)

Similar to Rice, in the *Princeton* categories "Professors bring material to life," "Professors make themselves accessible," and "Class discussion encouraged," colleges with faculty committed to teaching undergraduates always score very high, for example, Carleton, the Claremont (California) colleges, Reed, Rhodes, Sarah Lawrence, and St. John's (Maryland) on the late 1990s and 2000 lists. A recent history of American higher education explained their formula for success: these schools believe that "students do not need to be talked 'at' [in lectures], but 'conversed with,' preferably in small seminars and colloquia, recognizing that meaningful learning is inherently 'labor intensive,' and cannot be conducted on a large-scale, assembly-line basis."

Furthermore, the *Princeton* categories "Professors suck all life from material," "Professors make themselves scarce," and "Class discussion rare" turn up many of the usual suspects—research universities in big-time college sports, including those often high in the NCAA football and men's basketball polls: Arizona, Arizona State, Arkansas, Georgia, Georgia Tech, Michigan, Michigan State, Maryland (College Park), Minnesota (Twin Cities), Missouri (Columbia), Ohio State, Oklahoma, Penn State, Pitt, Rutgers, Buffalo, Texas A & M, UCLA, Virginia Tech, and West Virginia.

This guidebook also includes a category "Teaching assistants teach too many upper-level courses," and, in addition to many schools listed in the previous paragraph, Alabama, Boston College, Florida, Florida State, Hawaii, Illinois, Indiana, North Carolina (Chapel Hill), New Mexico, Purdue, Rhode Island, and Seton Hall score high here. *Princeton Review* does not include a "Worst overall academic experience for undergraduates" list, but it is easy to find candidates. Indeed, the school that ranked at or near the top of almost all of the negative academic categories in 1999 and 2000 was the University of Buffalo (see pages 65–68).

The *Princeton Review*'s methodology is not perfect—and universities earning negative ratings sometimes dispute its procedures—but because this guidebook bases its rankings on an enormous number of questionnaires, its results do not vary greatly from year to year. The schools committed to providing a quality undergraduate education for all of their students continually score high, and the large, public research universities, particularly the big-time college sports factories, consistently rate poorly in the academic categories. Considering the size of the *Princeton Review*'s poll, its results indicate important truths about the institutions that it examines annually.

The bottom line in terms of beer-and-circus—the party scene accompanying big-time college sports—is this: *A majority of schools earning very negative ratings in academic categories feature beer-and-circus; on the other hand, almost every institution achieving high positive rankings in academic categories is not involved in major intercollegiate athletics and none are on the "Party schools" list.*

11

THE FACULTY/STUDENT
NONAGGRESSION PACT

Guidebooks like the *Princeton Review* present evidence of the deplorable state of general undergraduate education at large, public research universities. For specific information on how these schools neglect this crucial enterprise—ironically, their most dependable source of income—it is necessary to examine what happens, or fails to occur, in undergraduate classes at these institutions. This chapter provides this information, as well as an inquiry into why many undergraduates accept beer-and-circus as a substitute for a meaningful education.

★   ★   ★

A mutual nonaggression pact develops between lazy students and lazier professors: "I won't bother you if you don't bother me."
—Anne Matthews, higher education writer

We encountered colleges where there was a general agreement that academics were weak, and faculty and students had a tacit agreement not to burden one another.
—Arthur Levine, president of Teachers College
at Columbia University

I think it's really sad that my friends and I didn't go to class much. I mean, we all go down there [to the University of Illinois at Champaign-Urbana] to get an education, and then we don't go to class. But you can get a good grade without going, so it's tempting not to go.
—Dorothy Puch, University of Illinois student

Big-time U's handle their undergraduate education problem by establishing a truce between faculty who want to spend a minimum amount of time on undergraduate teaching and students who want to obtain a degree as easily as possible. Sadly, this truce short-circuits students' natural curiosity and desire to learn. Many studies reveal that even the most collegiate or vocationally inclined students enter universities hoping to acquire an education. Often their wishes are inchoate, but, in a supportive academic environment, some of these men and women would fulfill their hopes and talents. However, no one ever accused a Big-time U of being supportive and nurturing: "impersonal" and "mean" are the adjectives that undergraduates most often use to describe these schools.

As detailed in chapter 7, because Big-time U's reward faculty primarily for research, not teaching, they assign professors to teach massive undergraduate lecture courses, and these classes severely restrict student learning. For example, in all parts of the country, introductory courses in psychology, an inherently fascinating subject for undergraduates trying to establish adult personalities, consist mainly of huge lecture classes. Indeed, at some universities with high-powered research departments in this discipline, administrators increase the size of basic psych courses to many hundreds of students to generate more money for research programs, and to provide employment for large numbers of graduate students—they work as teaching assistants in these mammoth courses. However, for most undergraduates, exploring one's identity along with hundreds of other people in the same room is not a learning experience—indeed, it turns the vast majority of students away from this field. But as one psych professor remarked, "That's the whole idea. Who wants a lot of undergrad psychology majors hanging around a research department?"

Across the curriculum, many introductory courses, including in such foundation subjects as math and English, are frequently taught in large lecture courses. If the lectures also contain a discussion section component, or the courses enroll only a moderate number of students, usually an inexperienced TA or underpaid part-timer is in charge of the smaller group (see pages 78–80). The recent Boyer Commission study noted that, "ironically, the first years of university studies . . . the most formative years [for students], are usually the least satisfactory." Professors dislike teaching introductory courses because the material is so far from their research, and TA's "rarely come armed with serious training in pedagogy" (nor do most faculty, for that matter). "As a result, freshmen—the students who need the very best teaching—may actually receive the worst."

Another view of this situation suggests that because of the finances of the research university, and its pursuit of the "nonaggression pact" between faculty and undergraduates, Big-time U's try to persuade entering students to accept inferior education as the norm. The mammoth lecture classes during freshmen year help accomplish this task, reducing students to passive and cynical attitudes about these courses and, soon, their entire undergraduate education.

It is important to note that some regular undergraduates at research universities fight the system and gain meaningful educations—a testament to their extraordinary determination. Similarly, some faculty members at these schools teach their undergraduate courses conscientiously, spending long hours on this activity—an indication of their idealism and career foolhardiness. In addition, one other group avoids the nonaggression, nonlearning trap: honors students. However, when large, public research universities siphon off their best students and substantial resources for special honors programs and colleges, they confirm and even increase the woeful conditions of general undergraduate education. (See chapter 13.)

Despite Big-time U's shabby treatment of regular undergraduates in the classroom, they need their tuition dollars and often offer a substitute for genuine learning: a diploma, plus a "fun experience," including beer-and-circus. Because many students arrive on campus predisposed to the collegiate subculture or immediately become immersed in it, they accept the university's deal. A University of Missouri (Columbia) undergraduate explained:

> Most students here, except for the journalism majors, feel they don't need to try hard [in classes] and they can get by and get their degree. You find that out when you walk into your first class here. . . . Most Mizzou students are satisfied with easy schoolwork because other things are much more important to them, mostly partying and following the Tigers.

The *Insider's Guide to the Colleges* confirmed these comments in its review of Missouri:

> Like many large state schools, the University of Missouri is defined by an active frat life and a relatively loose attitude toward academic life. . . . Academics are not a great source of stress for many Mizzou students. . . . [However,] athletics plays a big role in Mizzou life. There is a lot of spirit behind the Tigers. . . .
>
> What should be the campus mascot? *The drunken frat boy.*

*

The need for as many undergraduate tuition dollars as possible—Missouri accepts 90 percent of its applicants—as well as Upward Drift and empire-building propel schools to what one critic calls "gigantism—the sheer size and complexity of the modern university," which "militates against . . . closeness and intimacy" and a student-centered approach to education. Indeed, even before entering a classroom, the size and impersonality of a Big-time U intimidates and turns off many incoming freshmen, as do the indifferent advising system and the mammoth high-rise dormitories and research buildings. One student told Anne Matthews, "This school is the anti-'Cheers,' where nobody knows your name."

On the questionnaire for this book, an Ohio State female freshman wrote:

> I feel like just another number at a large state school. I have to use my social security number for everything here. Many of my friends here and at other state schools say the same thing. Also academics is not at the top of my priority list anymore, although it was when I came here, and I've started to live for the weekend parties and Buckeye Fever [rooting for the school's football and basketball teams]. . . . For me and my friends here, our courses would be lucky to make the middle of our priority lists.

A comprehensive survey of student attitudes at Indiana University, conducted by that school's administration, confirmed the anti-academic and alienated feelings of undergraduates. In response to the statement "Students come first" at this school, only 14 percent strongly agreed; and the same small percentage affirmed the statement "Students are intellectually engaged in their academic work" here.

In a more graphic manner, a columnist in this school's student newspaper discussed the common undergraduate problem of staying awake in class: "I've seen people bring Big Gulps of [caffeine-laden] Mountain Dew, liters of Jolt and mugs of coffee as thick as milkshakes to class," then consume them, "only to slip into unconsciousness as soon as the overhead projector lights up" and the prof starts talking. This writer admitted that the "typical college student's lifestyle (pizza at 11 P.M.)," and so on, influenced class alertness, but finally the lack of engagement with undergraduate education was the main culprit.

A folklorist studying college life noticed that the comments students carved into desktops in all parts of the country mainly "express boredom or frustration" during classes. One of the most common inscriptions—a cry for total escape—was the line from the TV show *Star Trek*: "Beam me up, Scotty!" Yet these sentiments seem old-fashioned—recalling the historic hostility between most undergraduates and their professors—compared to contemporary student comments on the new "mutual nonaggression pact."

★   ★   ★

> The entire discussion [in the apartment living room] began after someone mentioned a student who walked in five minutes late to class, then slept through every class [in that course] last semester. . . . Then someone interrupted [the discussion], articulating the sentiment of our generation: *"Teachers should be happy that people just show up for class at all."*
>
> I pondered that idea—that we placate ourselves by lowering educational standards to the point where simply arriving at class equals valuing school. . . . The sentiment now is that since students "paid" for the class, they also "own" the rights to do with it what they will while in that class.
>
> —Amy Webb, *Indiana [University] Daily Student* columnist

This writer protested the consumerist trend in university life, but she blamed her fellow students for this situation. She titled her article, "Students Should Respect Professors," yet many undergraduates would respond to her declaration by listing the ways that profs "diss" students. A story in *U Magazine* captured undergraduate attitudes on this issue: a student in a theater course had to learn a dramatic monologue to deliver during the next class meeting, but he lost his tape of the speech. He could only rent a tape of a different monologue, so he rented it, claiming that "the professor was so far gone she'd never notice." She never did, awarding him a high grade on this exercise, her "only comment [was] that he shouldn't be afraid to pause longer between phrases."

This student's description of the professor as "far gone" needs translation: probably she was neither demented nor absentminded; instead, she was mentally detached from teaching and, in student vernacular, "didn't give a shit" about what occurred in her courses or whether individual students accurately fulfilled her assignments or not. She gave them high grades so that she could get through her teaching as quickly and easily as possible.

U Magazine included this story in an article headlined, "WHAT ME STUDY?"—illustrating it with a photo of a male college student asleep on a park bench, a copy of a *Cliffs Notes* pamphlet covering his face. A major flaw exists in this symbolic photo: many undergraduates no longer need the *Cliffs Notes* shortcut to mastering reading assignments, as numerous professors now supply "study guides" that furnish everything a student requires for a course, including exam questions and answers. The *Chicago Tribune* quoted undergraduates who explained that the study guides sum up the course material, and "if they [students] put question marks at the ends of the topic headings in the study guide, they have the exam" questions followed by the answers.

A similar "dumbing down" of university courses occurs when faculty members, not even bothering to dispense study guides, recycle the same exam questions year after year. Student organizations, particularly fraternities and sororities, assemble "test files" (called "test banks" at some schools) for these profs' courses, and the Greeks and their friends use the old exams. A Purdue undergraduate commented, "It's not what you know in a course, but who you know. Who's got the 'test files,' even for profs who don't let students keep their exams. Some students always sneak out copies for the 'files' and so the exams are out there somewhere."

Under these circumstances, many undergraduates feel that attending class is worthless, and studying anything other than the guides or the old exams makes no sense. This system seduces even conscientious students, and various reports on the amount of time per week that undergraduates spend studying reveal amazingly low numbers of hours.

Almost every university, in its official handouts to freshmen, suggests a minimum of two hours of studying for every hour in class, therefore a student with a standard fifteen-hour course load should put in at least thirty hours per week studying. However, many surveys on this topic reveal that most students at Big-time U's study far fewer than thirty hours per week. The responses to the questionnaire for this book indicate that 18 percent of undergraduates spent one to five hours a week "studying and doing course assignments"; 35 percent logged six to ten hours a week on these activities; 29 percent, eleven to fifteen hours; and only 18 percent, sixteen or more hours per week. Women studied more than men but not significant amounts of time more.

As always, the results varied from school to school, but again correlated with the *Princeton Review*'s categories on this topic. For "Their students (almost) never study," in the late 1990s and 2000, Alabama, Arizona State, Arkansas, Auburn, Florida, Florida State, Georgia, Georgia Tech, Hawaii, Kansas, Louisiana State, Miami (Florida), Michigan State, Missouri (Columbia), Mississippi, Rhode Island, Seton Hall, Tennessee (Knoxville), Wisconsin (Madison), West Virginia, and, inevitably, the University of Buffalo rank very high. In the questionnaire for this book, respondents from these universities as well as other big-time college sports schools spent the fewest number of hours per week "studying and doing course assignments."

The category, "Their students never stop studying," listed Carleton, the Claremont (California) schools, Cal Tech, Swarthmore, Reed, Grinnell, Middlebury, and similar institutions. The questionnaire for this book revealed parallel results: only 12 percent of the respondents from "never stop studying" schools spent less than eleven hours a week on this activity; 27 percent logged eleven to fifteen hours; 36 percent, sixteen to twenty hours; and 25 percent, over twenty hours per week, many over thirty hours. The only universities in NCAA Division I-A with undergraduates spending comparable hours were Rice and the University of California, Berkeley.

Yet, the one statistic shared by students in both of the *Princeton* "studying" categories were similar grade point averages. *Whether they never studied or always worked hard on their courses, almost all of the undergraduates received high grades.* Did these GPAs, averaging 3.3 (out of 4), indicate that the students at the big-time college sports schools were smarter than those at the more academically oriented institutions, and therefore had to study less to learn as much? No. The answer is what the *Chronicle of Higher Education* termed *Education's Dirty Secret: Grade Inflation.* Not only does it rule public universities, but it also exists at many excellent private schools—except, at the latter, some undergraduates learn something on their way to high grades, whereas at beer-and-circus universities, the inflated grades tend to be handed out as part of the tuition deal, a key element of the "mutual nonaggression pact."

> The nub of the problem seems to me to be the customer-supplier model that has been adopted by academia . . . [because of] relatively high tuition, there is considerable incentive to give the customer what he or she wants, with no hassle. If a substantial majority of students want good grades without commensurate effort and preparation, then it's easiest to give them what they want—after all, they're paying for it. Never mind that the universities become credentialing agencies rather than institutions of learning.
> —Frederic A. Lyman, Syracuse University professor

Before the consumerist model overtook higher education, faculty at large universities did not regard ordinary students as customers; they mainly tolerated them as necessary guests in the "groves of academe." Hence, professors awarded A's only to academically talented undergraduates, usually their "professional children"; they doled out B's to students who completed course work competently; and they gave C's and lower grades to all others in their classes. In the 1970s and 1980s, as higher education adopted the student-consumer model, grade inflation accelerated, continuing full throttle into the 1990s.

In that decade, the topic also moved from anecdotal report to researched phenomena. In a comprehensive survey of thousands of transcripts for selected years from 1969 to 1993, Arthur Levine discovered that "the gentleman's C has become the gentleman's A as the percentage of C's and A's given to students in college has reversed itself." In 1969, only 7 percent of undergraduates in Levine's sample earned A range GPAs, whereas 25 percent possessed C range averages; in 1993, only 9 percent had C range GPAs, versus 26 percent with A range averages. The number of B range averages—the majority of GPAs—also grew because, by the 1990s, very few D's and F's were awarded; thus, the 1960s C students had become B or better students, replaced in the C cohort by formerly D and F students.

Within academia, scientists tend to blame humanities faculty for this "lowering of standards," but a biology professor informed the *Chronicle of Higher Education* that "grade inflation is not limited to the humanities but is very prevalent in the sciences as well," especially at schools and within departments that pressure faculty to fill their classes with as many students as possible to generate as many tuition dollars as possible. What better way to please students than by giving them high grades for little work?

But pressure on faculty to inflate grades is generally more subtle than direct orders from college administrators or department heads. The promotion, tenure, and salary system of the research university exerts the maximum amount of pressure (see pages 76–77). Many faculty believe that every hour spent on undergraduate teaching is an hour stolen from research, and they become skilled at cutting corners in all phases of their teaching, especially grading. Even in upper-division classes, they move quickly when grading papers or exams, often only putting a brief comment or a letter grade on each student's work. (In lecture courses, most professors never see student papers or exams; the TAs or the scantron machines do all the grading.)

In determining specific grades, faculty frequently take the path of least resistance, and also direct their TAs to this route—*inflate*. No student ever complained after receiving an A+ or an A, although some now whine about an A−. Many students object to B's, most protest C's and become angry at D's. If a professor actually flunks a student, or allows a TA to do so, that faculty member must have documentation to justify the F, not only that student's papers and exams throughout the course—all carefully marked, with each grade fully explained—but, for comparison, samples of the work of other students in the course who earned similar and higher grades, also thoroughly marked.

A professor who wants to grade hard embarks upon a very time-consuming and labor-intensive course of action: throughout the semester, he or she must respond accurately and at length to the work of every student in the class. Moreover, to fight grade inflation, a faculty member must be prepared to answer complaints from students and their parents, inquiries from department heads and deans, requests to appear before various student committees, and even lawsuits. Predictably, few faculty members at research universities choose to go down this lonesome road or, as a cinema studies professor called it, The River of No Return.

(One exception to grade inflation exists: those faculty who teach subjects in which many students want to major, for example, in this era, business. As a result of this demand, these professors can grade "on a [statistical] curve" and determine beforehand how many A's, B's, et cetera, they will dispense. In addition, because they mainly use scantron exams requiring no writing from students—or reading by instructors—they can arrive at numerical point totals that undergraduates cannot easily challenge. However, for faculty using this pedagogical model to condemn professors in other disciplines for inflating grades is absurd. Designing a multiple-choice business exam is an efficient process; creating a multiple-choice exam for an English composition class is impossible because it cannot test a student's writing ability and progress.)

Conservative critics of grade inflation like William Cole argue that on this issue faculty must act individually, and that "solving the problem of grade inflation . . . requires simply [to] acknowledge the problem and act responsibly." O that academic life were so simple! Because grade inflation connects to the finances of research universities and their bottomless hunger for tuition dollars, as well as their privileging research over undergraduate education, asking each professor at these schools to "act responsibly" is a myopic request. These schools would have to transform their internal culture and values to truly fight grade inflation. Moreover, the administrators of Big-time U's, as well as the research faculty, have far too much invested in the "nonaggression pact" with student-consumers to change it.

Only a major shift in the missions of research universities—an earthquake in higher education equaling the end of the Cold War—could halt grade inflation. The dismantlement of the Soviet empire terminated the nuclear arms concept of mutual nonaggression; however, it is hard to imagine a similar event occurring in American higher education. Therefore, the faculty/student nonaggression pact will remain in place for the foreseeable future and, along with it, grade inflation. Eventually, every student will receive at A+ in almost every course.

12

CHEATING

J ust as the internal culture and values of the modern research university prevent an end to grade inflation, they also block a solution to the problem of student cheating. According to many studies, cheating by undergraduates has reached epidemic levels, but many faculty at research universities neither attempt to curtail it nor even seriously discourage it. Details on this situation—the hidden clauses in the "nonaggression pact"—follow.

★ ★ ★

> One factor often overlooked is the relationship between cheating and the grading and testing environment. . . . Students frequently report that cheating increases . . . when instructors are viewed as inattentive and inaccessible, when papers are not read and graded carefully, and when students perceive a very high level of cheating on the part of their classmates.
> —Richard A. Fass, professor of ethics

In the history of American higher education, undergraduates have cheated in a large variety of ways: "ponies" (primitive *Cliffs Notes*) to facilitate studying for exams; "crib" sheets and notes for the exams themselves; and the constant recycling of essays and papers. One historian noted that "at Yale in the 1860s, perhaps less than half of the compositions were actually written by the supposed author." Because of the collegiate subculture's aversion to academics, matched by professorial disdain for most undergraduates, cheating was normal behavior at many schools. This tradition continued through the twentieth century, faculty and administrators usually blaming the "deficient moral standard of our students" for the cheating, and never considering the connections between undergraduate dishonesty and a deeply flawed pedagogical system.

In the final decades of the twentieth century, by all measurements, student cheating accelerated at many colleges and universities to the point where, in 1999, an authoritative poll stated that "three-quarters of college students confess to cheating at least once." On some campuses, officials estimated the number of one-timers as high as 90 percent, with repeat offenders topping 50 percent of their undergraduates.

These statistics prompt the question: Why is cheating so widespread at a time of grade inflation? It seems counterintuitive that these two phenomena would occur simultaneously: if high grades are so easy to obtain, why bother to cheat for them? This paradox contradicts the students-cheat-out-of-desperation hypothesis, as well as the moral-decay-in-society explanation: high grades are so common that, like pennies, they are not worth bending over for or stealing. But the paradox points directly to the abysmal state of undergraduate education at Big-time U's—by most accounts, the schools with the highest number of student cheaters.

The 1990s studies on this issue contain some version of the following conclusion from a survey of thirteen thousand undergraduates: "A major factor determining whether a student will cheat or not is the academic culture of the specific institution that he or she attends." Students at large, public research universities that treat them as tuition dollars, not individuals, and that channel them into mammoth lecture courses with distant, frigid professors or inexperienced and overworked TAs, tend to cheat. They cheat for a variety of reasons, including as a show of contempt for a contemptible system. Or, as a Michigan State sophomore described his conduct in lecture courses—he rarely attended, bought lecture notes from an off-campus service, and cheated on papers and exams—"It's an eye for an eye, it's my insults for the school's insults." The name of a popular website that facilitates a variety of cheating practices also sums up the attitude of many undergraduates at Big-time U's today: www.SCHOOLSUCKS.com—its motto is, "Download your workload."

Michael Moore, a Rutgers student and the author of *Cheating 101: The Benefits and Fundamentals of Earning an Easy A*, admitted that students also cheat because they "want to spend more time partying and meeting people instead of burying their heads in books," but he placed much of "the blame on professors, [citing] their laziness in using the same teaching methods every year." Such comments prompt the question: Where do student indolence and rationalization end, and faculty laziness and contempt for undergraduates begin? Rutgers professor Michael Moffat answered the query, in part, by noting that "undergrads who know their professors and respect them are less likely to cheat in those classes" than students in huge lecture courses.

No observer can or should condone cheating and, finally, every student can and should act as a responsible and ethical individual. However, the neglect of undergraduate education by research universities begins to explain some of the increase in student cheating.

Predictably, most faculty and administrators regard cheating differently than do undergraduates. A professor of anthropology, also an associate provost at his university, denounced all forms of cheating, including the form "perpetrated" by off-campus companies posting course lecture notes on the web—he termed this an "assault on the integrity of higher education." Surprisingly, *USA Today* weighed into the debate with an editorial:

> *Net Notes Trump Boring Lecture*
> Quick, a test: You're a freshman and you're running late for Psych 101. You could drag yourself over to the lecture hall and strain to hear the tiny professorial speck down at the lectern impart wisdom. Or you could clock on www.StudentU.com and download the speck's course notes. . . .
>
> Students who download notes are right. The notes are adding value to the assembly line of undergraduate education, where grad students and minor [faculty] lights, not earth-shattering geniuses, lecture, and where traded paper notes have long been the order of the day.

A University of Texas (Austin) student columnist confirmed *USA Today*'s argument: "The unwritten UT philosophy," exemplified by the mass lecture courses at the school and the arrogant faculty, is: "We [professors] are smart, you [undergraduates] are stupid. We lecture, you take notes." Obviously, this system generates undergraduate cynicism, the purchase of lecture notes, and more serious forms of cheating.

A dissident professor at the University of Virginia offered a sensible but biting solution to the lecture note controversy:

> Maybe the course should be distributed as a book, rather than having this charade of somebody standing up and going through a lecture

that, for all purposes, doesn't change from year to year and doesn't allow students the possibility of discussion.

Most academics who oppose course notes appearing on the web have considered the book option—for that reason, they generally cite copyright issues, not pedagogical ones, in opposing the web note-taking services. Indeed, many faculty members publish the book and require the hundreds of students in their lecture classes to buy it. The professor then makes a profit from these forced purchases and still lectures from the book! This prompts the question: Who is cheating in this situation?

Anthony Scimone, a high school teacher, neatly summed up the debate about the new websites: "I suspect that the best teachers are not threatened by the new note-taking services. These teachers . . . encourage students to generate ideas and engage in scholarly discourse." The current studies on why students cheat confirms Mr. Scimone's intuition; one authority commented, "It's clear that when students really care about learning, they're much less likely to cheat." An official at a large public university noted that "In the 100 and 200 level [lecture] classes you see much more cheating" than in small upper-level courses; in the latter, "students take greater pride in their work because it is more important to them," and because they have direct contact with a professor.

The most striking proof of how a low faculty/student ratio short-circuits cheating comes from a study of schools with honor codes—where students can cheat easily and constantly if they choose to do so. Because these institutions emphasize undergraduate education, have few lecture courses, and because the "honor codes [are] rooted in a campus tradition of mutual trust and respect . . . between faculty members and students," they succeed in eliminating almost all student cheating.

At Rice University, for example, professors hand out exams and allow students to return to their dorm rooms or apartments with the exams in order to use their computers there to write their answers. Faculty trust students to take the exam without seeking any outside aid, without even opening their course books or notes. According to a current Rice undergraduate, "I've never seen anyone or heard of anyone breaking the honor code. Anyway, you'd mainly be cheating yourself [out of a good education]. . . . Also you become friendly with your instructors, and so cheating on them is like stealing from someone you know."

Rice University and other schools with low faculty/student ratios try to provide their undergraduates with quality educations. But what occurs at large public universities with high ratios? A faculty member at the University of Central Florida, a school that recently moved to NCAA Division I-A, has research ambitions, and features many lecture classes, explained that "The increasing casualness with which students seem to be cheating and committing plagiarism is just another symptom of the paradigm shift . . . to education as a consumer product—something that must be handed over on demand to all who pay their tuition." But the paradox reappears here: Why would students cheat if, after paying their bursar bills, they are simply handed what they want?

One answer, suggested by P.S. notes on the questionnaire for this book, is that some undergraduates cheat as a primitive, inarticulate form of consumer protest: they feel that because their U cheats them out of their money by giving them worthless classes, their dishonesty is justified. "This place constantly screws me over and takes my money," wrote a student at the University of New Mexico. "So why should I have a conscience about cheating in class?" Nevertheless, primitive individual actions—unlike the organized student protests in the 1960s—fail to disrupt the current system in any way; indeed, they deflect attention from its failures and allow college officials to place the blame for the cheating problem on "student immorality."

An Indiana University undergraduate offered his view of student dishonesty in a caustic article in the campus newspaper. He described "The Only Syllabus You'll Ever Need" at this school, and his cynicism about the huge lecture courses and indifferent professors premised his approval of student deceit. Under "Cheating" on his mock syllabus, he noted:

> Students caught cheating will be dealt with swiftly and severely by the Dean of Students, although you have to be practically brain-dead to get caught cheating in a huge lecture class. There's like, 300 kids in there—it's easy.

Under "Grades," he wrote: "Your grade in this course will be determined by two fifty-minute tests," no papers, no writing assignments.

As this student noted, cheating during lecture course exams is not difficult: in addition to the time-worn methods of copying from the person next to you and using crib sheets, undergraduates now employ such high-tech devices as cellular phones to dial multiple-choice answers into alphanumeric pagers, for example, 1C-2B-3A, to exchange answers with friends. One teacher remarked, "I get the sense there's a thrill to it, that [students think] 'my teachers are too dumb to catch me.' "

Probably some undergraduates hold this belief; however, dumbness does not prevent most professors from catching student cheaters—deafness does. Faculty simply do not want to hear about it. Tolerating cheating is a hidden clause in the nonaggression pact between many faculty members at research universities and their students. A classics professor at Northwestern University explained: "Most professors at a place like Northwestern can't be bothered [about undergraduate cheating]. They're not rewarded for teaching; they're rewarded for research. There's no future in pursuing cheating from the standpoint of a professor's self-interest."

As for students cheating for "the thrill of it": undoubtedly some undergraduates do it for the risk-taking thrill, but others also regard cheating as an active, engaging experience, far superior to passively ingesting the lectures and, without retaining anything from them, dumping them out on the exams. An undergraduate at the University of Iowa explained, "I'm into gambling and I'm into cheating in lecture classes. The only times when I feel alive in those courses is when I'm cheating. I'm really concentrating then, like when I'm on a river boat [casino]." This student was disappointed to learn that probably some of his professors did not care whether he cheated or not. "That sorta takes the fun out of it," he admitted, "but that explains why it's often so easy."

★　　★　　★

A few years ago, a professor at a southern university suspected a student of plagiarism. What did the professor do? Absolutely nothing. The messy case didn't seem worth the anxiety or aggravation, so he graded the assignment as usual and passed the student on.
—Allison Schneider, *Chronicle of Higher Education* reporter

Catching cheaters, like fighting grade inflation, requires a large amount of a faculty member's time and energy, and because the promotion, tenure, and salary system of the research university never rewards a professor for detecting a student plagiarist, or any other species of academic thief, why would a faculty member spend precious minutes, hours, even days or weeks in this endeavor (tracking down the exact source of a plagiarized paper can be a trek across a desert)? Moreover, apprehending the cheater is merely the first step in a very laborious process: countless reports to fill out, many faculty and student disciplinary committees at which to appear and present the evidence in the case, and always the threat of the accused student suing the accuser.

If grading student work puts faculty on the path of least resistance, resulting in grade inflation, then discovering a plagiarist or exam cheater often triggers a sprint down that path. As the southern professor told the *Chronicle of Higher Education*, exposing a cheater is not worth "the anxiety or aggravation" or time. Therefore, the best course of action is to do nothing. But what happens to faculty who—out of pride, honesty, or perversity—try to expose a cheater?

Many faculty members interviewed for this book on this issue told a horror story about a professor who accumulated lots of evidence of a particular student's cheating, then reported the student's dishonesty to the proper university authorities. After a year of hearings before various university judicial groups and no judgments, the student sued the accuser. The professor's school provided no legal aid for him or her; then, in a triumph of Johnnie Cochran–like lawyering, the student got off scot-free, and the professor had to pay exorbitant court costs and damages. He or she was financially and emotionally ruined by the case.

Faculty repeated versions of this anecdote so often—usually with the besieged professor as "a colleague of a friend at another university"—that the tale took on the character of an urban legend. A few cases like the professor's have occurred, although never in this extreme form, but the accuracy of the story is much less important than the fact that so many faculty members believe it and invoke it as a reason for doing nothing about student cheating.

Even professors who actually want to combat cheating discover that their universities will not help them in this endeavor. James Karge-Taylor teaches a lecture course in the history of jazz at the University of Arizona, and, in 1998, he discovered in a poll in his class that, of the 368 enrolled students, 25 percent had cheated on the first quiz. He had a simple request of his school, "I would like more help reading papers." Apparently help never arrived. A late-1999 article about websites selling papers for students to submit as their own work mentioned: "The paper mills are keeping customers happy. Tim, a University of Arizona senior who buys around four papers a semester, recalls ordering an essay on Louis Armstrong [for a jazz lecture class]. . . . Five minutes later, he got a call from the company urging him to reconsider. One of his schoolmates had already ordered the same paper."

Nevertheless, in the bleak research university landscape, some faculty members at Big-time U's manage to prevent cheating and plagiarism in their courses. However, their methods are very labor intensive. An Indiana University professor puts the following note in all of his course syllabi:

A warning on original work vs. plagiarism

An experienced teacher can easily tell the difference between original student writing and plagiarized work. Because you will have to write various exercises in class, I will have an excellent idea of your true writing abilities. Thus, when you turn in your major papers in the course, your writing—although more careful and polished than your in-class work—will still reflect your abilities. Your writing is like your signature, unique to you. To turn in someone else's writing—professional critic, friend, tutor, website doofus, etc.—is foolish, easily recognized, an insult to your instructor and fellow students, and a good way to get yourself into serious trouble.

NOTE: When you turn in your major papers in this course, you must also turn in your original notes, outlines, and drafts—be sure to print out the drafts after you do them. I will not accept a major paper without this material (it helps me gauge the quality of your research as well as the amount of work that you put into the paper).

This instructor admits that he would not know what to do if a student actually turned in a plagiarized paper, but, fortunately, he has not discovered one since he added these paragraphs to his syllabi many years ago. Admittedly, his teaching methods are time-consuming—he has to read all of his students' in-class and out-of-class work—but he believes that this is the only way to teach people to become better writers.

In addition, he finds that requiring "notes, outlines, and drafts" is a useful pedagogical device, and one that also short-circuits plagiarism. The instructor remarked, "The plagiarist would have to deconstruct the bought or stolen finished product into draft, outline, and note form. He or she would learn far more about writing from doing this than writing the paper straight."

This instructor is not a typical faculty member at a major research university. Some of his colleagues at Indiana and other Big-time U's also try to prevent cheating—but mainly with seating strategies in lecture halls, such as handing out various versions of the scantron exam so that no student sits next to another student with the same version of the exam. However, the new cellular phone technologies tend to defeat these strategies.

Similarly, some faculty have embraced the new anti-plagiarism search engines on the web. In theory, they take a suspect paper and locate the original already posted somewhere on the web. In practice, as a reporter discovered, the search engines "fail to detect [papers] . . . with even the slightest amount of rewriting," and, more to the point, they can only find papers listed in html and free to all (many of which are atrociously written). The anti-plagiarism engines cannot penetrate websites that require passwords, i.e., those that sell excellent recycled essays or, for a fairly high price, that supply an original paper to clients. Therefore, the best antidote to plagiarism on the web remains a teacher who requires writing in class and knows his or her students and their work well.

★   ★   ★

At a time when many universities tolerate student cheating, some institutions have gone a step further and have created a culture where staff members write the papers and take-home exams for some undergraduates, particularly intercollegiate athletes. A national magazine remarked:

> Sometimes the schools are directly responsible [for cheating]. . . . A former tutor for the University of Minnesota revealed that she had written 400 papers for 20 [varsity men's] basketball players between 1993 and 1998.

The University of Minnesota academic cheating scandal was large in scale but not exceptional in occurrence. Indeed, athletic department tutors at every NCAA Division I school have approached or crossed the line between tutoring a student and actually doing some of the student's course work. For example, in helping an athlete correct writing errors, the tutor rewrites the entire paper, and then the jock submits it as his or her own work; or, in typing a paper for an athlete, the tutor makes so many changes and corrections that the final product—submitted as the jock's original work—is, at best, a collaborative effort, and more often a ghost-written one.

In the Minnesota academic cheating scandal, three tutors, encouraged and rewarded by athletic department officials, brazenly composed whole papers and answered take-home exams for many basketball players, sometimes on subjects about which the athletes knew nothing, and in polished prose that some of these academically challenged jocks were incapable of writing. Not surprisingly, faculty members receiving these papers and exams were suspicious, but, in true Big-time U fashion, they ignored the alarm bells and graded the papers as if they were original student work.

However, one assistant professor did complain to University of Minnesota authorities. He pointed out that in one of his courses, basketball "star forward Courtney James had [recently] turned in a paper that was the best he [the instructor] had seen in his nearly forty years at the university," and that he clearly "suspected academic fraud." Nevertheless, Minnesota administrators would not investigate or support the instructor, and so he gave the paper and the player a passing grade.

Eventually, due to the competitive nature of the two daily newspapers in the area, the details of academic fraud in the men's basketball program at Minnesota emerged, including this assistant professor's experiences. UM administrators then pledged a total cleanup—as they had after every public revelation in the long history of UM athletic department scandals. Yet, NCAA officials called the recent UM incident an idiosyncratic event; in reality, many tutors at other Big-time U's could tell the press about academic dishonesty in their athletic departments (unfortunately, these revelations rarely emerge because most college towns have only a single daily newspaper, resting snugly in the local athletic department's pocket, and the paper refuses to investigate the U's college sports program or listen to tutors brave or foolhardy enough to come forward).

Finally, however, it is important to take a step back and to place athletic department malfeasance—not only academic fraud but also cheating in recruiting and retention of athletes—within the context of the entire university. The Carnegie Foundation noted that:

> The tragedy is that the cynicism that stems from the abuses in athletics infects the rest of student life, from promoting academic dishonesty to the loss of individual ideals. We find it disturbing that students who admit to cheating often excuse their conduct as being set by college examples such as athletic dishonesty.

Interviews for this book and P.S comments on the questionnaire support this Carnegie comment. A surprising number of students, particularly male sports fans, justified their academic dishonesty by referring to college coaches who cheated to win or ignored illegal off-the-field conduct by their players so that the offending athletes could remain on the team and help it win. During fall 1999, many students cited Peter Warrick's involvement in a shoplifting incident at Florida State, for example, "Hey, this All-American thief [Warrick] should be in the slammer, not leading the 'Noles to the national football championship. When King Bobby [Bowden, FSU coach] lets his jocks cheat like this, why should Joe Blow college student act differently?"

In addition, the student sports fans, unlike those undergraduates who regarded cheating as "an insult for an insult," tended to see it as an element in "the game of going to college," a contest that they were determined to win "by any means necessary" (the two phrases kept recurring). These students are only one cohort—albeit a rapidly growing one—of the undergraduate population, but their attitudes definitely contribute to the general cynicism of the student body. As do the unethical coaches and the never-ending scandals in intercollegiate athletics.

An undergraduate at Indiana University suggested a survey question to probe the connections between student cheating and college sports:

> A star athlete at your school asks you to help him/her cheat on an important exam. A passing grade in this course will determine whether the athlete remains eligible to play or not. Would you help the athlete cheat? If not, what would you do (turn the athlete in, etc.)?

The question was included in the survey and produced interesting results. At schools with Division I college sports programs, 59 percent of the respondents said that they would help the athlete cheat, men outnumbering women in positive assent almost two to one. Of the 41 percent no vote, a large majority came from women. However, on the second part of the question—"what would you do (turn the athlete in, etc.)?"—84 percent of respondents at Division I schools said they would not turn the athlete in, and only 16 percent said they would. (This statistic parallels a *U.S. News* poll finding that only 18 percent of their responding students said that they would "turn in a classmate" who is cheating.)

Of equal interest were the written responses prompted by the question. A typical yes explanation from a male student was: "Cheating is o.k. If I have the answers to the exam, sure I'll give them to a star jock." Other males explained with versions of the following: "I'd help. It's not hurting me," and: "No big deal here. I'd tell him, 'Let's go for it.' " However, more nurturing and judicious yesses came from some females. One wrote:

> I would help the athlete prepare for the exam but probably wouldn't help him cheat in it. Unless he was the absolute star of the team—then I'd first make him sign lots of stuff for my kid brother. But I'd never turn him in.

The no answers held some surprises, but rather than showing student idealism, they usually revealed cynicism. A large number of males replied with a version of this response: "No, I won't help. Why bother? If he flunks the class, you better believe he'll still remain eligible." Some males, particularly at Sunbelt football schools, replied with versions of this formulation, "No. I'd tell the athlete no-can-do, but I sure wouldn't turn him in for fear of being assaulted by the student population." However, in a more ethical and emphatic refusal, an intercollegiate athlete wrote:

> I'd tell him to eat shit. As a jock myself I realize that it takes a lot of effort to study after a hard practice but you don't learn anything by cheating. I've had teammates ask me to help them cheat lots of times and I always tell them to "mange merde" (I took French).

A number of the female no answers had rather complicated responses; one of the more tortured was: "I wouldn't help him. Maybe I'd even tell the professor or, at this school, the TA. Then again, the TA has no power. It would be a total mess. Maybe I'd try to forget the whole thing, pretend that he never asked for help." But a few vocational women had strong and clear answers, like the following: "No help for this pathetic moron from me. I'm also turning in the son-of-a-bitch. I work too damn hard outside and inside this university to ignore this!"

Many critics of college sports claim that athletic department academic fraud stems from the fact that most intercollegiate athletes are dumb jocks, and that they do not belong in higher education. Some dumb jocks exist on college campuses (a number of Minnesota basketball players were in this group), but, in reality, the physically and mentally exhausted and academically underachieving athlete is much more common than the dumb jock (some UM b-ball players and the vast majority of other athletes at the school were in this category).

As discussed elsewhere in this book, most Division I athletic scholarship holders are vocational students, working full-time at very demanding jobs and also trying to carry regular course loads. Many of these young men and women, because their coaches and sports require extraordinary amounts of their time and energy, experience academic problems. And athletic department tutors—under orders from coaches to "keep the jocks eligible any way you can"—sometimes cheat to keep players academically afloat. However, for some critics of college sports to regard the athletes as the source of athletic department academic fraud is to blame the victims (often willing but always shortsighted) of a complex and exploitative system.

To their credit, a minority of athletes fight the athletic department system as soon as they enter college, and they manage, through amazing effort,

134 | BEER AND CIRCUS

to obtain a good education while playing sports—often they have to defy athletic department attempts to steer them to "gut" courses and "mickey" majors. Other athletes, when they realize that they will never play at the pro level, begin to work hard on their education; nevertheless, because of time and physical constraints, they often academically underachieve. And some athletes, after they end their college athletic careers—either because of injury or the completion of their playing eligibility—become excellent students. At last able to concentrate full-time on their studies, they bring the discipline that they learned in sports to their academic endeavors.

Finally, the reasons why athletes commit academic fraud are as complicated as the causes of regular undergraduate cheating. Nonetheless, in every case the individual student can refuse to commit the crime. Numerous athletes and regular students do not cheat. That some honest undergraduates exist—despite their schools generally ignoring student cheating—is a testament to the morality of these young people.

13

UNDERGRADUATE EDUCATION TRIAGE:
HONORS PROGRAM LIFEBOATS

Honors programs and colleges, with their striking contrast to ordinary undergraduate classes, offer the best proof of Big-time U's neglect of general undergraduate education. The comments from honors program directors and in their guidebooks provide a clear view of the triage scene.

★　　★　　★

In every case, catering to the [honors] student as an individual plays a central role in honors course design. Most honors classes are small (under 20 students) and discussion oriented—giving students a chance to present their own interpretation of ideas. . . .

All honors classes help students develop and articulate their own perspectives by cultivating verbal and written style. The classes help students mature intellectually and prepare them to engage in their own explorations and research.

—Dr. Joan Digby, editor of *Peterson's Honors Programs*

Every description of honors programs stresses the small size of honors courses versus the usually enormous regular undergraduate classes. For example, at the University of Minnesota (Twin Cities), honors students "cite class size as their primary reason for choosing the special program. Classes in the rest of the university . . . [are] notoriously large. Some are so big that they use television monitors" so that students in the back half of the lecture hall can see what the professor looks like and can hear him or her better.

At many universities, honors students "place out of" or skip the massive introductory courses; at others, the university sets up special honors sections of these courses for them, almost always taught by full faculty members, not graduate teaching assistants. Miami University of Ohio, in describing its honors program, takes a sarcastic swipe at the lecture course tradition, both at its school and others: its honors "program empowers students to see themselves as generators of knowledge rather than as passive transmitters," taking notes and regurgitating information on exams. The University of Maryland (College Park) honors program makes the same point when it tells potential freshmen applicants, "You'll be creating knowledge with the faculty, not memorizing a zillion facts to throw back on some test." This prompts the question: If administrators at Miami, Maryland, and other schools condemn the lecture course method, why do Big-time U's continue teaching the vast majority of their undergraduates in these courses? This tradition is pedagogically bankrupt, as these administrators and almost all of the studies on the topic indicate, but research universities keep it alive and flourishing for noneducational reasons—it is the most economic means for Big-time U's to pursue research prestige.

In its honors program material, the University of Connecticut also offers a damning statement about regular undergraduates at the school; it states that its honors program—enrolling only a small percentage of all undergraduates—"is for enthusiastic and energetic students who enjoy small classes, extensive discussions with professors, and the challenge of articulating and refining their ideas." Do the vast majority of UConn students dislike small classes, personal contact with professors, etc.? *U.S. News* profiled an honors freshman at the school who took science seminars with as few as fifteen students as "compared with more than 300 [students] in the non-honors" equivalent classes. Surely, regular UConn students would have preferred the seminars?

In its admissions material for regular students, UConn does not mention the discrepancy between its honors program and general undergraduate education one. However, it stresses the UConn Huskies men's and women's basketball teams and their national championships as well as the accompanying campus festivities. The *Insider's Guide* says of UConn: "Well known as a party school, students find that it is hard to find good places [on campus] to study"; however, the honors students have special, quiet places reserved for their use.

Many honors programs also advertise: "*The Honors college emphasizes the development of fundamental rhetorical skills: writing, reading, speaking, and listening* [emphasis added]. Enrollment in any course rarely exceeds 25 students, and many courses are seminars where each student is encouraged to play an active role in discussion" (University of Oregon). Again, the implication is that regular courses at Big-time U's do not teach these essential "rhetorical skills," and that an undergraduate's best chance of acquiring them is in an honors program. This theme is repeated so often in the guidebooks that the conclusion is ominous: Big-time U is admitting that it is not teaching regular undergraduates to read and write at a college level. Many experts in the field of "outcomes and assessments" also confirm this fact. Therefore, when honors programs emphasize their ability to teach literacy, they are pointing the way to their lifeboats.

Instead of acknowledging this triage of undergraduate students, research universities try to sell honors as a wonderful enhancement of their entire educational mission, and a great boon to *all students*.

> *An Elite Education at Public School:*
> *Honors Program at College Park*
> *[University of Maryland]*
> The program is a key element in the campus' much larger ambition to move into the upper echelons of public universities nationally. . . . "These programs set the pace for the entire undergraduate experience here," says University [of Maryland] Provost Gregory Geoffrey. "They attract to the campus the very best students and their presence enriches all students."
>
> —Michael Hill, *Baltimore Sun* reporter

> The University of Massachusetts [at Amherst] is proposing a $15 million complex to house a new academically exclusive [honors] college within UMass-Amherst. . . . The complex would give an identity, as well as distinct residences, classrooms, and a student center to Commonwealth College . . . conceived as part of a broad plan to enhance the prestige of a public university . . . [and] establish tangible evidence of the state's commitment to academic excellence at UMass. . . .
>
> It will be a breeding ground for Rhodes and Marshall scholars—honors never bestowed on a UMass student, and ones that UMass president William M. Bulger is eager to have distinguish his school.
>
> —Kate Zernike, *Boston Globe* reporter

That the pursuit of "prestige" motivates research universities—particularly Upward Drift ones like Maryland and UMass—is not news. Indeed, many rating services and annual guidebooks consider the number of

Rhodes, Marshalls, and other famous scholarships won by a university's undergraduates as an important "school prestige" item. However, for Big-time U officials to pretend that an honors college or program will benefit all undergraduates is worse than hypocrisy, it is bold-faced lying. How can an honors program help "the entire undergraduate experience" at Maryland or any other school when it siphons off the best students as well as many of the best faculty teachers? Numerous experts have commented on the well-known phenomenon of removing the brightest and most articulate students from a course, and leaving the rest, as well as the instructor, to sink. Similarly, at many schools with honors programs, faculty members willing and able to teach regular undergraduates often decamp to honors courses, diminishing the already low level of pedagogy in general undergraduate classes. One observer noted, "The bright students better fit the faculty ideal" of what undergraduates should be, and they help "keep faculty morale high," allowing professors to ignore the insurmountable problems of teaching often hostile students in mass courses.

In UMass's new honors college, enrollment in courses—all taught by full faculty members—is limited to no more than twenty students, with many classes much smaller. However, regular UMass undergraduate courses are often very large, with hundreds of students in some introductory classes. One freshman commented, "It is really scary. . . . I attend two classes that are bigger than my whole [high] school put together," that's more than 400 in each UMass class. Another student complained about the school using *undergraduate teaching assistants* in some lecture courses: "I'm paying the university . . . to get the best education possible, and an undergraduate from down the hall is grading me"—although the complainant admitted that the undergrad TA graded really easy. The chair of the psychology department defended the use of undergraduate TAs as a way of allowing huge classes to have more human-sized discussion sections. "It's not possible to have professors provide this [discussion] experience for a class of 300 to 500 students. There isn't enough time in the day or money in the budget."

This school, along with an increasing number of other Big-time U's, does not even put enough money into regular undergraduate education to staff all discussion sections with graduate student TAs; instead, it uses unpaid undergrad teaching assistants. The UMass student griped that in his discussion sections, "People would ask simple questions and the [undergrad] TAs had absolutely no idea how to answer."

Nevertheless, there is enough money in the UMass pot—$15 million worth—to fund Commonwealth College, a Lexus on a campus surrounded by ordinary general undergraduate education programs. But not everyone on campus loved the new Lexus, one student writing the *Boston Globe*: "The elitist ideology of Commonwealth College is a danger to public higher education. Isolating the 'smart kids' is a bad idea, reeking of selfish administrative illusions of greater prestige." A *Globe* columnist also articulated this argument, adding: "This [honors college] is about image," and UMass pursues it at the expense of ordinary undergraduates. "What is the message to every" UMass regular student? "It's not subtle at all. It screams out to those who don't make the honors cut: You're just not worth that much."

The recent Boyer Commission report funded by the Carnegie Foundation put the UMass situation in national perspective, particularly the fond hope by the president of UMass for Commonwealth College to produce Rhodes, Marshall, and other scholarship winners:

> Universities take great pleasure in proclaiming how many of their undergraduates win Rhodes or other prestigious scholarships and how many are accepted at the most selective graduate schools, but while those achievements are lauded, too many baccalaureate students who are not in the running for any kind of distinction may get little or no attention.

The University of Texas at Austin must have been pleased when *U.S. News*, in its 1999 college issue, included the UT honors program, Plan II, and one of the program's graduates, a Rhodes Scholar, in a laudatory article. The magazine also claimed that the students admitted into this UT program "rival those accepted at Houston's Rice University, one of the nation's best private institutions." However, what happens to the more than thirty-four thousand UT undergraduates not in the honors program? Unlike Rice, where all undergrads take small classes and have personal contact with faculty members, UT features many lecture courses, some with five hundred students in them and, over the years, a constant stream of student criticism about the size of classes at the school and the remoteness of professors from the average undergraduate (see page 139).

Nevertheless, because honors programs gain prestige for research universities, and also camouflage the failure of their general undergraduate programs, Big-time U's pump money into them—dollars that could better go to improving educational conditions for all students. In addition, schools have diverted funds into generous scholarships to attract honors students to their campuses, whether these students need the financial aid or not. Again, this money could help regular undergraduates in the traditional form of need-based aid; the *New York Times* disclosed that "as a result" of these new scholarships, universities "have less to spend on many needy applicants." The *Boston Globe*, in writing about UMass's new honors scholarships, noted: "Nationwide, more and more second-tier schools [like UMass] have begun offering similar scholarships . . . to lure top students"; these universities claim that "the better the students they can get, the higher their rankings rise and the more applicants they can attract—which in turn raises their rankings even more."

Again the question occurs: If this applications phenomenon actually exists (it has never been proven), how does it help regular students? If a high school senior in New England sees that UMass has gone up in, say, *U.S.News*'s rankings, and she enrolls at the school but is not accepted into the honors program, how has she advanced her educational opportunities? In fact, is this not another Admissions Office scam, an academic bait and switch? Of course, she could tire of the large lecture classes and distant faculty, and embrace the facet of the school nicknamed "ZooMass," the large party scene, much of it revolving around the school's intercollegiate athletics program.

The administrators at this university claim that the "ZooMass" image is unfair, and that Commonwealth College will soon obliterate it. Yet, they proudly told *USA Today* that after the basketball team's success in the NCAA men's tourney in the early and mid 1990s, "out-of-state applications increased 50 percent"; they also tried to smile their way through a major scandal involving the abysmal GPAs of many players on those NCAA tourney teams. Then the school newspaper, after a snowball pelting by UMass students of nearby Amherst College caused $10,000 in damage, admitted, "How can we change the University's ZooMass reputation . . . when we re-enact scenes straight out of *Animal House*?" Also there were the "Right to Party" demonstrations when the Massachusetts Board of Higher Education banned alcohol at all public colleges and universities in the state. "Save our beer," UMass students chanted at their rally.

UMass remains a beer-and-circus school, and, appropriately, *Insider's Guide* 2000 quotes its students as proclaiming that "the most popular beverage on campus [is] Busch Lite." Predictably, many UMass faculty members prefer to teach in Commonwealth College than in the general undergraduate education units. And this school, like many others promoting honors programs, rewards them for this work. Because Big-time U's generally advance professors for research, not teaching, this seems contradictory, but, always pursuing ever elusive "prestige," these schools are willing to compensate faculty for working with honors students. For this reason and some less tangible ones, many professors eagerly migrate to honors programs and colleges.

> The heart of the [Temple University honors] program is a set of courses open only to honors students and typically taught by specially selected, full-time faculty members, many of whom have won the Temple University Great Teacher Award. The program features small classes of about 20 students and encourages a lively, seminar-style classroom atmosphere.
> —Temple University's honors program official description

This university, as well as most others, accompanies the honors program written material with photos of famous professors sitting at seminar tables with small groups of lively and engaged undergraduates. National magazines like *U.S. News* also feature these shots in their annual issues. Indeed, these icons of great teaching and learning—along with the photos of professors and attentive students on grassy knolls—also appear in the Admissions Office material for regular, nonhonors students, prompting the Boyer Commission to complain about "an advertising practice that [universities] would condemn in the commercial world": in reality, multitudes of "students graduate without ever seeing the world-famous professors or tasting genuine research." Regular Temple students discover this when they try to enroll in a seminar with a Great Teacher Award winner. Finally, Temple's honors program does not change this school's top-ten rating for "Least happy students" in *Princeton Review* or help its legions of undergraduates.

Not only do many universities like Temple divert internal funds into special honors programs, but they also try to generate outside grant money for them. A campus of the University of Wisconsin received a large foundation grant to fund three visiting professors a year "to teach exclusively in the [honors] program for three year terms." In addition, according to the school's honors material, some of its "best teachers and scholars teach regularly in the program, offering undergraduates the opportunity to work with faculty members often available only to graduate students." Obviously, the missing words in this sentence are "a few" as in: "offering a few undergraduates the opportunity. . . ." Like other public universities, the tuition dollars of regular undergraduates provide this school's main source of revenue, but, as increasingly occurs in higher education, these students are neglected for the honors program few.

> Honors students are easy. They're motivated, inventive. They never complain about homework, extra reading, or deadlines. They are better read than most and want to read more. We have spirited discussions in these groups because the students themselves are so good and so eager.
>
> —Richard Moll, higher education expert, quoting an unnamed honors program director

Honors students embody one of the oldest university traditions: the academically talented students who become the intellectual children of the professoriate and, subsequently, the future faculty. Unlike regular undergraduates who enter required lecture courses as a conscripted army—unhappy, frequently shuffling their feet, closing their notebooks with ten minutes to go in the lecture, sometimes leaving before the professor finishes speaking—honors students volunteer for their classes (usually seminars) and listen carefully to the faculty member, then eagerly ask and answer questions. According to a longtime honors instructor, "They are a joy to teach, especially after wrestling with and being thrown out of the ring by average students, never mind when in lectures they look like they want to hit you with their chairs."

A high school senior on a college visiting tour, after sitting in on an honors class at a Big-time U, said, "They spent the hour on the professor's specialty. The kids had done all the required reading and even the supplementary stuff. They asked the professor constant questions, interrupted him, argued all the time with him and each other. It must be so hard for profs to teach them." The interviewer replied, "No, it's like teaching graduate students. Most faculty members could roll out of bed at 3 A.M. and do it. But try teaching regular undergraduates who haven't done the reading and won't say a thing. Now that's hard teaching, straight uphill." Regular undergraduates can also crush faculty egos, whereas honors students flatter the professorial psyche and give faculty the illusion of being great teachers (some educators term honors students "pre-learners," in other words, they master most things on their own, with no need of formal instruction).

In addition, traditional academic snobbery enters the faculty/honors student equation. A typical professorial pronouncement on regular undergrads versus honors students came from a faculty member commenting on the cheating issue: "I'm not here to prevent [ordinary] students from cheating. I'm here to help the genuine learners catch fire. Spending my time listening to appeals or [making] accusations of cheating is not my idea of spending it well." Possibly if faculty members did not have to deal with hundreds of students in huge lecture classes, they might help regular undergraduates "catch fire" too; blaming and dismissing them solves nothing.

Not only do Big-time U's monetarily reward professors for doing honors courses, but many faculty members gain other professional benefits. The University of Maryland honors program brags that "most of the faculty [in it] are teaching courses they created just for honors students—courses they are especially eager to teach." Often faculty are keen because they are mutating their research into the topic of the honors seminar, and gaining valuable research time—as they do in graduate courses—by focusing their energy in this way. In addition, faculty members regularly turn their honors undergraduates into free research assistants.

Honors programs boast that their students have frequent opportunities to work directly with professors, and often they accompany their lists of "research projects and internships" with photos of undergraduates in labs examining test tubes with their instructors. At their best these research exercises engage and train future faculty members. However, as with all aspects of Big-time U's, the reality behind the glossy photos of profs and students sharing a lab beaker is often different. One honors program professor admitted, "A lot of this directed research thing is a sham. I have my honors students doing scut work for me for free, but they don't seem to mind, and it definitely lowers my research costs."

Because Big-time U's promote their honors programs, some schools fund the student assistantships and internships, and faculty quickly glom onto these dollars. An English professor remarked, "My honors kids get minimum wage and I have them digging into databases for references for my projects and grant applications. It's great for me and saves me research costs. I'm not sure what they learn from it, other than the fact that lots of research is totally boring and tedious but has to be done."

Commonwealth College at UMass also boasts of its honors research opportunities, and how it "provides assistance to students in identifying faculty members with whom they can form mentoring relationships." Not only does this fulfill many professors' need to have academic children, but, for some, it also salves their consciences. Demographically, a sizable percentage of faculty members at research universities did not attend Big-time

U's as undergraduates; instead, they went to small schools like the ones clustered near UMass—Amherst, Hampshire, Mount Holyoke, and Smith—and they received excellent educations and faculty mentoring. This seminal experience often propelled them into academia, and, as professors, they wish to reproduce it for their students—except they work at Big-time U's and mainly encounter undergraduates by the hundreds in lecture classes. These faculty members go along with the research university system but sometimes their consciences bother them—hence their fondness for honors programs and their work there.

In honors program brochures, usually written by the faculty director, a constant theme is: "The program means the opportunity [for faculty] to teach bright students in inventive, interdisciplinary, and small-class settings, and advanced or intensive classes devoted to particular disciplines" (Indiana University). These professors are often among the best teachers at their schools because, from their undergraduate experiences, they have a sense of what excellent teaching/learning entails. However, this prompts the recurring question: How does this situation help regular students at Big-time U's? It doesn't; indeed, it drains many of the best teachers away from regular undergraduate classrooms, impoverishing them even more than they need be.

When honors program brochures discuss the perks that students receive when entering their lifeboats, they provide a clear view of some of the other difficulties that regular undergraduates encounter at the same universities:

Clemson University
Calhoun College, Honors Program . . .
Some of the advantages of membership in Calhoun College are priority class scheduling and registration, the option of honors housing, extended library loan privileges, and special lectures and cultural events.
—Clemson University's honors program official description

In an era when regular students at many universities, including Clemson, have difficulties obtaining places in courses, and, due to closed class sections and red tape, some undergraduates have to postpone graduation because they cannot complete all of their course requirements, Big-time U's give honors students "priority . . . scheduling and registration," allowing them to sign up for classes before opening registration to regular undergraduates (intercollegiate athletes also receive this privilege, see pages 244–46). Gaining entrance to lecture courses is rarely a problem, but sometimes honors students snap up spaces in smaller upper division courses, preventing regular undergraduates from taking these required classes in their major field.

Honors housing is also a desirable perk. At Clemson, honors students can live in "Holmes Hall, a converted hotel of four-person suites, complete with a kitchenette, two bedrooms, and a bathroom." Not only are the physical accommodations in honors facilities at Clemson and most other schools usually better than the ordinary dorms, but living conditions—particularly the low noise level—make honors residence halls much more pleasant than the often zoolike regular dorms. Even universities that do not provide separate residences for their honors students always have "centers or lounges where students gather together for informal conversations, luncheons, discussions," and so on (*Peterson's Honors Programs*).

Another major perk for honors students, particularly valuable at huge campuses, are faculty advisors. Instead of receiving the fast shuffle from the lowly paid staff advisors given to regular undergraduates, honors students discuss their class schedules with faculty members who steer them into the best courses available, and who also know the system and its loopholes. In an interview at the University of Texas, Austin, an honors student commented:

> I have many privileges here which make my undergraduate education particularly strong. But I hear awful stories from my high school friends who came with me to UT (nonhonors students) about poor advising, about being signed up for the wrong courses, and about wasting whole semesters and years not fulfilling graduation requirements. It sounds grim, and I'm thankful that I have a great faculty advisor.

At some schools, regular undergraduates resent the perks of the honors students. The University of Iowa has an elaborate wall-to-wall four-year honors track called the Unified Program, with all the standard perks, whereas regular undergrads at this school encounter the usual Big Ten treatment, including large lecture classes, "which can have as many as 800 students." In 1999, *Insider's Guide* wrote that for regular Iowa students, "the most unpopular administration regulation" concerned "some of the selective programs like the Unified Program. They tend to siphon off the best students from mainstream college life."

In interviews at this school, nonhonors undergraduates complained about the large lecture classes—a number of interviewees said that they had attended small Iowa high schools and "were completely lost" in the immense freshmen UI courses, and some honors students from similar backgrounds admitted that they felt "very lucky" to be in Unified Program seminars. However, both groups mentioned their affection for Iowa's college sports teams, including the women's basketball squad, and their participation in the lively on—and off—campus party scene. A number of honors students from the Chicago area said that they chose Iowa over more academically prestigious institutions because of the "Unified Program and Big Ten sports." These comments underline the fact that although Big-time U's continue the traditional separation between academically talented students and other undergraduates, the walls between these subcultures are more permeable than ever before.

A University of Maryland honors student articulated this when she explained that in her honors dorm: "You're living and learning together"; however, we also "like to have fun and party. But we know when it's time to hit the books," unlike many collegiate students at Maryland and other schools. In fact, because many honors undergrads fear being called "dorks" and "nerds" by regular students, most universities with separate honors housing make living there optional for participants in the program.

In terms of the University of Iowa's situation, UI trails behind the honors colleges, intercollegiate athletic teams, and party scenes of a number of other Big Ten institutions. Indeed, this conference features a school with one of the strongest honors programs in America, top football and men's basketball teams, and a consistently high ranking on "Party school" lists. Bring on the Spartans.

★   ★   ★

The Honors College at Michigan State University . . .
—Exempts its members from the standard curricular requirements and . . . [allows them to] bypass prerequisite and limited enrollment stipulations [in undergraduate courses]; and also enroll in graduate courses . . .

—Features faculty advisors in the majors . . .

—Promotes early access to research opportunities . . .

—Makes available, but optional, honors housing in four different residence halls.
—Michigan State's self-description in
The College Guide for Academically Talented Students

The most interesting aspect of this statement about MSU's honors program is where it appeared and what it did not say. The College Guide is an advertising booklet sent to high school students who score in the upper range of the PSAT, SAT, and ACT exams. The publication features self-descriptions by universities and colleges that stress undergraduate education—Rice, Emory, Washington of St. Louis, Kenyon, etc.—as well as ads for some Big-time U's and small Division III colleges. The fascinating element in Michigan State's entry is the fact that the school focuses entirely on its honors program—it never mentions regular undergraduate education at MSU except by negative implication, e.g., it "exempts" honors students from "standard curricular requirements," etc. A naive reader of *The College Guide* might think that the MSU Honors College is the only educational establishment in East Lansing, Michigan, surrounded by cherry orchards, with the state capitol in the distance.

For a description of the actual school and its more than thirty thousand regular undergraduates, the reader must turn to publications like the *Insider's Guide*: "huge lecture classes"; some "TAs can barely speak a word of English"; "difficult [for students] to get individual help"; mainly "multiple-choice tests," and so on. In recent years, the *Princeton Review* has placed Michigan State near the top in its "Long lines and red tape" category, and also revealed what undergraduates do instead of fighting the MSU anti-educational system. In two categories, "Their students (almost) never study" and "Party school," Michigan State ranked third in the entire country in 2000, earning these high finishes with a multitude of parties, even some riots, often accompanying Spartan sports events. Indeed, MSU undergraduates claim that the "Right to Party" movement of the 1990s originated at their school.

From the 1980s through the late 1990s, MSU students held tailgate parties before and after football games at Munn Field, near Spartan Stadium ("Biggie" Munn was a win-at-all-costs MSU football coach who took his teams to national prominence in the 1940s and 1950s). Because of the increasingly chaotic, sometimes violent, always drunken nature of the tailgate parties, MSU officials decided in the fall of 1997 to ban alcohol from Munn Field. This sparked student demonstrations at the time that exploded the following spring into a large-protest-rally-turned-major-riot. The MSU students rallied under the "Right to Party" movement, to the amusement of outside observers and the consternation of MSU officials.

Evoking the student protests of the 1960s, a newspaper columnist wrote that "the demonstrators weren't agitating for a better tomorrow, they were agitating for a better Saturday afternoon." Gary Trudeau in his "Doonesbury" comic strip mocked the MSU students, and the university president claimed that Trudeau and the rest of the media were uninformed and unfair. In fact, the *Chronicle of Higher Education* reported that Michigan State "led the nation for campus alcohol violations" the previous year; moreover, throughout the 1990s, many MSU students went to the emergency rooms of local hospitals with close to lethal doses of alcohol poisoning. Inevitably, in 1998, a MSU undergraduate died of an alcohol overdose, and to underline the horror of the story, when he passed out—but was still alive—his friends wrote "24 shots" on his body and painted his nose red.

The MSU president led a campus "Alcohol Awareness" campaign but the massive partying and drinking continued, much of it occurring before, during, and after intercollegiate athletic events. In fact, in 1999, after the men's basketball team lost in the semifinals of the NCAA tournament, thousands of students, many of them drunk, rioted in downtown East Lansing, trashing cars and stores. Columnist Robert Lipsyte of the *New York Times* went to Michigan State to examine this phenomenon, particularly the connection between sports and drunken behavior (beer-and-circus). He remarked, "Sports was clearly some kind of excuse, a permission to go mad. Alcohol was a fuel, and this is the Bud Light generation to which beer, breasts, and ball games are inextricably bound."

Without mentioning the mascot of Bud Light, Spuds MacKenzie, his entourage of "beautiful babes," and their constant appearances in beer commercials tied to athletic events, Lipsyte connected the dots from the late 1980s to the late 1990s. Possibly the young men and women rioting in the Right to Party movement had, as children, worn Spuds MacKenzie T-shirts and even played with Spuds toys. Now they had grown up, enrolled in college, many had joined fraternities and sororities, and they drank lots of Bud Light and other cheap beers.

Finally, for all of Michigan State's promotion of its outstanding honors program, the vast majority of undergraduates at the school exist far from it, uninterested in academics and consuming their college years in beer-and-circus. A similar situation occurs at most Big-time U's with honors divisions, and like Michigan State's entry in *The College Guide*, these schools publicly promote their excellent and well-funded honors programs and never mention their deteriorating regular undergraduate education ones— as if somehow the flashy honors colleges compensate for the poverty of ordinary classes. At the beginning of the twenty-first century, the enrichment of already affluent honors programs increases, and the impoverishment of regular undergraduate education also continues. This trend will prove hard to reverse.

PART THREE

BEER-AND-CIRCUS

RULES

14

CHEAP BEER:

THE OXYGEN OF THE GREEK SYSTEM

A cultural icon that connected 1990s undergraduates to their collegiate predecessors was the film *Animal House*—its hold on the imagination of many students, especially fraternity men, remaining undiminished during the final decade of the century. The film also provides a way into an examination of the contemporary collegiate subculture, particularly the infatuation with alcohol and the escalation of the drinking phenomenon known as binge drinking.

★   ★   ★

My father would always get very excited when WPIX [New York TV] would show *Animal House*, and would make sure that I would see it, even though [I was a child] . . . Now that I'm here [in college in 1997], I realize that fraternities, instead of consisting of drunk, rude womanizing morons in a decrepit, shoddy house, in fact, consist of drunk, rude, womanizing morons in cookie-cutter, antiseptic corners of university dormitories [where this school has placed them]. . . .

Luckily this film can be appreciated for its depiction of freewheeling, late-'50s college life . . . when you could go through life "fat, drunk, and stupid," and nail random passed-out women when—well, I guess some things never change.

—A student film reviewer's contribution
to an *Animal House* web page

Throughout the 1990s, as binge drinking by college students became a national issue, many commentators referred to the late 1970s film *Animal*

House. Editorial writers termed it "a defining moment in many Americans' perception of college fraternities and sororities," and even Minnesota governor Jesse Ventura, representing the "common man," invoked it in explaining his opposition to new federal tax credits for university tuition charges: "What are we asking for [with these credits], *National Lampoon's Animal House?* What kid at eighteen wouldn't say, 'I can go to college for two years, drink beer, chase women.' Whether he wants to go to college or not, who wouldn't go?"

Thus *Animal House,* set in the pre-Vietnam era and filmed after the war, provided a bridge for the collegiate subculture, particularly its alcoholic and sexual excesses, to span the last half of the twentieth century. When the 1990s media dug into the binge-drinking story, they spotlighted scenes of contemporary collegiate life that replicated the *Animal House* version of the 1950s, and even echoed the drinking culture of earlier decades. The *Kansas City Star* examined the Big-time U's in its region, reporting that at Missouri (Columbia), and Kansas (Lawrence), "Students brag about going to a university with a 'party school' reputation," featuring many Greek houses and big-time college sports teams. According to a KU internal poll, 92 percent of undergraduates there drank, 60 percent binged, and 40 percent had passed out one or more times from overdrinking. Another publication noted that at Kansas State at Manhattan, the Greeks have their annual "Patty Murphy" bash, "a party named after a fraternity member who allegedly drank himself to death during Prohibition, which features tombstones . . . as decorations."

In the 1990s, when across the country increasing numbers of college students died from alcohol poisoning, and more than fifteen students at Kansas schools died in alcohol-related incidents during the decade, the "Patty Murphy" party seemed in poor taste—yet the university never ended this collegiate tradition. In fact, with the rise to national prominence of the Kansas State football team in the 1990s, the party scene at this university accelerated, the students having more to celebrate.

Television networks and national newspapers also focused on the collegiate drinking scene. *USA Today,* in a front-page feature, explained the connection of the past to the present: "Epic acts of alcoholic stupidity form the basis of a rich oral history, and the most legendary excesses are burnished and passed down like treasured heirlooms" by one generation of collegians to the next. The main storytellers are often alumni, and they frequently gather in their old fraternity houses to narrate the tales and, on occasion, to try to relive them. Their universities support this subculture in various ways, including large displays in campus bookstores and gift shops of beer mugs, shot glasses, and other party paraphernalia—all with the school's logo on them—as well as T-shirts and sweatshirts commemorating famous parties, particularly annual bashes.

In addition, even as some universities, upon the advice of legal counsel, banned alcohol from student housing units on their campuses, they allowed alumni to hold tailgaters on their property, and they entertained important grads at on-campus cocktail parties. Undergraduates quickly spotted the hypocrisy, one telling *USA Today*, "This is supposedly a dry campus, but you see people drinking on the porch of the president's house. The rules only apply to some people."

A senior at the University of Mississippi noted that his school's alumni "would go ballistic" if Ole Miss actually enforced its liquor ban. That university, enveloped in its history, maintained its drinking customs throughout the 1990s. A Greek there described an important fraternity rush custom: houses have slide shows of "what their parties are like, and how crazy they can get." This Greek admitted, "You think, 'I want to be that crazy. I want to be in some of these pictures next year,' " and you join to party.

The last few years, the *Insider's Guide* has run a section on the University of Mississippi titled, "Party, Party, Party," including the student boast: "We may lose a game" in intercollegiate football or basketball, "but we never lose a party." Ole Miss Greeks organize and run the school's party scene, and alumni often return to their fraternities for drinking weekends; an undergraduate remarked that "husbands bring their wives and you see forty-year-olds passed out on the floor! It gets a bit ridiculous."

Similar scenes occurred at many other beer-and-circus schools and indicated the immense volume of alcohol consumed by students and alumni in the collegiate subculture. Indeed, when researchers began to study this subculture, they discovered both its vitality and the large impediments to changing it. Not only does beer-and-circus have immense historical momentum, but, in terms of fraternities and sororities, those people most responsible for the members' behavior—alumni officials and current chapter leaders—often drank the heaviest and caroused the most wildly.

Most studies indicated that alcohol consumption by Greek organization members escalated in the 1980s and 1990s and that many students belonging to other campus subcultures joined the party. One researcher even charted the drinking games popular with undergraduates and "found that previous generations of students knew of drinking games, but did not engage in the frequency and variety of games of today's students," nor did past collegians consume as much alcohol as contemporary undergraduates did.

In the 1990s, *The Complete Book of Beer Drinking Games* became a national best-seller. The book, according to its authors, began "during a beery evening," and grew into a publishing phenomenon, with multiple reprintings and over a half-million copies sold, as well as "scores of angry letters from college administrators, and prudish Bible-thumpers." Most of all, the book provided readers with detailed instructions on fifty beer-drinking games, including "all the old favorites" and many newer ones. In fact, the book probably prompted the consumption of more beer than any other single media source—except possibly Spuds MacKenzie.

The success of *The Complete Book of Beer Drinking Games* generated imitators and parallel volumes, including ones with college drinking songs. The most famous of these tunes—originating well over a century ago and capturing the essence of the collegiate subculture—with the name of the fraternity or sorority inserted in the blank space is:

> Bring out that old silver goblet with the _____ on it,
> And we'll open up another keg of beer,
> For it ain't for knowledge that we go to college,
> But to raise hell while we're here.

★   ★   ★

In the 1990s, not all of the songs or comments published about Greek drinking were as cheerful or mindless as the famous song. Many newspaper and magazine headlines announced:

SIGMA DIE

CAN'T FRATERNITIES EXIST

WITHOUT BINGE DRINKING?

The death of a Louisiana State University student from alcohol poisoning this week again calls attention to the irresponsible and destructive behavior long associated with many college fraternities.

—Houston Chronicle

ALCOHOL CONTRIBUTED TO DEATH

AT IU [INDIANA UNIVERSITY]

FRATERNITY

A 19-year old Indiana University student choked to death on his vomit after drinking alcohol at a party at his fraternity, a Monroe County coroner's report said.

—Indianapolis Star

BELLYING UP TO THE BAR

Are colleges doing enough to crack down on risky drinking? The stakes are high . . . alcohol poisonings kill an estimated 50 students annually.

—*Newsweek* magazine cover story

The newspaper adage—"If it bleeds, it leads"—definitely applied to the topic of student drinking in the 1990s. The more sensational the calamities from overdrinking, the more the media focused on the issue (similarly, when the mishaps became less dramatic, media interest declined—even though student binge drinking increased). One ancillary and positive result of the 1990s media spotlight was the attention that various researchers, quietly studying the subject for many years, finally received.

Raymond A. Scroth began his work on the connection between fraternities and drinking decades ago, and he ascertained that media and public interest in the topic was cyclical, following a definite pattern: "First the horror stories, [including] death and binge drinking statistics"; "Second: impassioned defenses" by fraternity and sorority members, particularly alumni, often in the form of "angry letters-to-the-editor [that] testify to the deep friendships Greeks form, and [that] accuse journalists of persecuting the Greek system." The defenders become especially shrill when a commentator proposes banning fraternities and sororities from specific campuses or abolishing them nationally.

Scroth described the arguments about the Greek system, and also participated in them (as an abolitionist). Like most combatants on this topic, he ignored the wider university context within which fraternities and sororities exist. Greek houses can serve a useful function at some schools, particularly mammoth Big-time U's, by providing students with human-sized residencies and immediate friendship networks. A young woman at the University of Washington explained:

> Through my sorority, I found a group of friends who became a surrogate family for me and who made the hard times I experience at college bearable. The sorority is a home where I am a name and a face and not just another social security number, the only way this school relates to me. During my years here, I have felt totally alienated by the university, the teachers, and academic things in general. All I have are my sorority sisters. This house, with its social opportunities, friendships, and fun times, is what saves college for me, definitely not my academic endeavors.

However, fraternity and sorority friendships usually come with a price tag: conformity to group demands, including participation in drinking rituals and games. Yet, as the woman at UW explained, the academic aspects of her school "totally alienated" her, whereas the collegiate subculture embraced and engrossed her.

Professor Scroth's third and final phase of the Greek-drinking-and-media-attention cycle is a cooling-out period during which university and Greek officials make "promises of reform." They offer:

> Proposals [that] imagine that a little tinkering with the system will make fraternities a creative force compatible with a school's intellectual and spiritual goals. Yet, radical reform is impossible because fraternities, which have no purpose outside themselves—beyond their own bonding—can survive only by reinforcing their own traditions . . . particularly their drinking ones.

In the modern era, Greek proponents answer charges like Dr. Scroth's with lists of their charity work and, sometimes, their "house GPAs." In an on-going attempt to change their image and to generate positive PR, fraternities and sororities engage in highly visible philanthropy, and they also publicize their group grade point averages—if those numbers are higher than the average GPAs of students in university dorms (at many schools, fraternity GPAs are lower than the student average and go unmentioned). Similarly, some Greek altruism is real, but sometimes it consists of fund-raising events for local charities featuring great quantities of alcohol and loud music.

Thus, Dr. Scroth's critique of fraternities is narrowly correct, but, finally, he overlooks the main purposes of Greek organizations at public Big-time U's—institutions without "intellectual and spiritual goals" for their undergraduates. In addition to providing housing and friendship networks for a significant percentage of undergraduates, the Greek system is central to a school's "party scene." Cheap beer provides the oxygen that keeps the Greek system functioning, and, in turn, this subculture pumps essential blood into a Big-time U, helping it maintain its beer-and-circus heartbeat. Without this synergy between the Greeks and Big-time U's, the party scene would expire, and research universities would lose a large percentage of their main source of income—undergraduate tuition dollars—and probably wither and die.

A student columnist for a Big Ten campus newspaper glimpsed this alternate future while contemplating what would occur if his university actually banished alcohol from all on- and off-campus Greek housing units: "It would literally destroy the school. Frats with no alcohol would quickly lead to frats with no members (I know, I know, people don't join frats to drink, they join frats to improve their grades and get involved in community service). A housing crisis of unforeseen proportions would occur," and this university would be depopulated.

Big-time U's, for all of their current pronouncements about curtailing student drinking, will never allow their schools and the surrounding areas to become dry. Officials of these universities know that if their institutions became deserts without alcoholic irrigation, this terrain would not sustain undergraduate student life.

★   ★   ★

> Binge drinking is not evenly distributed across all student groups. Some, like fraternity and sorority members and students involved in athletics [particularly as super fans], are more often binge drinkers. Nor is it distributed evenly at all colleges. Indeed, binge drinking ranges from 10% of students at the colleges with the lowest rate to 70% at the highest. Colleges with Greek houses and [collegiate type] dormitories, with NCAA Division I teams and with alcohol outlets within one mile of campus have higher binge-drinking rates.
>
> —The Center for Science in the Public Interest

Health professionals define binge drinking as an average-size male consuming five or more drinks within a fairly short period of time, and a female, four drinks (body weight, not gender, is the determining factor here). To speed up alcoholic intake, sometimes bingers dispense with glasses and bottles, and "funnel"—pour quantities of alcohol into a funnel attached to a rubber hose, aiming the hose spout at the throat. In the 1990s, a number of major studies discovered that over 80 percent of all college students consumed alcohol, and over half of this group binged on occasion. However, the key finding was the fact that almost 20 percent of college drinkers binged once a week or more. And throughout the decade—during and after the immense media attention to the problem—the number of frequent bingers grew. A dean at the University of Colorado at Boulder, a famous party school, admitted, "More kids drink every day, they stagger from party to party."

Nevertheless, as the Center for Science in the Public Interest and other authorities indicate, student alcohol consumption varies from campus to campus and according to type of school. Yet, student drinking is so widespread that experts do not divide institutions into Drinking U's and Nondrinking U's, but High Binge Schools versus Low Binge Schools. Similarly, researchers do not separate students into Drinkers and Abstainers, but Bingers versus Non-Bingers. Nationally, college students buy $6 billion worth of alcohol products a year—more money than they spend on books, snack foods, and all other beverages combined. In terms of beer, each student averages sixty six-packs annually.

Predictably, a majority of bingers belong to the traditional collegiate subculture and attend beer-and-circus schools, notably those with big-time college sports teams. Moreover, members of fraternities and sororities lead all collegians in the consumption of alcohol. Conversely, a majority of nonbingers do not participate fully in the collegiate subculture and many attend academically oriented schools, particularly those in NCAA Division III. In addition, unlike bingers, most nonbingers are not alienated from the academic aspects of their institutions, and usually they have responsible adults, even faculty members, to turn to when encountering personal difficulties, including alcohol-related ones. On the other hand, bingers mainly respond to peer pressure from other bingers, and if their drinking evolves into alcoholism, often they will not seek outside help, or it is not a viable option at a Big-time U.

(It is important to note that some students at the best small colleges in America, as well as at Ivy League universities, binge drink, and that a number of Division III institutions have reputations as "hard-drinking" places. However, the Center for Science in the Public Interest, and the Harvard University School of Public Health—the main researchers on this issue—examined extremely large samples of undergraduates at hundreds of schools and, despite the above exceptions, their studies indicate that the schools with the highest percentage of binge drinkers also had large Greek systems and big-time college sports teams, in other words, Big-time U's where beer-and-circus rules.)

> When people ask me why college students [binge] drink, I say, "Why not?" People in the "real world" have too little time and too many responsibilities to drink heavily night after night. They have to get up early five days a week, work all day, then go home to their families. College students are usually only responsible for themselves. All they have to do is go to a few classes and study when it's convenient.
>
> —David Hanson, professor of sociology at
> the State University of New York

This portrait of undergraduate behavior excludes all the vocational students who work at full-time jobs and/or head families and, predictably, tend not to binge drink. However, students who work part-time and belong mainly to the collegiate subculture engage in a certain amount of binge drinking, and spend a proportion of their income on this activity. In addition, rebel students sometimes indulge in heavy drinking, and even some academically inclined undergraduates consume their portion—although they rarely binge more than once a week and, even more rarely, on weekday nights. Their explanation is usually, "We work and study hard all week, and party hard on Friday and Saturday nights."

But finally, Professor Hanson's comment on average student drinkers having too much time on their hands and too little to do academically is accurate for many undergraduates in the collegiate subculture at beer-and-circus schools. The faculty/student nonaggression pact allows these undergraduates to spend a majority of their time and energy in extracurricular activities; sometimes these pastimes are organized, such as playing recreational sports and attending college sports events, but often they are pure leisure, watching TV and boozing (for a breakdown of hours per week spent by regular undergraduates in these activities, see pages 195–96).

In contrast, a recent study found that "nonstudents of the same age . . . 17- to 24-year-olds" did far less binge drinking than average undergraduates. The reason is obvious—most nonstudents have the same work pressures and responsibilities as others in the "real world"—but the finding is important because of the class background of a majority of nonstudents. Usually working class, they live in a culture where binge drinking has long existed and, to some extent, is tolerated. On the other hand, college students are mainly middle class, and, historically, this culture has not fostered binge drinking. Therefore, as a university president remarked after reviewing this study, "It's very clear from the data that something is going on at college campuses, and in the college experience, that makes the problem very significant for us to get hold of."

Dr. Henry Wechsler of Harvard has studied college-student binge drinking more intensely and for a longer period of time than any other researcher in America. His most recent work reveals that, despite 1990s public and university campaigns to solve this problem, binge drinking is increasing. Wechsler has long argued that Greek organizations are central to the problem; not only do "four out of five" fraternity members binge, half of them on a regular basis, but they "play a prominent role in campus [social] life" far out of proportion to their numbers within the student population.

In a period when the collegiate subculture is more inclusive than ever before, fraternity parties attract many non-Greeks, particularly collegiates living in dorms and apartments. As the *Insider's Guide* explained in the introduction to every edition in the 1990s, the Greeks have "an important role in campus social activity . . . [because] at most schools," as the saying goes, " 'frats don't card' "—ask party-goers for proof that they are twenty-one or older. And, according to the *Chronicle of Higher Education*, when schools ban alcohol from frat houses, usually the Greeks move "the parties off-campus, to unofficial fraternity houses rented out by upperclassmen" (see pages 165–66 for more on this phenomenon).

Wechsler urges universities to clamp down on Greek drinking and Greek-sponsored parties, but he admits that "many administrators" hesitate to do so "for fear of angering [Greek] alumni donors who fondly remember their own college years of partying." Moreover, he indicates that another major "impetus for binge drinking on college campuses—one rarely mentioned publicly—involves alumni at tailgate parties during homecoming activities and sporting events," and undergraduates participating in or imitating these celebrations. He wants schools to ban alcohol on these occasions, but he fails to acknowledge that booze-plus-college-sports is at the core of Big-time U's culture. Prohibiting alcohol from stadium and arena parking lots would be like barring athletes with low SAT scores from playing inside those venues. "Logically, Wechsler makes sense," said an official at the University of Kentucky about the researcher's proposals, "but it ain't gonna happen, Henry. . . . Any president of a SEC school who tells his alums that they can't tailgate would be lynched, then roasted in little pieces on their barbecue grills." (Ironically, Big-time U alumni give much less money to their alma maters than do alums of non-big-time college sports schools, see pages 256–58.)

The main patrons of Greek organizations will never change the drinking culture and, as a 1998 study discovered, future Greek alumni leaders—today's house presidents—the people "who ought to play responsible roles in helping address" the binge drinking problem, "are by far the heaviest drinkers on campus." This study included more than twenty-five thousand undergraduates at sixty-one colleges and universities, and also revealed that "fraternity house members averaged 20.3 drinks per week compared with 7.5 drinks for all other male students" in the sample—thus, the fraternity leaders consumed more alcohol than any other cohort of undergraduates.

A similar pattern emerged for sorority women and their leaders: "Sorority house residents averaged 6.2 drinks per week," much less than their male counterparts, but almost twice the rate "for all female students." And sorority leaders paralleled male house presidents and officers with a higher alcohol consumption rate than regular "sisters."

The news about Greek women is particularly negative because it reveals one of the major changes in collegiate culture in the final decades of the twentieth century: female college students are drinking, and binge drinking, much more than their mothers and grandmothers did while at university. In other words, although the alcohol consumption of all students has increased during the last two decades, and dangerous kinds of drinking, especially binge drinking, have escalated, the rate of increase for women has exceeded that of men. The reasons are complex and connect to the changing role of women in American society; nonetheless, the statistics are depressing.

★　　★　　★

At 1 A.M., paramedics rush into Scorekeepers [an Ann Arbor, Michigan bar]. A young woman has thrown up and passed out. As police and rescue workers try to help, spectators encircle the prostrate woman. Most have drinks in their hands . . . the crowd dismisses the woman as a "dumb drunk" who didn't know her limit. Meanwhile, others [students] crowd around the bar three deep, holding out money and trying to get the bartender's attention.

—Ron French, Jodi S. Cohen, and Wendy Case,
Detroit News reporters

The young woman at Scorekeepers survived, but, increasingly, college women binge and end up in life-threatening situations. Nationally, the number of female students who binge more than tripled from the 1980s to the 1990s and, as with fraternity men, sorority women drank more and faster than all other female undergraduates—Wechsler's Harvard study found that 62 percent of Greek women binged versus 35 percent of non-sorority women. Wechsler also commented that "50 years ago, drinking by college women was not considered a problem" but, today, female college students are catching up to the alcoholism rate of male collegians.

Anecdotal evidence supports Wechsler's statement. "In the 1950s and 1960s," a sorority woman of that era recalled, "it was very sociable to drink a cocktail or two during the weekends at a party, a Pink Lady or an Old Fashion." Another "co-ed" of that period remembered, "We never drank beer at all. It tasted awful and was considered really low class." Even in the 1970s, when the legal drinking age was eighteen, few college women consumed the quantities of alcohol that female students do now, and only a small minority binged.

Fast-forward to the beginning of the twenty-first century: many college women favor a highly potent drink with the innocuous name of Long Island Iced Tea—a mixture of rum, vodka, tequila, and triple sec containing 400 percent more alcohol per volume than the average Pink Lady or Old Fashion. In addition, college females toss down much more beer than ever before, beer drinking games often introducing them to the "strange brew"—not an immediately pleasant taste, but no longer déclassé. As a researcher explained, the games serve as initiation rituals for younger students, particularly women, and while playing them, females feel "more at ease drinking beer and engaging in publicly assertive behavior," including public drunkenness—conduct that their mothers and their grandmothers would have avoided.

Sometimes sororities formalize the alcohol initiation rites by requiring their pledges (new, probationary members) to consume drinks in hazing ceremonies. On occasion, the drunken pledges attract the attention of campus police and university authorities, resulting in fines and other penalties, but, more often, the drinking initiation is merely a "fun part" of collegiate life, only noticed by the participants and their friends. One young woman described her sorority's "pledge night," held off-campus— beyond the reach of college officials—in the party room of a local Chinese restaurant:

> Jennifer, our president, brought out a big basket decorated with pink ribbons and threw handfuls of pink condoms to every table. We all started cheering and screaming "More, more!" The chapter advisor [an alum], a nice but clueless suburban type, looked like she was going to faint, but the sisters were pretty drunk and she intelligently did not interfere with our revelry.

In an era of gender equality, women will be women, but, unfortunately, some boys, hormones raging, will remain boys. One reporter began a story on drunken college student behavior with, "If the legendary Sweetheart of Sigma Chi were an undergraduate today, she'd probably be in court bringing charges against the brothers for date rape." Many studies indicate that binge drinkers, both male and female, "engage in unplanned sexual activity" far more frequently than nonbinge drinkers, and this activity is not only unplanned but often "unwanted," including, in its most extreme form, "date rape." In addition, despite the distribution of pink and other colored condoms, bingers "have unprotected sexual relations" much more often than nonbingers. *Rolling Stone* magazine, in its fall 1999 college issue, featured a vivid article about sorority life at Ohio State University that concluded with a number of the sisters totally drunk and on the verge of unprotected and unpleasant sexual misadventures.

Campus police officers deal with many cases of "unwanted sexual advances," and they indicate that a large majority of perpetrators and victims have high alcohol blood levels when the incidents occur. Not only does alcohol lower inhibitions, but according to one researcher, " 'I was drunk' is [considered] a get-out-of-jail-free card by college students who act like idiots." Men often use this excuse to explain their sexual advances, and according to this researcher, "women, who still face a double standard when it comes to sleeping around, can blame one-night stands on alcohol." Indeed, a common student expression on many campuses is "the Walk of Shame": the trip home from the male's housing unit, often a fraternity house or dorm, that a woman takes the morning after a one-night stand. (On a few campuses, the term also applies to a man's trip from a female's room.)

In this emotionally charged collegiate world, thoroughly befogged by far too much booze, date rape also takes place. "No" must mean no, and when uttered, it should end the predatory advance. However, most date rapists deny ever hearing the word *no*; many victims feel guilty about stumbling into a situation where they need to say the word; and the authorities despise the paperwork, the legal hassles, and the bad publicity that results from the word being uttered. An administrator at Ohio State University commented:

> Date rape is a nasty part of the school's cost of doing business. It's awful, it's obscene, but it will never end as long as students allow themselves to get drunk out of their heads and end up in locked bedrooms. . . . The school puts on countless Awareness Clinics, but students are sober and rational when they attend them. Binge drinking is wholly irrational and that's when date rape happens most often.

Another part of a university's cost of doing business is borne directly by undergraduates in the path of student drunks, and indirectly by the school. The Center for Science in the Public Interest indicates that "student vandalism, including trashing dormitories, stealing property, and writing graffiti goes hand-in-hand with heavy drinking." Henry Wechsler has also studied this side-effect, pointing out that 82 percent of all students in his large sample had experienced "secondhand binge effects." An undergraduate at the University of Connecticut complained to the student newspaper that, at 2:30 A.M., some drunk had pulled the fire alarm in his dorm:

> An event that doesn't happen more than, I'd say, 17,000 times a week. So, in the middle of a snowstorm I had the great honor of standing outside in my pajamas . . . as various parts of my brain froze while firefighters risked their lives and the lives of everyone else out on the roads by driving heavy trucks as fast as possible on ice-covered roads.

At Seton Hall University in January 2000, the plague of false alarms claimed a number of victims: when an actual dorm fire occurred, many students ignored the alarm and were caught in the blaze, three dying and sixty-two injured.

At High Binge schools, a majority of students report frequent "secondhand alcohol-related" incidents. At Low Binge colleges, only a minority experience these problems, as well as such other effects as "personal property damaged" by drunks. As a result of secondhand problems, some High Binge schools have established substance-free housing, entire dorms or parts of dorms where residents agree to ban all alcohol products and illegal drugs. The Center for Science in the Public Interest points to these dorms as proof of "student willingness to pass up some conveniences (being able to drink in their rooms) in exchange for a safe and sure place to live and study."

In reality, only small numbers of undergraduates sign up for these dorms (and many of these students are pressured into doing so by their parents). At one eastern university with championship hockey teams and a well-earned "party school" reputation, the students conducting campus tours for visitors and prospective applicants refer to the alcohol-free dorm as "the place where the geeks live." The university official in charge of this school's substance-abuse program admitted that, at his institution and similar ones, "It is more acceptable to come out of the closet as a gay than to come out of the closet and say you're a nondrinker."

A few years ago, the University of Wisconsin at Madison, one of the country's premier beer-and-circus schools—an article in the *New England Journal of Medicine* estimated that 65 percent of UW undergraduates binged—instituted substance-free sections of Witte Hall and Adams Hall. About one hundred fifty students chose to live in these areas, out of about seven thousand in all UW dorms, and almost thirty thousand UW under-graduates. Unfortunately, the substance-free dorms did not help all the residents. Early one Sunday morning, a drunken student wedged himself into a small garbage chute in Witte and fell nine floors to the bottom, almost dying as a result. School officials admitted that it was difficult to change the drinking culture of the school, particularly the weekend party scene, even for those undergraduates in the substance-free dorms.

In the last decade, many colleges and universities have discovered what administrators at Wisconsin have long known—that it is very hard, if not impossible, to alter or even slow the huge drinking culture at their schools. The president of Indiana University spoke at the national student convention of a major fraternity, and he asked these Greek leaders "to consider an alcohol ban" in their houses across the country. The president described the response to his suggestion: "They booed me."

Subsequently, the IU president officially banned alcohol from all university dorms and Greek houses on his campus. However, like Prohibition in the 1920s, the ban prompted widespread disobedience, much of it covert but some so overt that campus police intervened. In autumn 1999, after the police "busted" one fraternity for repeated alcohol violations, and the school put the house on "disciplinary probation," the chapter president said, "We were irresponsible about what we were doing," allowing lots of people to leave our parties very drunk, some requiring medical attention. But the fraternity leader did not consider this a crime, just carelessness and bad luck, because "this kind of stuff happens in every fraternity [here], but we happened to get caught."

Not only does a disjuncture exist between the current policies of school administrators and the drunken reality of collegiate life on their campuses, but there is a major disconnect between the national policies of many Greek organizations and the members of their chapters throughout the country. The executive vice president of Phi Delta Theta, one of the oldest and largest fraternities, claimed that "we have refocused on a message . . . [of] good fellowship, good opportunities for academic excellence, leadership opportunities. . . . We [also] insist that no alcohol or drugs be in the houses." Yet, the Phi Delta Theta official admitted that changing the *Animal House* image of Greek organizations will take time because the public sees fraternities as "houses with goofy-looking letters that basically say 'bar.'"

This Greek official added, "I've often kidded that if somebody wants to party, they ought to rent an apartment, not join a fraternity." But most

Greeks do both during their university careers: they live and party in the fraternity or sorority for a year or two, and then, along with their closest Greek brothers or sisters, they rent a house or an apartment off-campus and party on for their remaining college years. In fact, a large majority of American undergraduates, including those at schools in small college towns, live off-campus (one study put the number at 85 percent of all nonfreshmen students).

As a result, the off-campus party scene, although connected through Greek and dorm affiliations to the campus one, has become the true center of party action at most Big-time U's. On-campus parties continue, but the hosts now run the risk of campus police intervention, and the participants, if under twenty-one, of arrest for underage drinking. Therefore, just as the sorority women with the pink condoms held their pledge night in the private room of a Chinese restaurant, many other Greek organizations rent off-campus facilities for parties or gather their members and friends in private houses or apartments. Furthermore, university authorities are pleased with the party scene moving off-campus because it absolves schools of many legal responsibilities, and it distances them from negative incidents. A University of Michigan administrator said:

> If the girl in the *Detroit News* story had never come out of Score-keepers alive, legally that's the bar's problem, not U of M's. It occurred on their property, not ours. They served her, they should have seen that she was drinking too much. You know, there's an excellent and expanding body of case law for just such eventualities.

Changing the off-campus drinking culture is almost impossible; in addition, most beer-and-circus universities have no desire to alter it; they just want to keep it at a safe legal distance. For all of the official pronouncements about "cracking down on student drinking," most administrators realize that alcohol, particularly cheap beer, is the oxygen of the Greek system and the party scene at their schools.

In the 1980s, most Big-time U's practiced "benign neglect" in regard to student alcohol consumption. In the 1990s, "benign harassment" became the policy: administrators used the campus police to control excessive drinking in dorms and Greek houses, and to move large parties off-campus. But officials did not discourage drinking to the point where their institution gained a reputation as, to use *Princeton Review*'s category name, a "Stone-cold sober school."

No Big-time U wants to make the top twenty in this category. If that occurs, applications will decline, students will transfer to less sober schools, and tuition dollars will plummet. Big-time U's willingly allow Brigham Young University and similar institutions to head the "Stone-cold sober" list, while Big-time U's retain their reputations as "fun" and "happening" places, the new code words for beer-and-circus.

15

DRINKING OFF-CAMPUS
AND FAR OFF-CAMPUS
(SPRING BREAK)

In the 1990s, school authorities, prompted by university lawyers, prodded the party scene to off-campus bars and apartments. Not only did this increase student alcohol consumption and binge drinking but, during Spring Break, it turned various far off-campus locations into mammoth bacchanals. This chapter details this phenomenon.

★   ★   ★

> Visit some fraternity houses these days and you might be hard pressed to get so much as a cold beer. The venerable beer keg that has served so long as a centerpiece in fraternity houses has fallen into disgrace—a victim of the times, not to mention lawyers and risk managers.
>
> No, college kids haven't quit drinking. They're just doing it on someone else's property. More and more, fraternity officials are advising their chapters to move drinking parties out of the house—preferably to bars, which are licensed, staffed, and insured for such debauchery.
>
> —Steven Girardi, *Tampa [Florida] Tribune* reporter

In the late 1990s, after *Playboy* named a bar in Tampa as one of the top college bars in the United States, Tampa Bay newspapers started examining the local college-student drinking scene. The *Playboy* award surprised Tampa/St. Pete residents who thought of their area in terms of tourists and retirees rather than college kids boozing year round. However, the University of South Florida in Tampa, in its attempt to rise in the academic world, had created a strong collegiate subculture with many fraternities and sororities as well as college sports teams elevated to NCAA Division I-A. By the late 1990s, USF had gained beer-and-circus status, and various newspapers described its party scene.

The *St. Petersburg Times* reported that "many USF students say the week begins Monday with song and beer at the Greenery Pub next to the University Townhouse Apartments. The bar's proximity to campus attracts" students, as do the sports events on the large-screen TVs. The reporter followed USF students through their drinking week: "On Tuesdays . . . Goodfellas not far from the USF campus turns into a college sports bar, offering 2-for-1 drink specials"; "On Wednesdays, the Oak Barrel hosts Liter Night, with a liter of beer, about 34 ounces, for $4." A nearby bar—the one on *Playboy*'s list—also does a huge Wednesday and Thursday night business by hosting " 'Out of Control College Night' . . . a couple of hours of free draft beer and bargain-priced [liquor] drinks." But some students, particularly USF women, spend Thursday nights in Fat Tuesdays (Mardi Gras), because of the $1 drinks, including "18 varieties of daiquiris churning in vats built into a pink neon wall."

The reporters dropped out before the Friday, Saturday, and Sunday night festivities, however, for many USF students, these encompassed the usual college weekend fun. In interviews for this book, USF undergraduates described frenetic weekend parties, including at bars in St. Pete Beach and along the Gulf in St. Petersburg, and at private beach houses and condos. A fraternity man added, "I can't wait until our football team gets good, and we can show the Gators [University of Florida] and the 'Noles [Florida State] that we outparty them and outplay them."

If the party scene at this school begins on Monday and runs through the following Sunday, the question occurs: When do USF undergraduates study? "This school is a joke, it's unbelievably easy," said a female vocational student. "It makes Florida State, the all-time party school, look like Harvard in comparison. I'm only here because I'm from Tampa and can live at home and work my way through, but I really worry if my degree will be worth anything. Why can't this school become famous for something educational instead of rowdy students and now big-time sports."

Playboy, in its article on the top college bars in the country, explained the beer-and-circus value system: "Why study when you can work on critical social skills? The best part of a college education is not included in the tuition. The facts of life are learned not in a classroom but in a college bar." Then why bother paying tuition *and* a bar bill? Why not just pay the latter? Indeed, if research universities were honest and acknowledged that they could not provide meaningful educations to most undergraduates, then many young people could attend college elsewhere, or they could keep their tuition dollars, spending all of them on fun and games. *Playboy* described how beer-and-circus works at Big-time U's: "Early afternoon happy hours draw students straight from the lecture halls," where they have learned little or nothing; and throughout the week, "theme nights prevail, creating the feel of perpetual Saturday—how can a Tuesday study session compete with two-for-one margaritas and free tacos?"

Other national magazines also list the top college bars, usually overlapping with *Playboy*'s choices. *ESPN The Magazine* began its list with, "If they held a national championship for college sports bars, the Esso Club would be our pick to win it all. This converted gas station on the edge of the Clemson University campus" has great deals on drinks and food, and patrons can "taste-test the beer in a niche dubbed the 'Educational Corner'" (this theme—drinking is the true education—runs through all the college bar literature and lore). Trailing the Esso Club on ESPN's list are such famous watering-holes as State Street Brats in Madison, Wisconsin; Ivar's in Baton Rouge, Louisiana; McDuffy's Sports Bar in Tempe, Arizona; 44's in Syracuse, New York; and Harpo's in Columbia, Missouri. Not surprisingly, all of these bars are attached to Big-time U's with famous Division I-A sports programs and party scenes. The bars contain large screen TVs perpetually showing sports events, particularly intercollegiate contests, and feature large displays of college sports memorabilia.

Outstanding in the memento category, and also high on the *ESPN* and *Playboy* lists, are Nick's English Hut in Bloomington, Indiana, and the Touchdown Club in Ann Arbor, Michigan. Nick's hangs jerseys from former IU basketball players from its rafters and serves beer in large buckets—committed patrons earn personal silver ones. The managers of the Touchdown Club at Michigan, after years, according to *Playboy*, of "hard partying at Indiana University," migrated to Ann Arbor and installed Nick's-like memorabilia in the bar there, including "bench seating from the school's original football stadium."

These bars and the ones in other college towns are the temples of beer-and-circus, testimony to its current dynamism and its storied past. Every Saturday before and after home football games, and in the evenings before and after home basketball contests, crowds of worshipers line up outside these shrines, waiting for a chance to enter and to drink the sacramental liquor. Alums and undergraduates mingle in the lines, and many of the older people have made pilgrimages of thousands of miles to reach the sacred places.

A reporter for the *Los Angeles Times* traveled around the country examining this religious phenomenon. In Lincoln, Nebraska, home of the University of Nebraska Cornhuskers, he noticed that "at Barry's Bar and Grill, two blocks from the stadium . . . the doors open at 10 A.M. and the premixed Bloody Mary's start flowing out of 20 gallon containers." Thirty-seven bars cluster in this area of Lincoln, and students call the sidewalks in front of them "the most puked-upon stretch of concrete in the United States."

The *L.A. Times* writer journeyed on, chronicling such traditions as Saturday morning "kegs and eggs" at Ohio State, and the drinking and college football scene at the University of Georgia at Athens. Beyond the fun and UGA (the bulldog mascot), an official of this school's health service pointed out: "There are at least fifty-two businesses that serve alcohol within walking distance of this campus. The simple fact is [that] it would be impossible for them to stay in business if they sold just to students who were twenty-one" or older, and to alumni; thus the undergraduate drinking culture at this school and similar ones raises serious public health questions. Georgia undergrads told the *Insider's Guide* that their "campus mascot" should be "a drunk person," not UGA.

Yet in the fall of 1999, for ESPN's coverage of the Georgia-Florida football game, Chris Fowler, the lead announcer, constantly called the contest "The World's Largest Outdoor Cocktail Party," and the cameras frequently focused on student and alumni fans of both schools, spotlighting their drunken antics and lubricated happiness. Therefore, when the same university administrators who embrace ESPN and other TV coverage of their college sports teams announce a school campaign against student drinking, many undergraduates spot the hypocrisy and consider the effort absurd. Living in a collegiate subculture that glorifies drinking, reinforced by the national media, students know that university officials are either lying to them or to themselves when they encourage temperance.

Hip sarcasm is the mode with which some student commentators approach the drinking problem on their campuses, and, in this way, they hope to communicate with their fellow students more effectively than do "out of it" administrators. A woman at the University of Connecticut at Storrs, recent NCAA champion in men's and women's basketball, and a contender for "Party school of the East," if not the nation, wrote an article in the student newspaper mocking the bar scene at her school. Her advice to those undergraduates not yet involved, "Get a fake ID":

> Although it's illegal, and you will end up with $7 in your bank account by the end of the semester, it can be a whole lotta fun. Having

> a fake ID is the underaged undergrad's ticket to a whole new social world otherwise known as "the bars." With many options ranging from Wednesday's Nickel Nights to Friday's Happy Hour, with a fake ID one can find something to do involving alcohol almost every night of the week. And when you can go to the bar whenever you want, you always have a reason not to study. . . .

The reader wonders if the average UConn student caught on to this criticism of "the bars"? In tone and content, the writer is so close to *Playboy*'s and *ESPN*'s hip laudatory style that the sarcasm might be lost on the average student, particularly those who want to participate in the bar scene and neglect their studies.

An unambiguous approach to "the bars" characterizes *The Real Freshmen Handbook*, published nationally by Houghton Mifflin. In the section "How to Get a Fake ID," the author suggests finding an upperclassman who "resembles you," and then "offering to buy or borrow [your look-alike's] old IDs." If this method fails, "Ask around campus: you should be able to find someone who either makes fake IDs himself or knows how to order them." In fact, in an Internet age, entering the keywords "Fake IDs" into various search engines turns up many firms specializing in them.

Some bars in some college towns—particularly if they have had licensing problems with local or state authorities—require an authentic-looking ID for admittance. But at many other bars in most college towns, amazingly hokey IDs will usually work for underage drinkers. The student head of the Panhellenic [Sorority] Association at the University of Kansas said that in Lawrence, "All bars card, but there are some bars where you can practically scribble, 'Yes, I'm twenty-one,' on a piece of paper in crayon and get in."

A bar manager in East Lansing, Michigan, explained why some bars accept obviously phony IDs:

> It's capitalism in action. Running a bar in a college town is a very competitive business. Students can be very fickle, they love your place one year and then think that it's "radically out of it" the next. But you always have the option of "going loose" on carding [not closely checking IDs], and when you do that, pretty soon lots of kids who can't get into other places start showing up and paying full price for drinks. . . .
>
> Sure, you run a risk, but you didn't make the fake IDs, the kids

did, and you just were trusting human nature when they showed it to you and you believed them. At least that's what you tell the authorities if they bust you, and you hope that they believe you.

Even when law enforcement agents crack down on bars and liquor stores selling alcohol to underage clients, often they cannot obtain a conviction. In Columbus, Ohio, on the Saturday night of the 1998 Ohio State–Penn State football game, the police raided an out-of-control party, and, subsequently, the authorities went after the distributor who sold thirty-nine kegs of beer to the student party-givers. The headline in the *Columbus Dispatch* related the outcome: "CASE AGAINST BEER VENDOR IS DOWN DRAIN WHEN NO ONE SHOWED UP TO TESTIFY ABOUT KEGS SOLD FOR PARTY." A story in that paper the previous week headlined, "NO ID NEEDED TO BUY BEER [in Columbus]. MANY STORES DON'T ASK, STUDY FINDS," and the lead began, "Minors in Franklin County can buy beer more easily than they can buy cigarettes."

In fact, the consumption of alcohol is much more socially acceptable at the beginning of the twenty-first century than is smoking. Corporate America promotes alcohol much more assiduously than it does tobacco, and with marketing strategies more pernicious and effective than were the Miller Lite ex-jocks and Spuds MacKenzie in the 1980s.

★   ★   ★

> The campus drinking environment has changed noticeably since the 1980s. Brewing companies, once heavily visible and sponsoring many campus events and activities, now maintain a more subtle presence.
> —The Center for Science in the Public Interest

The amount of money that alcohol beverage companies spend pitching their products to college students has increased significantly since the 1980s; however, they have traded in their old advertising vehicles for new and sleeker ones. Instead of the full-page Bud Light and Miller Lite ads in student newspapers, readers now find publicity for local bars (often these ads are "co-ops," paid for by the bar, the local beer distributor, or the national company). In addition, because most college dorms, Greek houses, and off-campus apartments are now wired for cable TV, and because college students watch ESPN, ESPN2, MTV, VH1, and Comedy Central more than any other channels, the national brewers advertise heavily on these networks and reach college students in this way. Moreover, for the first time in broadcast history, liquor companies now promote their products on TV, most frequently on Comedy Central. And the national magazines most read by college students—*Rolling Stone, Spin, Sports Illustrated*, and *ESPN The Magazine*—contain many pages of beer and liquor ads.

But the alcohol beverage companies are not the only part of corporate America promoting student drinking. In its 1998 back-to-school catalogue, Abercrombie & Fitch—a clothing brand popular with contemporary undergraduates—had a section called "Drinking 101," with recipes for such concoctions as a "Woo-Woo" and a "Brain Hemorrhage." In addition, A&F arranged photos of these drinks and others in a circular chart that, with a spinner, functioned as a drinking game (spin and land on the photo of the Brain Hemorrhage, and toss one down). Groups like M.A.D.D. criticized A&F for the "Drinking 101" section, and, in so doing, they fell into the advertisers' trap of transforming paid material into a free news story, attracting far more attention to the catalogue than it normally receives, and making it a must-see item on many campuses.

In the words of the East Lansing bar manager, the A&F ploy is "capitalism, in action," and when critics of binge drinking attack this social problem, not only must they consider the deeply entrenched collegiate subculture that nurtures and promotes heavy alcohol consumption, but also the wider society that supports this activity in a multitude of ways, including joking about the risks, such as calling a highly potent drink a Brain Hemorrhage.

Because massive advertising, direct and indirect, produces excellent sales, the rate of student alcohol consumption increased every year in the 1990s, and it shows no signs of slowing in the twenty-first century. Contributing to the rate, and as effective as the national advertising campaigns, are the promotions by local bars catering to students. As noted during the Tampa drinking tour, college bars often run "cost-leader" specials on weekday nights. Bar managers know that if they can get students inside the door, they will sell them enough alcohol and food to make a profit off of them by closing time. Bars offer "All-You-Can-Drink-Specials" on the cheapest beer available, and limit the time frame, e.g., from 7 P.M. to 9 P.M. Similarly, "Two-for-One" specials often have limited time frames, as do, by definition, "Happy Hours." But most customers stay in the bar long after the specials have passed; sometimes drinkers remain in place because they can no longer move—all of the specials invite rapid consumption of alcohol.

Another popular inducement is "Ladies Night." Female customers receive deep discounts all night, with two main results: more males patronize bars on Ladies Night than on any other weekday evening, and females consume far more alcohol that night than during their other trips to the bar. "We've never lost a dime on account of a 'Ladies Night,' " said a bar manager in Iowa City, Iowa, "The guys pack in here paying full price, and we also sell a ton of food at regular prices, plus we get a reputation as a 'happening place,' and everybody comes back on the weekend and pays full price then. I love the ladies and Ladies Nights."

College newspapers are filled with ads for "Ladies Nights" and other special evenings at the local bars. "Lose Those Midweek Blues," a college town nightclub recommended in a Big Ten student newspaper; "Get over the HUMP NITE," and coast downhill to the weekend. The inducement was a "$1 cover charge and 10 cent Miller" beer. A bar in a SEC college town advised, "Ease your mind before FINAL EXAMS with our MIND ERASER drink specials." The Center for Science in the Public Interest noted that for some student newspapers, ad money from local bars constitutes a significant part of their revenue.

This prompts the question: Why do college administrators, now decrying student drinking, permit massive local bar advertising in newspapers that their universities own and subsidize? Banning the ads by official fiat would create free speech problems; however, encouraging student newspapers not to run the ads and agreeing to supplement the lost revenue dollar-for-dollar is a feasible solution. (Universities cover athletic department deficits; it is hoped they could find the money for this more worthy cause.)

Every day, almost every daily paper in America declines to run some sort of ad, thus student newspapers rejecting advertising that so clearly promotes binge drinking will not abrogate their readers' First Amendment rights. Yet university authorities never explore this option, leading some observers to question whether schools are serious about curtailing binge drinking, or mainly seek to move it off-campus.

An even more direct challenge by local bars—rarely answered by administrators—are the tons of advertising leaflets that bars distribute on campus. The fliers usually announce week-night specials, and they are handed out, stapled to bulletin boards and kiosks, taped to lampposts and sidewalks, replicated on sidewalks in chalk, plastered on other public spaces, and even placed in student mailboxes. Universities, including public ones, could ban this advertising from their campuses—they forbid other kinds of commercial material—but they have been slow to react to the blizzard of bar leaflets.

In recent years, the bars have added another campus publication to their advertising arsenal: the ubiquitous weekly ad sheets (often yellow in color) that trumpet special deals at local pizza houses, Chinese take-outs, tanning salons, travel agencies, and, most prominently, bars. Distributed by the thousands on many campuses, the full-page bar ads contain such copy as: "Kilroy's on Kirkwood. We Throw the Best Party in Town. Every Thursday enter contests and win prizes. Participants are [also] entered to win a trip to whatever bowl game our team plays in." Again, universities could move the ad sheets and their distributors off their property, but they rarely do.

In the fall, the travel agency ads in the yellow sheets increase before Christmas, and then, early in the second semester, they begin to feature many pages with Spring Break promotions. The Spring Break phenomenon—originally a cheap, one-week student trip to Fort Lauderdale, Florida—has become an elaborate and expensive multiweek sojourn involving various locales. Spring Break originated in the collegiate subculture of pre- and post-WWII America, but, in the final decades of the twentieth century, it escalated in both drunken revelry and corporate involvement. In many ways, Spring Break is the apotheosis of the collegiate subculture and any discussion about beer-and-circus must consider it.

       ★   ★   ★

Spring Break 1995 looks something
like an endless commercial break.
Corporate sponsors will spend a record $20 million trying to reach students on break from college during March. That's nearly five times what was spent a decade ago.

Among 1995's biggest spenders: Chevrolet's Geo division and Coca-Cola. Each is expected to spend more than $2 million to get their message to the estimated 1 million students who are piling in to one of four spring break hot spots: Panama City and Daytona Beach, Fla; Lake Havasu City, Ariz; and South Padre Island, Texas.
—*USA Today*

Ironically, the corporations that spent the most on Spring Break promotions in the 1980s—the beer companies—pulled out of direct sponsorship in the 1990s (although they now do many "co-op" deals with bars and distributors in the Spring Break areas). Into the void came other national corporations, and, since the mid 1990s, many other businesses have joined them, particularly junk-food companies and banks hawking credit cards to undergraduates. In addition to "imprinting" their logos on college students and building brand loyalty, corporate America loves the "product placement" that Spring Break provides: with the festivities covered extensively by MTV and other cable networks, viewers watch as the cameras pan across beaches full of young bodies, with corporate logos always in the background. In 2000, corporations put an estimated $50 million into Spring Break advertising and promotions, and at least 1.25 million students, spending over $1 billion, participated in the festivities at American and off-shore locations.

This large industry owes its origins, as well as its current beer-and-circus connections, to college sports. In the mid 1930s, a number of intercollegiate swimming coaches at Northeastern colleges took their teams to Fort Lauderdale, Florida, to train during their schools' spring vacation period. In 1935, they added a swim meet to the training, and the event became popular, attracting more teams as well as some student supporters. The latter also partied on the beach. World War II ended the swim meets and the trips to Florida, but, after the war, Fort Lauderdale began to attract college students on Spring Break. In the 1950s, major partying involving thousands of undergraduates occurred in that town. A popular 1958 novel, *Where the Boys Are*, described the scene, Hollywood filmed a version of the book, and Spring Break developed into a collegiate tradition, eventually becoming as deeply embedded in the subculture as hazing and the huge Greek letters on the front of chapter houses.

By the 1980s, the residents of Fort Lauderdale, now a part of the Miami metro area, had tired of weeks of drunken kids on their beaches, and, with strict police enforcement of municipal ordinances, the city removed itself from the Spring Break destination list. Daytona Beach, a few hundred miles north and that much closer to Northeastern, Atlantic Coast, and Midwestern schools, became the 1980s student vacation spot; subsequently, Panama City in the Florida Panhandle, with the help of MTV, emerged as an attractive locale, as did South Padre Island, Texas. Meanwhile, college students in far western states who had gone to Palm Springs, California, for many years began to migrate to the more hospitable Lake Havisu, Arizona, area.

In the 1990s, corporate travel agencies moved into the Spring Break business and began offering package tours to U.S. and off-shore spots, mainly in Mexico. That country, with a legal drinking age of eighteen and reasonably priced hotels, proved very attractive to American collegians, with the beach resorts of Cancun and Mazatlan becoming the most popular Mexican destinations. *Rolling Stone*, in its 1999 guide to Spring Break, noted in the category "Chances of getting served using a fake ID," that in Cancun, the chances were "very high. A note from Mom will pass," and bars in Mazatlan were almost as casual. Other off-shore locations, particularly in the Caribbean, also became popular, as did Spring Break cruises.

The travel agencies made handsome profits from their Spring Break "packages"—many off-shore ones began at $1,000 per person (door to door) and with decent accommodations approached $2,000. But in case a collegian did not want the sun-and-surf, the agencies and some airlines offered ski packages—Steamboat Springs, Colorado, becoming the South Padre Island of the student ski crowd.

In some ways, Spring Break resurrects the traditional walls between the collegiate subculture and other student groups. Hard-core vocational students lack the extra income for even the least expensive vacations; a senior woman at Ohio State remarked, "I always go home for Spring Break because I don't have the money to go anywhere else. Anyway, I have to work full-time for my dad that week. My close friends don't go anywhere either, and usually work that week." On the other hand, semivocationals who work part-time at college often use some of their job money for a Spring Break trip.

However, highly vocational students on athletic scholarships—the undergraduates who helped start Spring Break—often have to work full-time during this period. In many sports—basketball, hockey, etc.—players are in NCAA tournaments; in spring sports like baseball and outdoor track, athletes begin intensive training periods; and even Division I-A football players have to prepare for their April weeks of "Spring Practice."

Finally, rebel students and academically inclined ones often have their own versions of Spring Break. In the early 1990s, a Big Ten newspaper ran an article about "Students [Who] Spend Break in Search of the Dead," i.e., join the Grateful Dead tour. Today, many rebels spend the week following other bands and/or making the rebel scene in various cities.

Similarly, some academic undergraduates take trips of special interest to them. An Iowa State senior female revealed:

> For the last three years, I've spent Spring Break staying with a close friend who goes to the University of Chicago. I sleep in her room in the dorms, work on my term papers in the wonderful library there, and go to concerts and lectures on campus. It's the most stimulating week of the year for me, and I hate to come back to Iowa State just as much as the sorority women hate coming back from the beaches.

Other academic students spend Spring Break in such activities as working for Habitat for Humanity, quietly engaging in charity work while the Greeks who trumpet their philanthropy party in the vacation spots.

During the school year on individual campuses, members of the different subcultures sometimes party together, but Spring Break, attracting hordes of Greeks and similar collegians, tends to alienate undergraduates who belong mainly to the vocational, rebel, or academic subcultures. "I can handle a party full of frat rats every so often here," a University of Maryland honors student remarked, "but a beach full of thousands of them for an entire week would be way too much."

For the collegiate subculture, Spring Break has become a major event on the calendar, more important than Homecoming Weekend, but less significant than a bowl game trip or a journey to the NCAA Final Four. However, unlike bowl games and NCAA tourneys, every collegiate student can participate in Spring Break and almost every one does at least once in her or his university career, generally more than once.

Planning the Spring Break trip usually begins at the start of the second semester. Student newspapers run special Spring Break supplements at this time, and they include inserts from travel agencies as well as from Chambers of Commerce in Spring Break locales. In recent years, the Convention & Visitors Bureau of South Padre Island has distributed over 10 million copies of its brochures to college campuses around the country, its photos featuring handsome young collegians in skimpy swimsuits frolicking on beaches and giving the party salute.

After planning the trip, preparing for it consumes many weeks, if not months. Student newspapers run articles entitled, "Start Working Out Now [January 15] for Pleasing Spring Break Body," and "Tanning Salons Work Overtime" (apparently, it is best to go on Spring Break with a tan in case it rains at the beach and a tan is unobtainable).

The actual trip can be anticlimactic—although most students will not admit that. A Florida bartender who has worked at Spring Break locales in the state for many years described spring breakers as much "crazier" than other tourists: "The whole concept of Spring Break is that kids come away on vacation and they want to drink and have sex." They have no problem getting totally drunk and staying that way for days, but often a sexual hookup never occurs, and that leads to anticlimax or, more specifically, nonclimax.

But the return to university is usually excellent. For many students the vacation has consumed almost two weeks (they left days before school officially closed, and they returned days after classes resumed), and they "scope out" who has the best tans, and swap tales of adventure, particularly of binge drinking. They also bring back souvenir T-shirts, such as these from Mazatlan: "I'M NOT AS THUNK AS YOU DRINK I AM," and "THE FOUR STAGES OF DRINKING: (1) I'M HANDSOME. (2) I'M RICH. (3) I'M INVISIBLE. (4) I'M BULLET-PROOF."

In the questionnaire for this book, to the query, "After you graduate from and/or leave your university, what do you think you will remember most vividly about your time here?" many students replied with a version of "Going on Spring Break with my friends, and the wild things we did at _____ [name of Spring Break location]." These responses did not appear to answer the question until it became apparent that for these students, "here" was a concept that transcended ordinary space and time. Even though for Spring Break they had traveled far from their home campus, they never left their collegiate subculture; in this way, Spring Break formed a crucial part of their university experience.

One of the most interesting answers from this group of respondents was written by a senior male at Pennsylvania State University:

> By far my most vivid college memory will be a spring break one that has happened every year (it's now 4). I'm looking over the balcony of the hotel in different places in Florida or Texas where we're staying, and I'm seeing every single balcony in the place full of college kids yelling and drinking.
>
> It always strikes me as very weird, because usually when you go out on a hotel balcony, all the other ones are empty. But at spring break, they're full of people drinking and screaming. Floor upon floor of them on all sides. Packed. That's what I'll always remember about college.

★   ★   ★

Finally, collegiate drinking has not only moved off-campus and into the bars and apartment complexes that surround all beer-and-circus schools, as well as further off-campus to various Spring Break sites, but, as the above questionnaire answers suggest, it has become a way of life for many young people. They transport the drinking culture with them when they return home from school, and they take it to public occasions, particularly sports events and rock concerts, in their hometowns and when they travel.

At Woodstock 1999, drunken collegiates trampled the peace-and-love folks. One of the organizers (a veteran of the original Woodstock), viewed the 1999 scene and commented sadly, "This is a frat party to a large degree." Most newspapers and TV networks had the same take on the spectacle, one reporter summing up: "Forget peace. The rallying cry among the predominantly white male crowd was 'PARTY!' Aggressively." And after partying, RIOT. The riots that ended the event resembled the 1990s "Right to Party" riots at Michigan State and other universities, and the main participants were similar collegiate types. In all probability, in future, more "frat boy" riots will occur in college towns, in vacation spots, or wherever large numbers of collegians gather and consume amazing quantities of alcohol.

★ ★ ★

This chapter attempted to take the reader on a bar tour of college towns and Spring Break locations, paralleling the informal bar tours that many college students regularly undertake during the school year, and the scheduled "pub crawls" that travel agents include in Spring Break vacation packages. On all of these occasions, many students drink to their capacity and beyond.

The bar tours reveal that large corporations and a multitude of small businesses encourage and benefit from student drinking. Universities claim that they want to control undergraduate alcohol consumption, but they never challenge the on-campus presence of these corporations and businesses, nor do they seriously attempt to diminish the off-campus drinking scene. The question becomes: Are the current university anti-alcohol campaigns empty rhetoric to appease parents of students and concerned government officials, or are they sincere attempts to change undergraduate behavior?

Focusing on the beer-and-circus aspect of this situation—drinking in conjunction with big-time college sports events—provides one answer, and the topic of the next chapter of this book.

16

PARTY ROUND THE TEAM

In the late 1990s, as public concern about student alcohol consumption and binge drinking increased, a number of important government officials addressed these problems. Donna Shalala, U.S. Secretary of Health and Human Services, had encountered them in her previous job as president of the University of Wisconsin. She saw a link between beer and circus and offered her suggestions on loosening it at the 1998 annual convention of the NCAA:

> I believe that the time has come for schools to consider voluntary guidelines that say, "No alcohol advertising on the premises of an intercollegiate athletic event. No bringing alcohol to the site of an event. No turning a blind eye to underage drinking at tailgate parties—and on campus. And no alcohol sponsorship of intercollegiate sporting events."
>
> I know that there has been stiff resistance—both inside and outside the NCAA—to these kinds of tough guidelines in the past. But the time has come to reconsider them, especially in light of the recent alcohol-related deaths [of students], and some research suggesting that advertising may influence adolescents to be more favorably disposed to drinking.

Secretary Shalala, when questioned after her address to the NCAA, also declared that the association and all athletic conferences and schools should insist that TV and radio broadcasts of their college sports games exclude alcoholic beverage advertising. To say that her proposals "fell upon deaf ears" is to portray the reaction at the NCAA convention as positive. In her audience sat university presidents, faculty representatives, and athletic directors, as well as almost all NCAA officials, conference commissioners, and many other leaders of intercollegiate athletics. According to observers, they dismissed her recommendations before she had finished uttering them, their main concern being how to spin their negativity to the press.

The commissioner of the Pac-10 conference spun his answer for the *Chronicle of Higher Education* by noting that the NCAA, the conferences, and individual schools sign multiyear television and radio contracts—for example, the Pac-10's deals extended for another eight years—and said, "We would not be in a position to go back and do restrictions" on the advertising that the broadcasters sell for the games. Moreover, "the beer industry is one of the major interests in sports broadcasting" and, the unstated but omnipresent premise, every school in big-time college sports needs every dollar that the TV and radio deals produce.

Some university presidents also considered Donna Shalala's remarks hypocritical. "After all," one pointed out privately, "she was president of the University of Wisconsin before taking her present job, and her athletic department there accepted beer ads, and her campus police allowed tailgating and drinking in the stadium. And I mean serious, dangerous drinking."

Yet her recommendations make sense, particularly coming after the Harvard Public Health and the Center for Science in the Public Interest studies on binge drinking. Possibly, if she still headed UW, she would try to implement her ideas; then again, as a member of the Big Ten conference, probably she could not convince her fellow presidents and the commissioner to redo the national TV and radio contracts to exclude beer advertising.

However, praise for her suggestions came from a longtime supporter of big-time college sports who attended the NCAA meeting—Furman Bisher, sports columnist for the *Atlanta Constitution*:

> Of all that took place this week, what I liked most was the challenge by Donna Shalala to turn off the beer money. It has always seemed to me to go against everything that college sports is about when a game is interrupted for a commercial delivered by a bunch of varmints pushing beer.

Fisher represents the traditional view of intercollegiate athletics, with its deep faith in the student-athlete ideal. On the other hand, the men and

women now running big-time college sports worship "Media Demographics," and they know that networks and advertisers crave the young male
audience that college sports events attract—the very fans who dismiss the
student-athlete ideal and who believe that intercollegiate athletics is about
winning at all costs and enjoying beer-and-circus. A PR executive for the
beer industry explained, "If you had to choose the best audience in the
world for a beer advertiser, it is twenty-one-to-thirty-four-year-old men
who participate in sports and are avid sports fans. . . . [Our] fit with the
college sports audience is hand in glove." (Note the "twenty-one-year"
reference in his comment: he carefully avoided saying "sixteen-to-thirty-
four-year-old men" but that is the target audience: if the brewers sold no
beer to sixteen-to-twenty-year-olds, they would have to downsize considerably.)

Furman Bisher ended his piece by referring to a number of brewery PR
men at the NCAA convention "running around the hotels wearing
Anheuser-Busch T-shirts and beneath the brewery's name, 'We'll Fight for
a Better Future.' " Apparently the T-shirts were one brewer's mocking response to Secretary Shalala's recommendations.

After her keynote speech, Donna Shalala returned to Washington, D.C.,
and turned her attention to other social problems, but the alcohol beverage
people continued working full-time for their version of a "better future,"
and the leaders of college sports fully cooperated with them.

In that future, two years after the Shalala speech, college football held
the greatest extravaganza in its history, the championship playoff game
between Florida State University and Virginia Tech in the New Orleans
Superdome. The scene was a triumph of beer-and-circus, *USA Today* noting that many fans came to the game "staggering, soused with spirits,"
and, in front of the Superdome, "a rock band—on a huge stage between
a pair of giant Budweiser cans—played. . . ."

Historically, only two Division I-A universities have adamantly refused to
allow alcohol or alcohol beverage advertising in their home arenas and
stadiums, or to permit beer ads on the TV and radio broadcasts that they
control: Brigham Young University and Baylor University (as strict Mor-
mon and Baptist institutions, they disapprove of alcohol consumption).
From time to time, other schools have instituted similar bans, but neither
they, nor BYU and Baylor, ever objected to their teams playing in out-of-
town arenas and stadiums that displayed beer signs and sold beer to spectators. By 2000, these contrary policies amplified: an increasing number of
schools now prohibit spectators from bringing alcohol into campus arenas
and stadiums (although the hidden flask continues as an essential "game

item" for many fans), and some universities have removed the beer signs; however, all of these schools eagerly seek bookings for their teams in out-of-town facilities, particularly in large cities, that flash beer ads and also sell beer during games, often to underage drinkers. Moreover, every member of Division I-A wants to play in a bowl game and almost every one of these venues has brewery ads and sells beer. And no school would have objected to the giant Budweiser cans outside the Superdome if their team had played inside. Again, the ambiguity of the situation produces a clear message to undergraduates: university officials who ban alcohol on campus are hypocrites and fools, to be ignored or, if that is impossible, defied.

Experts in alcohol abuse indicate that these mixed signals also encourage students to disregard all warnings about binge drinking, and, ironically, they make alcohol beverage ads more effective. The beer message is distinct and relentless: it constantly "creates the impression," according to the Stanford University director of alcohol abuse prevention, "that everyone is drinking all the time, and [it] leads some students to assume that if they are not drinking alcoholic beverages, they are missing an important part of collegiate social life." The Stanford authority also agreed with Donna Shalala that collective action was necessary, that universities could not change student mores with individual bans. Thus far, the beer companies have won, their advertising has forged "this link . . . through the years between sports—college and professional—and beer," and it will not uncouple easily.

Yet, thanks to the Robert Wood Johnson Foundation, a number of universities, including such Big-time U's as the University of Iowa in Iowa City, are acting unilaterally and attempting to change student attitudes about drinking on their campuses. They also hope to nullify the effect of national and local alcoholic beverage advertising upon their undergraduates. This experiment is worth examining.

★　　★　　★

My hat's off to Iowa for participating in the Johnson program. They call it "Stepping Up," and that school really stepped up. They went public with the fact that they have a binge drinking problem in their student population, and they want to do something about it. . . .

Many schools refused to participate in the program. I know we did—we didn't want to touch it at all, we were worried that it would give us lots of bad publicity. But the Iowa folks did what people with an alcohol problem should always do—take the first step and admit that you have a problem, and then go from there. Most schools in

Iowa's situation just won't do that, and so they dig themselves a
deeper hole. You'd think that the student deaths and near-deaths
from bingeing would wake everyone up, but that hasn't happened
yet. I say, good for Iowa.
                            —An Indiana University administrator

In 1996, the Robert Wood Johnson Foundation, in conjunction with the
American Medical Association, gave the University of Iowa a substantial
grant to try to combat college student binge drinking on its campus. The
Des Moines Register proclaimed that the school "has been chosen to lead
a national effort" to fight this widespread problem but, as significantly, UI
president Mary Sue Coleman acknowledged that "the national figures and
our own figures on binge drinking provide vivid confirmation that we have
a serious problem with the number of college students who are drinking
to get drunk." Comprehensive surveys of the Iowa student body confirmed
her words: almost 64 percent of UI undergraduates regularly engaged in
binge drinking, as opposed to the 42 percent national student average.

A spokesperson for the Robert Wood Johnson Foundation, in announcing the grant to Iowa and a number of other universities, explained "the
profile of schools with drinking problems . . . [They are] schools with big
athletic programs and big Greek systems." A journalist specializing in medical issues also emphasized the link between big-time college sports, the
collegiate subculture, and bingeing: "The highest-risk campuses . . . [those
with] big sports programs, fraternities, and sororities . . . got that way for
two reasons: They attracted binge drinkers and they turned non-drinkers
into binge drinkers."

In this period, some of the college guidebooks aimed at high school
seniors described the University of Iowa in beer-and-circus terms. The *Insider's Guide* reported:

Drinking? Awwwww Yeahhh!

Undergrads party hard. . . . Drinking is a large part of student life. . . .
Greek life at the university is also strong: the frats sponsor parties
open to all students for a small fee. . . .

Big-Name Sports

A member of the Big Ten Athletic Conference, the University of Iowa
has a strong sports program that captures student enthusiasm. During football season, tailgate parties bring students together to bolster
school spirit.

One of Iowa's first steps to counter binge drinking was ordering all Greek units on campus "to go dry." But in a concession to their party traditions, the university gave the fraternities and sororities two years, from 1997 to 1999, "to taper off" before completely shutting their booze taps. Similarly, the university did not ban beer from its football stadium parking lots but created an "alcohol-free area" for tailgate parties without alcoholic beverages. The *Des Moines Register* reported that the typical Hawkeye fan considers " 'tailgate' . . . a verb meaning 'to drink beer,' " but some students venturing into "alcohol-free . . . parking lot No. 14" enjoyed the free soft drinks, hot dogs, and volleyball games.

Then, in 1999, the school refused Miller Beer's offer for advertising rights to the Hawkeye logo, and for ad space on the weekly TV programs of UI's football and men's basketball coaches. Throughout the 1990s, Stroh Brewery held this contract and Miller wanted it. A university spokesperson explained that these beer ads were not "consistent with trying to reduce consumption of alcohol within the student population," and by rejecting a brewer's top-dollar sponsorship, the school had to settle for less money from other advertisers. Despite this laudable unilateral move, Iowa cannot alter the Big Ten or NCAA television contracts, or the regional and national beer ads that stream across the TV screens viewed by its students.

In April 2000, the UI student newspaper examined the Stepping Up program, "formed in 1996 with a five-year $830,000 grant to combat UI's binge drinking rate. Nearly three years and almost $400,000 later," a recent UI campus survey of binge drinking revealed that "the rate hasn't budged." The program had encountered the intransigence of the collegiate subculture and its resistance to change. During the three years, campus drinking had increasingly migrated to off-campus locations. The *Daily Iowan* report is discouraging news: the single most ambitious anti–binge drinking campaign ever conducted at an American university has not yet dented the problem.

Iowa undergraduates clarified this result: one woman commented that some of the non-alcoholic activities sponsored by Stepping Up were interesting but, "I have a lot of friends who won't go out with me if it doesn't involve alcohol." Other UI students noted the proliferation of sports bars in the Iowa City area, and their popularity with female as well as male students.

Joel Eskovitz, the 1999 editor-in-chief of the *Indiana Daily Student*, explained part of the attraction of binge drinking for undergraduates at Big Ten schools like Indiana and Iowa, and how the pleasures sometimes rivaled those gained from sports:

Binge drinking is often very competitive. Some students try to outdo each other in drinking games. . . . There's also a large bragging element to it. Students constantly boast about their drinking feats: how much they drank and how fast, and how many crazy things they did while drunk, even how they passed out. They can't wait to see their friends the next day and tell them their stories. That is a huge part of the student drinking subculture.

Indeed, the depth of the collegiate subculture, its participants' sense of bingeing as a game and a rite of passage, and the media's frequent glorification of these customs create maximum undergraduate resistance to university officials attempting to stop bingeing.

An added impediment to changing the student drinking culture is the laissez-faire attitude of many residents in the communities surrounding a university, including numerous businesspeople who profit from student alcohol consumption. When the Stepping Up program began at UI, there were 94 establishments with liquor licenses within a mile radius of the campus, and 149 in the surrounding towns of Iowa City and Coralville. Three years later, more liquor license holders exist in these areas. In 1999 and 2000, during a number of visits to the campus and the town, this writer found a drinking scene very similar to those at other beer-and-circus schools, with crowded off-campus bars, as well as apartment complexes that, according to student residents, were the "new center of the party scene." UI president Coleman acknowledged the flourishing off-campus drinking scene to the *New York Times* in March 2000.

But University of Iowa administrators keep working on the binge drinking problem. A vice-president for student services explained that, among other measures, UI had instituted a plan "to reclaim Mondays and Fridays," specifically, to persuade faculty to treat those days as regular school days and to end the tradition of "making fewer academc demands on students on those days because students are less alert after partying," which, at Iowa and similar schools, gains full force on Thursday night and continues through Sunday evening.

In fact, many undergraduates are not even in class on Fridays and Mondays, particularly if the Hawkeyes are on the road that weekend. "Lots of students here," explained a fraternity man, "consider road games as a reason to take off for the weekend and join in supporting the Hawks away from home. We do it for all football and basketball away games on weekends. But my friends at other Big Ten and Big 12 schools do the same thing."

The "road trip" is an old fraternity tradition, not only prompted by sports events but by other reasons "to take off" for the weekend or even during the week; for example, every year, tens of thousands of students from many schools drive to New Orleans for Mardi Gras, often journeying thousands of miles. However, for away football and weekend basketball games, the road trip usually begins Friday morning and ends in the early hours of Monday morning. Friday and Monday classes are "washed out" for road trippers, as they are for many students on campus who begin their weekends Thursday afternoon and end them late Sunday night.

As indicated by the Iowa vice president, often faculty are complicit in the "lost weekend" tradition; indeed, many professors at research universities want to do all of their teaching on Tuesdays and Thursdays. The College of Arts & Sciences at Indiana University requests instructors in its departments to sign up for Monday-Wednesday-Friday classes to balance the excessive faculty demand for Tuesday-Thursday, and to use classroom space more efficiently, particularly the large lecture halls.

Iowa's attempt to reclaim Fridays and Mondays will encounter more obstacles than the designers of this initiative contemplated. Not the least of the problems are student contempt for undergraduate courses, particularly lecture classes, and faculty disdain in return. A professor at a championship beer-and-circus school, Florida State University, remarked:

> The only time to teach a regular undergraduate class at this school is Wednesday early afternoon. Students here stretch the party weekend into Tuesdays, and begin again late Wednesday afternoon. Because they sleep late every day, the only "window of opportunity" to catch them alert is Wednesday early afternoon. . . . That's when I schedule my main lectures. . . . But many students still fall asleep in them, and some never do show up.

Another Iowa antidrinking proposal is university sponsorship of "more campus social activities that do not feature alcohol, such as movies, concerts, speakers, and street dances." On paper, this seems like an excellent idea, easily implemented and potentially successful. However, it is a plan conceived by members of the academic subculture for large numbers of collegiates. The latter attend movies, but they want to see the latest hit feature at the mall, not reruns available on videotape or, least of all, serious domestic or foreign films, the kind that most schools show on campus and that mainly attract academic and some rebel students.

As for concerts, popular musicians generate large crowds, but many undergraduates want to consume alcohol or drugs while they listen to the music. The *Princeton Review* received a large number of student comments about university-sponsored concerts, summing them up with: "Few students are interested in any campus-sponsored activity if they know security guards will be actively enforcing the no-drinking [and no-drugs] rules." They veto campus "street dances" and other official "parties" for the same reason. "A UI-sponsored party is a contradiction in terms," said an Iowa honors student. "Most of us define 'a party' as meaning 'to be free, to let go.' Whoever heard of a good party given by a school?"

As for attending speeches, even those given by famous speakers: most undergraduates so despise their lecture courses that they have minimal interest in hearing a university-sponsored speaker. Again, administrators belonging to the academic subculture conceived of this diversion for collegiates, and as a result, these talks attract few regular students. An Iowa official disputed this point, indicating that, for example, Bob Knight, the Indiana University men's basketball coach, gives an annual public lecture at his school that attracts thousands of undergraduates. In fact, this is not an exception to the students-won't-attend-speeches rule: for Indiana undergraduates, Knight represents big-time college basketball, a major part of their collegiate subculture, and they revere him even more than they do the Budweiser Frogs—whom they also would turn out to see.

A *Los Angeles Times* health reporter visited Iowa City and investigated the effect of the school's Stepping Up program. She listened patiently to the official explanations but then did her own inquiries, concluding, in part:

> It's even hard to know whether students—many of whom have moved their parties to residences off-campus—are paying attention to the efforts going on around them. Dormitory literature making students aware of their rights to a clean, quiet, alcohol-free dorm seems to have stirred little interest or opposition.

The comment about student life in the dorms connects to a phenomenon that this writer frequently encountered at Iowa and elsewhere: when administrators were asked how often they had been inside a student dormitory or a Greek housing unit in the last year, a majority admitted that they had not done so within that time frame or, in fact, in many years. (When faculty at research universities were asked the same question, most admitted that they had never visited a student housing unit—including professors who had taught at the same university for decades.) When administrators and faculty were asked whether they had ever been inside an off-campus student apartment, almost all acknowledged that they had not. Finally, when asked how far their own homes were from their school's student dorms, Greek houses, and off-campus apartment complexes, most administrators and professors said that they resided in the "faculty ghetto," an older residential area in the college town or, more often, in the new suburban tracts far from the university.

The conclusion is obvious: For all of their talk about transforming undergraduate culture, particularly the drinking aspects, most university officials and almost all faculty do not possess a clue about how—and sometimes even where—their students live. When administrators establish policies intended to change student behavior, they imitate blind people attempting to describe and then lead the proverbial elephant.

★   ★   ★

Signs outside Bobby Dodd Stadium at Georgia Tech say, "No alcohol."

Inside, students drink Cokes spiked with smuggled liquor, and lustily sing the school's "Ramblin' Wreck" fight song [which includes] . . . the words, "I drink my whiskey clear."

When the band strikes up a favorite tune in the second half of Tech's homecoming football game . . . they [the students] loudly join the chorus, "When you say Budweiser, you've said it all."

The divide between stated policy and reality points out the mixed messages about alcohol at Tech and other college campuses. Even with the drinking age at 21, stricter school policies regulating consumption, and more attention on the issue, drinking is still a favorite college pastime.

The *Atlanta Constitution* investigated the late-1990s drinking scene at Georgia Tech and confirmed what the national studies had reported about similar schools: at this university, massive student alcohol consumption connected to a strong Greek system and big-time college sports. Moreover, at Tech, drinking was so deeply embedded within the collegiate subculture that it was essentially immovable. Students described how they snuck liquor into games—tying a flask to a shoestring and hanging it inside a pants leg was especially popular—and they bragged that their fraternities served all drinkers, including underage ones. Furthermore, the off-campus bar scene was huge and vast—it included hundreds of establishments all over Atlanta and neighboring Buckhead.

In the 1990s, Georgia Tech put a substantial amount of money into its intercollegiate athletics program, upgrading its facilities and also paying its football and men's basketball coaches enormous sums to turn out championship teams (on occasion, they succeeded or came close). And successful college teams produced large crowds, including students with flasks and other drinking devices. Yet the school officially banned alcohol in undergraduate housing units, and sometimes campus police enforced the prohibition. But student drinking at Georgia Tech, including binging, did not diminish.

The *Princeton Review* edition of 2000 commented on this phenomenon nationally:

> We'd like to add an editorial comment based on numerous essays from angry students: CAMPUS WIDE DRINKING PROHIBITIONS DON'T WORK!

The bottom line is clear: many Big-time U administrators want to have it all ways—big-time college sports and *no* beer—but that is an oxymoron. University officials welcome the circus, but now they wish to keep the beer wagons away; however, the collegiate subculture, aided and abetted by the alcohol beverage industry and the people who run college sports, demands beer. Whether college presidents and their hordes of assistants like it or not, beer-and-circus is a done deal, as permanent a part of their campuses as their Collegiate Gothic-style buildings. Whatever policies they conceive to combat alcohol consumption will only work in the most limited manner; indeed, more often they will trigger the law of unintended consequences. For example, if administrators force the drinking far enough off-campus, the number of drunk-driving accidents, even deaths, involving their students will increase.

One of the arguments that the *Princeton Review* offers against the new campus-wide drinking prohibitions is that "students resent what they consider the school's intrusion into their personal lives." As noted, college administrators rarely speak to undergraduates about this problem; instead, they talk to so-called "student leaders," but often these leaders have no followers, and generally they try to please administrators, not inform them of unpleasant, often brutal truths. The isolation of administrators is not only cultural—often they come from the academic subculture, and they have to deal with their natural antagonists, the collegiates—but also self-imposed. They refuse to closely examine the collegians on their campuses.

At this point in this chapter, it seems best to listen at length to students themselves, particularly their comments in interviews, and their responses to the questionnaire for this book.

*　　*　　*

Everything this school [Purdue University] does socially revolves around football and basketball games. To tell you the truth, I know very little about the rules and regulations of those games. They are purely an outlet for social functions with friends for me. . . . I guess that I have been taught and socialized to use college athletics as an excuse to party with friends.

—A Purdue University senior female

Queries probing the connection between beer and circus on the questionnaire and in interviews for this book prompted this comment from a Purdue senior, and statements from many other students, as well as some revealing numerical results. To the question: "At this school, college sports events are central to the party scene," males and females responded in almost identical numbers: 64 percent "strongly agree" or "agree"; 10 percent "neither agree or disagree"; and 26 percent "disagree or strongly disagree." When respondents were divided according to whether they attended a NCAA Division I or Division III institution—the standard separation between schools running big-time college sports programs, and those conducting low-profile, nonathletic scholarship ones—the Division III respondents accounted for almost all of the neutral and "disagree" answers.

In their written responses, undergraduates at NCAA Division III schools provided such comments as, "Only the actual players and their friends party after games," and "People here wouldn't know how to tailgate if you gave them a demonstration in the stadium parking lot. Then again, we don't have a stadium or a vast parking lot."

At big-time college sports schools, the written responses from men and women differed, the latter often offering comments similar to the Purdue senior's. A University of Texas female explained,

UT men are ultraserious about college sports and about drinking, but women here tend to take them at face value. We enjoy the thrill and hype associated with big games, but we view sports more as a social opportunity, as a reason to party, not as the center of your life, like my boyfriend and his fraternity brothers do.

A Clemson woman remarked: "Sororities attend football games for the simple pleasures of drinking and tailgating. It seems to be more of an image thing than enjoying the football games themselves." An Oregon State sophomore woman commented that "it all begins for female students here their freshmen year. They get caught up in the pre-, the during, and the postgame partying involving college sports games, with alcohol lowering their inhibitions, making it easier for them to meet people and socialize."

A senior female at North Carolina State distinguished between male and female students at her school: "Women like the party atmosphere around college sports games, but the men are totally into the sports and into the booze. If you write a book from this poll about how men love college sports, you should call it *Big-time College Sports: A Tradition of Boozing and Brawling*."

Male respondents explained themselves somewhat differently than did the females. An Indiana University male senior commented:

> B-ball games here are always sold out, and students often cannot come up with tickets. . . . But many prefer to watch the games in one of the B-town [Bloomington] bars rather than "the alcohol-free arena." . . . Drinking with your [fraternity] brothers is a big part of watching a game and a whole lot better than cheering when dumb-ass cheerleaders tell you to.

For away men's basketball games, often scheduled on weekday nights, large numbers of students pack the bars at Indiana and other big-time college sports schools. A University of Iowa male remarked, "When the Hawks are on the road, the whole [fraternity] house goes down to the Sports Column [a local bar]. An away game during the week is a great time to party. If UI loses, then we drink to forget the loss. If we win, then we sometimes celebrate all night."

Even at some NCAA Division I schools without powerhouse men's basketball teams, students go to bars to watch college sports events. An Ohio University male junior wrote, "Why go to OU basketball games when we can make the bar scene and watch a *real* college game on ESPN." Another Ohio U student made a similar remark about not attending OU football games, but instead going to the bars in Athens and "catching top teams and staying warm and drinking with your [fraternity] brothers."

Some of the male respondents detailed their game-watching rituals, an Iowa senior noting that "if there is an away basketball game, my fraternity brothers and I usually arrive at Mondo's [an Iowa City bar] at least two hours before the game. This assures us of a seat. Then we watch the game, and this translates into another three or four hours of drinking. This does not take into account the amount of partying that goes on long after the game, 'specially if the Hawks win."

Other students noted the amount of time spent drinking on football weekends, a Washington State senior commenting: "The day of a football game here is at least a fifteen-hour day of partying—usually until you drop." However, a more systematic way of assessing the amount of time undergraduates at beer-and-circus schools spend partying is to calculate the totals from the queries on this subject on the questionnaire for this book.

★   ★   ★

Question 15

On average, during the school year, how many hours a week do you spend partying—at private functions and in bars—*in conjunction with college sports events* (include time spent arranging the party, traveling to and from the party, and at the party). Try to calculate your daily totals and then add on your weekend total. Mark the appropriate weekly amount.

The totals for men and women differed, as did the numbers from respondents at Division I and Division III schools. From the latter group came most of the low totals, i.e., 22 percent of men and 30 percent of women marked "0 hours per week" spent partying in conjunction with college sports events; and 16 percent males, 18 percent females checked "1–5 hours." Only a minority of respondents from Division I schools were in those time brackets, but these students dominated the remaining ones: 23 percent males and 28 percent females marked "6–10 hours per week," and 19 percent males, 16 percent females, "11–15 hours." After this, almost all females dropped out, only 8 percent spending "more than 15 hours per week" on this activity. However, a cohort of males continued strong, 14 percent at 16–20 hours and 6 percent at "more than 20 hours per week."

Nevertheless, this is only a partial photo. The numerical responses to the next question, when added to the above one, provide a more complete picture:

Question 16

On average, during the school year, how many hours a week do you spend partying—at private functions and in bars—*NOT* in conjunction with college sports events (include time spent arranging the party, traveling to and from the party, and at the party)? Try to calculate your daily totals and then add on your weekend total. Mark the appropriate weekly amount.

Adding up the numbers on both questions indicate that men outpartied women; thus, females dominated the lower time brackets: 2 percent of males and 11 percent of females spent "0 hours per week" partying; 10 percent males, 22 percent females, "1–5 hours"; and 11 percent males, 26 percent females, "6–10 hours." The "11–15 hours" time bracket—39 percent males, 23 percent females—included many men at Division III schools and women at Division I schools. The "16–20 hours" cohort mainly contained men (17 percent) and women (14 percent) at Division I schools. At "21–25 hours," all but 4 percent of the women dropped out, whereas 15 percent of the men partied on, with another 6 percent of the males continuing "above 25 hours per week."

In examining these totals, a number of conclusions emerge: many students, particularly at Division I schools, spend far more time partying than they do studying (see page 117 for these numbers); and students at Division I institutions spend more time partying "round the team" than they do at nonsports-related festivities. However, even students at Division III schools devote a fair amount of time per week to partying, usually nonsports related. In addition, the totals parallel the Harvard Public Health and the Center for Science in the Public Interest studies on High Binge and Low Binge schools, and also indicate that although women, particularly at Division I institutions, party a great deal, they have thousands of hours to spend, and oceans of alcohol to consume, before they catch up to male undergraduates at these schools.

The above numbers and conclusions provide an abstract indication of the party scene at American colleges and universities, especially big-time college sports schools, but personal comments from students put human faces on the statistics. A senior woman at the University of Illinois, Champaign-Urbana, wrote:

> Many students party throughout the football and basketball seasons to support the Fighting Illini, completely forgetting their studies. Many of these students develop serious alcohol problems, and as the seasons roll along, so does their substance dependency, and their party nights get closer and closer, particularly if they start hitting the sports bars regularly.
>
> Soon these students lose track of school and they start spiraling out of control. This may seem extreme, but it happens all the time here. . . . The U of I tries to inform freshmen of these risks, but the drinking culture here keeps producing more student alcoholics. Somehow schools have to get the anti-alcohol message across, but they aren't doing it.

A fraternity house president at the University of Maryland explained how student drinkers can lose control:

> I think a lot of people [students] go out with the intention of getting drunk. . . . I don't think they know that they are binge drinking. . . . They go out to drink and have a good time with their friends, and, in their minds, they're not doing anything wrong. They feel that they are completely in control, that they are on top of the situation. They don't consider that they are actually doing something which is quite a problem and could lead to some very dangerous things.

Probably the University of Michigan students at Scorekeepers had similar rationalizations and feelings of omnipotence when, while observing the passed-out woman on the floor, they kept ordering more drinks. The U of M students, like their counterparts across the country, believed that they personally were immune from the effects of alcohol poisoning. No doubt the passed-out woman shared this belief.

"Drinking in college is all an elaborate game," said an Indiana University fraternity member. "And we get so wound up in it that we completely lose sight of the bigger picture. It's like we've never heard of human physiology. I've taken [fraternity] brothers turning blue to the E.R." This student then detailed the "elaborate game": how his fraternity built a special "keg room" in its house basement so that the members could hide beer kegs and cases during raids by the dean of students and the police; how it arranged for false IDs for pledges; how it rented houses off-campus as "party centrals"; how the "game" consumed enormous amounts of undergraduate time and energy; and how winning the game—"drinking until you puke and pass out . . . finally didn't make a whole lot of sense."

The IU student added, "At least I try to go to the Rec Center [recreational gymnasium] to work off my hangovers. I try to spend as much time there as I do in the bars." This comment connects to one of the most intriguing conclusions of the Harvard and Center for Science in the Public Interest studies on binge drinking: students who frequently play intramural sports, who exercise, and also engage in superfan activities, often binge drink. In one respect, this seems contradictory: people who work out regularly and respect their bodies usually do not poison themselves by consuming too much alcohol. However, in reality, the beer-and-circus subculture has a large participatory component, not only in actively drinking and cheering for one's team, but in playing sports and exercising. The results to the following question confirmed this:

On average, during the school year, how many hours per week do you spend in athletic activities (intercollegiate athletic training and games, intramurals, jogging, aerobics, exercising, etc.)? Try to calculate your daily totals and then add on your weekend total. Mark the appropriate weekly amount.

The intercollegiate athletes—8 percent of the female and 5 percent of the male respondents—immediately identified themselves by marking "more than 30 hours per week," significantly higher than all other students (some of the college athletes added in the P.S. section that they spent 40, 50, sometimes 60 hours per week in their sports). At the other extreme were 6 percent females and 3 percent males who spent "0 hours per week . . . in athletic activities."

Over a third of the students—38 percent females, 36 percent males—marked "1–5 hours." Undergraduates at Division III schools dominated this time bracket, whereas many students at Division I institutions marked "6–10 hours": 33 percent females, 42 percent males. Written and interview comments revealed that in the "1–10 hour" range, women tended to exercise, and men played on intramural and pickup teams in various sports. In the "11–20 hour" range, both women (12 percent) and men (14 percent) worked out *and* played on intramural teams. In addition, many women and some men regarded the exercise areas, jogging tracks, and swimming pools of their school's recreational facilities as "social scenes," "pickup areas," and "great places to meet people." Finally, the numbers indicate how much time supposedly busy college students spend in the gym as well as in other sports related activities (see page 104 for the numbers on sports spectatorship). An Arizona State male senior remarked:

> After doing your poll, I was amazed by how much sports occupies my college life. When I add up the time spent watching TV sports, going to games, working out, playing on my frat's teams, and then partying in conjunction with sports, it is an unbelievable 34.5 hours per week. That's almost five hours a day! Imagine what my GPA would be if I spent that time in the library studying (my GPA is high now, but they'd have to put me on a special 8 point scale).

A tour of Arizona State University places these comments in context: the school has lavish, state-of-the-art recreational facilities, including the latest exercise machines and a number of Olympic-size swimming pools; on the other hand, the library is underground, a dark, forbidding place. Predictably, on a typical weekday, undergraduates fill the recreational buildings, and the library is deserted. At night, students pack the off-campus bars in Tempe, as they do the stadiums and arenas when the Sun Devils play at home.

Another ASU undergraduate explained his sense of his institution and its beer-and-circus core:

> Sometime in your freshmen year, you go through a transition where the college sports scene becomes your environment, rather than something that you observe from a distance as you did in high school, or as people who go to smaller schools do. You realize that being a Sun Devil, from cheering to drinking, is crucial to experiencing college life.

A sophomore male at ASU's main rival, the University of Arizona in Tucson, put another twist on the question of time spent in sports related activities: "I'm well over the thirty-hour-a-week mark, but a lot of it is following my bets on TV and the web." As an earlier question on sports spectatorship discovered (page 105), many male students, particularly those belonging to the collegiate subculture at beer-and-circus schools, bet frequently on college sports events, and consume many hours per week tracking the games on which they have money "down." The next chapter of this book examines campus gambling, and also the mind-set of contemporary student fans.

★　★　★

The results of the "hours spent" questions on the survey for this book highlight a major difference between students at NCAA Division I schools and those at Division III institutions. Big-time college sports not only plays a much more important role in the daily lives of Division I undergraduates than their counterparts in Division III, but the ancillary effects, particularly time spent in sports-related activities, especially partying, indicate significant differences in student life at these schools.

An equally important contrast occurs when responses from undergraduates at Division I-A football universities are separated from those at Division III and Division I institutions not in I-A football (mainly schools with big-time basketball programs but small-time football ones). Division I-A respondents, particularly males, spent many more hours partying, watching, betting on, and playing sports than students at all other types of schools.

Most Division I-A universities contain two essential elements of the criteria that researchers use to define High Binge schools: big-time intercollegiate athletic programs and large Greek systems. Similarly, most Division III and some smaller Division I schools have Low Binge characteristics: institutions with mainly low-key college sports programs and few or no Greeks. In addition, as discussed in previous chapters, High Binge institutions tend to be large, public research universities that neglect general undergraduate education, whereas Low Binge schools are often smaller-sized private universities and colleges that attempt to provide all of their students with quality undergraduate educations.

Finally, every college student in America has freedom of choice, and even at the highest binge schools, every undergraduate chooses how to spend his or her time. Sadly, far too many students at NCAA Division I-A universities devote numerous hours per week to drinking and big-time college sports entertainment. In fact, the main time difference in the responses to the "partying" questions from students at most Division I-A schools and those at all other institutions were the added hours that the undergraduates at I-A's spent drinking in conjunction with the college sports circus. In many ways, I-A student devotion to beer-and-circus is the difference between a school being a High Binge or Low Binge institution.

17

RALLY ROUND THE TEAM—
AS LONG AS IT WINS
AND COVERS THE SPREAD

T his chapter examines the mind-set of contemporary student fans, including those who bet on college sports teams. For most undergraduates, a winning team is paramount, but for an increasing number of student fans, winning is not enough; the team must also help them win their bets.

★ ★ ★

One of the most annoying things about being a UConn [University of Connecticut] student is that people constantly come up to me [in my hometown] and ask all kinds of questions about the [UConn men's and women's] basketball teams, as though the only reason that I came to college was to become a screaming, drunken fan of the Husky dog [the UConn mascot]. When I politely answer that I have no time to watch basketball due to a sordid desire to graduate on time, people look at me as though I might be a hippie, or a Communist, or both.
                        —Matthew Decapua, in a 1999 article in the
                        UConn student newspaper

This undergraduate admits to being unusual in placing academic ambitions above rooting for his college team, and, as he suggests, many of his fellow UConn students are "screaming, drunken fan[s] of the Husky dog." The questionnaire and interviews for this book discovered a similar situation at most Big-time U's: a majority of students embrace their college teams, particularly if they are championship caliber like the UConn basketball squads, and they fully enjoy the beer-and-circus atmosphere surrounding the teams.

However, a downside exists for universities and athletic departments: student fans, like most contemporary sports fans, are increasingly obsessed with winning, and they define triumph as not simply an "above .500 won-loss record," but winning it all—winning national titles. An Ohio State senior stated, "For every Big Ten champion, there are ten losers [the conference has eleven members since Penn State joined]. Anyway, league titles don't count for much anymore, it's the national championship, or you lose."

Nevertheless, students will party on whether their team wins or loses, but often they will not support losing squads by attending games or showing any school spirit toward them. "We have an awful football program," a Ball State University junior said. "On game days, it seems like there are more students tailgating in the parking lot outside the football stadium than inside watching the game, and there are lots of frat and off-campus parties taking place while the game is going on."

Psychology professor Robert Cialdini has long studied the fans of winning teams like those at UConn, and of losers like those at Ball State. He describes their attitudes as "basking in [the] reflected glory" of winners, and "distancing themselves" from losers. Student fans want "to associate themselves with winning teams . . . to boost their image in the eyes of others," especially outside their universities; and "they believe that other people will see them as more positive if they are associated with positive things, even though they didn't cause the positive things." Hence, the Flutie Factor in applications for college admission—the desire by applicants to attend schools with winning college teams, even though as students at Big-time U's, they will probably never meet the athletes or coaches responsible for the victories (see chapter 6).

Equally important to the fans' psyche is the fear of failure, of their teams' losing and being called, along with them, that most dreaded of contemporary epithets—"LOSER." After the 1999 football season, a University of Iowa junior male felt that he was experiencing this nightmare:

> This has been an absolutely humiliating year for me. Our football team lost almost all its games and were pathetic. It's a *personal* embarrassment to me because all of my friends back home in Chicago are going to call me during [Christmas] vacation and harass me about the pitiful Hawkeyes. They're going to rag on me for supporting a bunch of losers and going to a loser school.

The Iowa student's comments reflected those of many other undergraduates. In interviews for this book, when asked whether loyalty to their university and its teams would keep them rooting through losing seasons, many students stated that loyalty was much less important to them than winning, and, if their teams became or remained "losers," they would stop attending games or even watch them regularly on TV. But almost all said that they would "party on, win or lose," although they much preferred victory celebrations to wakes. Moreover, as the Ball State student indicated, schools with mediocre or bad teams usually have trouble filling their football stadiums and basketball arenas; some athletic departments in this situation have even given free tickets to students and had few attend.

The contemporary college student fixation on winning was echoed—and sharpened—by *ESPN The Magazine* when, after the 1999 men's and women's championship basketball games, won by UConn and Purdue over Duke teams, it proclaimed in its hipper-than-thou manner: DUKE UNIVERSITY—Two teams. Two finals. No [championship] rings? Yeah, more like Loser University."

ESPN The Magazine also did one of its mock gambling charts on "College [Football] Fans" versus "Pro [Football] Fans," the entries reflecting its—and its readers—doublethink on college sports: it's wonderful/it's ridiculous, and even championships have questionable undersides. Among the entries were:

Category	College Fans	Pro Fans	Advantage
Tradition	119 years of Michigan football	Ladies and Gentlemen, your Oakland, I mean Los Angeles, I mean Oakland, I mean, the Raiders	College fan
Stadium Ambiance	Your own vomit	Someone else's vomit	College fan
Best way to meet your [football] hero	Take a class with him—if you can afford to waste a credit on "Dynamics of Napping"	Encourage your wife to work at Jugg City	Pro fans
Your champions are crowned	By a bunch of sportswriters between pressbox Rob Roys	On the field of battle in the Super Bowl	College fans. Kids, have you ever tried a Rob Roy?

Despite elements of sentimentality about college football ("119 years of Michigan football"), the ESPN writer also mocks it: the heroes are dumb jocks and the championship game is decided by drunken sportswriters voting for the top teams. Alcohol also envelops college fans in the stands, including in their own vomit. A college football championship is great and simultaneously tarnished. But ESPN's most important message is: *As ESPN viewers and readers, you are hip to it all.*

Another ESPN commentary—and influence—on contemporary college sports fans occurs when, during games, it focuses its cameras on students displaying various body parts painted in their school colors (other networks also spotlight the painted fans, but ESPN features them more frequently during telecasts and in clips on news shows, particularly *SportsCenter*). *ESPN The Magazine* also glorified these fans in a feature titled "War Paint." Next to a full-page photo of a male student wearing gold paint and little else, and another photo of a male student similarly dressed in garnet (deep red) paint, the text explained:

> Some fans wear their hearts on their sleeves. But when Florida State meets Florida, who needs sleeves? Or sanity? Two FSU scholars— magna cum gaudy—dipped themselves in team colors to spur the Seminoles on to . . . victory. Their parents now know they're getting their tuition money's worth.

Unfortunately, not only might the parents of these two FSU students question the "money's worth" of their tuition payments, but many other Americans, while watching TV shots of similar student antics during college games, might wonder whether undergraduate life is merely fun and games, and whether they should support higher education with their tax dollars and charitable donations. Indeed, public and private aid to America's colleges and universities has dropped significantly in the last few decades; probably the constant stream of images of bizarre student behavior at college sports events has contributed to this erosion of support.

ESPN constantly promotes the beer-and-circus aspect of higher education. Every Saturday during the football season, it places its *GameDay* announcing crew on location at a Big-time U and in close proximity to drunken undergraduates. As a result, every shot of its announcers' discussing the featured game as well as other games around the country includes, in the background, obviously drunk students acting rowdy or goofy. Because the ESPN *GameDay* broadcasts go on for over nine hours each week—and drunken students always clog the background in the hopes of being on TV—almost every American who subscribes to cable-TV sees them during the fall. Then, in the winter and spring, the network's basketball broadcasts also place the announcers in front of frenetic, often painted students. ESPN imprints this image of undergraduate life upon the public, and also "normalizes" this behavior for students already on campus, as well as for those planning to enroll at Big-time U's.

> Most students who attended games [in the 1950s] dressed much differently than do those at today's games. Almost all guys wore collared shirts, some with ties and jackets. Girls wore blouses and skirts down below their knees. . . . This is a far cry from the obscene T-shirts and torn jeans which some students wear to games today.

These observations came in an essay comparing college sports fans in the 1950s versus those in the 1990s. The writer included photocopies from school newspapers and yearbooks to illustrate the then-and-nows, the more formal 1950s attire contrasting to contemporary T-shirts exhibiting such statements as "Muck Fichigan," and "Penn State Sucks, Purdue Swallows." In addition, although 1950s rooters wanted their school teams to win and they had little patience with losing coaches and players, they did not taunt the opposing team with obscene signs and chants, nor try to distract them during play, particularly when kicking field goals and point-after touchdowns, and shooting free throws.

In another then-and-now contrast, the essayist remarked that, according to the press, fights between fans of opposing schools rarely occurred in the 1950s. This is accurate, but historically, college sports rivalries often prompted brawls among spectators, and their general absence in the 1950s was exceptional, mainly due to that era's "buttoned-down" ethos. In subsequent decades, primitivism returned to most football stadiums and basketball arenas, partly fueled by increasing undergraduate consumption of alcohol before and during games. By the end of the century, at some beer-and-circus schools, fan devolution had reached a Neanderthal stage, *USA Today* describing it in a feature article that began:

> ADD A THIRD CERTAINTY TO DEATH AND TAXES.
> FANS BEHAVING BADLY.

> When Florida beat Tennessee in September, 141 fans were ejected. Florida State visits the Swamp [the nickname of the University of Florida's home field] this Saturday. Trouble waits.
> [The University of] Florida will increase its usual police contingent

from about 150 to 190 officers. The combustible mix of rivalry, alcohol, and hype will make their job a difficult one. It is much the same across the land.

The causes of students "behaving badly" at college sports events differ markedly from current fan misbehavior at pro games. At the latter, fans often resent the gargantuan salaries of professional athletes and consider the players fair game for verbal and even physical attacks. However, because of NCAA rules, the salaries of college athletes are not an issue for fans. The student conduct described by *USA Today* results from other causes, mainly the collegiate subculture that, with alcohol erasing inhibitions, allows members to act out their aggressions.

Binge drinking and brawling are dangerous ventures, but risk-taking is central to the collegiate subculture, not only in these activities but also in a more subtle but often just as hazardous preoccupation with gambling. One expert believes that betting, mainly on intercollegiate athletic events, "is probably a worse problem. . . . on college campuses [today] than alcohol or drug abuse." Unfortunately, unlike the drinking and drug problems, very few studies on student gambling exist, and the actual extent of the problem is difficult to measure.

Nonetheless, a large body of anecdotal evidence and some research indicate that a substantial number of undergraduates gamble regularly, and that more join them every day. In addition, of all students at American colleges and universities, males belonging to the collegiate subculture at beer-and-circus schools appear to be the most frequent gamblers. Any study of beer-and-circus must consider this topic.

★   ★   ★

> Meet the Juice generation. For them, finance isn't a major, it's knowing how to spread $1,000 in wagers over 10 Saturday college football games. . . . Class participation is sitting in the back of a lecture hall with Vegas-style "spreadsheets" laid out, plotting a week's worth of plays on games.
>
> —Tim Layden, *Sports Illustrated* reporter

Five years ago, *SI* published an excellent series on sports gambling on college campuses, terming the young, predominantly male bettors, the *Juice generation,* after the bookmakers' term *juice*—the 10 percent surcharge on losing bets (also called the *vigorish*). *SI* reporters visited numerous campuses and found that, particularly at beer-and-circus schools, gambling was "rampant and thriving," involving many students, notably from the collegiate subculture: "Put simply, lots of college sports bettors are clever frat-boy jocks who like to watch games with a crowd and get pumped up by betting on them." A former bookmaker, with ties to organized crime, explained: "College kids bet everything. They pick the phone up and they call, especially after a couple of drinks. . . . They make a bigger bet and a bigger bet. They can do it seven nights a week." But by betting so often, and frequently on "sucker parleys," they tend to lose, anywhere from a few dollars to many thousands, hence their regular payments of "juice."

One of the few research studies of undergraduate gambling asserted that "23 percent of students gambled at least once a week." The study was done in 1990, and experts believe that a decade later the percentage of student gamblers has increased considerably. In the questionnaire for this book, a respondent at Michigan State wrote in a P.S.: "I have noticed a betting problem on this campus. . . . I believe that five out of ten [male] students gamble at least once in awhile," and many of them do it more often. An undergraduate at Indiana University wrote about the "serious betting scene at this school. . . . The real joke of it is that most of these people are betting their parents' money away." Like the parents of the Florida State painted fans, undoubtedly the parents of student gamblers are not amused.

An undergraduate at the University of Maryland discussed another element of student gambling:

> Betting on games undermines school spirit here. Many students go to games or watch them on TV, and all they care about are their bets. I've been to games here where we've won and lots of fans sat on their hands at the end because the team "didn't cover the spread." Can you believe that some idiots even booed our players because of that?

Sports Illustrated used Duke University, like Maryland an ACC (Atlantic Coast Conference) member, as an example of the point-spread phenomenon: "Some small corner of Cameron Indoor Stadium," the Duke basketball arena, "is crazy because a few of the Crazies took Duke, minus 4 for $25," and won their bets (Duke fans call themselves "Cameron Crazies"). There is yet another side to point-spread mania: on occasion, home fans cheer when their team loses but beats the spread, and they win their bets. (The point spread is the bookmaker's attempt to make betting more interesting by equalizing the differences between teams. Bookies assign the supposedly superior squad a handicap of various points, and they "give" points to the underdog. The assigned point totals are the spread. Bookies pay off bets on the favorite when it wins by more points than the spread, and on the underdog when it "beats" the spread—loses by less points than the spread or wins the game. For example, if Duke is a four-point underdog to Virginia, and it loses by a single point, the Cameron Crazies with Duke "minus four" win their bets. But the Virginia bettors, needing their team to win by five or more points, lose.)

An ACC athletic department official admitted:

> It's impossible to build a solid fan base on such people [as student gamblers]. It's easy enough to predict low student turnouts when the team is losing, but who knows when and if bettors will come. Personally, I think that most stay home and watch as many games on TV as they can, all at the same time. . . . I wonder what will happen when these people become alumni? They'll keep betting and we won't see any of their money.

When student bettors view games on TV, frequently they have one eye on the "crawl" at the bottom of the ESPN2 screen or, on occasion, CNN Headline News. The constant stream of the latest scores provides gamblers with updates on their bets, and the "crawl" is particularly useful for bettors "in action" on a large number of games. In addition, ESPN.com provides minute-by-minute updates, as do other sports websites. At the beginning of the twenty-first century, many student bettors simultaneously watch TV and scan the sports websites on their computers to follow their bets. Some also wager at one of the many Internet gambling sites; however, most undergraduates prefer local bookies—the latter extend credit on bets, whereas at a website, the bettor must pay immediately with a bank card to make the wager official. As a result, by dealing with bookies—often fellow students—many undergraduate gamblers go deeply into debt before considering the consequences of their betting and its negative effect on their lives.

Yet gambling—or "gaming" as its proponents term it—has become so accepted and mainstream in contemporary American society that few college students consider it a social malady and potential addiction, similar to alcohol and drugs, and, in some cases, as destructive. Reinforcing its acceptability are the ubiquitous TV, print, and billboard ads for lotteries, on- and off-shore casinos, and gambling meccas like Las Vegas and Atlantic City.

Obviously, in this social climate, the average student bettor sees nothing wrong with putting down money on a college game or, if inclined and enterprising, becoming a student bookie for a few years, often affiliated with a professional bookmaker.

Compare student drug-taking and gambling: Many undergraduates dislike the current drug laws, but every student in America knows that selling, buying, and possessing narcotics is illegal and risky; also, no daily newspaper publishes the "street prices" on marijuana or any other "controlled substance," or advertisements from drug dealers. On the other hand, *USA Today* and many local papers feature the daily betting lines on college and pro games; they also display large ads from betting "touts" with 800-numbers and websites. In addition, many TV and radio sports commentators, particularly on the ESPN networks and SportsTalk radio, regularly discuss the "betting situation" and "point spreads" on college games. "I don't see a single thing wrong with betting on college sports," a University of Florida student declared. "Everywhere you look it's promoted like crazy by the most popular media in this country."

Nevertheless, betting on intercollegiate athletics is illegal in all states except Nevada, and a recently introduced congressional bill aims to ban it in that state, as well as increase the penalties on all illegal bookmakers who accept bets on college sports events. Like the prohibitions on student drinking, for undergraduates the mixed message on gambling is clear: When politicians and university officials condemn betting on college sports—as many are now doing—they exhibit the usual hypocrisy, and should be ignored or, if that is impossible, defied.

How much money is actually bet on college sports games? A few years ago, the *Omaha World-Herald* asked a Las Vegas bookmaker to estimate the total on the 1998 University of Nebraska versus Kansas State football game: the legal betting in Nevada on this contest was almost $500,000, and the Las Vegas rule of thumb is that the illegal betting nationwide is usually fifty times the Nevada total—almost $25 million on this one game. Multiply that number by twenty other major games that Saturday; factor in thirty less-important but nevertheless bet-upon Division I-A contests; also add one hundred lesser college contests, as well as the popular "parley plays" on multiple games; and a total of $1 billion for that college football day seems a reasonable amount.

Multiply $1 billion by approximately fifteen weeks of full college football schedules; add a "huge take" during the bowl game season; factor in another fifteen weeks of college basketball of at least $1 billion a week;

then add the "colossal action" on March Madness, the NCAA Division I basketball tournaments; and a bottom line of $75 billion a year bet on college sports becomes a conservative estimate.

With this much money "in play," inevitably some of it will touch college athletes. The NCAA publicly worries about athletes betting on games and, as occurred during past betting scandals, players accepting money from gamblers to fix games ("shaving points"—athletes trying to make sure that their team does not "cover" the point spread—is the most popular way of fixing games). Nevertheless, the association has placed only a pinkie finger in the dike to hold back the $75 billion sea and the potential tidal wave of fixes. It assigns a single staff member to work part-time monitoring athletes' betting, and trying to persuade them not to gamble in any way.

But the recent findings of a University of Michigan study sounded an alarm and, in so doing, called into question the NCAA's commitment to combating gambling on college games. According to the U of M research on current athletic scholarship holders:

> More than 5 percent of football and men's basketball players have either given inside information to gamblers, bet on games in which they played or [have] shaved points. Also, 72 percent of athletes had gambled in various other forms [i.e., at casinos, in lotteries, etc.].

An Indianapolis sportswriter translated the Michigan statistics into game situations: "Assuming a college football team has 100 student-athletes [including walk-ons], that's five players" involved in betting. "What if one is the free safety" who "accidentally" trips while defending on a long pass? Or "the tailback" who fumbles just before the goal line as Northwestern University's Dennis Lundy did to save his bet in a Big Ten game a few years ago. Or "the quarterback" who throws an interception at a key moment in the contest. "Or all three?" Additionally, in basketball, players have a warehouse full of fixing devices, including blown shots and missed defensive assignments.

All of the college athletes involved in gambling scandals during the 1990s—at Northwestern, Boston College, Arizona State, and other schools—subsequently discussed the betting atmosphere on their campuses, the large numbers of regular students placing bets and asking athletes for "inside information," and also offering players some "free bets"—if the wager wins, the athlete receives money; if it fails, it costs the player nothing.

In this college gambling world, surrounded by the gaming mania of contemporary America, it is a small step for athletes to start placing their own bets, then a larger but not insurmountable step to trying to win those bets during games as Dennis Lundy did, or shaving points as Northwestern and Arizona State basketball players did. Such actions are immensely stupid, and, if detected, they destroy athletic careers and personal reputations; however, as the Michigan study indicated, they are neither idiosyncratic nor highly aberrant. Moreover, unless a radical change in American attitudes on gambling occurs, in all probability more intercollegiate athletes will bet on college games, and a growing number will attempt to fix them. A Big Ten athlete, when asked for his prognosis on future college fixes, replied, "You can bet on it."

The single NCAA employee in charge of gambling investigations explains athlete betting as one more evil caused by contemporary American culture: "Something has happened to lower their [athletes'] respect for themselves and the game." However, this explanation omits the most frequent target of athletes' disrespect—their coaches.

Often college players feel abused or exploited by their coaches, and they resent the endless training regimens as well as their coaches' often huge annual incomes. Many college athletes also feel powerless, constricted by NCAA rules on transferring and losing year(s) of eligibility, and unable to express their discontent without reprisals from their coaches or athletic departments. According to the *Chicago Tribune*, a number of Northwestern basketball players involved in that school's 1990s point-shaving scandal had become "embittered" by their coach's high-handed and often erratic treatment of them, and, in part, this made them willing to shave points. These players were also betting on college sports games and wanted to pay off their gambling debts. They were perfect targets for their bookmaker's suggestion to shave points.

Northwestern University's 1990s hopes for athletic fame and fortune from its big-time college sports teams—and the football squad rode a high wave after its Rose Bowl appearance—crashed with the gambling scandals. Robert Lipsyte of the *New York Times* commented that the confessions by the NU football and basketball fixers "nullified Northwestern University's bet that the millions it spent on" intercollegiate athletics "would pay off in national happy news, increased enrollment, and alumni donations."

Lipsyte's gambling metaphor is apt: universities wager fortunes on their college sports teams but never contemplate losing their bets. Northwestern, after its Rose Bowl season, did experience some Flutie Factor application increases—only to see the Flutie cohort disappear in the wake of the gambling scandals. The revelation of the fixes also enraged many Northwestern alumni, and they privately and publicly complained. Such prominent NU grads as journalists Rick Telander (*Chicago Sun-Times*) and Andy Bagnato (*Chicago Tribune*) wrote long columns expressing their anger and embarrassment about their alma mater's involvement in sordid gambling scandals. Other alumni vowed not to contribute money to NU until it returned to a "sane athletics policy."

Not only do the administrators of Big-time U's like Northwestern fail to understand the campus gambling subculture that spawns fixes, but they totally miscalculate the long odds of winning their institutional wagers on intercollegiate athletics. Undoubtedly, one of the events that blinds them is the massive media attention to, and popularity of, March Madness, the NCAA Division I basketball tournaments. Success in the men's tournament can trigger the Flutie Factor; however, of all intercollegiate athletic events, none is more dependent on the public's and the media's infatuation with college sports betting.

★   ★   ★

> One disturbing factor is the media hype surrounding the [office and campus gambling] pools. . . . The media seems to cater to pool-hungry fans. Newspapers conveniently create NCAA tournament brackets at the standard paper size of 8.5 by 11 inches [that] . . . handily photocopy onto a regular sheet of paper. The tournament brackets can even be downloaded off ESPN's web site and printed without adjusting a thing. The Nike ad campaign's logo is not a swoosh, but the brackets.
> —A 1999 editorial in the Rutgers University *Daily Targum*

Many events reveal the NCAA's hypocrisy on gambling, none more than March Madness. Most of the association's revenue comes from the sale of television rights fees to its Division I men's and women's tournaments, but these TV payouts—now in the multibillion-dollar range—depend on millions of people watching the games. Why do a large percentage of viewers tune into this NCAA event? Because they have bet money on the outcome of the games, anywhere from ten dollars to tens of thousands of dollars. A similar viewers-watching-their-bets principle effects the TV ratings of bowl games and regular season contests, but to a much lesser extent than March Madness.

A bookie in a Big Ten college town explains:

If everyone who bet money on college games, especially the NCAA b-ball tourney, stopped watching the games on TV and only followed their bets by looking at scores on the web . . . then the TV ratings would go into the toilet and out into the sewer system and never be seen again. . . . The same thing would happen to all the money the NCAA receives from CBS.

When NCAA officials campaign against betting on college sports, and lobby in Congress for bills to strengthen anti-betting laws, one wonders if they have a suicidal impulse. More likely, they know that such legislation probably will not pass, and, even if it did, the new laws will have minimal impact because the illegal bookmaking industry is so well entrenched and web gambling is growing so quickly. As with so many NCAA initiatives, public relations—in this case, wanting to appear high-minded and reform-ist—dictates policy.

However, the NCAA should care deeply about betting on college sports, for pragmatic as well as ethical reasons. The horrendous point-shaving scandal in college basketball during the late 1940s–early 1950s illustrated a simple fact: When the media and the public believe that games are fixed, the popularity of the sport declines. Ironically, professional bookmakers, because they depend on a level playing field, have always shown much greater concern about fixing than has the NCAA. In the late 1940s–early 1950s scandal, the bookies were the whistle-blowers; and, in the 1990s, Las Vegas bookies spotted the Arizona State basketball fix.

Opposing the NCAA's legislative proposals is the powerful gaming in-dustry; its head lobbyist argues that if the NCAA were serious about its anti-betting campaign, its members "should do more to crack down on illegal gambling on their campuses, including using proceeds from lucrative television network contracts to fund gambling-prevention programs."

The NCAA and some schools do produce videotapes on the dangers of gambling, but most students pay as much attention to these official pro-nouncements as they do to the brewers' "drink responsibly" ads. A much more persuasive source of information for college students is ESPN in all of its forms. Not only does its website provide March Madness "pool" forms and other betting paraphernalia, but it celebrates gambling in many other ways. For example, in a Special Summer Double Issue of *ESPN The Magazine*, titled "99 WAYS TO LIVE THE LIFE OF THE ULTIMATE FAN," the fifth best was, "Watch the Big Dance [March Madness] at Caesar's Sports Book" in Las Vegas.

ESPN recommended that the "ultimate fan" obtain a "seat at Caesar's

Race and Sports Book on the two greatest days in spectator sports—the opening round of the NCAA tournament." For ESPN, these days are "great" because all sixty-four teams in the men's field play, and the games produce some upsets as well as frequent failures to cover the spread. In terms of traditional basketball viewing, these contests—most are predictable and lopsided—cannot compare with the games in the final rounds when the best teams emerge and often play excellent basketball. But for gamblers seeking "action," the first two days are heaven—and hell.

The ESPN reporter described the emotional atmosphere at Caesar's as bettors "fall to the carpet in anguish as a meaningless buzzer-beater by some third-string chucker from We-Don't-Have-a-Chance U closes his team to 98–69," beating the thirty-point spread, and "killing" the fallen bettors. In the world of college sports gambling, so celebrated by ESPN and other media outlets, no athletic contest transcends the money bet on it; and gamblers much prefer winning their bets to viewing outstanding play, particularly if the latter costs them money.

★   ★   ★

This is the world of college sports over which the NCAA and member athletic departments preside. For all of their rhetoric on "ending the curse of college sports betting," they must know that as gaming grows in popularity, more college students, more college athletes, and many more fans will bet increasing amounts of money on college sports events. The $75 billion annual "handle" will soon surpass $100 billion, and soar from there. And the media will provide more gambling information and glorify college sports betting more than ever before.

CBS-TV did not sign a multibillion-dollar contract with the NCAA for television rights to March Madness through 2013 because the network believed that the association will succeed in its campaign to end betting on college sports. Television executives probably hope that the gaming industry will triumph and legalize sports bookmaking nationally, and that legal Sports Books, as well as illegal bookies and office pools, will continue to thrive. For the networks, the equation is simple: More bettors equals more eyeballs watching college sports, especially more eighteen-to-thirty-four-year-old viewers, the beloved demographic. Only one element can imbalance the equation—if the Internet overtakes television, and sports viewers switch to it.

But this possibility has pushed TV networks to begin merger talks with Internet companies. At the beginning of the twenty-first century, as the TV ratings for March Madness rest on a slippery slope, the new NCAA/CBS-

RALLY ROUND THE TEAM—AS LONG AS IT WINS . . . | 215

TV contract indicates that the network will actively seek Internet tie-ins for the tournaments. One expert explains that CBS regards the NCAA events as "software" in case of "a transition of television to the Internet."

This is the contemporary college sports industry as presided over by the NCAA. A detailed examination of its financial condition—beyond the megabucks from the March Madness deal—as well as its impact upon its member universities, is the subject of the next chapter of this book.

18

COLLEGE SPORTS MEGAINC.

Ten years ago, the big-time college sports entertainment industry could be termed College Sports Inc. Since that time, its revenue has exploded, and it has become College Sports MegaInc.

★   ★   ★

Six Billion?
Where's Mine?
Six billion dollars over 11 years [that's the new NCAA deal with CBS-TV]. It comes out to about $545 million per year. . . .
    College basketball players watch the coach roaming the sidelines in his $1,500 custom-made suit. They read about his $500,000 salary and $250,000 per [year] from some sneaker deal. They watch the schools sell jerseys with the players' [names and] numbers on them. . . . They see the athletic director getting rich and the college president getting rich and NCAA officials getting rich and the coach's dog getting rich. And you wonder why they might ask, "Hey, where's my share? What am I, a pack mule?"
    There is no other show business in which the actual entertainers don't get any money. . . . Even our Olympic teams pay the athletes above the table now. Believe me, the NCAA is not getting six billion dollars so we can watch [Duke University's] Mike Kryzewski coach a bunch of chem majors.
                    —Tony Kornheiser, sportswriter and broadcaster

Beyond the sarcasm and outrage, this writer makes a crucial point: How can the NCAA and member schools continue the pretense of student-athlete amateurism when the people running big-time college sports amass fortunes from this huge entertainment business, whereas the actual performers—the young men and women who put fans in the seats and viewers in front of their TVs—receive only athletic scholarships, the most generous of which top out at $30,000, with the majority below $20,000 per year?

USA Today led its front-page story on the new NCAA/CBS-TV March Madness deal with, "Amateurism has never been more lucrative" for the NCAA. As Tony Kornheiser indicated, Division I basketball players are rarely "chem majors," but, most often, minor leaguers in training for the next pro level. And CBS-TV is not paying the NCAA for TV rights to games where the players take difficult majors, such as an Emory versus Rochester contest, which feature truly amateur athletes in action. Yet, the NCAA works hard to maintain the amateur facade of big-time college sports—without it, the association would lose its tax exemptions, and the IRS would place it in the same category as all other professional sports enterprises.

To maintain its nonprofit status, the NCAA employs full-time lobbyists in Washington, D.C., and it locates their office in a building on Dupont Circle that also houses the most reputable higher education associations in America. The NCAA's head lobbyist explained the decision to rent space at One Dupont Circle as a strategic move: "Because of our office location, we are perceived as and treated as one of the higher education associations."

But the NCAA emperor has no clothes: When USA Today and other media outlets discussed the new March Madness TV contract, they put it within the context of "professional sports TV rights deals," placing it third on the television contract list, behind the NFL and NBA, but ahead of Nascar, major league baseball, and the NHL. And when the TV deals of NCAA Division I-A football schools are added to the basketball money, the annual television revenue of "amateur" college sports surpasses that of every professional league in the world.

In addition, the athletic directors and coaches who work in big-time college sports tend to forget the NCAA's official line on amateurism, and they usually speak in sports business terms. In a typical comment in January 2000 the AD at North Carolina State justified his slow time-table on hiring a new football coach by arguing, "We are part of a corporate group bigger than N.C. State called the Atlantic Coast Conference," and we have to consider the collective corporate interests before acting on our own.

Mike Kryzewski, the men's basketball coach at Duke University, another part of the Atlantic Coast Corporation, uses similar language. He has long complained that "the marketing of our product [college basketball] is at a really low level," and has urged the NCAA to bring in top corporate marketers to sell the college game better. Kryzewski, with an annual income of over $1 million, has marketed himself into the elite level of college coaches and, ironically, part of his success is the image of his players as authentic students, placing their academic goals ahead of their athletic ambitions. (In recent years, as some of his best players left school early to enter the NBA, this marketing ploy has eroded.)

Many college sports fans, particularly those over thirty-five, enjoy the student-athlete trappings of intercollegiate athletics. However, as Tony Kornheiser and other journalists constantly point out, the "big bucks reality" is omnipresent, and fans increasingly require a willful innocence to ignore the dollar signs.

> Compare the BCS' [football Bowl Championship Series] $100 million [a year revenue] to the $545 million a year the NCAA basketball tournaments will get from CBS, and you can see why everyone's spinning in his boots. They [college sports administrators] say, "Wait a minute. I thought football was the king of college sports."
>
> —Jim Wheeler, vice president of an international sports marketing firm

One hundred million dollars a year revenue from the BCS bowls—Rose, Orange, Sugar, and Fiesta—is not "chump change"; however, according to Wheeler, if the bowls were reconfigured into a playoff system, culminating in a College Super Bowl, "you'd be looking at $250 million" a year for the final games. To back this argument, his company, Swiss-based International Sports and Leisure (ISL), has offered BCS football schools a multiyear, multibillion-dollar contract for the rights to produce and market the college football playoffs. (The BCS encompasses the top six conferences in Division I-A football and Notre Dame.)

Many of the opponents of the ISL proposal cloak their objections in the rhetoric of amateurism—they claim that a playoff will stretch the football season too far into January, and players will have trouble starting their second semester classes—but the real roadblock is money. BCS officials believe that the current system works fine, and that other formats would render all games but the championship match meaningless, hurting overall bowl attendance, TV ratings, and the money flow.

That's exactly what occurred in late 1999 and early 2000 when the media focused primarily on the Sugar Bowl game between No. 1 Florida

State and No. 2 Virginia Tech. Probably a sixteen-team playoff series would produce more positive results: it could include many bowl games and, like the NCAA basketball Sweet Sixteen and final rounds when every game counts, college football playoff games would fill the stands, earn excellent TV ratings, and generate maximum revenue.

If, in future years, the BCS format continues to hamper the lower-tier bowls, the main participants in those games—the runners-up in the BCS conferences—might support a playoff system. The BCS television contract extends through 2005; however, a TV network insider explained that the executive in charge of the Bowl Championship Series, Roy Kramer, is always receptive to new ideas for postseason college football, particularly when it involves billions of dollars: "Money is what drove Roy to put together the BCS, and money can drive him to a better version."

When that occurs, you can bet that no BCS or NCAA official will argue that "college football players should not suit up in late January." Indeed, as an alternative proposal to the sixteen-team playoff, ISL suggests that after the current bowl season ends, a four-team billion-dollar playoff take place, adding more weeks to the winter football season.

> [Bowl game] life is good—if you're part of the BCS. On the outside, rumbles of discontent remain. . . . Schools in the six major [BCS] conferences—the Atlantic Coast, Big East, Big Ten, Big 12, Pacific 10, and Southeastern—figure to pull in just under 94% of the total $144.6 million paid out by 23 bowls this season.
> —Steve Weiberg, *USA Today* reporter

More than 110 schools play Division I-A football; however, unless they reside within the BCS fold, they remain at home during the bowl season or collect spare change in such marginal contests as the Motor City Bowl and the Las Vegas Bowl. In addition, although more than 300 schools play Division I basketball, the six BCS conferences hog the largest proportion of payout dollars from March Madness. According to a recent analysis of the finances of big-time college sports, the average annual revenue of the BCS conferences was $63 million, whereas the amount for the other twenty-three leagues in Division I averaged less than $3 million per year.

Those are the revenue totals in big-time intercollegiate athletics. But the expenses numbers are higher, resulting in the amazing fact that *most college sports programs lose money*. Most extraordinary of all, the losers include many schools in the BCS conferences, including those playing in the most lucrative bowl games and advancing deep into the final rounds of the NCAA basketball tournaments. In late 1999, the athletic director of the University of Michigan—a school with an always full 110,000-seat stadium and 20,000-seat basketball arena—acknowledged that "the Wolverines intercollegiate sports program . . . last year ran a deficit," more than $2 million dollars of red ink. If Big Blue loses money in college sports, what hope is there for smaller programs?

Historically, and contrary to popular myth, almost all colleges and universities have always lost money on their intercollegiate athletics programs. Moreover, athletic departments ran deficits long before the federal government's Title IX mandated equality for women's intercollegiate athletics, and male athletic directors seized upon their Title IX costs to excuse their overall money losses. Historically, the main causes of athletic department red ink were waste, mismanagement, and fraud, and this situation continues today.

Of course, these annual deficits preclude paying the players: journalists like Tony Kornheiser have logic and ethics on their side when they demand that the athletes receive their fair "share" of the TV payouts—except, after the athletic directors, coaches, and athletic department staff spend the revenue, nothing remains for the players. Before the athletes can obtain their share, the entire athletic department finance system must be overhauled. But the people who run intercollegiate athletics, and benefit so handsomely from the corrupt system in place, will not willingly overturn the red ink trough.

The NCAA, in its regular financial reports, provides an indication of the profit-and-loss situation in big-time college sports. The most recent edition revealed that a majority of Division I athletic departments lost money in the 1990s, running larger deficits at the end of the decade than at the beginning, even though their revenue increased every year. However, because of the accounting tricks used by almost all athletic departments, the NCAA reports are only partially accurate, and the actual annual deficit numbers are much higher than the NCAA and member schools admit publicly.

Some accounting experts multiply the NCAA's deficit numbers by a factor of three. They point out that almost all athletic departments routinely move many legitimate costs from their ledgers and place them on their universities' financial books. These items include the utilities, maintenance, and debt-servicing bills on their intercollegiate athletic facilities—multimillion-dollar annual expenses for most big-time programs. Economist Andrew Zimbalist, after in-depth research on the finances of intercollegiate athletics, recently concluded that, despite all the accounting maneuvers, "the vast majority of schools" still "run a significant deficit from their athletic programs," and "only a handful of schools consistently earn surpluses," often small ones.

Athletic department deficits impact on host universities in many negative ways. Not only are millions of dollars siphoned from schools when athletic departments move expenditures onto university books, but more millions depart when schools cover the annual athletic department deficits. At the end of each fiscal year, universities "zero out" athletic department books; to do so they divert money from their General Operating Funds and other financial resources to cover the college sports losses. Money that could go to academic programs, student scholarships and loans, and many other educational purposes annually disappears down the athletic department financial hole.

The bottom line is clear: Big-time intercollegiate athletics financially hurts NCAA Division I schools more than it helps them. For every dollar that a few of these institutions acquire through college sports phenomena like the Flutie Factor, many more Division I members annually lose millions of dollars as a result of their athletic department deficits and other negative college sports factors. One inescapable conclusion appears: *College Sports MegaInc. is the most dysfunctional business in America.*

But neither the media nor the public focuses on this fact. Even Tony Kornheiser, one of the savviest sportswriters in America, says that the schools, as well as the individuals in charge of intercollegiate athletics, amass fortunes from the fun and games. Other media personalities also state this loudly and frequently.

The myth of college sports profitability not only masks the deficits of intercollegiate athletic programs, but it generates other negative financial consequences:

> The public hears about the millions that universities rake in from the NCAA basketball tournaments and bowl games, and people conclude that higher education doesn't need their tax dollars or private contributions. They believe that universities are doing great from their big-time college sports teams. . . . At Illinois, it couldn't be further from the truth, and that's also the situation at most other schools.
> —Howard Schein, professor at the University of Illinois, Champaign-Urbana

During the last two decades, legislative and taxpayer support for higher education has declined considerably. The role of big-time intercollegiate athletics in this decline is difficult to ascertain, but some observers believe that the never-ending college sports recruiting and academic scandals have made the public cynical about intercollegiate athletics, and stingy toward the universities that promote it. Additional evidence suggests that the myth of college sports profitability also closes taxpayers' wallets. In interviews for this book, a number of respondents offered comments similar to Professor Schein's. Common sense suggests that the myth of college sports profitability is a factor, possibly an important one, in the decline of public support for higher education; it certainly appeared to be so in the state of Illinois in the 1980s and 1990s. (For a discussion of the myth that college sports generates increased alumni donations, see pages 256–59.)

Not only is the public unaware of the financial reality of college sports, but it knows even less about the causes of this situation. The media trumpets the huge payouts from bowl games and the NCAA basketball tournaments, and the public sees the high dollar numbers, but rarely does the media go beyond the myths and explore the financial facts.

A discussion of the following myths and realities helps explain why College Sports MegaInc. is the most dysfunctional business in America. It also explains how and why the men and women who administer universities and supposedly control their schools' athletic departments are totally complicit in the deficit financing of College Sports MegaInc.

★   ★   ★

Myth: Schools make millions of dollars when their teams play in football bowl games.

Reality: Most universities lose money when their football teams appear in bowl games. In a typical case, the University of Wisconsin received $1.8 million for participating in the 1999 Rose Bowl, but racked up almost $2.1 million in expenses on this event, close to $300,000 of rose-colored ink. The Rose Bowl payout could have helped the UW athletic department balance its books—its announced deficit at the end of the 1998–99 fiscal year was $1.1 million—but its excessive spending on this trip turned potential profit into real loss.

The cost of flying the football team, the coaches, and the team's support staff to and from Los Angeles, and housing and feeding them while there came to $831,400. In addition to this cost, like all schools going to bowl games, Wisconsin took along the families of the coaches, as well as babysitters (six) for the coaches' kids. Also a large number of other athletic department personnel and their spouses made the junket. Also on the "gravy plane" were members of the University of Wisconsin Board of Regents and spouses, school administrators and spouses, plus the so-called Faculty Board of Control of Intercollegiate Athletics and their spouses, and many hangers-on (termed "friends of the program") and their spouses. Then there was the marching band and cheerleaders, and not one but *three Bucky Badger mascots*—possibly in case the school-sponsored New Year's Eve celebration, costing $34,400, incapacitated one or two Buckys and the third one had to suit up on January 1.

The official Wisconsin traveling party numbered 832 people, including well over one hundred university officials and spouses. The Wisconsin group journeyed in the usual athletic department deluxe-class-for-all style, staying at a very expensive Beverly Hills hotel, wining and dining in an extravagant manner. After the UW athletic department paid all the bills from the trip, the expenses totaled $2,093,500. The travel manager of a major corporation, after examining a breakdown of the Wisconsin expenses, concluded:

> They could have done this trip for at least a fifth the cost and still stayed at nice hotels and eaten well. And that's with all the extra people—I've never seen so many free-loaders on a trip before and it appears completely unjustified. . . . These athletic department administrators could give lessons to drunken sailors on how to throw money around.

In the amazing world of college sports finances, Wisconsin's losses were not an anomaly: most athletic departments lose money on their bowl game excursions, and often they incur greater losses than Wisconsin's because few payouts equal or top the $1.8 million the Badgers received from the Rose Bowl Corporation.

With bowl paydays so fat, why do athletic directors pass up these excellent opportunities to help balance their books? The answer is twofold: Despite all the corporate jargon that ADs spout, their management style has never been lean and mean. Because Big-time U's always sop up the red ink at the end of the fiscal year, most ADs spend in an extravagant and wasteful manner and allow many of their employees, particularly their football and men's basketball coaches, to do the same.

The other reason ADs sanction lavish bowl trips is self-protection: Long ago, they learned that by spending money on university officials and faculty boards of control, taking them and their spouses to bowl games and on other junkets (as well as providing them with free skyboxes or excellent seats to all home football and basketball games), athletic departments obtained insurance policies—they persuaded the people within the university who have direct oversight over intercollegiate athletics to back it enthusiastically. The potential critics of the financial and other abuses of big-time college sports climb onto the gravy planes and become complicit in the wasting of large sums of money. As a result, these university officials rarely question the specific expenses or the general financial operations of their athletic departments, nor do they hesitate to cover the annual deficits.

Not only are most university officials intimidated by powerful ADs and coaches and fear displeasing them, but, in the current era, many administrators seem to believe the NCAA and athletic department propaganda about the wonderful benefits that College Sports MegaInc. bestows upon the university (see chapter 21 for refutations of these supposed benefits).

Is this the total explanation? It accounts for athletic department behavior—ADs and coaches are merely doing what comes naturally—but beyond the obvious causes of administrative complicity in the deficit spending, a more complex reason for their official conduct exists. Many Big-time U officials, knowing that their schools cannot provide the vast majority of undergraduates with meaningful educations, try to distract and please these consumers with ongoing entertainment in the form of big-time college sports. For all of its high expenses, an intercollegiate athletics program costs far less than a quality undergraduate education program. University officials deny employing this strategy, but their denials are less important than the current reality: Many Big-time U's supply their students with an abundance of college sports events and accept the drinking culture that accompanies the fun and games; meanwhile, these schools offer their undergraduates few quality educational opportunities, reserving those for the honors students (usually a single-digit percentage of the student body).

An administrator of a Sunbelt university, when presented with this thesis, replied:

> There's certainly no plot or conspiracy by school officials on this. You have to remember that most universities are always in a money bind. We sure as hell can't get enough money out of our state legislature or anyone else to turn our undergraduate education program into one big honors college. But we need every undergraduate tuition dollar we can get . . . and we can swallow the million bucks a year

that the athletic department costs us. . . . Maybe that's how it all happens. I can assure you that we never thought any of this out beforehand, nor did any other school.

He also mentioned, somewhat defensively:

Yes, I've been to bowl games and the NCAA tourney with our teams, and I'm not going to apologize for enjoying those trips. I see them as rewards for me working hard on behalf of the athletic department. . . .

He concluded:

I don't know how it all happened, how our athletic department never stops growing, and how this school always rates high on the "Party School" lists in the college guides, but I'm not going to carry the can for it, and my president sure wouldn't. Anyway, he's mainly concerned with our research and graduate programs which have really improved under his leadership.

Finally, in an age of accepting personal responsibility, college presidents and administrators at beer-and-circus schools should assume some of the blame for the current situation. They make frequent pronouncements on "refocusing student life" and "curtailing drinking" on their campuses, but they sanction, promote, and sometimes even participate in the beer-and-circus culture out of which student sports fandom and partying comes. Remarkably, they never acknowledge their hypocrisy, even when they tailgate with alums before and after college sports events.

In the 1960s, rebel students often accused university administrators of "selling out" undergraduate education to gain power and perks for themselves, and to keep their institutions running efficiently. Thirty-plus years later, the activities of university officials in charge of beer-and-circus schools adds a new dimension to the term *selling out*.

Another illustration of presidential and administrative misconduct concerns their dealings with the NCAA. Deconstructing a popular myth about the March Madness money provides a way into this subject.

★   ★   ★

Myth: Thanks to the NCAA's billion-dollar TV contract for its Division I basketball tournaments, schools make millions when their teams participate in March Madness, and college officials put this money into academic pro-grams.

Reality: The association distributes the tournament revenue through a complicated formula that sends most of it to the conferences of the partic-ipating schools. Because the BCS football conferences also form the big-time college basketball leagues and dominate the NCAA tourney, they receive the highest percentage of the money. As a result, when a school in a minor conference makes a brief appearance in the men's tourney—thirty-two of sixty-four teams lose in the first round—it receives a low-six-figure check.

On the other hand, if several teams from the same conference enter and reach the final rounds, they and their fellow conference members gain low-seven-figure payouts. With more than three hundred schools in NCAA Di-vision I men's basketball, the minority who receive the million-dollar checks resemble lottery winners. But, like addicted gamblers, all three-hundred-plus schools spend big bucks to enter the Division I basketball season lottery, and most end up holding losing tickets. Athletic directors and coaches drive this process, and university presidents and administrators approve it.

But financial reality never deters fanatic lottery players, especially when they are playing with other people's—in this case, their school's—money. After the announcement of the recent NCAA/CBS television deal, a national newspaper predicted that the increased payout will prompt "a continued migration of schools from lower divisions into the NCAA's Division I to more fully share the wealth." Probably the migration will occur, but the NCAA wealth is a mirage. Economist Andrew Zimbalist states bluntly: The new "CBS contract will have precious little impact on the economics of college sports." According to this expert, of the three-hundred-plus ath-letic departments in Division I basketball operating under the current miltimillion-dollar CBS contract, a tiny percentage "generate black ink in any given year. The prudent bet is that college sports will be in the same financial mess or worse in 2003," when the new NCAA/CBS deal begins, and that the red ink will continue to flow for the length of the contract until 2013.

But, thanks to the media, the public only hears about the NCAA's fab-ulous deals with CBS, and it considers March Madness a financial bonanza for American higher education. The public also believes that the colleges and universities who belong to the NCAA run the association, and they use the TV money to help their academic missions. In reality, the NCAA is a large, autonomous bureaucracy acting primarily out of self-interest, and because almost all members lose money on their college sports programs, they rarely have excess revenue to put into academic programs.

Finally, the March Madness money is not an NCAA share-the-wealth plan with higher education, but trickle-down economics in a slow-drip phase. The bottom line for almost all NCAA members is simple: *Belonging to the NCAA costs much more money annually than they receive from the association.*

Every year, the largest financial drain on NCAA members results from the association's requirement that schools field a minimum number of teams to remain in good standing—for Division I, at least fourteen teams in seven sports. This is a compulsory stake in a very expensive poker game. The motive behind this rule is self-interest: NCAA executives, mainly former athletic directors and coaches, regard the NCAA as a trade association, in business to promote college sports; they are empire-builders, they want athletic programs to be as large as possible, and to employ as many athletic administrators and coaches as possible.

Because, throughout Division I, almost all of a school's fourteen teams lose money every year, the minimum team requirement locks athletic departments and universities into huge annual expenses. Within the context of American higher education, this NCAA rule is an anomaly—no other outside agency forces universities to spend money in this way. Only the NCAA, with its minimum team requirements, totally ignores the financial autonomy of colleges and universities. Currently, this situation occurs during a period of severe financial constraints within higher education, when many parts of the university are experiencing drastic cutbacks.

Ironically, the presidents and administrators who wield the sharpest financial axes at their schools, slashing undergraduate programs and services, are often the men and women on the gravy planes to NCAA events. When these administrators cut academic programs, and then underwrite ever-escalating athletic department costs, they weaken the educational fabric of their schools and increase the beer-and-circus aspects. Furthermore, in the last decade, not one of these officials asked the NCAA to consider changing its team minimum rules, allowing schools to spend less money on their college sports programs. This sends a signal to people inside and out of the university system that, at many Big-time U's, intercollegiate athletics comes before undergraduate education.

Beyond the NCAA minimum team requirements, a huge part of the stake in the association's poker game concerns facilities, not only stadiums and arenas but training structures and state-of-the-art equipment. For a school to remain in Division I-A, the NCAA requires it to have large stadiums and arenas, and to meet attendance levels (see page 34). In the 1990s, many athletic departments either upgraded their facilities or built new ones, often moving the expenses, including the debt-servicing, off their books and onto university ledgers. As always, athletic directors and coaches pressured presidents and administrators to approve the construction—whether the institution could afford the costs or not. Often the ADs and coaches enlisted the sports media and fans in their campaigns.

In 1999, University of Minnesota football coach Glen Mason lobbied for a new stadium for his team, arguing that his program needed to keep up with the recent stadium upgrades at Penn State and Ohio State ($100 million each), and new structures at other schools: "When you look at what is happening nationally with the amount of investments these great academic institutions are making in athletics and football, it's mind-boggling." It is particularly mind-boggling when these investments are compared to the proportionally lower ones that these supposedly "great academic institutions" put into their undergraduate education programs.

Virginia Tech AD Jim Weaver was more honest than Glen Mason about his department's construction spree, not bothering to put academic ribbons on it: "If you are not upgrading your facilities, you are going backward. In college athletics today . . . we're in the game of keeping up with the Joneses. I don't like it, but it's a fact."

Sociologist Harry Edwards calls this the "Athletics Arms Race," and although the Cold War competition ended, College Sports MegaInc. has intensified its version. According to ADs, coaches, and the executives who run their trade association, the NCAA, athletic departments must never stop expanding, and should never reach a spending equilibrium—even though they run continual deficits. A former athletic official at the University of Nebraska explained:

> When we won the national [football] championship at Nebraska in 1994, what we did instantly was continue to expand. That's when we started the project to build skyboxes and expand the stadium and continue to improve facilities.

★   ★   ★

Colossal new football stadiums and basketball arenas, as well as luxury skyboxes, are the most visible symbol of College Sports MegaInc. In addition, in many college towns, big-name coaches build enormous mansions, part of the harvest from their million-dollar annual incomes. As Tony Kornheiser indicated, every coach and administrator in big-time college sports is "getting rich," if not already enormously wealthy. Predictably, the association in charge of College Sports MegaInc. also takes care of its own, and overpays its personnel, particularly its top officials. For example, NCAA executive director Cedric Dempsey receives an annual salary of $650,000, plus multiple perks: his pay is about $450,000 more per year than the average salary of CEOs at America's two hundred largest non-profit organizations, and his perks far exceed most of theirs.

The only consistent financial losers are the schools that belong to the NCAA and furnish the stadiums, arenas, and facilities for its operations. Contrary to one of the most tenacious myths in American society, *the vast majority of colleges and universities do not make money in big-time intercollegiate athletics*. But the myth will never die as long as university officials use it to justify their affection and need for beer-and-circus, particularly as a substitute for quality undergraduate education.

19

COLLEGE SPORTS MEGAINC.
VERSUS UNDERGRADUATE EDUCATION

W hat does College Sports MegaInc. have to do with the undergraduate education programs of the host universities? This chapter considers this crucial issue through the opinions of students across the country.

★   ★   ★

ASK JIMMY JOHN,

Q. HEY JIMMY JOHN: Why is the University president's house so big?

A. The president represents all that is important to our school as an institution of higher learning. These hallowed and noble academic grounds are the fertile fields upon which the future of our nation is grown. And the University president and the house he lives in must demonstrate to all the priority we place on this important mission.

Q. Why is the coach's house even bigger?

A. No comment.

—A college newspaper advertisement for
Jimmy John's Sandwich Shops

This ad for a Midwestern fast-food chain popular in college towns was written by a student. The ad copy is edgy, capturing undergraduate cynicism and unease with the current priorities of Big-time U's. The writer mocks the official line on "higher learning," and then uses a punchline based on the money reality of big-time college sports. But, at the end, like many contemporary undergraduates, this student refuses to engage the implications of the situation.

Similar responses characterized a plurality of replies to a statement in the questionnaire for this book: "Your school emphasizes its intercollegiate athletics program more than its undergraduate education program." Neither positive nor negative answers achieved a majority, and the neutral plurality reflected student uncertainty, cynicism, and doublethink on this issue. Many of the positive responses were also in the doublethink mode.

Men and women, often for different reasons, registered almost identical numbers on the question, but the entire pool of respondents divided sharply according to type of school attended. All of the positive replies came from students at big-time college sports universities: 16 percent "agreed" and 13 percent "strongly agreed" that their schools emphasized sports over education, though some males in the latter cohort added in P.S.'s that they liked it that way. A Clemson senior male articulated a frequently repeated "strongly agree" position:

> Rooting for our teams teaches me a lot more than I've ever learned in class. I've seen coaches and athletes do great things, and I've seen the same people cheat and steal. College sports has introduced me to the real world and, thanks to the Tigers, I'm ready to leave this place and enter that world.

But not all students at Division I-A schools agreed with the questionnaire statement. Negative answers came from undergraduates throughout the Pac-10, Big Ten, and other conferences, particularly students at Stanford, Cal-Berkeley, Northwestern, Duke, and Rice, but a majority of negative respondents attended Division III schools. The total "disagree" number was 11 percent, and "strongly disagree," 24 percent. Some P.S.'s from the latter group also "dissed" the question: "This is dumb," wrote an Emory woman, and "You can't be serious," from a NYU man.

This left 36 percent who "neither agreed or disagreed." Almost all of these respondents were at Division I universities, some at so-called Public Ivies (North Carolina, Virginia, Michigan, and UCLA), but most at other ACC, Big Ten, and Pac-10 institutions. In the P.S. notes of these respondents, many wrote versions of "It's a toss up here," and, "Maybe yes, maybe no, I can't say for sure." Even some honors students at these universities could not decide, a University of Maryland male remarking: "The excellent honors classes begin to balance the mammoth athletic department, but when you consider all the terrible regular courses and the awesome tailgating, it's difficult to say which way the emphasis goes."

Many "neither agree or disagree" respondents also expressed cynicism, offering versions of a University of Kansas junior woman's comments:

> KU knows that being a Jayhawk fan is a lot more fun than going to classes. It doesn't care what we do as long as we pay our money for season tickets, tuition, and everything else. It lets us choose our life here, although sitting at games is a lot more pleasant than sitting in lectures. But we get to choose.

In the entire survey, no other question prompted as high a number of neutral responses. But neutrality on this issue also gives a signal. When students refuse to affirm that their school emphasizes undergraduate education over intercollegiate athletics, they make an adverse comment about their universities. If an institution of higher learning truly carries on that activity, then undergraduates should not have to reflect on this proposition, or respond cynically, or call it a "toss up."

Not a single student at a Division III school agreed with or claimed neutrality on the statement. Some echoed a DePauw University student who remarked, "Classes here are not as great as the administration claims, but the school sure doesn't make a big deal about our college sports teams, even the guys playing on them don't." But most Division III undergraduates offered a version of this Emory junior male's comment: "It's clear that academics come first here. If you don't want it that way, this isn't the school for you."

On the other hand, a majority of respondents at universities in the SEC, Big 12, and Big East conferences, as well as lesser leagues like the Atlantic 10 and Big West, agreed with the statement that their schools overemphasized sports at the expense of education. However, many of the P.S.'s from these positive respondents, particularly women, complained rather than praised this situation. A freshmen female at Kansas State noted, "They treat the jocks a whole lot better than they do regular students here, and it just shows their priorities." A sophomore woman at UMass (Amherst) commented, "This school has brand-new intercollegiate athletic buildings and meanwhile classroom ceilings fall on you. That's where this place is at." In fact, a majority of women who assented to the statement criticized their school's stress on college sports.

*

The answers to another question on the survey—one requesting a written response—also reflected the mixed reactions of Division I undergraduates to their institutions' big-time college sports programs:

> When you are in your hometown or traveling, and you tell someone that you attend your school, what is her or his first comment?

Almost all respondents at Division I universities with famous football and/or basketball teams offered a college sports–related answer. "How's the team look for the coming season" recurred, as did comments about famous coaches. Most Indiana University students offered versions of "Inside the state of Indiana, people say 'I love coach Knight,' " or, "I'm from out-of-state and the first thing non-Hoosiers say is 'Bob Knight is an asshole.' " Some IU students added, "I always reply, 'I love him because he's an asshole, that's why he wins.' "

Another common response concerned the nickname of the school: University of Texas (Austin) students wrote that, as a first comment, many people say "Hook 'em Horns," accompanied by the hand signal; University of North Carolina undergraduates wrote, "Go Heels"; but some students at schools with off-the-field athletic problems encountered negative nicknames. For example, a Florida State senior noted that, instead of "Go Seminoles," many people say, "Go Criminoles." This FSU student also made a cynical prediction: "I tell people that, in today's America, Peter Warrick will soon be doing ads for Dillard's, telling people about the store's special discounts" (Warrick, a FSU football star, was involved in a shoplifting incident at a Dillard's department store).

Students at NCAA Division I institutions with less-controversial championship football and/or basketball teams than FSU's received frequent congratulations for the victories, which they valued. But if their schools' teams were mediocre or worse, they often encountered derision, and despised these remarks. In addition, a significant number of undergraduates, particularly women, at schools with losing *and* winning squads added P.S.'s, typically, "I wish this place was known for something other than its sports teams." Some of these students also commented: "When I go for job interviews, sometimes they only want to talk about the _____" (the team's nickname), and "I wonder if people think that my degree from this place has any value?" In interviews for this book, other students at Division I schools made similar remarks (see page 169).

Students at Division I universities that clearly emphasize academics provided more mixed responses to the open-ended question. A typical Rice

University answer was, "In the Southwest, people say, 'You must be really smart,' but in other places they say, 'I hear Rice is getting good as a school.' " Some Notre Dame students encountered, "Your university is so hard to get into," but many others heard "Go Irish," as well as people singing or humming the "Notre Dame Fight Song." A number of UC-Berkeley undergraduates were asked, "How do you compete against the Asian kids?" and Stanford students, "Have you met Chelsea Clinton?" The latter query contrasts to all the undergraduates at big-time college sports universities who receive, "Have you met _____?" (the name of a famous coach).

Another frequent first comment received by students, particularly those at beer-and-circus schools, were versions of: "Is the tailgating as great as everyone says?"; "Are there still kegs on all the frat house lawns every football weekend?"; and "Has the party scene really moved off-campus?" Students at some big-time U's also encountered location and appearance-of-campus remarks, especially if their school had invested heavily in the look of its buildings and grounds. University of Wisconsin respondents mentioned, "Your campus is really beautiful," as well as alcohol-related remarks, "I hear that beer flows like water at Wisconsin."

In contrast to the Division I responses, students at Division III institutions almost never heard a college sports comment first. Most often, variations on "Your school has a great _____" (the name of an academic program) occurred: a Middlebury College senior filled in "foreign language program"; a number of Emory University students wrote "pre-med" and "business school"; and a Washington of St. Louis sophomore put, "school of architecture." Only one Kenyon College male contradicted this pattern, writing, "great swim teams." In addition, a few Division III students received party comments: a Washington & Lee male wrote, "I hear you guys drink like fish." And some Division III students offered location remarks, usually "Where's _____?" (the name of their small college), especially if in the Midwest.

Finally, despite the mixed nature of the first comments for Division I schools, the overwhelming number of college sports–related remarks about these institutions (87 percent) proves that the NCAA and Division I athletic programs have triumphed. For many Americans, the big-time athletic department *is* the university, and its teams have so imprinted their images upon the public that intercollegiate athletics eclipses the academic programs of the host universities, even those with well-known research departments.

Since the beginning of college sports in the late nineteenth century, a majority of Americans have known more about the football and basketball teams of many universities than about those institutions' educational programs. Nevertheless, for most of the twentieth century, the general public believed that the academic parts of Big-time U's should have priority over their sports entertainment divisions. In the twenty-first century, thanks to the wall-to-wall television coverage of college sports, the traditional education-first view seems to be fading, particularly among younger Americans.

The president of Kansas State University recently remarked that college sports is "the window through which your particular university is viewed. Not that it should be that way, but that's the way it is." The media maintains the window, opening it wide for big-time college sports events and the accompanying festivities, but only offering glimpses of the academic side of these universities. The three-to-four-hour telecasts of major college football games, with their two-minute promo spots on the academic aspects of the schools, indicates the disparity in emphasis. The subtext for viewers is: At these universities, college sports is far more important than undergraduate education.

Kansas State president Jon Wefald understands this phenomenon, and, in his years as head of this school, he has spent millions of dollars on intercollegiate athletics and proportionally little on undergraduate education. As a result, his Wildcat football team managed to achieve national fame in the 1990s, and his general undergraduate education programs continued to limp along. A brief examination of the impact of the K State athletic department on the rest of the university charts the distance between media/public perception and on-campus reality.

The *Chronicle of Higher Education* spotlighted Kansas State in a feature article in 1999. Reporter Welch Suggs discovered that the football team's bowl appearances and high poll rankings had *not* prompted a Flutie Factor jump in admission applications, or a discernible increase in alumni contributions to the university's undergraduate education programs. (See chapter 21 for a discussion on whether big-time college sports programs actually prompt alumni donations.)

The Kansas State president did boast that football success had erased the "loser image" of his school. But that is a circular argument. Kansas State's "loser" reputation resulted from years of losing football teams; if the school had never entered Division I-A college football, and had emphasized undergraduate education, it might have developed another kind of fame, possibly as an outstanding agriculture and technical school.

However, once in the big-time NCAA poker game, K State had to live with losing hands and winning ones, forever strapped into its chair at the table, its national reputation based mainly on sports results.

One element at K State that continued from the losing football years through the winning ones was the party scene. Kevin Allen, an alum of the university, noted that "beer-and-circus is a very accurate description of the atmosphere when I was in school there (1987–1992), and especially for the last six years since the football team has started going to bowl games." Allen added, "Yes, I'm one of those forty thousand fans who follow KSU to bowl games," but he worried that beer-and-circus undermined undergraduate education at his alma mater.

A number of students currently at the school raised similar concerns in their P.S. remarks to the questionnaire for this book. A sophomore male wrote:

> The JUCO [junior college] transfers that star for the Cats have to be among the dumbest students in America. I was in a class with some of them and they could barely read or write. I was embarrassed that they attend the same college I do. But I still bleed purple [the school color] and go on the road with the Cats. . . . I got so drunk at the Alamo Bowl last year that I couldn't remember a single thing. I found out afterward that we lost.

A sophomore female at Kansas State made a more direct comment on the quality of undergraduate education at the school:

> I applied here after I read in the [Yale] *Insider's Guide* about how good and serious the College of Architecture was and how students in it have to spend twenty hours a week in studio. When I came, it turned out that architecture majors take about 9 credit hours of studio work each semester, and so twenty hours a week is not very much. And the program turns out to be fairly mediocre. . . . An architecture major at Rice University told me she spends at least forty hours per week in studio, usually a lot more. And I've found out that Rice is rated one of the leading programs in the country, and K State is way down the list. . . .

Despite her discontent, this student offered a shrewd analysis of academics at K State:

I don't think K State tried to fool me on purpose. What happened in architecture is all part of how K State deludes itself into thinking that it's a good school. They call architecture a "weed out" major and say that it's one of their best. It's true that it's ten times harder than most of the majors here. But so what? Most of the majors are a joke and most K State students spend their time cheering for the Cats and partying, and they couldn't care less about going to school . . . Then the school prints all this stuff about "Excellence in Sports Equals Excellence in Education." They might even believe it but it's complete b.s.

The responses of these Kansas State insiders present a less glowing and positive picture of this university than does the national media. Other than the *Chronicle of Higher Education*'s investigation of the educational and athletic aspects of K State, and *U.S. News*'s ranking the school in the third tier of national universities (institutions that place between 121 and 176 in its ratings), the rest of the national media only peers through the K State college sports window, praising what they call—without irony—"Purple Haze."

In January 2000, *USA Today* applauded K State's rise to football fame, noting that the university had used a clever "formula" for intercollegiate athletic success:

A supportive president, quality coaching, blue-chip recruiting, TV exposure, selling tickets to keep the cash flowing, and "upgrading facilities," jargon for bigger stadiums and fancier locker rooms and weight rooms.

In the corporate world of *USA Today* and College Sports MegaInc., this formula makes perfect sense. The only problem is its disconnection from education, and its dependence on fielding winning teams.

Crucial to winning in college sports is blue chip recruiting and, if the high schools in a state do not produce a sufficient number of blue chip athletes in a sport (the football situation in Kansas), the coach often brings in former JUCO players. Kansas State's rise in the football world parallels the athletic quality of its JUCO transfers, but recruiting these athletes is always a two-edged sword: their athletic talent can produce sports victory, but their educational deficiencies, as mentioned by the K State undergrad above, can generate academic embarrassment.

Undergraduates at Kansas State and many other Big-time U's expressed unease and doublethink about College Sports MegaInc., many of them loving it, particularly the accompanying party scene, and simultaneously questioning its corrupt practices, including star athletes who can "barely read or write." Like all major corporations, College Sports MegaInc. has plans for future expansion and revenue, and it usually projects today's students as tomorrow's fervent rooters. However, the undergraduate responses to the survey for this book indicate very shallow support for big-time college sports among a large segment of the undergraduate population. If these fans do not become future supporters, College Sports MegaInc. could cost Big-time U's even more money than at present.

20

WHO LOVES THE JOCKS?

Recruiting JUCO players reveals the underside of College Sports MegaInc., and their presence on university campuses often prompts negative reactions from regular undergraduates. This chapter continues to explore this situation as well as the surprising student responses to a number of survey questions probing their attitudes toward intercollegiate athletes.

★   ★   ★

We've never admitted junior college athletes to Notre Dame because we don't believe they're real college students or could ever become ones. . . . Maybe we're too strict and we sure miss out on lots of great players that way, but cripes, these guys are pros, hired by schools to play sports. . . .

The NCAA is always talking about student-athletes. If it's really serious about that, it would bar JUCO transfers. The big football and basketball schools will never let that happen because they believe that JUCOs can help them turn around their programs if they hit a bad stretch. And it helps some of the little guys move up in the world.

—Edward "Moose" Krause, former coach and athletic director at
the University of Notre Dame.

"Moose" Krause raised basic questions about the nature of student-athletes on many campuses and, by implication, the conflict between big-time college sports and authentic undergraduate education. An examination of JUCO transfers provides a path into these issues; it also dramatizes the conflicting feelings of regular students about "special admits" for all athletes—a practice that allows intercollegiate athletes to enter universities with ACT/SAT scores far below regular students, and that permits some JUCO transfers to enter without ever taking the ACT or SAT exam.

JUCO athletes usually belong to the cohort of high school athletes who fail to meet the NCAA's minimal academic requirements for playing intercollegiate athletics as freshmen. As a result, they attend junior colleges and, after receiving graduation certificates there, move on to an NCAA school (they lose two years of NCAA playing eligibility in the process). Most important, these athletes are not required to take the SAT/ACT exams or to prove to anyone outside their junior college and the welcoming NCAA school that they can read, write, and count past ten.

Because of the JUCO loophole and the fact that many junior colleges do not provide quality educations, numerous JUCO transfers cannot do university work, even in "gut" courses. In the eyes of regular undergraduates, these athletes come closest to the "dumb jock" stereotype; in interviews, many students express resentment and cynicism about the admission of these athletes to their schools.

A number of questions on the survey for this book also revealed these undergraduate feelings, not just on JUCO transfers but concerning special admissions for all intercollegiate athletes, and concerning the academic privileges that all intercollegiate athletes receive while in college. The large majorities in response to these questions were the most unexpected results on the survey.

Question 11
All intercollegiate athletes should meet the same university entrance requirements as regular students.

Twenty-nine percent of respondents "strongly agreed" with this statement, and 31 percent "agreed." A majority of these positive responses came from students at Division III colleges and women at Division I schools; nevertheless, many men at big-time college sports universities also assented. Almost all the negatives were from males at Division I schools—10 percent "strongly disagreed," and 18 percent "disagreed." In addition, 12 percent were neutral, split evenly between Division I and III schools.

An interesting correlation occurred at Division I schools between the responses and the differences in the average SAT/ACT scores of athletes and regular students: the larger the spread, the higher the percentage of students opposed to special admits for athletes. At the University of North Carolina at Chapel Hill, a school that accepts only 35 percent of all applicants, men's basketball players average 905 out of a possible 1600 on their SATs, and regular undergraduates, 1220. At this university, 82 percent of female, and 60 percent of male respondents disapproved of special admits for athletes. Similar percentages occurred at other schools with situations paralleling UNC–Chapel Hill's. These results imply that if regular students have to work hard to gain admission to their university, they resent other students, even athletes, entering with significantly lower SAT scores. (In contrast, at the University of Alabama, Tuscaloosa, accepting 94 percent of all applicants and with less of an SAT and ACT differential between regular students and athletes, the disapproval numbers were 59 percent female, and 43 percent male.)

In addition, at many schools with selective admissions policies, student doublethink existed on this question. Despite their dislike of special admits, North Carolina undergraduates love and cheer wildly for their "Heels," particularly when they are winning. A Georgetown University junior offered a typical explanation for student doublethink on special admits:

> I busted my ass in high school to get into this place, and I know that some of the basketball players here got almost half the SAT score I did. I also know that there aren't many outstanding athletes with 1600 SATs, or even 1100, and I want our teams to win. So I accept the fact that these low SAT guys are in Georgetown, but I think the system stinks. Then again, our team would be terrible if only regular Georgetown students played. Who knows? *Go Hoyas.* Meet you at the Tombs or Chadwicks [off-campus sports bars].

The following question on the survey prompted an even greater surge of hostile feelings toward the jocks than did the admissions one:

> Regular students should have the same access to academic assistance as intercollegiate athletes (free unlimited tutoring, priority scheduling of classes, et cetera).

Possibly the lack of academic assistance available to regular undergraduates, or jealousy over the perks that athletes receive, caused 43 percent to "strongly agree" and 35 percent to "agree" to equal assistance for all students (these numbers were the most one-sided on the survey). Only 7 percent "strongly disagreed" and another 9 percent "disagreed," with a mere

6 percent remaining neutral. Agreement encompassed almost every respondent at Division III schools, a large majority of women in Division I, and a sizable majority of men at the "Public Ivies" and similar private institutions.

Only some men and a few women at big-time college sports universities in the SEC, ACC, Big 12, and Pac-10 disagreed, often arguing a version of "The jocks work really hard here and deserve extra help." Male respondents from these schools also appeared in the neutral category, adding such cynical P.S.'s as, "Why should academic assistance matter—the jocks pass their courses no matter what?" Also:

> I can't answer this question because I can't believe that schools will ever give the same assistance to regular students that they give to athletes, like having tutors write papers for them, [team] managers take exams for them, and everything else I've seen given to jocks.

A few years ago, *U Magazine* conducted a poll on this topic and discovered similar positive and negative results. It asked, "Athletes—should they be given special treatment?" and only 21 percent of respondents answered yes, versus 79 percent replying no. The comments to *U Magazine* also paralleled many of the P.S.'s to this question on the book survey. A University of Georgia student told *U*, "Yes. It's hard to fit an athletic [training and playing] schedule with an academic schedule." But many more undergraduates replied "No," an Illinois undergraduate recognizing the vocationalism of an athletic scholarship, but showing no sympathy for the jocks' work-filled days: "Athletes should look at their role as a forty-hour-a-week job. I work forty hours a week, and I don't get special treatment."

For all the apparent clarity of the student responses on special admits and academic perks for athletes, the results require an important qualification: They reflect undergraduate attitudes to intercollegiate athletes in the abstract. When students at Division I schools were questioned about specific athletes on their campuses, their opinions shifted and the celebrity of the player became important to them, often triggering a doublethink response.

In chapter 12 of this book, "Cheating," the results to the question on helping "a star athlete at your school . . . cheat on an important exam" revealed much less hostility than the inquiries on perks for abstract intercollegiate athletes: 59 percent of the respondents at Division I schools agreed, sometimes for cynical reasons, to help the star cheat. Even after factoring in the highly negative Division III responses on this question, the "yes" percentage was still higher than the pro-athlete responses to the more general inquiries on special admits and aid for jocks.

Sports journalist Teri Bostian observed this phenomenon at the University of Iowa:

> Regular undergraduates always complain about the special deals the jocks get, and then they turn around and tell you how thrilled they were when they saw Jess Settles [an UI basketball player] or some other star athlete in the student union. They have a real split personality on this one.

Student doublethink can take another complete revolution: undergraduates will speak cynically about star players but almost swoon when they actually meet them. A faculty member at Georgetown University noticed that when basketball star Allen Iverson briefly attended the school, undergraduates "talked about his questionable high school academic record and about [his] run-in with the law," as well as his "cruising around campus in a Mercedes and wearing a Rolex" (Iverson came from a very poor background). Then "when he left the campus for the NBA, students felt not that a fellow student had dropped out, but that an athlete had won an early exit from a basketball camp"—Georgetown's men's basketball program.

Yet, not only did many of these same undergraduates proudly wear their Hoyas basketball regalia, attend home games, and cheer mightily for Iverson when he played for their university, but, in interviews for this book, a number of otherwise cynical Georgetown students almost gushed while telling stories of seeing Iverson in D.C. clubs and following him on club-hopping tours.

At what point does student doublethink about college sports become schizophrenia, so unstable that student fans cannot distinguish between their fantasies and reality? It is also unstable because the media iconography of star college athletes merges with the reality of the athletes' campus lives, and, for many undergraduates, the mixed images make no sense. Do students love the jocks? Yes, no, maybe—sometimes all three reactions at once.

In many ways, intercollegiate athletes possess a saner and more coherent vision of big-time college sports than do the student fans. Their attitude on special admission tends to be straightforward, practical, and vocational. They also show some contempt for regular students, particularly those mired in the collegiate subculture. In a typical comment, a Tulane female tennis player explained:

> I've been practicing and training since I was a little kid. If I had put a tenth of that time into studying, I'd have more than enough SAT points to get in here regularly. But this school brings me to New Orleans to play tennis, *to do a job*, so they should cut me some slack on admission.

The Tulane athlete added: "My SAT scores weren't that much below regular students here, and most of them trained for Tulane by drinking their way through high school . . . [And] that's what they do now while I work at tennis."

Basketball and football players from less privileged backgrounds than the Tulane tennis player offered versions of the same justification. A Boston College football player remarked, "I'm at BC to play football, and the coaches make sure that I do it. If BC let me in with low SAT scores, don't blame me, bitch at the school. Anyway, I made my NCAA number [850]." Paralleling the Tulane athlete's complaint about regular students at the school, the BC player remarked:

> At least I'm not in the bars every night like most of the nonathletes in my dorm. I even go to class in the morning, that's more than you can say for some of those clowns. . . . Don't get me wrong, they're not bad guys, they just don't know the meaning of work.

Similarly, on the issue of special academic privileges, athletes employ the vocational justification, offering a version of "I work hard at my sports job, and I think it's only fair that I get tutoring and other help." They also frequently say, as a University of Texas (Austin) female distance runner remarked: "The tutors are there for you, but by the time I get to their offices at night, I'm so tired that I can barely stay awake. I've been up since 5 A.M. when I hit the roads. . . . I've also run all afternoon."

As for "priority scheduling"—the opportunity to gain places in a class before regular students can register for the course—the web page of the Ohio State athletic department explains that "priority scheduling allows student-athletes to arrange their classes around [sports] practice times." This can help the academic careers of some athletic scholarship holders, but it also places sports ahead of education in other athletes' lives. Because almost every coach holds mandatory afternoon practices, usually from 3 to 6 P.M., this schedule eliminates the possibility of an athlete majoring in or taking classes in any subject that requires lengthy afternoon labs or studio sessions (pre-med, architecture, and many others). Robert Smith, the All-American runner at Ohio State in the early 1990s, complained that the OSU athletic department would not allow him to be a pre-med student; as a result, he left the Big Ten school.

A more common problem for athletes occurs when their hopes and dreams of playing their sport at the professional level conflict with their academic aspirations. As discussed in chapter 11, many Division I athletes have to—and often want to—spend so much time in their sports that they have trouble obtaining a decent education. But every college athlete needs to maintain a minimum GPA to remain eligible for competition. Athletes tend to solve this problem the same way that many regular students, particularly those in the collegiate subculture, solve their eligibility dilemma (not flunking out of school): They take "gut" courses and "mickey" majors. The case of another OSU football star, Andy Katzenmoyer, illustrates this situation.

At Ohio State a few summers ago, priority scheduling enabled Katzenmoyer and a number of his teammates to enroll in three rather easy courses and to remain academically eligible to play that fall. ESPN and *Sports Illustrated* fell upon the story—it perfectly fit their current journalistic styles: classical sentimentality, long paeans to the Buckeyes' glorious football tradition, mixed with hip cynicism about a famous jock's classroom troubles. Overlooked in the media brouhaha was the fact that these courses were open to all Ohio State undergraduates, and, after the athletes' priority registration, regular OSU students filled the classes. Also overlooked was the fact that the average OSU course is not very difficult, and if athletes had more time or inclination for academics, and if hard-drinking undergrads were not so anti-academic or lazy, then neither group would need to take the "guts."

But the sports media rarely examines this reality. Instead in the Katzenmoyer case, it used the "dumb jock" cliché. In fact, he came from a family that stresses education (his parents are high school teachers), but he wanted to be a vocational athlete. He regarded playing college football as "a job, except I'm not getting paid [officially] for it." He noted that, as a freshman, "I came in here and learned the Ohio State defensive system and everything around that in a very short period of time. I wouldn't think they [the media] would say I'm a genius, but they wouldn't say I'm a stupid person." But most media members said exactly that—it fit preconceived notions and made for amusing copy.

Katzenmoyer was typical of many athletes in big-time intercollegiate athletic programs: his full-time sports job was much more engrossing and important to him than taking college courses. Why shouldn't it be? His dream since childhood was to play in the NFL, and he wanted to concentrate fully on his minor league training. The Ohio State franchise in College Sports MegaInc. was the logical place for him at this point in his career. And, after playing that fall, he realized that he was ready for the next professional level, and he entered the NFL.

The Andy Katzenmoyer case illustrates a profound and unresolvable contradiction: College Sports MegaInc. and its franchises insist that their main employees be amateur student-athletes, but these employers also demand that the employees train and perform at the highest possible level (no network pays to televise Oberlin College football games). One result of this contradiction is the infrastructure of questionable courses and majors available to athletes, as well as other Big-time U students.

At this juncture, beer and circus meet, the collegiate subculture and the athletic department joining to subvert the educational ideals of the university—and receiving assistance from the administration and the research faculty who tolerate the existence of academically dubious courses and majors for their own ulterior motives (see chapter 11, "The Faculty/Student Nonaggression Pact").

When reporters ask coaches and ADs questions about athletes taking easy courses, usually athletic department officials become defensive and invoke the Buckley Amendment—"It's against the law to discuss a student's academic file." However, if athletic department people were more savvy, and did not mind upsetting university administrators, they would tell the truth: After the athletic department fills as many slots as it needs in these courses, regular undergraduates jump in and register for the open places. An underenrolled "gut" course is an oxymoron. A Syracuse University professor told the *Chronicle of Higher Education*: "There are innumerable 'guts' on every campus, some of them specially designed for student-athletes," but all of those courses and many others are available to all undergraduates. Moreover, "There are empty degrees, totally hollow degrees out there" awarded to athletes and regular students.

Despite the common interest of athletic scholarship holders and beer-drinking students in their school's "College of Ridiculous Studies," the collegians usually resent athletic department priority scheduling. Perhaps undergraduate jealousy toward all athlete perks causes this hostility, or the more practical objection that priority scheduling allows the jocks first dibs on the easy classes. Whatever the reason, the result shows that many regular students, including those most enthralled by big-time college sports, have mixed feelings about the jocks—unless the team wins big, and it covers the spread, and they meet the athletes personally, and . . .

This contradicts one of the most cherished myths about big-time college sports: It builds school spirit and campus community. That fiction, as well as myths about the importance of big-time college sports in student recruitment, retention, and alumni donations, forms the basis of the "New 3 R's"—the topic of the final chapter of this book.

21

THE NEW 3 R'S

In the 1990s, as undergraduate enrollment and outside funding decreased, many colleges and universities turned to professional consultants to tell them how to solve these major problems. These gurus, always full of jargon, created the "New 3 R's."

        ★   ★   ★

> As an associate of a university planning firm that has assisted more than fifty colleges in developing quality-of-life facilities such as recreation centers and stadiums, I have concluded that these structures play a pivotal role for all students, not just jocks. These facilities are among the keys to the new three R's of higher education—recruitment (of students), retention (of current students) and renewal (of alumni support).
>
> —Jeffrey Turner, an executive with a consulting
> firm specializing in higher education

Brandishing their New 3 R buzzwords, the consultants convinced administrators to pour precious resources into recruitment campaigns for new students, retention efforts to stanch the huge freshmen dropout rate, and fund-raising drives aimed at alumni (renewal). In addition, as Jeffrey Turner explained, the New 3 R's required a commitment of millions of dollars for big-time college sports facilities and programs.

The New 3 R's continue to drive many Big-time U's. That the consultants and the university officials who implement their plans never mention the Old 3 R's—reading, 'riting, and 'rithmetic—indicates how far these schools have drifted from their historic missions. In the twentieth century, although most universities could not truly educate all of their undergraduates, they maintained that goal—at least for public consumption. In the twenty-first century, a growing number of schools will probably substitute the New 3 R's and sports entertainment for general undergraduate education. Whether presidents and administrators do this consciously, or it occurs because of their fixation on enrollment and external funding, the result is the same: Beer-and-circus rules many American campuses, and the Old 3 R's have become passé, as old-fashioned as their name.

Nevertheless, in an ultimate irony, the New 3 R's do not work very well. Recruitment campaigns tied to big-time college sports have very mixed results; for every Flutie Factor success, there are many more anti–Flutie Factor failures—all those losing teams at "loser" schools—and even some of the college sports winners like Kansas State fail to increase enrollment. Retention efforts to keep students at a school mainly succeed at Division III colleges and relatively small Division I universities, not at Big-time U's, and success has little connection to big-time college sports. Finally, contrary to the longtime myth, big-time intercollegiate athletics does not generate significant alumni contributions to the academic parts of a university; the evidence indicates that alumni giving is independent of college sports success or failure, and even national championships mainly produce money from booster fans—not alumni—for the athletic department, and for no other part of the university.

Deconstructing the New 3 R's is not only valuable for its own sake, but also for what it reveals about the present and future of the American research university.

*   *   *

[In recruiting undergraduates, schools should ask] can kids get the courses they want here? Are the classes and advisory system really personal [for students]? Do the teaching faculty and facilities stack up? . . . But instead of grappling with these questions, too many colleges respond by saying, "We can't do much about real value [in our undergraduate education programs]. . . ."

For places like Syracuse [University], this discussion raises the issue of whether we can continue to run a research institution on the back of undergraduate tuition. Is it not time to admit that we have perhaps been too faculty-centered, and will fall behind in today's hectic rush for undergraduates until we can prove that we are indeed student-centered?

—David Smith, dean of admissions and
financial aid at Syracuse University

The honesty and acuity of this college official is unusual. In the article that quoted him, the writer noted that, unlike this dean, most "admissions professionals appear less and less to be part of the academy; they now seem truly external, having little regular engagement with the central [historic] purposes of their institutions." Increasing numbers of admissions personnel do not even work directly for the university; they are outside consultants hired on short- or long-term contracts. The jargon for this procedure is "outsourcing admissions" and, in reality, many of these recruiters are bounty hunters, paid to find and bring back as many applicants for admission as possible, often paid per "warm body."

The bounty hunters do not lack for clients: for every "selective admissions" university like UNC–Chapel Hill, there are twenty de facto "open admission" schools like the University of Alabama, Tuscaloosa. Neither the bounty hunters nor their clients inquire about whether their student prey should attend these universities, or whether these young men and women should even enroll in college at this point in their lives, or ever.

The recruiters often behave like college sports recruiters, sometimes possessing the ability—like their athletic department counterparts—to admit a potential student at the moment he or she assents, bypassing regular admissions procedures. *U.S. News* discussed this technique within the context of the tremendous "pressure to win" that schools exert upon admissions deans, comparing these officials to athletic head coaches "who want to keep their jobs [and] need to chalk up one winning season after another."

So intertwined are the Admissions Office and the athletic department at many schools that they dictate major policy decisions. In 1999, Texas Christian University left the Western Athletic Conference to join Conference-USA, severing historic conference ties with nearby colleague and traditional rival Southern Methodist University, and in-state colleague Rice University. Instead of continuing relations with these similarly private and academically oriented universities, TCU moved to a league of mainly mediocre and far-flung public universities, including East Carolina, Louisville, and Cincinnati.

The TCU athletic director, speaking for the school, explained the decision:

> Most of our out-of-state students come from the midwestern corridor, and as a member of C-USA, TCU will gain exposure to an extremely high percentage of the nation's population, the media centers and large urban areas of the Central and Eastern time zones.

Apparently a recruitment consultant advised the TCU Admissions Office and the athletic department to make the move; the premise of the advice is that TCU will attract greater attention in, and increase the number of applicants from, these population centers. But for this strategy to succeed, the TCU football and basketball teams *have to win*. Otherwise, for many young TV viewers in these central and eastern cities, TCU becomes that religious "loser school" with the weird nickname, the Horned Frogs. (Despite its name, Texas Christian University is a secular institution.) For many decades, TCU has mainly fielded losing teams, and loosening its ties to Texas football might produce even worse squads (the state is one of the great high school recruiting areas in the country, and although TCU is far down the recruiting food chain, it is still on it).

Finally, what did TCU's move to C-USA have to do with the quality of undergraduate education at the school? Nothing. Even its traditional student base—74 percent of its undergraduates are from Texas—is ignored in the move to chase elusive out-of-staters. A more sensible institutional decision would be to copy Rice University: In the last decade that school has massively upgraded its undergraduate education program and put relatively little money into its athletic department; in the process, it often produced losing football and basketball teams, and gained a national reputation for academic excellence.

Rice now ranks sixteenth on *U.S. News*'s national university list, but TCU remains in the second tier, schools between 51 and 120. Texas Christian University is not as wealthy as Rice, but it is a well-funded institution; instead of pouring millions into its athletic department, TCU could put that money into undergraduate education. But it wants to chase the elusive Flutie Factor and hope that sports victories, if they come, will translate into increased applications for admissions. This tactic seems perilous and shortsighted, as well as anti-educational. Even in terms of the New 3 R's, the strategy seems counterproductive: Rice's current freshmen retention rate is 95 percent versus TCU's 80 percent, and most of the C-USA schools acknowledge even lower rates, some below the national average of 75 percent.

But tell that to the consultants who preach the New 3 R's. When pressed about the Flutie Factor, they quickly point to schools like Texas A & M and the University of Texas at Austin, and they correctly claim that these big-time college sports programs help attract students. The consultants leave out the part about how these schools have very old and successful—*winning*—college sports teams, as well as famous football weekends and year-long party scenes. In addition, for many applicants, part of the beer-and-circus attraction of UT (Austin) and Texas A & M are their

252 | BEER AND CIRCUS

famous rivalry games against each other and against Big 12 powerhouses like Nebraska and Colorado. What C-USA rivals will appear on TCU's schedule to attract large numbers of TV viewers and potential applicants for admission? Will the C-USA members mentioned above, or others like Memphis or Alabama-Birmingham, become TCU's big rivals and generate the high TV ratings? The chances of the annual TCU-Cincinnati game outdrawing Texas-Nebraksa are almost nil.

Finally, the first New R—recruitment—is mainly smoke and mirrors, not able to withstand scrutiny or the reality of big-time college sports.

★   ★   ★

Vanishing Freshmen
One in Four Nationally Does Not Return for Sophomore Year . . .
Retention is generally higher at private schools—where students tend to get more individual attention—than at public schools. It is higher at smaller colleges, where students are less likely to feel lost in the throng.

In some cases, the school imposes obstacles [to retention], such as requiring freshmen to attend . . . numerous large lecture classes.
—*U.S. News* college issue, 2000

The consultants maintain that big-time college sports programs help keep freshmen on campus and returning for their sophomore year. Big-time U's would be more likely to improve their retention rates if they ignored this piece of advice and imitated Division III colleges and small Division I schools like Rice. Those institutions employ a simple retention formula, one that has nothing to do with big-time intercollegiate athletics: They hire and reward faculty for teaching undergraduate courses; they limit class size and offer few lecture courses; and they build authentic communities of teachers and students. This final achievement contradicts *one of the major myths about big-time college sports: At huge, impersonal institutions, it provides a central rallying point, bringing all elements of the university together into a real community.*

This myth is the cornerstone of the consultants' argument for emphasizing big-time college sports: Not only will it keep freshmen on campus, but they will become so attached to the campus community—their fellow students and the faculty—that they will remain until they graduate, and then they will evolve into loyal and generous alumni. Examining this myth is the best response to the second New R.

*

On occasion, particularly when a school's team wins a national title, the myth appears to be true; in reality, because of the idiosyncratic and artificial nature of the championship—the necessity of sweeping through an entire season and tournament, and the immense amount of media attention—at best, great sports success helps Big-time U's develop random, occasional communities, not permanent ones. And annually, for every university with a NCAA Division I-A football title, more than 110 schools lose out; and for every Division I men's basketball champion, more than 310 also-rans exist.

The results to the questionnaire for this book revealed that at most Division I universities, undergraduates hold mixed and frequently incoherent attitudes about their school's big-time intercollegiate athletics program, and the athlete/performers on the teams. Students increasingly endorse the maxim: Winning isn't everything, it's the only thing. When the high-profile teams fail to win, undergraduates often become indifferent to their school's entire intercollegiate athletic program. Even when the football or basketball teams triumph, students exhibit a high degree of doublethink and cynicism. In addition, the best of times for athletic departments often become the worst of times for student fans: athletic departments with top men's basketball teams sell so many seats to alumni and boosters that large numbers of undergraduates cannot obtain tickets to games and become upset and angry. Added to these student grievances is the massive and ongoing undergraduate resentment toward "the jocks" and their many privileges and special deals: the resulting negativity heightens, rather than alleviates, student alienation toward Big-time U's. It certainly does not help the retention rate.

How does big-time college sports affect another key part of the university community—the faculty—and does it bring them closer to their students, aiding retention? At research universities, most professors live in the academic subculture and pay scant attention to their schools' sports teams. They hold the minority of their colleagues who are fans in contempt, especially those academics who serve on Faculty Athletic Committees, and they are indifferent to their students' college sports concerns. The one aspect of big-time intercollegiate athletics that attracts widespread faculty interest is the $1 million-plus annual income deals given to some of the coaches on their campuses. Unlike students who admire these men for their celebrity, most faculty regard them suspiciously, astounded by their entrepreneurial skills and the school's concessions to them. For faculty, the old-time image of the avuncular, unpretentious coach has been replaced by the

Armani-suited VIP traveling on a private jet to a $20,000-plus speaking engagement and, on the return flight, stopping and interviewing for his next job. (Some "faculty stars" at research universities show more envy than distaste for the contemporary celebrity coach.)

Even a national championship does not entice research faculty into the temporary, feel-good camaraderie on campus. A University of Kentucky professor remarked after that school's 1996 NCAA men's basketball title:

> The students love the championship and went crazy about it. But as far as I'm concerned, it just makes my professional life more difficult. When I go to meetings, colleagues from around the country constantly ask me how I can teach at a university that emphasizes basketball over everything else. I tell them that that isn't true, but they don't believe me. I'm a specialist in my field, and I want to talk to people about my work, not the Wildcats. . . . I'm embarrassed and angry that this school is known more and more for sports, and nothing academic gets any attention. It gets worse after every sports scandal and after every championship. There's no breaking the UK sports cycle.

The Kentucky professor had to live through another NCAA basketball championship in the late 1990s, as well as a controversy about whether to build a new state-of-the-art arena to replace a large and serviceable one. Nevertheless, at the University of Kentucky, many faculty members still feel attached to the school; at some other Big-time U's, a majority of professors are loyal to their research careers and little else. Whatever their feelings, big-time college sports definitely does not bind the faculty to the campus community, or attach them to their students, helping the retention rate.

Finally, even the athletic department and its employees, especially the athletes, often feel alienated from the rest of the university. At most Big-time U's, not only are the intercollegiate sports facilities on the geographic fringes of the campus, but the coaches create—and the athletes live in—a separate world. The physical part of Jockdom contains stadiums, arenas, training facilities, and athlete housing (usually off-campus apartment buildings or remnants of jock dorms). The mental aspect includes attitudes about work and frequent contempt for outsiders, particularly regular students. Coaches warn high-profile football and basketball players to avoid "jock sniffing" students; and coaches and most athletes harbor the traditional vocational contempt for "lazy collegians." In terms of the community created by big-time intercollegiate athletics, the men and women who should form its core are often the people on campus most detached from it.

Compounding this irony is the fact that the retention rate for freshmen intercollegiate athletes at most Big-time U's is below the national average of 75 percent for regular first-year students. This occurs because many coaches, after viewing new recruits at the intercollegiate level, decide that some of them will not help the team win, and "suggest" strongly that the athlete transfer to another school, freeing up the athletic scholarship. In addition, some freshmen athletes do not get along with the coach or cannot adjust to the work demands and stress of big-time college sports, and leave the school.

In contrast, the retention rate of athletes at Division III institutions is in the 90 percentile range. A female discus thrower at Ohio Wesleyan explained: "The Division III philosophy puts academics first. When I told my coaches that I was really interested in studying abroad" this summer, "their answer wasn't, 'You're going to miss preseason [practice],'" as it would be in Division I, "it was 'go ahead.'" As a result, this truly amateur student-athlete felt an attachment to her school that transcended the world of the athletic department, and she connected to the traditional and authentic values of college community. In Division I, the athletic department priority is to produce winning teams; in Division III, it is to allow athletes to develop as students.

In this way, Division III schools attempt to build communities based on shared values and goals, and to encourage open discourse among members. Sometimes these communities are fragile and they dissolve, but often they coalesce, providing all participants with extremely valuable experiences. In contrast, the best that a Big-time U can produce is the superficial coming together of fans in a stadium, arena, or bar for a few hours' time. If their team wins, they enjoy and share the experience; if it loses, the synthetic community quickly evaporates. If these fans consume enough alcohol in conjunction with the sports event, they achieve the false euphoria of a group of party-goers, some also lapsing into unpleasant or dangerous behavior.

Of all the justifications for universities to spend millions of dollars on big-time college sports programs, the second New R—it builds community and helps retention—is the shakiest.

Then there is the third New R—renewal. Many myths about intercollegiate athletics endured through the twentieth century and beyond, but the one most deserving of a silver stake through its heart is the contention that universities need big-time college sports programs to attract alumni donations, and the more the teams win, the more money the alums give to Old, now New Siwash.

★   ★   ★

Repeat after me: There is no empirical evidence demonstrating a correlation between athletic department achievement and [alumni] fundraising success. A number of researchers have explored this putative relationship, and they all have concluded that it does not exist. The myth persists, however, aided by anecdotal evidence from sports reporters who apparently spend more time in bars than in development [fund-raising] offices.

—Richard W. Conklin, vice president
of the University of Notre Dame

Many studies indicate that alumni giving is independent of college sports success or failure, and has no relation to whether a school has a big-time intercollegiate athletic program or not. Yet, the myth continues; central to its perpetuation are the University of Notre Dame Fighting Irish. Currently, many members of the sports media claim that because the famous Notre Dame football program is in a "down period," ND alumni are angry and closing their checkbooks to the school's fund-raisers. This is not true. Notre Dame alums feel intense loyalty to their university, in large part because of its historic emphasis on undergraduate education and the bonds that, as students, they established with faculty, staff, and fellow undergraduates. As a result, ND alums support their alma mater during good times and bad, and they give as much money—often more—during losing football seasons as during championship years. As Richard Conklin suggests, the sports media should exit the saloon and examine nonsports parts of the university.

A major element of Notre Dame's fund-raising success is its concept of "Notre Dame Family." The freshmen class, less than two thousand men and women, join it and remain within it for the rest of their lives. Many Big-time U's also try to use this concept of "family" but fail; they attempt to include legions of freshmen into a "family" of twenty-five thousand or more students on campus and a multitude of graduates. Freshmen at these schools cannot feel attached to more than a hundred thousand of their "closest friends." For many students at Big-time U's, alienation begins at entrance, continues through their undergraduate careers, and turns them into indifferent, often hostile, alumni. The size and success of the school's intercollegiate athletic program rarely changes this attitude.

Contrary to the myth that big-time college sports equals alumni donations, the formula for extracting maximum dollars from alums involves education. In addition to establishing an authentic sense of university family, a school must provide undergraduates with a quality education. Subsequently, if its graduates are pleased with what they learned and proud of their degrees, they want "to give something back" to their alma mater and continue a lifetime relationship with it. The "Alumni giving" rankings in *U.S. News*'s annual college issue indicate that schools using this formula raise much more money from their alums than do Big-time U's that neglect undergraduate education. For example, the magazine rates Notre Dame fourth in "Alumni giving" (it also ranks ND nineteenth on its national university list, and notes that the school has a 97 percent freshmen retention rate).

The proponents of the third New R should examine the *U.S. News* "Alumni giving" rankings. Other than Notre Dame and Duke, no other NCAA Division I-A football school makes the top-ten list (and some observers question whether Duke plays I-A football). Instead, the usual suspects—institutions famous for their quality undergraduate education programs and relatively small student bodies—dominate the "Alumni giving" list. From Number 1 to 10 are: Princeton, Dartmouth, Yale, Notre Dame, Harvard, Cal Tech, Duke, MIT, Penn, and Brown.

The schools through the teens also feature non-big-time college football teams, and although several are in Division I-A, only one, Stanford, has had outstanding football success in recent years. From Number 11 down are: Rice, Lehigh, Wake Forest, Emory, Chicago, Cornell, Stanford, Washington of St. Louis, and Brandeis. Again, all of these universities have relatively small student bodies and provide their undergraduates with a first-rate education.

Undoubtedly, that education helps their graduates gain good jobs, earn lots of money, and give some of it back to their alma maters. Yet, if big-time college sports universities also provided quality educations to all of their students, wouldn't they head the "Alumni giving" list? After all, these institutions graduate thousands upon thousands of students every year, and simply by weight of numbers, they should bulldoze the smaller schools in "Alumni giving." Instead, such Big-time U's with top college sports teams as Wisconsin (Madison), Michigan, UCLA, Texas (Austin), and the University of Washington rank, respectively, 126, 128, 134, 136, and 144 on the *U.S. News* "Alumni giving" list.

These statistics contradict the myth that big-time college sports generates alumni dollars. One of the reasons for the reality is the fact that many successful alums of Big-time U's obtained their education *despite* these institutions, not because of them, and these men and women were alienated as students and remain so as graduates. A University of Minnesota (Twin Cities) alum reflected on her experience:

> Minnesota was the meanest institution that I ever dealt with. It was large, impersonal, authoritarian, and downright mean. I managed to get a good education there, but I developed zero affection for the school. . . . These days Minnesota fund-raisers call me up all the time for money and I have given the school exactly $1 in the almost twenty years since I graduated. As for the football and basketball teams, I wish them well, but they have nothing to do with the academic parts of Minnesota and never have or will.

According to *U.S. News*, only 8 percent of Minnesota alumni give annually to the school, and its national ranking is off the magazine's charts.

Nevertheless, the big-time college-sports-equals-alumni-giving myth continues, in part because athletic departments claim to raise millions of dollars in donations to the university every year, and the media never examines this money, or asks why it is given, or where it ends up in the institution. This money trail begins with the alumni and the boosters.

At Big-time U's, a small percentage, usually in single digits, of alumni contribute annually to the school's intercollegiate athletics program (a similarly low percentage donate to its educational programs). However, often the main contributors to athletic departments are boosters—rabid sports fans who, unlike alumni, never attended the institution and whose interest in it focuses almost exclusively on its college sports teams. Within the context of college sports finances, because of the constant deficits, every alum and booster dollar obtained by an athletic department remains in its cashbox, soaking up a bit of red ink.

These alumni and booster dollars are clearly not gifts to the academic parts of the university, but are they donations at all? Only if one accepts a College Sports MegaInc. tax scam. In reality, the majority of this alum and booster money goes to purchase seats at football and basketball games. At schools where ticket demand outpaces supply, athletic departments call season tickets "priority" items, adding a large "priority" surcharge to the low face value of the seat and pricing the package as high as the market will bear. Because of the NCAA's lobbying power in Congress, 80 percent of the surcharge is now deemed a tax-deductible donation to higher education, and a similar deduction applies to the "priority" rental and purchase of skyboxes in college stadiums and arenas. No matter what the Congress, the NCAA, and member universities want to call this money, because Joe Alum and Booster Bob would not obtain their seats or boxes without paying the "priority" surcharge, their dollars are simply the cost of admission to a sports event—definitely not gifts to higher education.

Nevertheless, many Big-time U's claim these "priority" purchases as alumni donations and use them to inflate their fund-raising statistics. This ploy adds stadiums and arenas full of "priority" fans to the institution's "Alumni giving" totals. Yet, most of these Big-time U's still do not break into U.S. News' Top 100 in this category.

The final irony of the big-time college-sports-equals-alumni-giving myth is that, at many schools, the athletic department actively undermines efforts to raise money from alumni for educational programs. Often athletic department fund-raisers compete with regular university development (fund-raising) officers for dollars from the same alum. Because of the "Athletics Arms Race," intercollegiate athletic programs always need new and bigger facilities, and they try to get wealthy graduates to pay for them. After Joe Alum gives $250,000 for the "Joseph J. Alumnus Weight-Training Vestibule," usually he has no desire to donate $250,000 to the College of Arts and Sciences.

Big-time college sports hurts alumni fund-raising efforts in other ways. As many universities have discovered, publicity from intercollegiate athletics is a two-edged sword, generating attention and feel-good camaraderie when the teams are winning; but when a scandal occurs, the sword swings back, drawing buckets of negative media coverage and public scorn. During times of scandal, some alumni become embarrassed by and angry at their school; they blame its administrators for lack of control of the athletic department, and they close their checkbooks.

The alumni of Southern Methodist University, after enduring major football scandals in the mid 1980s, punished their alma mater for a number of years, contributing much less to its educational programs than they had during prescandal times. Moreover, the winning-while-cheating years at SMU had not produced an increase in alumni donations, but the scandals caused a significant decrease. (In addition, boosters, not alumni, caused the SMU debacle, and although athletic departments like to call these people "Friends of the University," boosters are usually the most dangerous and unreliable of associates, often causing scandals and other maladies, and doing nothing positive for the academic side of the university.)

All of these arguments should drive a silver stake into the heart of the big-time college-sports-equals-alumni-giving myth, but athletic department personnel and Big-time U administrators will not allow this to happen. Perpetuating the myth is in their self-interest—it provides one of the most popular justifications for big-time college sports. Its speciousness will never negate its power. As long as athletic directors want to grow their empires and university officials encourage them to do so, the myth will live on.

For all of College Sports MegaInc.'s endorsement of the myth, the real winners in alumni giving are those Division III and Division I institutions that provide undergraduates with quality educations and turn them into dependable and generous alumni. It never occurs to the proponents of College Sports MegaInc. that the Ivy League schools—the founders of intercollegiate athletics—had a reason for dropping out of big-time college sports, and that many wealthy Division III schools have a similar reason for not entering it. The officials of these institutions believe that a major sports entertainment enterprise on their campuses is incompatible with their academic missions.

But these schools, beyond their desire to give their students a first-rate education, also act out of self-interest: their institutional health depends upon their alumni, and they realize that if they provide mainly beer-and-circus to their undergraduates, this insubstantial diet will not build devoted alums, men and women whom the school can count on for ongoing contributions and support.

The most prominent alumni of a school often become members of its Board of Trustees, making general policy and guiding the institution through the present and into the future. In the 1950s, the trustees of Ivy League colleges and universities, in concert with a group of farsighted Ivy presidents, removed their schools from big-time intercollegiate athletics and, at the same time, committed them to excellence in undergraduate education. Unfortunately, both then and later, the trustees of public research universities allowed their schools to go in the opposite direction, enlarging their intercollegiate athletics programs and diminishing their undergraduate education ones. Indeed, many trustees of Big-time U's were (and are) rabid supporters of big-time college sports, not only condoning all of its sins but sometimes participating in them.

In late 1998, *Trusteeship* magazine—the main journal for American college and university trustees—warned:

Much of the public believes higher education institutions are com-
promising their academic integrity in the name of [big-time] intercollegiate athletics. . . . The public has come to view college athletics
as far more about entertainment and winning than about education.
As a result, more boards [of trustees] will face the unpleasant challenge of determining just how much damage to institutional integrity
the institution can absorb as a result of the perception that big-time
college athletics are out of control.

In addition, as this book disclosed, the party scene on many campuses—
the "beer" accompaniment to the college sports "circus"—is also out of
control, and extremely detrimental to undergraduate education.

Meanwhile the trustees and administrators of many Big-time U's react
to these problems by calling in the consultants with their New 3 R formulas. However, the solution is simple and proven daily at numerous Division III and some Division I schools: Bring back the Old 3 R's, and then
recruitment, retention, and renewal will take care of themselves.

CONCLUSION

WHAT SHOULD HAPPEN

VERSUS

WHAT PROBABLY WILL HAPPEN

This book has presented a detailed critique of current conditions at large, public research universities and in big-time college sports. Two logical questions arise: Can the neglect of general undergraduate education end, and Can genuine reform come to big-time intercollegiate athletics? The answer to both questions is yes, but that response immediately prompts two other questions: Are Big-time U's willing to alter their values and internal cultures in order to change, and Is College Sports MegaInc. capable of downsizing and allowing the majority of athletes to gain meaningful educations? Therefore, the book must conclude on two tracks: What Should Happen versus What Probably Will Happen.

The aim of the What Should Happen proposals is to nourish the academic ethos at large, public research universities and to dampen the collegiate subculture, particularly the drinking scene. However, eradicating alcohol consumption on American campuses is an impossible objective; the goal should be to transform High Binge student populations to Low Binge ones. This can occur only with the deflation of beer-and-circus at Big-time U's.

No matter what proposals are made, the one certainty is that current conditions within general undergraduate education and big-time college sports are so unstable that major changes will happen in the next decade whether Big-time U's want them or not.

★   ★   ★

What I would like to ask . . . the colleges and their professors is this: If you are so upset about the number of students who need remedial courses, why did you accept these kids in the first place?

Let's face it; there's only one reason: money. If these schools didn't take in kids from the bottom of the academic barrel, many [schools] would have to fire half their faculty and administrators; a few would have to shut down.

—Patrick Welsh, an Alexandria, Virginia, high school teacher

First Proposal: Large, public research universities must slim down, losing millions of students and, in a trim mode, offer quality undergraduate education to all students who legitimately qualify for entrance.

Diet experts constantly point out that going on a diet does not produce permanent weight loss—changing one's diet does. Patrick Welsh indicated that many colleges and universities accept applicants who need remedial work in basic subjects and who do not belong in higher education at this point in their academic careers. One survey ascertained that, in 1995, almost 30 percent of all incoming college students required remedial courses in English and math; more recent studies indicate that the number of freshmen in need of remediation has increased. College professors complain about having to "dumb down" many courses to accommodate these students, but faculty never insist that their schools admit only those applicants who demonstrate in SAT/ACT and college placement tests that they can do university work.

A corollary of the first proposal is this: Raise admissions standards and persuade applicants who need remedial work to go to community and junior colleges—institutions that specialize in remediation and will become better schools with the added tuition revenue. For these students, the extra years spent in improving academic skills will not only prepare them for university work but also permit them to mature and to value higher education. At present, too many unprepared and immature students enter universities, and, immediately turned off by the large lecture courses and other educational impediments, they embrace the collegiate subculture, never emerging from it. These students waste their tuition dollars and would be better off if, after high school, they attended junior college or entered the workforce. Later in their lives, when willing to acquire university-level skills and serious about earning a degree, they will benefit from higher education.

This proposal would mean a sharp reduction in enrollment at Big-time U's with residential campuses, and it would allow them to improve the quality of their undergraduate education programs. Indeed, the objective of Big-time U's should be to transform general undergraduate education into one large honors program. Crucial to this mission is the premise of the next proposal: Establish a clear distinction between researchers and teachers.

Second Proposal: Universities should separate pure research from graduate programs.

Because corporate America is increasingly involved in university research, schools should establish their pure research programs as profit-making institutes, mainly funded by corporations (as opposed to the current situation where universities often pick up the tab while doing corporate work).

A corollary of the second proposal is this: Allow the market to dictate the size and role of each university's research institute. Undoubtedly, this would cause a massive shake-up in higher education. The top research institutes would thrive, but mediocre and poor ones would fail, probably most of the research programs at Upward Drift universities would be becalmed and then sink, with very little loss to the world.

In this new system, some current graduate students would become well-paid research assistants at the successful institutes, eventually working their way up the corporate institute ladder. Schools can reward them with advanced degrees, but they cannot burden them by also requiring them to work as teaching assistants in undergraduate courses.

Third Proposal: Hire, promote, and reward faculty primarily for teaching undergraduates, and very secondarily for research, with some of their research devoted to pedagogy.

Big-time U's, as part of their massive weight loss, must shrink their graduate programs and stop pursuing ever-elusive research prestige with them. The money saved from reducing enormously expensive graduate programs should be shifted into undergraduate education, covering the shortfall of dollars in that area caused by the loss of tuition revenue (all those non-admitted students who went to JUCOs or entered the workforce).

The separation of pure research and undergraduate education will allow the remaining and slimmed-down noninstitute graduate programs to emphasize teaching above research, to have grad students take courses in pedagogy and, ultimately, to enable them to enter undergraduate classrooms willing and able to do a good job.

Fourth Proposal: Abolish teaching methods that turn undergraduates into passive receptacles; emphasize interactive, inquiry-based learning.

Abolish almost all lecture classes; establish small classes where students and instructor constantly interact. Undergraduate courses should teach students to retrieve information by using the new technologies—instead of passively receiving data in lecture courses. Classroom time should focus on process—not product—learning; in other words, learning to think critically and processing information.

In *Reinventing Undergraduate Education*, the Boyer Commission offered an excellent plan for each year of an undergraduate's academic career. It began with:

Construct an Inquiry-based Freshman Year
The first year of a [student's] university experience needs to provide new stimulation for intellectual growth and a firm grounding in inquiry-based learning and communication of information and ideas.

The Boyer Commission suggested the abolition of lectures for freshmen and an emphasis on interactive learning; but it also argued that faculty members should continue their serious research activities *and* teach freshmen in labor-intensive ways. As discussed in chapter 8, "The Great Researcher = Great Teacher Myth," very few professors can conduct important research and teach intensively at the same time. Therefore, in designing a system that serves the vast majority of undergraduates and faculty members, choices have to be made—in this case, on the side of teaching. Allow the great researchers to work full-time in the research institutes, and the great teachers to inhabit the undergraduate classrooms.

The Boyer Commission followed its recommendations for freshmen with:

Build on the Freshmen Foundation
The freshmen experience must be consolidated by extending its prin-
ciples into the following years. Inquiry-based learning, collaborative experience, [high-level] writing and speaking expectations need to characterize the whole of a research university education.

In addition to continuing interactive learning for each student, the commission suggested "long-term mentorship": a faculty member taking an undergraduate under his or her wing and serving as a faculty advisor and mentor. Obviously, this proposal would benefit student and professor. However, few activities are more labor-intensive and time-consuming for a faculty member, particularly because he or she would mentor a substantial number of students throughout their undergraduate careers. Again, the Boyer Commission has to acknowledge that for faculty members to engage in this activity, they must be teachers first and foremost, not full-time or even half-time researchers.

According to the commission, the student's undergraduate education should "culminate with a capstone experience: The final semester(s) should focus on a major project and utilize to the fullest the . . . skills learned in the previous semesters." Currently, honors programs require this of most of their students—an honors thesis is a typical and valuable "capstone" of the years spent in the program—but a faculty member must spend a significant amount of time working with each undergraduate on his or her major project. The current honors thesis system succeeds because an individual professor directs a small number of honors dissertations per year; what would occur when faculty have to direct many students in this endeavor? Only a full-time commitment to teaching would enable the average professor to undertake "capstone experiences" on a large scale.

Fifth Proposal: Require all undergraduates to attain a minimum score on the Graduate Record Exam (GRE) before they receive their bachelor's degrees.

Because of the current debasement of general undergraduate education, the questionable nature of many college degrees, and the lack of proof that a graduating senior has actually learned anything in college, universities should agree to a standard "outcomes and assessment" test. Despite the controversies surrounding all national tests, many authorities accept the Graduate Record Exam (GRE) as the best one in existence, presently required of graduating seniors for entrance to most graduate schools. In addition, the GRE is free of the controversies about cultural and racial biases that burden the SAT exam.

Alexander Astin, after testing more undergraduates than any other higher education expert has ever done, concluded that the GRE

> measures at least three cognitive skills that undergraduate education is supposed to facilitate: facility with language, scientific and mathematical skills, and analytic and problem-solving skills. . . . As a consequence, developing the undergraduate student's ability to perform well on these tests should be an important goal of any undergraduate program.

The GRE does not test information acquisition; for example, "Was *Taming of the Shrew* written by William Shakespeare or Christopher Marlowe? The GRE assumes that students wanting to know the answer to this and other factual questions can quickly retrieve them from electronic databases. The GRE attempts to test whether a person has learned how to process information, including the facts in databases; whether a student can make sense of verbal and mathematical entities; and whether a student can solve a large variety of cognitive problems.

Most important, the GRE assumes that after four years of undergraduate education, a student has attained a high level of cognitive skills. Universities now require minimum GRE scores for entrance to advanced-degree programs; they should also use a minimum score as a requirement for graduation. The GRE component will certify the value of the student's degree.

An ancillary benefit of the GRE graduation requirement would be the elimination of "gut" courses and "mickey" majors. To obtain a decent GRE score, a student would have to take meaningful courses; "guts" and "mickeys" would be a waste of time. Hopefully, under this system, these courses and majors would disappear from the university.

The proposal on the GRE exam provides an appropriate transition from What Should Happen at Big-time U's to What Probably Will Happen. If, in the year 2000, these schools instituted a minimum GRE score as a graduation requirement, probably many of their baccalaureate students would fall far below the minimum, revealing how little they had learned during their time in college, and the impoverished state of general undergraduate education at Big-time U's. In fact, the huge gap between the GRE scores of the honors students and the regular undergraduates would provide further proof of the current neglect of general undergraduate education.

★　★　★

> Big state universities are like ocean liners that set sail ages ago, and are somewhere on the ocean, and no one knows for sure where they're going. When you get to be president of one of these schools, you think that you can make major changes but, really, you are just a ship captain who gets his hands on the wheel in the wheelhouse, and as hard as you try, the best you can do is turn the ship maybe a half degree to starboard. . . . That's why these schools never really change, that's also why a president can never really get control of a big-time athletic department.
>
> —William Atchley, former president of Clemson
> University, and of the University of the Pacific

President Atchley made his comments a decade ago during a major economic recession and at a demographic low point in the enrollment history of the modern Big-time U. He believed that large, public universities required reforming, but he was pessimistic about whether fundamental changes would take place. Ten years later, the need for reform is greater, but because we live in one of the most unusual eras in American history—the longest period of prosperity on record—the current money flow and the increased enrollments mask the basic problems in higher education, temporarily paving them over with dollars.

Some Big-time U's have thrown cash at their general undergraduate education programs, hiring more part-time instructors, employing more graduate-student teaching assistants, sometimes even creating freshmen seminars taught by faculty—but then setting up large sophomore- and junior-level lecture courses to compensate for the seminars. These schools have also put more money into their honors programs than ever before. Many university officials claim that these changes—superficial and cosmetic—provide proof that Big-time U's are solving systemic problems.

The media, never inquiring deeply into higher education, has headlined the nips and tucks as substantive reforms. For example, *U.S. News* began its 2000 college issue with a feature article titled, "The Big Are Getting Better," and subheaded, "Research universities are working to put their undergraduates first." (The writers of this piece should have read *U.S. News*'s charts on the increasingly high faculty/student ratios at Big-time U's, and the growing percentage of classes with more than fifty students—statistics that contradict "the big are getting better.")

These days, economists discuss how the "wealth effect" generates improvident personal spending; an analogous term for the current attitude of higher education officials is the "fat, dumb, and happy effect." During the late 1980s and early 1990s, the crisis caused by economic recession and low enrollment did not produce significant changes in general undergraduate education; the current "good times" have had even less effect. However, as pointed out in this book, public funding for higher education keeps decreasing, and a future recession could hit colleges and universities much harder than did any previous one (see page 95).

Yet Big-time U's pursue "prestige maximization" for their research and graduate programs with a greater zeal than ever before, and Upward Drift universities are the worst offenders. As one expert noted: "Being at the top of the [research] heap is the quintessential *positional good*" for these institutions, but the top "is limited by its very nature to a few winners—but all can aspire." And degrade the quality of their general undergraduate education programs in the process.

For the above reasons, and all of the other ones stated in this book, fundamental change Should Happen at Big-time U's, but Probably Will Not

Happen. As a result, one possible scenario is a decline in importance of general undergraduate education: Big-time U's are delivering such an inferior product that corporate America might intervene and supplant them. John Chambers, the head of Cisco Systems, one of the most successful Internet companies, recently told the *New York Times*:

> If universities don't reinvent their curriculum and how they deliver them for an increasingly Net-driven economy, many students . . . will "go to school" on-line. Many big firms—Cisco, G.E., I.B.M., AT&T—are starting on-line academies to train new employees and to constantly upgrade the skills of existing ones.

In other words, many undergraduates currently receive educations of no use to them and their future employers. Therefore, unless schools radically retool, corporations will start to educate an increasing number of Americans, enabling them to skip a university education.

Higher education has survived challenges from other technologies, and accommodated to them. The industrial revolution in the nineteenth century did not end the American college system but forced it to change, making it stronger and more vibrant as a result. But this alteration took many decades; the Internet revolution is moving much more quickly and also leaping over national boundaries. John Chambers of Cisco Systems commented:

> Unlike in the industrial revolution when you had to be in the right country or city to participate, in this new era capital will flow to whichever countries and companies install the best Internet and educational capabilities.

Big-time U's, with their residential campuses in college towns like Boulder, Colorado, will either adapt or experience massive enrollment drops, with increasing numbers of students attending a web campus in cyberspace but based somewhere such as Manchester, England. All that will remain at schools like the University of Colorado and other Big-time U's will be beer-and-circus—not even the pretense, as now, of general undergraduate education. And big-time college sports will become even bigger at these schools.

★　★　★

For many years, critics of big-time college sports, including this writer in *College Sports Inc.*, have offered long lists of What Should Happen in intercollegiate athletics, only to see their ideas crash into What Is Happening—gargantuan growth and commercialization, along with increasing exploitation of athletes. Therefore, it seems best to confine What Should Happen to a core item, and then to focus on What Probably Will Happen, and why the latter will escalate beer-and-circus.

> If you want to change college sports instantly, forget about athletic scholarships and bring in "need based only" grants, like the Ivies give. And take them totally out of the hands of the athletic department. Put the Financial Aid Office in charge, like it is for every other grant to a student.
> —Edward "Moose" Krause, former coach and athletic director
> at the University of Notre Dame

Proposal: End athletic scholarships and allow only need-based grants.

"Moose" Krause is correct, the termination of athletic scholarships would eliminate the athletic department's current employer/employee relationship with an athlete, as well as the coach's power to renew or cancel the scholarship every July. In addition, elimination of athletic scholarships would decrease some of the tension between intercollegiate athletes and regular students, and it also would allow athletes the same control over their lives now possessed by average undergraduates; in other words, many jocks would become ordinary students.

Schools give money to regularly enrolled students mainly on the basis of financial need; Financial Aid Offices, using the U.S. government's FAFSA form and sometimes the private school PROFILE form, ascertain each undergraduate's money needs. Universities continue the need-based system for as long as the student remains in school. Many athletes would qualify for need-based grants, and, most important, the athletic department would have no input into whether they received them or not, and whether they were renewed or not. This system has long worked for Ivy League schools as well as all those in Division III. In the student-athlete equation, need-based grants put the emphasis on the student part, and cancel the employer/employee aspect of the athlete side.

In the history of college sports, athletic scholarships began during the 1930s when some have-not conferences of the era, particularly the Southwest and the Southeastern, adopted them to lure prime recruits to their athletic programs; the have-nots wanted to reach the same level as the wealthy conferences, particularly the Ivy League, Big Ten, and Pacific Coast. Many higher education authorities opposed athletic scholarships, calling them "play for pay." The Ivy League was adamantly against them, considering athletic scholarships antithetical to the mission of a university. The Ivies argued that athletic scholarships turned athletes into students brought to college for entertainment—not academic—purposes.

With this background as context, the debate within the NCAA on whether to institute athletic scholarships for all members continued through the 1940s and into the 1950s. Even important members of the sports media opposed them. Bill Stern, the radio "Voice of College Sports" in this period, wrote:

> Getting a higher education should be the primary reason for any youngster going to college. Athletic achievements, however sensational, should be secondary and should serve as a means to an end, namely a legitimate college diploma. Let's keep the record straight, when a college athlete plays for pay, receiving money through athletic scholarships, he's a professional no matter what uniform he wears.

In 1953, ironically the same year that NCAA executive director Walter Byers invented the term *student-athlete,* the association approved athletic scholarships across the board. For many people within higher education, this marked a crucial moment in the history of intercollegiate athletics: the shift from amateurism to professionalism.

The Ivy League, the founders of big-time college sports, responded by refusing to give athletic scholarships and continuing their policy of need-based-only aid to all students, including athletes. They also began to deemphasize their college sports programs in various ways, including prohibiting their teams from playing in bowl games and not allowing spring football practice. Their moves sharpened the line between college sports amateurism and professionalism.

On the Ivy side, and also at the schools that joined them and eventually formed NCAA Division III, were teams with players who were authentic students at their colleges and universities. On the other side were all the schools awarding athletic scholarships and hoping that their athletes could pass their institution's educational requirements; but if the jocks failed academically, the schools would accommodate them, including with "gut" courses and "mickey" majors. As a result, the higher education landscape divided between big-time college sports schools, and academic colleges and universities. A minority of institutions managed to straddle the line, but the majority did not.

From the perspective of the twenty-first century, it is clear that the Ivy League presidents and Boards of Trustees came to a fork in the higher education road and had to choose between big-time college sports or big-time undergraduate education. They chose the academic path, and this decision helped the Ivy League ascend to the pinnacle of American higher education. Other schools selected the other path and began the slow but inevitable degradation of undergraduate education at their institutions.

If the NCAA decided to reverse its history and end athletic scholarships, allowing only need-based grants, many other problems in big-time college sports would disappear; however, so would the quality of play, as well as the TV revenue for big-time college basketball and football games, for March Madness and the bowls. With the termination of athletic scholarships, the Division III model would prevail, but how many fans would rush to their TV sets to watch an Oberlin versus Antioch basketball game?

In an ideal world, even a logical one, the need-based-only grant proposal should prevail. In the real United States of America, it will not succeed. Nevertheless, if current trends within College Sports MegaInc. continue, more schools might accept this solution than the proponents of big-time college sports imagine. What Might Happen in intercollegiate athletics in the next decade presents the following scenario.

> If the package of [NCAA] proposals is passed [by the Division I membership] . . . high school prospects could receive pay or other compensation for athletic participation [while in high school] without jeopardizing their [college] eligibility. . . .
>
> The association's most radical recommendation is directed at prospects who choose to sign and play professionally right out of high school. . . . If they played no more than a year as a pro, they could opt to sign with a college, start playing immediately and have a full four seasons of eligibility. . . .
>
> Further, the NCAA is looking at allowing athletes to seek out loans based on future professional earnings.
>
> —*USA Today*, March 2000

College Sports MegaInc. is edging toward paying the players, whether with money disguised as "loans" or, as suggested by NCAA executive director Cedric Dempsey, monthly payments termed *stipends*. In addition, the association wants to overlook previous lapses in amateurism, such as earning money from sports as a high school student, or even playing in professional leagues before entering college. As one NCAA official says,

"Amateurism deregulation would fix many of the problems" in big-time college sports.

In many ways, this is true: paying the players would end much of the cant and hypocrisy currently surrounding College Sports MegaInc., particularly the enforcement of the amateur regulations, for example, penalizing players when they accept various gifts, some as trivial as T-shirts. However, professionalizing intercollegiate athletics would usher in many new problems and forever change big-time college sports.

Most of the current NCAA plans for professionalization include specific sums of money; for example, Cedric Dempsey has mentioned $200 per month for the stipend to athletes. Probably the "loans based on future professional earnings" will also have a dollar ceiling. In addition, some of the rules already passed include specific sums: e.g., athletes are allowed to work at part-time jobs but not earn more than $2,000 a year from this employment.

All of these fixed amounts, as well as the specific limitations on athletic scholarships, indicate that the NCAA is a cartel, arbitrarily setting the wages for the on-field employees of College Sports MegaInc. Economists have long attacked the cartel nature of the NCAA, and the U.S. Supreme Court, in a 7–1 decision in 1984, found that the association monopolized the TV revenue from college football games in a cartel manner, the court directing member schools to move to an open market in selling the telecast rights of their games.

Similarly in the 1990s, after the NCAA set an arbitrary salary scale for a group of assistant coaches, the courts found that the association had acted unfairly, and that these men and women should be paid according to the market value of their services. The NCAA had to settle the case—paying the assistant coaches for lost wages and damages—for a whopping $54 million dollars.

What will occur under the new NCAA "amateurism deregulation" rules if a college athlete sues the association, claiming that the arbitrary sum that he or she receives is, in fact, cartel control over his or her earnings and that market forces should prevail? Why is there an NCAA ceiling of $2,000 on part-time jobs? Why a limit on athletic scholarships? A University of Florida "full ride" in football is worth about $10,000 for an in-state player, but why this arbitrary ceiling, particularly when his services, along with his underpaid teammates, generate millions of dollars for his employer?

When an athlete sues and tries to break the NCAA's cartel control over his or her earnings, will a jury of twelve people—after years of watching highly commercial college football and basketball—decide, as undoubtedly the NCAA will argue, that the players are just ordinary students, mainly going to class and playing sports as amateurs? What if the athlete shows that he or she was paid to play sports as a high school student, and then played in professional sports leagues—all of these experiences approved by the NCAA under its new rules—before suiting up for more minor-league training in an intensive intercollegiate program? The jury would have to be dumb and dumber to buy the NCAA's "student amateur" argument.

Therefore, at the top of the What Will Probably Happen in College Sports MegaInc. list is professionalization: college athletes will be paid, either through the NCAA's own "amateurism deregulation"—its stipends and other payments will grow—or the courts will break the association's control over wages.

What Will Happen Then? Most probably, the rich conferences and teams will become fully professional, paying their athletes according to their market value, and all other members of Divisions I and II will have to decide whether they want to compete in professional college sports or not. Of course, because the athletic departments of almost all schools will still be losing money, paying the athletes will cost a fortune. This economic reality should end the dreams of big-time college sports glory for many schools, definitely all those below the NCAA Division I-A level, and even many in that group. The vast majority of institutions in Divisions I and II will have to fold their hands in the NCAA poker game.

In addition, some schools like Rice because of their academic traditions will probably choose not to play professional intercollegiate athletics. Other schools like Virginia will be on the bubble, not wanting to leave the highest level of college sports but also not wanting to field professional teams.

Ironically, the schools that dropped out of College Sports MegaInc. would do better than those that stayed. Probably the dropouts would accept the Division III model—why have expensive athletic departments if you cannot participate in the March Madness or bowl game lottery?—and they would save millions of dollars annually. Most important, they would signal the public, the various levels of government, the private foundations, and other benefactors of higher education that they are no longer in the sports entertainment business. Hopefully, many of these institutions would stress undergraduate education. As a result, if parents wanted their sons and daughters to obtain decent educations, and their children shared this goal, they would look at the non–Big-time U's, all those schools at the Division III level.

On the other hand, for the thirty to fifty schools that remain in College Sports MegaInc., the future becomes more problematic. The commercialism of their professional college sports programs will escalate: they will pay players openly but those athletes, particularly the stars, will have agents (presently they have "street agents"), and the tawdry world of pro sports will dominate college ball. In addition, the Big-time U's will so clearly operate pro sports franchises that the public and the higher education funding agencies will become increasingly skeptical about the academic aspects of these institutions. Inevitably, the collegiate subcultures at these schools will expand, and soon the vast majority of applicants and undergraduates will be students in love with beer-and-circus. This is a bleak scenario for those faculty members and other persons at Big-time U's who care about education, but it is a very possible one.

★   ★   ★

The present and future of Emory University in Atlanta, Georgia, is far different from that of most Big-time U's. In the mid-1990s, a number of people within and outside Emory called for the school to go from Division III college sports to Division I-A. They argued, in addition to the New 3 R's line, that Emory, with its huge endowment from Coca-Cola, was one of the few institutions that could easily afford to move to the top level of intercollegiate athletics. The president of Emory, William M. Chace, resisted the siren call of big-time college sports, and instead worked hard to improve the quality of undergraduate education at his school. Chace's reward was Emory's first appearance in the Top Ten of *U.S. News'* rankings of national universities.

As College Sports MegaInc. moves toward the bleak future of professionalization and greater beer-and-circus, the presidents of other research universities should follow Dr. Chace's example, particularly at a time when the U.S. economy is booming. In all probability, they will not.

A decade ago, the book *College Sports Inc.* concluded with the line, "The subtitle of this book is *The Athletic Department VS. the University*." If College Sports Inc. succeeds in its conquest [of Big-time U's], a future subtitle will read, *The Athletic Department IS the University*. That subtitle now applies to many Big-time U's, and college sports has evolved into College Sports MegaInc.

Unless the trustees, administrators, and other persons in charge of large, public research universities come to their senses, a future book title will read: *Beer and Circus: How College Sports Destroyed Undergraduate Education at Big-time U's*.

NOTES

The following notes provide references for quoted material in the book and further explanations for some of the comments in the text. The notes follow the order of material presented in each chapter of the book. However, when a source is clearly cited within the text, particularly magazines and college guidebooks along with their datelines, it is not repeated in the footnotes. For example, the many citations in the text to the *U.S. News & World Report* annual college issue for 2000 (formally subtitled *America's Best Colleges*) are not repeated below.

The quoted material from on-the-record interviews is footnoted according to name of interviewee, date, and place of the interview. However, in the case of interviewees who chose to speak off the record, I have noted this and included only the place and date. I regret that some university administrators and students chose anonymity. I understand their reluctance to see their names in print, particularly if they spoke critically of their schools, but in some cases they chose anonymity even when they praised their universities. I attribute this to the growing power of the public relations industry: increasingly they advise clients, including universities, to stonewall on every controversial subject, to not answer reporters' and researchers' questions, and if an interviewee feels impelled to respond, to do so off-the-record so that the interviewee can maintain maximum "deniability."

As a person who has always spoken his mind and put his name next to his remarks, I am distressed by this off-the-record trend, and I hope it ends soon. However, as an author who wants to do the best work possible, I felt that I had to use some off-the-record comments, although I tried to keep them to a minimum. In addition, before quoting them in print, I tried to get in touch with the interviewees, and urged them to go on the record. Occasionally, they agreed but most often they refused. My rule for using off-the-record comments became thus: if the person had spoken on tape, I would use the quote; if not, I would not. As a result, I have a verifiable record of the interviewee's comment. This rule seems the best way to assure readers of the authenticity of the off-the-record quotes in this book. Sadly for my research, a number of interviewees made very useful remarks after the taping session ended, but I have not quoted these comments.

As for the student quotes from the questionnaire for this book: because the survey asked for anonymous responses, no names were placed on the hard copies of the questionnaire (the ones handed out in classes and in campus gathering places, such as student union buildings). On the web survey, I assured respondents that I could not reveal their names because I was using a public server that does not maintain log files, identity codes, or return addresses.

The results on some of the questions on the survey differ slightly from those given in the final chapter of my book, *Onward to Victory: The Crises That Shaped College Sports* (New

York, 1998). After the publication of that book, I continued to distribute the questionnaire, including posting it on the World Wide Web. As a result, I received many more responses, and this changed the totals somewhat.

In addition, the reader will note in the text and in these footnotes a number of citations from the student newspaper and other publications of Indiana University, Bloomington. I am not singling out my employer for special praise or condemnation. IU is a typical, large, public research university, and because I happen to read its student newspaper and some of its other publications on a daily basis, and clipped and saved many items from those periodicals over the years, I ended up citing them in this book more often than I did items from any other single school. I am certain, however, that if I worked at another university, I would have included as many citations from that school in the book as I did from Indiana University.

Finally, for entries in the footnotes from college guidebooks, because of the erratic pagination in those publications but the consistent alphabetic listing, I have not always given the page numbers, instead referring the reader to the alphabetic listings. Similarly, because of the many editions that daily newspapers publish, and the frequent changes of the headlines on articles, I have given only the name of the periodical, the subject, author, and date. In a database age, this is almost always sufficient for retrieving articles.

Preface

Frederick Rudolph's comment is in his essay, "Neglect of Students as a Historical Tradition," in the anthology, *The College and the Student*, edited by Lawrence E. Dennis and Joseph F. Kaufman, published by the American Council on Education (ACE), Washington, D.C., 1966, p. 47. The Carnegie Foundation for the Advancement of Teaching funded the Boyer Commission and the latter group published *Reinventing Undergraduate Education: A Blueprint for America's Research Universities*, Stony Brook, New York, 1998; the quote on ordinary "baccalaureate students" is on p. 7. The argument that "You get out of this place whatever you put into it" occurs repeatedly at Big-time U's; for some printed examples of it, see *The Insider's Guide to the Colleges*, compiled and edited by the staff of the *Yale Daily News*, New York, 2000; for example, "Louisiana State is a large research university . . . introductory courses tend to be large. . . . As one undergrad said, 'You can get a lot out of an LSU education if you put a lot into it.' " The quotes about the University of New Mexico are from the same source, 2000 edition.

An American Imperative: Higher Expectations for Higher Education was published by the Wingspread Group, Washington, D.C., 1993. The material quoted here is on pp. 5–6. An explanation of Juvenal's "bread and circuses" phrase is in *Veni, Vidi, Vici* by Klaus Bartels, Darmstadt, Germany, 1999, pp. 130–31. My book *College Sports Inc.: The Athletic Department vs. the University* was published by Henry Holt and Company, New York, 1990. The administrator at the Sunbelt University spoke off the record, claiming that his bosses would not appreciate his comments about how beer-and-circus worked at his school. The junior at this university put his comment on the questionnaire that I handed out on campus at this school.

Introduction

The Clark and Trow passages in the introduction are from their essay, "The Organizational Context," in *College Peer Groups: Problems and Prospects for Research*, edited by Theodore M. Newcomb and Everett K. Wilson, Chicago, 1966, pp. 17–70. According to Clark and Trow, the essay "appeared first in unpublished form in 1960," and their conclusions are based on research done in the late 1950s and updated in the early 1960s. In their work, they go far beyond the descriptive passages used in the introduction to this book, and they present complicated social science matrices to analyze college students. Their work sparked a debate among sociologists and higher-education authorities, some seeing it as a valuable administrative tool, and others criticizing its statistical aspects and results. For a time, the Educational Testing Service used a version of Clark and Trow's work in college placement tests, but this infuriated many social scientists. In the end, the statistical formulas sank the entire essay, and the ideas in it disappeared from sight. (For a summary of the debate, see P. T. Terenzini and E. T. Pascarella's "An Assessment of the Construct Validity of the Clark-Trow Typology of the College Student Subcultures," *American Educational Research Journal*, 1977, vol. 14, pp. 225–48.)

However, by discarding the matrices and statistical formulas, and using the descriptions as historical insights, not social science, Clark and Trow's discussion of undergraduate subcultures proves a useful starting point for a book on this topic. Obviously, I use their remarks—with major emendations and additions—in this manner. American society and higher education have changed significantly since Clark and Trow did their research; nevertheless, their comments on student subcultures remain the single best explanation on record.

Very few historians have written about undergraduate life; the best studies are by Helen Lefkovitz-Horowitz, *Campus Life: Undergraduate Cultures from the End of the Eighteenth Century to the Present* (New York, 1987); in it, she calls the academically inclined students and the faculty the "outsiders"; Calvin Lee, *The Campus Scene, 1900–1970* (New York, 1970 [an anecdotal but factually accurate book]); and folklorist Simon J. Bronner, *Piled Higher and Deeper: The Folklore of Campus Life* (Little Rock, Ark., 1990 [his title originates in a student jest about university degrees: B.S. stands for "bullshit," M.S. is "more of the same," and Ph.D. is "piled higher and deeper"]). I have drawn from these sources, and some less important ones, as well as my own research, for the history of college life presented in this introduction and in the book.

A number of studies of vocational education exist, one of the best and most informative being Christopher J. Lucas's *American Higher Education: A History* (New York, 1994). The statistics of GI graduation rates are from Lucas's work; although the graduating class of 1949 was the first one dominated by vets, some ex-GIs graduated from 1946 through 1948 (they had attended college for a year or more before the war, resuming upon return). For a vivid portrait of the life of GI vets as college students, see Joseph Goulden's *The Best Years: 1945–1950* (New York, 1976); in addition, my book *Onward to Victory* (New York, 1998) focuses on the postwar era and discusses the GI vet college athletes. Clark Kerr was the president of the University of California who coined the phrase, the "Multiversity." He discussed it at length in his book *The Uses of the University* (Boston, 1964).

Clark and Trow do not use the term "rebel," instead employing "nonconformist." Their term seems bound by the 1950s—at the time called the "age of conformity"—and it is much less applicable in the twenty-first century. American culture is now so diffuse that there is no dominant culture to which to conform, whereas rebels can still find some things to rebel against, such as political apathy. Helen Lefkovitz-Horowitz also uses "rebel" for one of her student types, although she gives it a much wider meaning—she includes vocational students as rebels—than do Clark and Trow and other writers.

The college and post-college careers of the two most important Beat generation writers, Jack Kerouac and Allen Ginsberg, illustrate the progression of the student rebel. Kerouac came to Columbia University in 1940 to play football; he quickly pledged a fraternity, and was a collegiate student until he started reading voluminously on his own. He became a rebel, then dropped out of football, his frat, and Columbia, and lived with off-campus rebels on Morningside Heights.

Allen Ginsberg entered Columbia in 1943 as a vocational student sponsored by a labor union. From a lower-middle-class family in New Jersey, Ginsberg hoped to rise in the world and become a labor lawyer. However, his rebel nature, his love of poetry, and his homosexuality moved him outside the vocational mold, and he dropped out of Columbia, also living with off-campus rebels on Morningside Heights. From the 1950s to the beginning of the twenty-first century, many rebel students have seen these and other Beat writers as role models, and imitated their movement away from higher education to personal salvation.

1: Animal House

The title of *Animal House* is sometimes listed as *National Lampoon's Animal House* because the *National Lampoon* magazine spawned the movie. However, because most people refer to the film simply as *Animal House*, I use that title here. Kyle, the World Wide Web fan of *Animal*

House, posted his comments at: http://us.imdb.com. The production history and revenue of the film were discussed by director John Landis in an interview with Bruce Westbrook of the *Houston Chronicle,* 10/15/98. Harold Ramis, the main writer on *Animal House,* made his comments to Gene Siskel of the *Chicago Tribune,* 8/27/78. Gene Mustain of the *Chicago Sun-Times* speculated about the effect of *Animal House,* 9/3/78.

Helen Lefkovitz-Horowitz wrote about the revival of collegiate life in the 1970s (op. cit.), pp. 260–61; and Simon Bronner also discussed this phenomenon and supplied statistics on it (op. cit.), pp. 127–28. In 1984, Lisa Birnbach began publishing *Lisa Birnbach's College Book: The Inside Scoop, Straight from Students, on the Courses, Professors, and on- and off-Campus Life at over 200 Colleges* (New York, 1984); her comments about the University of Miami and the University of Illinois are in the 1984 edition. Gene Mustain quoted the comments of the U. of I. frat man in the *Chicago Sun-Times,* 9/3/78. Rudolph Weingartner in *Undergraduate Education: Goals and Means* (New York, 1992) commented about the noise level in the dorm, p. 130. I became aware of this phenomenon while visiting various student residence halls, and also seeing Indiana University publications advertising "quiet floors" in dorms. Rutgers anthropologist Michael Moffat wrote *Coming of Age in New Jersey: College and American Culture* (New Brunswick, N.J. 1989); his comment about "the floor party" is on p. 83. Penn State alum John Hall reminisced about "Happy Valley" in an article in the *Pittsburgh (PA) Post-Gazette,* 7/15/98.

Last Call: High-Risk Bar Promotions That Target College Students by Debra F. Erenberg and George A. Hacker, published by the Center for Science in the Public Interest, Washington, D.C., 1997, provides an excellent survey of undergraduate alcohol consumption during the final decades of the twentieth century. Much of my discussion of the situation on campuses during the 1970s and 1980s comes from this report, as well as from other sources, and my clear memory of Indiana University and other beer-and-circus schools during those decades.

The fan of *Animal House,* Justin Siegel, posted his comments on the web at http://us.imdb.com. Gene Siskel was the film reviewer who commented about "every parent's worst fears—that they are paying $5,000 each year to send their sons and daughters on a vacation called 'college' " (*Chicago Tribune,* 8/25/78). The most amazing aspect of his comments was the price of college for one year—only $5,000! Simon Bronner mentioned frats as "underage drinking clubs (op. cit.), pp. 127–28, and Ernest Boyer, head of the Carnegie Foundation, discussed the same phenomenon in *College: The Undergraduate Experience in America* (New York, 1987), p. 208. "Beer and Loafing [at Indiana University]: A Fifth-Year Senior Reflects on Years of Madness," by Robert J. Warren, appeared in the *Indiana* [University] *Daily Student* on 4/19/91. John S. DeMott of *Time* magazine discussed the student deaths from balcony falls, 4/7/86. The poll of college student attitudes begun in the late 1980s was done by this researcher: I mainly wanted to measure student opinion on intercollegiate athletics, and I started by handing out a questionnaire in my undergraduate classes at Indiana University, and similar schools. The most useful responses were to the question "After you graduate or leave your university, what do you think you will remember most vividly about your time there?" I kept this question for the survey used for this book.

Michael Moffat commented on the anti-academic ethos at his school (op. cit.), p. 91, "locating a good party," p. 26. Sociologist David Reisman in *On Higher Education: The Academic Enterprise in an Era of Rising Student Consumerism* (San Francisco, 1980), discussed the relationship of academic faculty to academically inclined students, p. 5; he also endorsed Clark and Trow in this discussion.

2: College Sports Winners and Losers

The Frederick Rudolph quote is in his classic history of American higher education, *The American College and University: A History* (New York, 1982), p. 381. Thomas Ehrlich's memoir is *The Courage to Inquire: Ideals and Realities in Higher Education,* with Juliet Frey (Bloomington, Ind., 1995); the quotes on the Bob Knight "rape" incident are on pp. 137–39. Many accounts of this incident exist, newspapers and magazines having covered it exhaustively. The best account between book covers is by Joan Mellen in *Bob Knight: His Own Man* (New York,

1988). She quotes Professor Robert Byrnes on "Ehrlich spoke of Knight as if he were a member of a different social class," p. 272.

The higher education writers who commented on the "three things" that can happen to a college president dealing with college sports were John R. Thelin and Lawrence L. Wiseman in *The Old College Try: Balancing Academics in Higher Education* (Washington, D.C., 1989), p. 66. Oddly, they do not explain what the three things are; therefore, I take full credit, or blame, for the three items in the text here.

Ira Berkow's comments came in a column in the *New York Times*, 5/21/90. My book *College Sports Inc.: The Athletic Department vs. the University* (op. cit.), has a section, "Toxic Waste," on the scandals of the 1980s, pp. 205–307, including a discussion of the New Mexico scandal, pp. 294–95. David Whitford wrote *A Payroll to Meet: A Story of Greed, Corruption, and Football at SMU* (New York, 1989); Benjamin Rader in *American Sports: From the Age of Folk Games to the Age of Spectators* (Englewood Cliffs, N.J., third edition, 1990) wrote about the NCAA's non-reaction to cheating, p. 273; and the 1988 edition of *Don Heinrich's [Pre-Season] College Football* guide worked out the percentages on cheating (np). Of all publications, the *Chronicle of Higher Education* has covered intercollegiate athletics more thoroughly and thoughtfully than any other; for the last three decades, it has printed periodic articles listing athletic programs under NCAA sanctions and the nature of their violations, for example, "20 Institutions Under NCAA Sanctions," 3/5/99. With these as a guide, the reader can go into the *Chronicle*'s excellent database, as well as Lexis-Nexis or Dow Jones and find detailed articles about specific incidents.

A number of books exist on athletic department finances during the final decades of the twentieth century. *College Sports Inc.* (op. cit.) is available in most college and public libraries; Andrew Zimbalist's *Unpaid Professionals* (Princeton, N.J., 1999) updates many items in *College Sports Inc.* and projects athletic department losses well into the twenty-first century. In 1993, the National Association of College and University Business Officers published an excellent report on the subject, *The Financial Management of Intercollegiate Athletics Programs*; and every two years, the NCAA publishes its *Revenues and Expenses of Intercollegiate Athletics Programs*, revealing some of the acknowledged deficits of athletic departments. In recent years, the NCAA has divided the reports into one for Divisions I and II, and one for Division III, and it plans to continue this format in future.

Isiah Thomas's quote was in *Newsweek*, 1/30/89. For a discussion on the NCAA's change from four-year guaranteed athletic scholarships to one-year renewable deals, see *College Sports Inc.* (op. cit.), pp. 207–10. For many chapters on this issue, see *College Athletes for Hire: The Evolution and Legacy of the NCAA's Amateur Myth*, by Allen L. Sack and Ellen J. Staurowsky (New York, 1998). An example of athletes being on one-year contracts based on athlete performance occurred at Auburn University in 1999. According to *USA Today*, new football coach Tommy Tubberville cut "players he didn't feel could help the team"; the unnamed reporter explained, in case the readers did not know, that "All NCAA scholarships are reviewed annually," 5/3/99.

Peterson's Guides, publishers of standard and non-controversial college guidebooks, commissioned two men inside the college sports world, Stephen K. Figler and Howard E. Figler, to write *Going the Distance: The College Athlete's Guide to Excellence on the Field and in the Classroom* (Princeton, N.J., 1991). Within this context, their comments are both reliable and startling; they commented on the "fifty hours or more each week," p. 12; "The label of student-athlete says it all," p. 1; "The team demands so much of your time," and "Coaches arrange aspects of your life," p. 95; and "WINNING VERSUS YOUR [ATHLETES'] WELFARE," p. 13. For a discussion of coaches' annual incomes, and deals, see *College Sports Inc.*, Part Two, "Greed City: College Coaches' Salaries, Perks, Deals, & Scams"; in addition, the databases contain hundreds of articles on these subjects.

The interview with Fred Akers, former NCAA Division I-A head football coach, took place in Lafayette, Indiana, on March 11, 1991; I interviewed him for another project, but I'm pleased to use some of his comments in this book. NCAA PR director Jim Marchiony made his remarks about the "voluntary" rules to Art Rosenbaum of the *San Francisco Chronicle*, 4/9/91. Jerry Eaves, the Howard coach, was quoted by Charles Farrell in *Basketball Times*, 10/15/92. The

Division I men's volleyball player was at Stanford and made his comments to me in Palo Alto, California, on 7/27/98; he asked to speak off the record because he was on athletic scholarship. David Leon Moore of *USA Today* wrote about U.S.C. football player R. Jay Soward, 10/5/99. Joe Abunasser, a former NCAA Division I assistant basketball coach, made his comments in an interview, 11/22/99.

3: *The NCAA, the Tube, and the Fans*

Athletic director Gene Slaughter of Capitol University in Columbus, Ohio, made the remark about "Greed," in the *Columbus Dispatch*, 9/16/82. William Atchley commented about the NCAA in an interview in Stockton, California, 6/10/88. Many books discuss the NCAA's self-interested rules and its manipulations of them; see Paul Lawrence, *Unsportsmanlike Conduct* (New York, 1987); also see former NCAA executive director Walter Byers' book of the same title (Ann Arbor, Mich., 1995); the Sack and Staurowsky book (op. cit.); and *College Sports Inc.* (op. cit.), Part Four, "The NCAA: The Fox in the Henhouse," pp. 309–44, with specific material on the MAC and its football stadium problem, p. 312. ESPN executive Loren Matthews remarked, "The bottom line is money," in an article by Rick Warner of the Associated Press, 8/22/90. J. A. Adande wrote about the importance of the 1979 NCAA final game in the *Los Angeles Times*, 3/25/99; Jack Craig discussed the broadcast history of college basketball in the *Boston Globe*, 7/14/91; Randy Minkoff commented on ESPN's role in popularizing the sport in the 1980s in a United Press International article, 11/15/86; and Richard Sandomir, who has covered the business of college sports extremely well over the years, outlined the TV revenue for the men's tourney in the *New York Times*, 9/10/99. Dana C. Caldwell of the *Tampa Tribune* discussed the NCAA's attendance requirement for Final Four games in the men's tourney, and also quoted John Wooden on playing in domes, 3/25/99; and Mal Florence of the *Los Angeles Times* quoted Jerry Tarkanian on the expanded field of sixty-four, 3/14/86.

Various writers have analyzed the NCAA's spending of the men's basketball tourney revenue; see *College Sports Inc.* (op. cit.), pp. 309–44, and Andrew Zimbalist (op. cit.), pp. 173–87. Rick Bozich's comments appeared in *Basketball Times*, 10/15/92 (no author given). For a discussion of the poll of college student attitudes begun in the 1980s, see above; the comment about "college culture today" also appeared as a student response to the first form of the questionnaire. The research of Dr. Robert Cialdini was quoted by Bob Andelman in *Why Men Watch Football*, (Lafayette, La., 1993), pp. 39–40. Allen Bogan, a psychology student at Indiana University, used the term "fandemonium" in an unpublished paper with that title, 12/12/93.

The Carnegie Foundation for the Advancement of Teaching sponsored a number of studies on intercollegiate athletics in the 1920s, culminating in the *Carnegie Foundation Bulletin Number Twenty-Three: American College Intercollegiate Athletics*, mainly authored by Howard Savage, New York, 1929. This study, the most comprehensive in the history of college sports, is popularly known as the "Carnegie Report." The *Miller Lite Report on American Attitudes Toward Sports* was published by Research & Forecasts, Inc., New York, 1983. In discussing the findings in this report, I treat "almost always," "often," and "sometimes" responses as qualified affirmatives, and the "rarely" and "never" as qualified negatives. For readers who wish to see the full breakdown of responses, please consult the *Miller Lite Report*.

The student who explained his fascination with ESPN was Charles Barksy, in an interview in Bloomington, Indiana, 4/4/94. Rudy Martze of *USA Today* had an excellent article on the synergy between ESPN and college basketball in that newspaper, 3/15/90. Jim O'Connell, Associated Press basketball writer, wrote about the early history of "Midnight Madness," giving Charles "Lefty" Dreisell credit for starting it, 10/13/94; and Will Parrish of McClatchy Newspapers Inc. discussed Joe B. Hall's 1970s open invitation to the University of Kentucky fans, 10/16/97. The late 1980s survey of how college students spent their time appeared in the *Chronicle of Higher Education* in an article by Susan Dodge, 10/4/89. Jodi Glickman of Indiana University described undergraduate reactions to ESPN's *SportsCenter* in an unpublished paper, "College Sports and Current Student Life," 2/1/94.

My book *Onward to Victory: The Crises That Shaped College Sports* (New York, 1998) has lengthy discussions on "Gee Whiz" and "Aw Nuts" sports journalism—see the index for the pages under those entries. The *New York Times* ran an article on the ESPN sports announcers and their favorite sayings, 11/1/98 (no author given); some of the quotes in the text are from that article and some are from my own viewing of the program. Bill Jeakle and Ed Wyatt wrote *How to College in the 1990s* (New York, 1989); the quote beginning "Come game time" appears on p. 106. The issue of *ESPN The Magazine* analyzed in the text appeared 11/02/98; Nick Bakay wrote the piece on "Halloween vs. Midnight Madness," p. 33; and Anne Marie Cruz did the one on the Tulsa recruit, p. 116. Michael Hiestand of *USA Today* discussed the marketing survey that charted the generational split, 12/10/91.

4: Corporate Beer-and-Circus

Of all mass-market college guidebooks in the 1980s and early 1990s, Lisa Birnbach (op. cit.) aimed hers most directly at prospective college students, informing them in detail about extracurricular life and the social scene at different schools. Birnbach's guidebooks were controversial within the higher education community, particularly in admissions offices. Dennis Drabelle of the *Washington Post* quoted one higher-education consultant: " 'She says all the things the respectable [guide] books are afraid to get into' " (11/1/87). Her comments, although sarcastic at times, reflect student opinions at the schools visited; in addition, they usually parallel the comments in another non-standard guidebook, the *Insider's Guide to the Colleges*, published by the staff of the *Yale [University] Daily News*, as well as other sources, including my own research in this period. As a result, Birnbach's comments seem accurate, and I have used them to illustrate various points in the text. Her comments about the University of Arkansas appeared in the 1992 edition, pp. 17–19; as did her remarks about the University of Southern California, pp. 73–77.

The Center for Science in the Public Interest booklet, *Last Call* (op. cit.), discussed the brewers' 1980s marketing campaign, pp. 4–11. The departure of Arkansas from the Southwest Conference, and the influence of that school's athletic department prompted many articles, including a lengthy analysis by Bob Boerg of Arkansas AD Frank Broyles's role in the move (*St. Louis Post-Dispatch*, 9/20/90). Diane Alters's piece in the *Boston Globe* appeared 6/25/89; she also quoted industry experts James Mosher on the "life-and-death battle," and Robert V. Shear, "Advertising doesn't create cultural trends." The *New York Times* described Bubba Smith's experiences at the Michigan State Homecoming, and his resignation from the Miller Lite ads, 9/18/86 (no author given). Beth Ann Krier wrote about the genesis and growing success of the Spuds MacKenzie advertising campaign in the *Los Angeles Times*, 7/16/87; she also noted that Spuds "quickly became a cult figure on college campuses." In reality, Spuds was a female bull terrier named Evie, owned by a Chicago suburban couple, *St. Louis Post-Dispatch*, 10/6/93 (no author given). The MacKenzie brothers were Rick Moranis and Dave Thomas, and their skit appeared on various TV shows and commercials; they also made a film appropriately named *Strange Brew* (1983).

The "Education Life Supplement" of the *New York Times*, 11/2/97, had an informative article by Linda Lee on the relationship between filmmakers, including those working for advertising agencies, and colleges and universities. The article discussed how USC and UCLA "have entire offices devoted to scheduling shooting of films, television pilots, and commercials." An inquiry to the USC office, 10/28/99, turned up the facts on the 1980s beer commercials. Cecelia Reed of *Advertising Age* discussed Spuds's and Budweiser's success at sports events, 4/27/87; and Matt Kilgore of the *St. Petersberg Times* described Spuds's appearance at a minor-league baseball game, 6/26/87. Paula Span of the *Washington Post* analyzed Spuds's sports connections, and discussed Spuds's "crossover appeal" to women, 1/7/89. The Associated Press ran an article by Skip Wollenberg about Miller Beer's clay figure animals, 12/8/88; *Last Call* (op. cit.) discussed the 1990 "Special Edition Coors Light Beer Can, Commemorating the University of Nebraska Cornhuskers' Championship Football Season," p. 9; and Melanie Wells of *USA Today* quoted Bob Lachky, Vice President of Brand Management for Anheiser-Busch, announcing Spuds's retirement, 1/21/99. In the late 1990s, Anheiser-Busch based another highly successful advertising campaign around a number of gravel-voiced frogs; according to an article by Seth Schiesel of the *New York Times*, 3/10/97, the brewer's website contained a biography of the lead frog, "Budbrew J. Budfrog . . . elected president of his college fraternity, and he likes to hang on the beach with a hot babe, a cold Bud and a folio edition of the Kama Sutra in the original Sanskrit."

Edward Fiske wrote about "a favorite indoor sport among educational pundits" in the *New York Times*, 9/7/88.

5: Admissions Office Scams

David Reisman discussed "the student as customer" (op. cit.), p. 9. Many articles in higher-education publications and the popular media detailed the 1980s and early 1990s demographic crunch in college applicants, see Larry Gordon's feature in the *Los Angeles Times*, 2/9/89; Pat Ordovensky's cover story in *USA Today*, 10/15/90; Devin Leonard's article in the *Bergen (NJ) Record*, 4/26/94. The quotes from *Peterson's Guide to College Admissions*, Princeton, NJ, are in the 1991 edition: "Colleges [and universities] . . . are business enterprises" on p. 196; "the flavor of student life," p. 47; and "Do you want an academically demanding college program," p. 14. Ernest Boyer in *College: The Undergraduate Experience in America* (op. cit.) quoted the admissions official who admitted, "If we didn't ask for the scores," and the ad with the "ability to close" phrase, p. 34; that book also describes the "college fairs" of this period, as does Anne Matthews, *Bright College Years: Inside the American Campus Today*, pp. 21–28. The statistics on acceptance rates in 2000 are from the *U.S. News* annual college issue of that year.

Larry Gordon of the *Los Angeles Times* wrote about U.S.C.'s enrollment crisis, 9/7/90; in this period, the school endured one of its regular athletic department scandals, this one involving academically marginal athletes receiving special favors from the university; see Bill Brubaker's article in the *Washington Post*, 10/1/91. Robert D. Hershey Jr. of the *New York Times* discussed "bait and switch" admissions office tricks, 9/20/98; Boyer (op. cit.) discussed "the appearance of the campus" and the typical campus tour, p. 17. The questionnaire results are from the survey for this book; see the "Preface" for a discussion of the questionnaire's methodology. The University of Oregon made the *Princeton Review*'s 1999 top "Party school" list; the full citation for this edition of the guidebook is *The Princeton Review: The Best 311 Colleges*, edited by Edward Custard with Tom Meltzer, Eric Owens, and Christine Chung (New York, 1998).

Linda Lee of the *New York Times* discussed the Oregon setting for *Animal House*, and quoted school P.R. director John Crosiar, 11/2/97; the AP carried an item on the Ducks' first bowl game in a quarter of a century, 11/21/89 (no author given). Lisa Birnbach described student life at Oregon in the 1992 edition of her guidebook (op. cit.), pp. 506–8; Louis Freedberg of the *San Francisco Chronicle* wrote at length about the higher-education enrollment and funding crisis in Oregon and California, 8/3/93; Mary Dieter of the *Louisville (KY) Courier-Journal* provided an overview of Myles Brand's career at Oregon, and the quote from Oregon Professor Charles Wright that he "can work the alums at a football game," 4/15/94. The article about Brand's emphasis on big-time intercollegiate athletics at Oregon appeared in the *Los Angeles Times*, 7/12/90 (no author given); and the AP wrote about the 20 percent jump in freshmen applications after the Rose Bowl appearance, 12/13/95 (no author given). That article also noted that the Ducks were about to go to the 1996 Cotton Bowl and the school "will spend more than $1.4 million in expenses to play" in that contest, and possibly "make a $50,000 profit."

6: The Flutie Factor

In this chapter, *Insider's Guide to the Colleges* (op. cit.) and the *Princeton Review* (op. cit.) are cited at length, therefore it seems appropriate to begin with the following notes about these student guidebooks. The *Insider's Guide* started in 1973 as a project of some *Yale Daily News* staff members and it surveyed mainly Ivy League schools. By the 1980s, it had evolved into a major annual guidebook, still connected to the *Yale Daily News*, and surveying over 300 colleges and universities. But it maintained the student point of view and, as a result, provided information that the stodgy traditional guidebooks ignored. It also outlasted its main 1980s rival, Lisa Birnbach's book. Dennis Drabelle of the *Washington Post* quoted a D.C.-area high school guidance counselor on the *Insider's Guide to the Colleges*: "It gives a good sense of a school from a student's point of view," 11/1/87. The *Insider's Guide*'s full-time staff updates the annual surveys, and sends many interviewers into the field. Again, as with Birnbach's work, the *Insider's Guide* seems accurate in terms of the schools that I know well, and also parallels my research. As a result, I find its comments to be quite accurate.

The most controversial of the current guidebooks (since Birnbach discontinued her series) is the *Princeton Review*, started in 1991. Famous for its rankings of schools in various categories, particularly "Party school," and despised by university officials whose institutions rank high on the negative lists, this guidebook works hard to back its findings with comprehensive research. It takes a huge sample of student opinion—56,000 questionnaires for its most recent edition, 2000—and determines its rankings based on the responses to its questionnaires. It explains that "the rankings are based directly upon what students on each campus tell us about their college," multiplied across the country. As a result, the *Princeton Review* is an accurate sampling of student opinion. Not only does it explain its technique in detail on its web page, but on 10/9/98 I interviewed one of its editors, Paul Cohen, in Indianapolis at length about its questionnaires and sampling techniques and was very impressed with his information; also see the discussion in the text of this book for more on its methodology.

Mary Burgan's comments came in her article "Academic Careers in the Nineties: Images and Realities," *ADE Bulletin*, fall 1990, p. 20. Many writers have tracked the "Flutie Factor" over the years: William H. Honan in the *New York Times* discussed it and gave the statistics for BC, 6/9/96; *Los Angeles Times* education writer Kenneth R. Weiss summed up, "The boost in applications or enrollment is usually short-lived, studies show. Swollen numbers usually recede the following year," 3/29/99. Lisa Birnbach's comments on Boston College appeared in her 1992 edition, pp. 246–49. The *Insider's Guide to the Colleges* (op. cit.) published its comments about "the game-winning field goal" in its mid-1990s editions, quoted here from 1996; according to the 2000 edition of the *Insider's Guide* as well as other guidebooks, BC is less of a party school than in the past. Apparently the debate about, and new legislation concerning, college student drinking in the State of Massachusetts in the late 1990s affected this school. A number of ESPN Radio announcers called BC "Notre Dame's Evil Twin," particularly Tony Bruno during and after the football point-shaving scandal.

Mike Dodd in a front-page story for *USA Today*, 4/11/97, quoted university admissions officers using the term "mission-driven athletics"; this story presents important statistics on a number of schools affected by the "Flutie Factor." Ernest Boyer in *College* (op. cit.) discussed the impact of " 'The [College] Game of the Week' " on applicants, p. 12. The results from the polling of enrolled students are from the survey done for this book (op. cit.). Another irony of the photos of classes held on lawns is that many students consider them "blow-off periods," often disappearing in the transition from regular classroom to lawn. The Syracuse sophomore made his comments in a P.S. on the web form of the questionnaire for this book, 10/10/99. Rebecca R. Dixon, an admissions official at Northwestern University, remarked on how "sports validates an institution" in an article by Mike Allen of the *New York Times*, 3/31/99.

Steve Weiberg and Jack Carey of *USA Today* dubbed Buffalo the "WORST TEAM" in college football, 10/13/99; Mike Harrington of the *Buffalo News* wrote about the defeat at Kent State, 10/31/99. Vice Provost William Fischer is the University of Buffalo official who commented in an e-mail on the faculty reaction to UB playing big-time college football, 11/10/99; despite the fact that his bosses might punish him after reading his comments, Professor Fischer agreed to stay on the record. He did the same in an article by Erik Lords on the UB Division I situation in the *Chronicle of Higher Education*, 12/10/99. Professor Fischer wins the Most-Stand-Up-Guy in Higher Education Award for his willingness to speak honestly and openly about big-time college sports.

UB president William Greiner spoke about the "quality of student life" in an article by Mark Gaughan of the *Buffalo News*, 7/13/99; and athletic director Bob Arkeilpane complained about "not having big-time college athletics at Buffalo" in an article by Jenny Kellner of the *New York Times*, 11/21/98. In the 1997 and 1998 editions of the *Insider's Guide* (op. cit.), Buffalo's out-of-state enrollment figures were 3 and 4 percent; however, in the 1999 and 2000 editions, the figures were "N/A" (not available). I wonder why?

Jay Oliva's comments on "Every school wants to believe" were in an article by Jeffrey Selingo, *Chronicle of Higher Education*, 10/31/97. The *Buffalo News* covered the financial costs of UB's joining the Mid-America Conference (MAC) in a number of articles over the years; particularly informative were pieces by Allen Wilson, 11/21/97; Mark Gaughan, 7/12/99; and Karen Brady, 4/16/97. The last named article also noted that the school passed on some of the intercollegiate athletics expenses to full-time undergraduates in the form of a $1.35 million increase in their annual fees—$200 per student per year—and the *Chronicle of Higher Education* article on UB (op. cit.) noted that the students were now paying $280 a year. Jerry Sullivan of the *Buffalo News* remarked that "Fans accustomed to seeing the [Miami] Dolphins won't be too thrilled about Kent State," 6/16/95. UB president William Greiner spoke about his ambitions for his intercollegiate athletics program in an article by Mark Gaughan of the *Buffalo News*, 7/13/99; in the same article, AD Bob Arkeilpane explained his parallel ambitions; these UB officials repeated their opinions in the *Chronicle of Higher Education* article (op. cit.).

The *Princeton Review* prints its rankings in part two of each edition; the *Insider's Guide* lists schools by state, and within each state alphabetically—it has never changed SUNY-Buffalo's name to the University of Buffalo, nor has the *Princeton Review*. William Fischer discussed the "negative halo effect" in an e-mail, 11/10/99.

7: Shaft the Undergraduates

Clark Kerr discussed "the mark of a university 'on the make' " in *The Uses of the University* (op. cit.), p. 90, and the "inevitable side-effect," pp. 64–65. His article, "The New Race to Be Harvard or Berkeley or Stanford," appeared in *Change* magazine, May/June, 1991, pp. 8–15. In recent decades, various critics of higher education attacked the emphasis on research at the expense of undergraduate teaching; the most widely read was Charles J. Sykes's *Prof Scam: Professors and the Demise of Higher Education* (New York, 1988). However, the most even-handed and well informed commentary on this subject appeared in Christopher J. Lucas's *Crisis in the Academy: Rethinking Higher Education in America* (New York, 1996); Lucas discussed not only "Upward Drift" universities, p. 214f, but also the critics and their positions, and he provided an excellent bibliography for all readers interested in the intricacies of this debate.

Stephen F. Aldersley wrote " 'Upward Drift' Is Alive and Well" for *Change*, September/October, 1995, pp. 51–56; he discussed the "potent drivers of institutional direction and decision-making" and provided many lists and charts on Upward Drift U's from the 1970s to the mid-1990s. Ronald Simpson and Susan Frost in *Inside College: Undergraduate Education for the Future* (New York, 1993) explained Clark Kerr's classification system for research universities, pp. 67–70. I used Aldersley's lists (op. cit.) for the correlation between Upward Drift U's and Division I college sports schools, and the *U.S. News*'s annual college issues (op. cit.) through the 1990s for the top 50 rankings of national universities. Many university administrators dispute the *U.S. News* rankings, particularly when their schools rate poorly on them, but almost everyone in higher education accepts the *U.S. News* lists as the standard poll and wants their school to achieve a high place on them.

Professor John E. Roueche of the University of Texas (Austin) discussed the "monolithic status system" in higher education in *An American Imperative* (op. cit.), p. 136. One of the best studies of Upward Drift and its effect on undergraduates appeared in the *Chicago Tribune*, 6/21/92 through 6/25/92. Reporters Ron Grossman, Carol Jouzaitis, and Charles Leroux studied the phenomenon at public universities in Illinois and adjoining states; the headline, "Colleges Find Follow-the-Leader is a No-Win Game," 6/25/92, sums up the study's conclusions. The *Tribune* series is far better than almost all articles in educational journals on the same subject, and it dramatizes the impact on individual students. Melinda Miller, editor of the U. of Illinois student newspaper at the time, was quoted in the 6/22/92 section of the series.

Rutgers professor Benjamin Barber wrote about his school in *An Aristocracy of Everyone: The Politics of Education and the Future of America* (New York, 1992), p. 196, and the "Ivy League university" with the "course off" prize, p. 197. Michael Moffat (op. cit.) wrote many chapters of his book on undergraduate education at Rutgers. Ernest Boyer in *College* (op. cit.) discussed the Carnegie Foundation's findings on the time faculty spent teaching undergraduates,

p. 121, and on the next page, the research prestige "goal" of Upward Drift U's; the Carnegie findings on faculty time on research are on p. 128. Christopher J. Lucas in *Crisis* (op. cit.) has an excellent discussion on the "Faculty Reward System," p. 195–96. Emeritus Professor Donald Gray of Indiana University recalled in an interview in Bloomington, Indiana, 10/19/99, that when he began his faculty career in the 1950s, the standard teaching assignment was four courses per semester, and salary went according to years in rank. In the transition from the old method to the new research imperative in the late 1960s and 1970s, some young faculty drowned in Upward Drift: the promotion and tenure rules changed during their probationary period; for example, when they were hired, the criterion for sufficient research for tenure was a series of scholarly articles; when they were up for tenure, it had become a major book. If drowning faculty protested that they had devoted much of their time and energy to teaching undergraduates, this plea almost never saved them.

Faculty wangle out of regular teaching responsibilities in a number of ways: straightforward appeals to their department chairs for "more time to do research"; agreements in their contracts when hired or retained by schools; and trading "a lighter load now for a heavier one during future semesters"—which rarely arrive. In addition, some departments, particularly in the sciences, allow faculty to "buy their way out" of teaching responsibilities. The *Chicago Tribune* (op. cit.), 6/23/92, explained the latter process: "A professor in the U. of Illinois' electrical engineering department . . . has a standard teaching load of three courses per year," and that professor "can buy his way out of one of those courses by bringing in research funds equal to at least 17 percent of his salary, or about $20,000 on average. For such professors, the teaching load drops to one class each semester, about three hours per week in the classroom."

Burton Clark described some professors as "cosmopolitans" and others as "locals" in his essay, "Faculty Culture," in *The Study of Campus Cultures*, edited by Terry F. Lunsford (Berkeley, Calif., 1963), pp. 39–54. The Carnegie Foundation findings on locals versus cosmopolitans are in Ernest Boyer, *College* (op. cit.), p. 239, and in Boyer's *Scholarship Reconsidered: Priorities of the Professoriate* (Princeton, N.J., 1990), p. 56. Christopher J. Lucas in *Crisis* (op. cit.) commented on "a single faculty reward structure," p. 192–93.

The interview with the Michigan State senior woman occurred in East Lansing, Michigan, 5/22/95; UCLA economist Emily Abel compared TA's to "McDonald's . . . part-time employees," in *Time* magazine's article, "Academia's New Gypsies" by Ezra Bowen, 1/12/87. *Academe*, the magazine of the American Association of University Professors (AAUP), had an excellent article, "Life on the 'Effectively Terminal' Tenure Track," by Martin Finkelstein, January/February 1986; I draw many of my ideas and statistics from that article, as well as from an interview with Paul Strohm, the editor of *Academe* from 1984 to 1992, conducted in Bloomington, Indiana, 7/7/99. Updates on the part-timers' increasing presence in higher education occurred throughout the 1990s, and a 1999 report, *Facing Change: Building the Faculty of the Future*, published by the U.S. Department of Education, Washington, D.C., summed up the situation, supplying excellent statistics. In addition, newspaper articles often gave a vivid picture of the life of a part-timer; see Joseph Berger's long piece in the *New York Times*, 3/8/98—the headline and subhead set the scene perfectly, "After Her Ph.D., the Scavenger's Life/Trying to Turn a Patchwork of Part-Time Jobs into an Academic Career."

Many writers within higher education criticized the increasing use of graduate-student teaching assistants—a result of the constant expansion of graduate programs at a time of shrinking economic resources for many universities. Christopher J. Lucas in *Crisis* (op. cit.) outlined the situation and supplied statistics, p. 10f; Cary Nelson and Michael Berube eloquently attacked graduate-school empire-building in the introduction to their *Higher Education Under Fire: Politics, Economics, and the Crisis in the Humanities* (New York, 1995). Ernest Boyer in *Scholarship* (op. cit.) disliked the use of TAs, p. 71, but Martin Anderson in *Imposters in the Temple* (New York, 1992), was vituperative about it, stating, "Children [TA's] teaching children is unconscionable," p. 65. Anderson continued his attack in other parts of his book; in so doing, he presented a powerful case against the exploitation of graduate and undergraduate students through the TA system.

On the bleak landscape of part-timers and TAs, there are a few positive developments; for example, in recent years my own department, English, at Indiana University, has significantly increased its teacher training for its graduate students (euphemistically called Associate Instructors) and instituted a number of graduate courses in pedagogy to connect to the AI's classroom work. Nevertheless, as I argue in the conclusion to this book, the entire graduate-school system is broken, and needs a total overhaul, not nips and tucks.

The total number of classes taught by part-timers and grad students is an elusive figure because very few studies include all of the courses where a professor is in charge but grad assistants do the bulk of the teaching, and do all of the grading and conferences with students. Invariably, to pad their statistics, most research universities list these courses as taught by full faculty, but in fact the professor teaches only about 20 percent of the course (the lectures). Whatever the actual numbers, even the conservative estimates in the 50 percentile range are appalling high.

Gail B. Promboin in the *American Imperative* (op. cit.) discussed how "The general public . . . sees teaching undergraduates as the primary mission of higher education," p. 128.

8: The Great Researcher = Great Teacher Myth

Former Indiana University president Thomas Ehrlich wrote his comments on "*Great Teachers and Teaching*" in *The Courage to Inquire* (op. cit.), pp. 25–26; I assume that he does not mind my taking his title to heart, and inquiring into the myth that he perpetuated here. Professors Patrick T. Terenzini and Ernest T. Pascarella debunked the "good teachers are good research-ers" myth in "Living with Myths: Undergraduate Education in America," *Change*, January/February, 1994, pp. 28–32; all of their quotes in this chapter are from this article. They based the article on their book, *How College Affects Students: Findings and Insights from Twenty Years of Research* (San Francisco, 1991); the interested reader can easily go from the topics in the article to the voluminous research behind it in their book, and I recommend this course of action.

Professor Lewis H. Miller wrote about "those rare few" faculty members who simultane-ously conduct intensive research and teaching in "Hubris in the Academy: Can Teaching Survive in the Overweening Quest for Excellence?" *Change*, September/October 1990, pp. 9–11, and p. 53; and in "Bold, Imaginative Steps Are Needed to Link Teaching with Research," *Chronicle of Higher Education*, 9/13/89, p. A52. The quote in the text is from the *Change* article, but some points in the paraphrase are from the *Chronicle* piece. Ehrlich (op. cit.) "underscore[d] that students benefit immensely," p. 25. The *Chicago Tribune* discussed the University of Mich-igan study and quoted the U of M science professor, 6/23/92. Paul Strohm wrote his comments in "The Ideology of 'Excellence,' " *AAUP Report*, a publication of the American Association of University Professors, Indiana University Chapter, Autumn 1991, pp. 2–5. Christopher J. Lucas in *American Higher Education* (op. cit.) discusses the myths surrounding research and teaching, p. 284f, and takes another run at them in *Crisis* (op. cit.), p. 198.

A majority of faculty at research universities consider themselves good teachers, thus buying into the administration's ideology on the subject as well as protecting their own egos. Some even cite those notoriously flawed indicators, student evaluations, as proof of their teaching excellence. However, most of these professors refuse to allow outside experts into their class-rooms to evaluate their teaching, and to assess what their students actually learned, if anything, in their courses. A charitable observer has to conclude that some of these professors are prob-ably adequate teachers but nowhere near as good as they imagine themselves and their col-leagues to be, and many other faculty members are mediocre to awful teachers. Finally, in the interest of full disclosure, before I began the research for this book, I believed that I was an excellent teacher and I had the student evaluations to "prove" it; I subsequently had my teaching evaluated by outside experts and I have discovered that, although it is quite good, it is far from outstanding. The experts suggested that I devote more time to preparation, student conferences, and marking papers and, in this labor-intensive way, try to become an excellent teacher. I know that many other faculty members at research universities are in the same situation.

The visit to the "freshman psychology lecture" is in Boyer, *College* (op. cit.), p. 140. Many commentators have discussed the lecture-course method: Christopher J. Lucas in *Crisis* (op. cit.), p. 169f; Simpson and Frost in *Inside College* (op. cit.) have an excellent chapter, "How Professors Teach," and a section, "Interactive Methods," of that chapter on these issues; and

Robert Nielsen in the *AFT Newsletter* (American Federation of Teachers) offered insights into the history of lecturing, "Putting the Lecture in Its Place," December 1990/January 1991, p. 16. Simon Bronner (op. cit.) related the folklore joke, "During a lecture," p. 183. Christopher J. Lucas in *American Higher Education* (op. cit.) commented on St. John's in Annapolis, Maryland, p. 280. Many authors have discussed the higher-education reforms suggested by rebel students in the 1960s; an excellent anthology on this topic was *Beyond Berkeley: A Sourcebook in Student Values*, edited by Christopher G. Katope and Paul G. Zolbrod (Cleveland and New York, 1966).

The *Chronicle of Higher Education* discussed the financial crisis in higher education and its impact on class size in various articles over the years, including Karen Grassmuck's analysis of administrators' reasons for placing faculty in lecture courses, 1/31/90. Arthur M. Cohen in *Shaping of American Higher Education: The Emergence and Growth of the Contemporary System* (San Francisco, 1998) explained the "$15,000 or more per class taught by a full-time professor," p. 347. Ernest Boyer in *College* (op. cit.) quoted undergraduates on classes with "more than one hundred students enrolled," p. 145; Rutgers professor Michael Moffat noted "classes of 300 and 400 were quite common," p. 292; University of Illinois political science professor Robert Weissberg discussed his class sizes and his "lounge act" in the *Chicago Tribune* (op. cit.), 5/21/92; that newspaper also reported that "students find themselves in lecture halls seating 1,200," 5/21/92; and quoted U of I student Dan Lillig on the mechanical engineering professor who "faced the blackboard the entire time," 6/23/92. The interview with the Ohio State student took place in Columbus, Ohio, 6/6/88, while I was doing research for *College Sports Inc.*; the interviewee began complaining on tape about his undergraduate courses.

Indiana University student George David related the story of the professors and the overhead transparencies, 11/14/94. Anne Matthews in *Bright College Years* (op. cit.) quoted the student remarks, and discussed the evaluations, pp. 198–99. The cross-country survey of the *Insider's Guide to the Colleges* is from the 1999 edition. Many studies contrast "lecture/discussion classes" with "active learning" situations; a classic work, still valid, is *Involvement in Learning: Realizing the Potential of American Higher Education*, National Institute for Education (Washington, D.C., 1984).

Randolph H. Weingartner in *Undergraduate Education* (op. cit.) included the study that "found lecturing to be the mode of instruction of" most faculty, p. 102. The day that I wrote this footnote, I passed by a seminar room at Indiana University and, through the open door, I saw a professor standing at a lectern, lecturing four students! Mary Beth Marklein reported on the study that calculated the number of questions from students per classroom hour in *USA Today*, 10/9/90. An undergraduate at the University of Iowa remarked that "lectures frustrate me" in an interview in Iowa City, 10/19/99.

The Carnegie Foundation has tracked faculty attitudes toward students for many decades: Ernest Boyer in *College* discussed some of their findings, pp. 140–45; and individual universities, including my own, have discovered similar faculty complaints over the years. The interview with the University of Texas (Austin) junior occurred in the student union, 11/21/98. Ernest Boyer in *College* summed up, "If faculty and students do not see themselves as having important business to do together," p. 141. A comment as powerful as Boyer's came in *What Matters in College: Four Critical Years Revisited* by Alexander Astin (San Francisco, 1993), p. 419. Astin, a UCLA professor, has conducted the most extensive polling of undergraduates ever undertaken; he concluded that "the net result of these trends [emphasis on research, de-emphasis on teaching undergraduates] is a large physical and psychological distance between the research university faculty and their undergraduate students." The latter feel that they are "not regarded as important enough to merit the personal attention of the university community's most esteemed members: the faculty. No wonder, then, that student satisfaction with faculty is lower in the public university than in any other kind of institution."

9: New Siwash in Red Ink

Arthur Levine's comments came in an op-ed piece for the *Chronicle of Higher Education*, "Higher Education's New Status as a Mature Industry," 1/31/97, A48. *USA Today* did a good job of tracking the escalating costs in higher education and printing the comments of the corporate critics (it did not explain the main reason for the costs—Upward Drift): see Mary Beth Marklein's article on the costs, 2/5/97; Jon C. Straus's op-ed piece on the same subject, 5/17/97; and the editorial complaining about the costs, 3/5/98. All of these pieces provided excellent and accurate statistics, and I have used them in the text; the Marklein piece noted the increase in research expenses of "157% between 1981 and 1995," and the item about George Mason University; and the Straus one, "bureaucratic bloat." Nancy J. Brucker wrote about "50 percent of their time to fund-raising," and "States now typically supply," in the *Washington Post*, 2/22/98. She also noted that when the job performance of administrators is reviewed, they are "graded on their fund-raising ability, and those who won't do it, or don't do it well, don't get promoted"; indeed, some get fired.

Christopher J. Lucas in *American Higher Education* (op. cit.) wrote about the history of state universities and their late-twentieth-century predicament, chapters 5 through 7; and he discussed the topic in his *Crisis* (op. cit.), pp. 110f. From a market point of view, raising tuition made some sense, but in terms of higher-education history—public universities were established to allow bright students within the state to attend, regardless of their economic status—raising tuition changed the nature of many student bodies, particularly at residential campuses, with poor students increasingly priced out of the school and relegated to urban institutions and community colleges. Sara Hebel of the *Chronicle of Higher Education* wrote that the Clinton administration's tax credits for tuition were not helping competent but poor students enter and stay in four-year universities, 10/22/99.

Patrick Healy of the *Chronicle of Higher Education* reported the prediction by Harold A. Hovey of State Policy Resources Inc. on the decline in "state spending on higher education" in the twenty-first century, 7/27/99; in the article, David Breneman, a high official at the University of Virginia, seconded this prediction: "The basic message is a sobering one—we're acting like everything's just wonderful right now [during the current prosperity] and all the problems are solved for higher education," but we're living in a fool's paradise. Lisa Guernsey of the *Chronicle of Higher Education* reported the U.S. General Accounting Office's figures on the 234 percent increase in tuition fees of four-year public universities, 9/6/96. *Time* magazine did a cover story on the escalating costs in higher education, 3/17/97, and discussed the University of Pennsylvania numbers, as well as the "Chivas Regal effect." No doubt, that effect has transmuted into the "Glenlivet effect," and keeps changing names as tuition and the cost of rare brands of Scotch whiskey escalate.

Financial World, 3/15/94, carried the report by Katherine Barrett and Richard Greene on the rise in tuition versus educational quality. Just as the media loves and focuses on the "horse race" aspect of politics, it does the same with the "admissions competition." In a typical example, the front-page feature article in *USA Today*, 4/16/96, by Kavita Varma, headlined "Top Colleges Reject Top Kids," and subheaded, "More students than ever are turned away/Better than 1500 on the SAT is no guarantee of an Ivy League education." Nowhere in the feature article is there a discussion of the lack of selectivity of the colleges and universities beyond the Ivy League. In its 1998 college issue, *U.S. News*, in a prominent place at the front of the "How to Apply" section, listed some important statistics, including, "Schools that accept over 90 percent—205." Yet most readers ignored this reality.

Gordon C. Winston wrote about "*prestige maximization* in an article for *Change* magazine, "The Decline in Undergraduate Teaching: Moral Failure of Market Pressure" (September/October, 1994) pp. 9–14. The quotes from *U.S. News* about its criteria for rating universities are in the 2000 edition; the comments of Angela Browne-Miller, California higher-education expert, about "students graduating who cannot write a business letter," were in her book, *Shameful Admissions: The Losing Battle to Serve Everyone in Our Universities* (San Francisco, 1996), p. 12. Rudolph H. Weingartner in *Undergraduate Education* (op. cit.) complained about the student concept of "*having been* to college . . . [as] the important" thing," pp. 126–27. The Boyer Commission's *Reinventing Undergraduate Education* (op. cit.), remarked about "undergraduate programs as sideshows to the main event," p. 37. The male senior at Ohio State put his remarks in the P.S. section of the survey form for this book on the web, 8/12/99.

10: Student Mix and Match

In the mid-1990s, in my advanced expository writing classes at Indiana University, Blooming-ton, I used Clark and Trow's essay (op. cit.) as the basis of a writing assignment. I asked students to read the essay carefully, and then to respond to the following question: "In what ways, if any, do Clark and Trow's four student subcultures apply to current undergraduate life at Indiana University, Bloomington? Feel free to illustrate your argument with personal examples—however, be sure to focus on the question, and do not write a memoir of your college experiences." This intentionally open-ended assignment received a variety of responses and I quote from some of them in this chapter. Because the students in this class were typical IU under-graduates, I believe that their responses reflected the opinions of many students at their school and at similar universities across the country. However, I claim only anecdotal, not scientific, validity for these responses. Finally, for obvious reasons, I cannot use the students' names but, if they read their comments here, I wish to thank them, as well as all of the other students who wrote such good and thoughtful essays on this assignment over the years.

A number of historians and sociologists noticed that the campus turmoil of the 1960s broke down the barriers between student subcultures, often unifying undergraduates from various groups against the administration or the national government. Helen Lefkovitz-Horowitz (op. cit.) remarked that "the boundaries between groups became more permeable," and this continued in subsequent decades, p. 290. Patrick T. Terenzini and Ernest T. Pascarella remarked on this phenomenon in their late-1970s article on Clark and Trow's subcultures (op. cit.), pp. 245–46. Alexander Astin's comment about "the student's peer group" is in his *What Matters in College?* (op. cit.), p. 398.

The most authoritative study on intercollegiate athletes engaging in antisocial behavior is the ongoing "National Initiation and Athletics Survey," conducted by Alfred University in up-state New York. Educational journals and the national media have printed the results of this survey, for example, *USA Today*, 8/31/99. In addition, the national media has increasingly covered specific incidents at various colleges and universities, for example, the Associated Press, 11/25/98, carried a story about a party involving North Carolina State athletic scholarship holders that resulted in a murder, and *USA Today*, 2/4/00, featured a hazing incident involving the University of Vermont hockey team.

The *Insider's Guide* (op. cit.) discusses the LSU student dress code in the 2000 edition, and an on-campus visit to Ohio State made me aware of the "Cake Lady" tradition. The question-naire for this book (op. cit.) revealed how students spent their time during the average school week; the statistic that 32 percent of male students spent more hours per week as sports fans than they did studying and doing course assignments was ascertained by comparing each re-spondent's totals for the question on studying versus the one on sports fandom. The Ohio University student attending Bristol University put his comment in the P.S. section of the web survey form, 9/10/99. Scott Edelstein's remarks are in his book, *The Truth about College: How to Survive and Succeed as a Student in the Nineties* (New York, 1991), p. 103.

Lou Harris announced the results of his polling in a talk to the National Alliance for College Athletics Reform at Drake University, 10/22/99; he also supplied the audience with a handout of his results. The Boyer Commission's comment, "At many universities, research faculty and undergraduate students do not expect to interact with each other" is in *Reinventing Under-graduate Education* (op. cit.), p. 9. A good example of undergraduate contempt for professors was provided by Chris Edwards, a student columnist for the *Indiana [University] Daily Student* newspaper on 10/18/99: "In small-town Indiana the guys who stagger around town in cheap suits and blather incoherently about things that no one cares about are called town drunks. Here [at Indiana University] we call them professors."

William Tam's letter appeared in the *Indiana [University] Daily Student* on 3/28/95; *Mea culpa*—as a faculty member at IU, I did not attend this university-wide Founder's Day ceremony. I cannot remember what I did during that time period; however, I did attend my department's Founder's Day ceremony held later that day. *U Magazine* reprinted the cartoon entitled "Uni-versity X" by James Lasser of the University of Michigan in the 3/96 issue.

The *Princeton Review*'s explanation of its rankings are from its website: www.review.com/

college; it offers a brief explanation of its methodology at the front of each edition but provides a much more complete one on its website. Julie Mandelbaum, guidebooks editor of the *Princeton Review*, provided me with a copy of every set of rankings for every year of the guidebook's existence, and also explained how some of the categories have mutated during the past decade. In terms of the "Party school" list, although the big-time college sports schools have dominated it over the years, some minor Division I institutions and some not in that division have appeared on it: in 1999, SUNY-Albany headed it, but was followed by major athletic powers, and in 2000, California State at Sonoma snuck on. Their presence seemed more anomalous than trend-like, although the University of Rhode Island's high ranking in 1996 heralded its debut in big-time basketball.

The *Princeton Review*'s comments on Rice University appeared in its 1999 edition. Rice was thoroughly researched for this book, including extensive on-campus visits in November 1995, August 1997, November 1998, and June 1999. Christopher J. Lucas commented that "students do not need to be talked 'at' " in lectures in *American Higher Education* (op. cit.), p. 293; he titled this section of his book "Neglect of Undergraduate Education." In addition to the big-time college sports schools on the *Princeton Review*'s negative academic lists, other institutions made the top twenty in recent years: some of the military academies, probably because of their relentless lecturing; a number of historically black institutions, again probably because of their historic commitment to lecturing; and Canadian schools like the University of Toronto and McGill—again, these institutions feature massive lecture classes, and very few small discussion ones. Even the exceptions to the big-time college sports/beer-and-circus rule prove that lecturing deadens education.

11: *The Faculty/Student Nonaggression Pact*

Anne Matthews's comment on the "mutual nonaggression pact" is in *Bright College Years* (op. cit.), p. 206; Arthur Levine's "tacit agreement" is in his book, *When Hope and Fear Collide: A Portrait of Today's College Student* (San Francisco, 1998); and Dorothy Puch's remark came in the *Chicago Tribune*'s series on higher education (op. cit.), 6/23/92. The Boyer Commission report *Reinventing Undergraduate Education* outlined many of the maladies discussed in this chapter, and also provided the quotes beginning, "Ironically, the first years of university studies," p. 29.

In doing research for this book on the topic of class size for introductory and/or freshmen courses, I was amazed at how schools, particularly public universities, stonewalled on this subject. Psychology departments seemed especially sensitive, and even the one at my university was reluctant to divulge class sizes. However, for the spring semester 2000, the numbers appear to be 255 students enrolled in the smallest lecture class and 377 in the largest; also department chair Joseph E. Steinmetz acknowledged that the department employs an adjunct lecturer—not a regular faculty member—to teach "one section of P101 in the fall [semester] and one section of P102 in the spring to about 450 students [for each section] using a lecture hall," 11/29/99. To be fair to the IU psychology department, nationally ranked for its research, its large introductory lecture courses are the norm across the country, not an IU aberration. In addition, this department, like an increasing number of others, uses unpaid undergraduate students as teaching assistants to lead discussion sections; Ms. Holly Welker, a student at Indiana University, described her experiences as a UTA (undergraduate teaching assistant) in sociology, and the experiences of some of her friends as psychology UTAs, 3/23/00. The psychology professor who remarked, "That's the whole idea," explained: "Going public with my comments would do me zero good. I benefit from the current system and do not want it changed."

The University of Missouri (Columbia) undergraduate filled in the P.S. section of the questionnaire on the web (op. cit.), 9/17/99. The 2000 edition of the *Insider's Guide to the Colleges* had the comments on Ol' Mizzou quoted in the text here, as well as the 90 percent figure for this school's acceptance rate. Christopher J. Lucas wrote about "Gigantism" in *American Higher Education* (op. cit.), p. 289; Anne Matthews (op. cit.) quoted the "anti-'Cheers' " remark, p. 51; and the Ohio State female wrote her comments on a hard copy of the questionnaire filled out on the OSU campus, 11/17/98.

The Indiana University survey of student attitudes, "Senior Satisfaction Study," was published by the IU Office of Institutional Research, 1/20/99; I am indebted to Deb Olson of that office for a copy of the survey. Emily Chui, a columnist for the *Indiana Daily Student,* wrote about staying awake in class, 3/6/98. Folklorist Simon Bronner (op. cit.) studied the desktop carvings, p. 203. Amy Webb published her column on student attendance in the *Indiana Daily Student,* 1/20/97. *U Magazine*'s article, "WHAT ME STUDY?" appeared 9/94 (no author given); and the *Chicago Tribune* discussed the study guides, 6/21/92. Student newspapers often discuss test files and test banks; Christopher Smith wrote a revealing article about the subject for the Texas Christian University paper, *The Skiff,* 10/1/07; and Pauline Vu of the UCLA *Daily Bruin* explained how exams are stolen from examination rooms, 1/14/99. The Purdue undergraduate put his comments on the web questionnaire for this book (op. cit.), 6/6/99; the questionnaire asked respondents to state their cumulative GPAs, and these averaged 3.3 (out of 4)—this number is slightly above the national average.

The *Chronicle of Higher Education* headlined a long letter-to-the-editor from Syracuse University professor Frederic A. Lyman, "Education's Dirty Secret: Grade Inflation," 2/10/93, p. B3. Christopher J. Lucas in *American Higher Education* (op. cit.), chapter 6, wrote about faculty attitudes toward most undergraduates; Joseph C. Goulden in *The Best Years* (op. cit.) commented on the GI vets' scorn for traditional faculty attitudes, one ex-GI saying that if the student vets could grade the average professor, they "would give him a big red 'F' and rate him as insipid, antiquated and ineffectual," p. 79f. Arthur Levine discussed the results of his research on grade inflation in an op-ed piece, "To Deflate Grade Inflation, Simplify the System," *Chronicle of Higher Education,* 1/19/94, B3; and biology professor Rose Morgan informed the *Chronicle of Higher Education* about grade inflation in the sciences in a letter, 1/27/93.

In addition to the causes of grade inflation discussed in the text, other factors contribute to it. At some schools, instructors do not have a plus/minus option for grades, and teachers tend to bump high C students into the B range, and high B's into A's. In 1999, the faculty at the University of Maryland at College Park—a school without plus/minus grades—debated this issue, with some professors arguing that plus/minus grades would enable faculty to make greater distinctions among students in a course, and deflate grades. John Henderson, a reporter for the student newspaper, *The Diamondback,* covered the debate, 4/27/99. Unfortunately, at many schools with a plus/minus option, grade inflation has never abated.

Some critics of grade inflation also argue that fear of bad student evaluations motivate faculty to give high grades. Possibly this occurs at some schools; however, as Anne Matthews points out, page 88 in the text here, few officials ever read these evaluations, and even fewer act upon them. Moreover, student evaluations—good, bad, or indifferent—tend to be neutral items in promotion, tenure, and salary decisions. A faculty member's research is the key factor in these decisions, and student evaluations are used to confirm already-decided-upon judgments; for example, good evaluations for a good researcher adds to that person's success, and bad evaluations for a bad researcher seals failure; however, bad evaluations for a good researcher tend to be ignored, as do good teaching evaluations for a bad researcher.

Indiana University, Bloomington, introduced an interesting anti–grade inflation plan in 1998 called "Expanded Grade Context." Student transcripts now reveal, in addition to the grade for each course, the "complete distribution of all grades awarded in the class" (how many A's, B's, etc.), and various other items placing the student's specific grade within context. This tends to reveal whether the course was a "mickey" or not. Students decide whether to have the university send the expanded transcript or the standard, grades-only one to prospective employers, etc. Sarah Rupel of the *Indiana Daily Student* reported on the plan, 3/10/98; in the years since its inception, the average GPA of the student body has not declined.

The late Dennis Turner, a cinema studies professor at Wayne State University, often used the expression "The River of No Return" in the context of grading hard, referring to one of Marilyn Monroe's films and her suicide. William Cole wrote an op-ed piece, "The Perils of Grade Inflation," for the *Chronicle of Higher Education,* 1/6/93, B1. Undergraduate opinion on grade inflation is very mixed. For example, Baylor University student Paul Gibson wrote in his student newspaper, "Looking at my GPA and knowing how easy some of my classes were . . . I'm inclined" to complain about grade inflation. "Not that I didn't like getting the grades. So-called blow-off courses help revive some low grades . . . [from] more serious courses" (*The Lariat*, 3/31/99). Going into the Lexis-Nexis database with the U-Wire file (a collection of college newspapers) reveals this ambiguity from coast to coast.

12: *Cheating*

Professor Richard A. Fass wrote his comments in an essay, "Cheating and Plagiarism," in the anthology, *Ethics and Higher Education*, edited by William W. May, published by the American Council on Education (Washington, D.C., 1990), p. 180; on that page, he also commented on administrators blaming the "deficient moral standard of our students" for the cheating. Helen Lefkovitz-Horowitz (op. cit.) related the cheating at "Yale in the 1860s," p. 33; and Simon Bronner (op. cit.) discussed some of the traditional cheating methods, p. 31f.

U.S. News polled a huge sample of students and placed the results on its website, 11/13/99. Marie Miller, director of Undergraduate Affairs for the Indiana University School of Business, noted, "Cheating is so commonplace at IU that for every student caught and reprimanded, one hundred more get away with it" (*Indiana Daily Student*, 4/10/92); by all accounts, the situation became worse at this school and others like it through the 1990s. Marie Miller's comment connects to another result from the 1999 *U.S. News* poll: "Ninety percent of college kids believe cheaters 'never pay the price.'" Donald L. McCabe and Patrick Drinan wrote an op-ed piece, "Toward a Culture of Academic Integrity," for the *Chronicle of Higher Education*, 10/15/99, in which they cited the research on 13,000 undergraduates. The Michigan State sophomore left his "eye for an eye" comment on the web survey for this book, 10/10/99. Julie Farren of *USA Today* quoted Michael Moore, the author of *Cheating 101: The Benefits and Fundamentals of Earning an Easy A* (Brunswick, N.J., 1992), and Prof. Michael Moffat, 1/7/92.

Anthropology professor Peter Wood of Boston University saw the course lecture notes on the web as an "assault on the integrity of higher education" in *USA Today*, 9/15/99; that newspaper printed its editorial on the subject the same day. The *New York Times* tracked the topic through the fall of 1999 and into 2000, even putting an article on it by Jacques Steinberg and Edward Wyatt on the front page of the Sunday "News of the Week in Review" section, 2/13/00: again, the main issue for faculty was whether they owned the copyrights to their lecture notes or whether their universities did; both sides saw big bucks in the e-commerce involved, and neither considered the possibility that this form of pedagogy might not succeed on the web.

University of Texas (Austin) student columnist Rhys Southan wrote his comments in the *Daily Texan*, 11/3/98; he also described the UT lecture situation of "sitting in a bolted-down chair, staring forward for endless hours." Jacques Steinberg reported on the lecture notes on the web controversy in a front-page article in the *New York Times*, 9/9/99; he quoted Mark Edmundson, an English professor at the University of Virginia; and Anthony Scimone, in a letter to the editor responding to the Steinberg article, gave his views on the new websites, 9/12/99. Kim Porter, an official at the University of North Dakota, told the student newspaper, *Dakota Student*, about cheating in lecture classes versus small upper-level courses, 3/25/99. Carolyn Kleiner and Mary Lord wrote a cover story on student cheating for *U.S. News*, 11/22/99; in it, they quoted Bob Corbett, an expert on the subject, "when students really care about learning"; Donald L. McCabe and Patrick Drinan (op. cit.) discussed the research on honor codes. The information about Rice University was gained from an on-campus visit, 6/28–30/99; the Rice student who commented on her school's honor code was Giselle Everett, 6/30/99. Mary Beth Marklein of *USA Today* wrote an excellent feature on honor codes as the solution to cheating, 1/5/00.

Professor Ronnie Hawkins of the University of Central Florida complained about "the increasing casualness" of student cheating in a letter to the *Chronicle of Higher Education*, 2/26/99; the student at the University of New Mexico left her comment on the web survey for this book, 7/17/99. Indiana University undergraduate David Vrabel created "The Only Syllabus You'll Ever Need" for the *Indiana Daily Student*, 2/7/97. The *U.S. News* cover story on cheating (op. cit.) discussed the use of alphanumeric pagers, and quoted English teacher Connie Eberly about the "thrill" of cheating. The University of Iowa student "into gambling" was interviewed on campus, 5/29/99; the student admitted that he was in debt to student bookies and did not want his parents to find out.

Alison Schneider of the *Chronicle of Higher Education* reported on the faculty reaction to student cheating, 1/22/99; she quoted Northwestern University classics professor Daniel H. Garrison and other academics on the difficulties of pursuing student plagiarists and other cheaters. Stephanie Corns, a student reporter at the University of Arizona, wrote a story about James Karge-Taylor's problems in his history of jazz course in the *Daily Wildcat*, 9/21/98; the *U.S. News* cover story on cheating (op. cit.) contained the anecdote about "Tim, a University of Arizona senior" buying a paper for his jazz lecture course. *U.S. News* did not identify the course as Prof. Karge-Taylor's, however, the university's schedule of classes on the web disclosed that he was the only professor teaching this course, and so probably Tim was in it. David Plotz of *Rolling Stone* discovered the flaws in the anti-plagiarism search engines (10/14/99). The Indiana University professor with the note in his course syllabi is the author of this book; hopefully, the reader, like an experienced teacher, recognized the telltale stylistic signs—particularly sentences containing dashes—and overuse of such conjunctions as "however."

U.S. News commented on the academic scandal in the University of Minnesota athletic department, 11/22/99; that article also quoted sports expert Richard Lapchick stating that "in the past year alone, [he] counseled tutors and former players at six different schools to report cheating, only to have every athletic director—and one college president—investigate and deny there was a problem." The *St. Paul (MN) Pioneer Press* and the *Minneapolis (MN) Star Tribune* covered the Minnesota scandal in voluminous detail—unfortunately, the website of the former paper does not provide free access to its back issues. However, the *Tribune* does, and the reader can follow all the twists of the story there. Of particular value are the following articles: the long summary of the university's report on the scandal, 11/20/99; Jay Weiner's history of athletic scandals at the university, 11/22/99; and Chris Ison and Paul McEnroe's piece on the never-ending recruiting problems of coaches in a state without many blue-chip football and basketball players, 12/17/99. Ison and McEnroe quoted faculty member Sander Latts on "star forward Courtney James's" paper, 3/14/99, and the lack of administrative follow-up, 3/18/99. Apparently, as a result of the investigation, the president of the university, Mark Yudoff, has reprimanded some administrators and faculty members for their roles in the academic fraud but, as of March 2000, the first anniversary of the scandal, these penalties have yet to be enforced.

Ernest Boyer, the head of the Carnegie Foundation, commented on "the cynicism that stems from the abuses in athletics" in *College* (op. cit.), p. 184. The comment about Peter Warrick's involvement in a shoplifting incident came from a student at the University of Georgia, 11/19/99. IU student Andy Short suggested the survey question to probe the connections between student cheating and college sports, 2/20/94; and the *U.S. News* poll statistic of 18 percent on turning in a classmate was on the magazine website, 11/15/99. The respondents quoted at length in the text on helping the athlete cheat were a freshman female at Illinois: "I would help the athlete prepare"; a Tulane senior male intercollegiate athlete: "I'd tell him to eat shit"; a junior female at Ohio State: "It would be a total mess"; and a sophomore woman at Temple University: "No help for this pathetic moron from me."

In the ongoing debate as to whether intercollegiate athletes gain meaningful university educations, many observers note the higher graduation rates for female athletes than for their male counterparts. The reason is obvious: female athletes, less burdened by the fantasy of playing pro sports, place a higher value on their free educations and try to beat the training system to obtain them. The further away the female athlete is from a pro sports career, the higher the grad rate; as a result, women basketball players have the lowest grad rates for female athletes, and field hockey players have very high rates. Whether the female grad rates will erode as professional women's sports expands is an open question.

13: Undergraduate Education Triage: Honors Program Lifeboats

The quote from Dr. Joan Digby, editor of *Peterson's Honors Programs* (Princeton, N.J., 1997), is on p. 2 of that book; the comments about honors classes at the University of Minnesota (Twin Cities) is in the 2000 edition of the *Insider's Guide to the Colleges* (op. cit.); the description of Miami University of Ohio's honors program is in *Peterson's Honors Programs* (op. cit.), p. 203; and the comments on the University of Maryland (College Park) honors program are on the university's website, honors program section. The University of Connecticut describes its honors program in *Peterson's Honors Programs* (op. cit.), pp. 332–34; the 2000 edition of *U.S. News*'s college issue profiled the honors freshman at UConn; and the 2000 edition of the *Insider's Guide* (op. cit.) had the comments on UConn, "well known as a party school." The University of Oregon's honors program pitch is in *Peterson's Honors Programs* (op. cit.), p. 376.

Michael Hill's article about the University of Maryland honors program appeared in the *Baltimore Sun*, 2/22/99; Kate Zernike's article about the UMass (Amherst) honors program was in the *Boston Globe*, 1/6/99; Arthur M. Cohen, in *Shaping of American Higher Education*, noted that "the bright students better fit the faculty ideal," p. 222. UMass freshman Thu Mai commented on class size in the *Boston Globe*, 12/6/98; she graduated from St. Clare Academy in Boston, a school with a total student population of 200. UMass student John Goodwin complained about the school using undergraduate teaching assistants in a *Boston Globe* article by Alice Dembner, 1/20/97; UMass Psychology Department chair Melinda Novak explained her position in the same article.

UMass student Timothy Dalton wrote the *Boston Globe* about the "elitist ideology of Commonwealth College," 1/21/99; columnist Joan Vennochi of that paper argued that the UMass honors college is "about image," 1/19/99. The Boyer Commission report *Reinventing Undergraduate Education* (op. cit.) commented on how "universities take great pleasure," p. 7. The University of Texas at Austin is so large that it has a number of honors programs, some based on major fields such as business and engineering, and some interdisciplinary ones, such as Plan II. The *New York Times* discussed the new scholarships in a front-page article by Ethan Bronner, 6/21/98; and Kate Zernike of the *Boston Globe* wrote about UMass and other "second-tier schools . . . offering similar scholarships," 5/20/99. Mike Dodd of *USA Today* reported on the UMass "out-of-state applications increase," 7/17/97; the *Boston Globe* covered the UMass men's basketball GPA scandal thoroughly, including a staff article revealing each player's GPA, 10/19/94. Paul Sullivan of the *Boston Herald* reported on the snowball pelting by UMass students of nearby Amherst College and quoted the UMass student newspaper, the *Daily Collegian*, 12/13/96. Carla Haworth of the *Chronicle of Higher Education* reported on the UMass student "Save our Beer" campaign, 10/31/97.

Temple University described its honors program in *Peterson's Honors Programs* (op. cit.), pp. 305–6; the Boyer Commission report *Reinventing Undergraduate Education* (op. cit.) complained about "an advertising practice," pp. 5–6. Temple has earned the dubious distinction of being on *Princeton Review*'s list of schools with the "least happy students"—originally just "unhappy students"—for every year from 1993 to 2000—in other words, every year that the guidebook has published this list.

The University of Wisconsin at Milwaukee discussed the foundation grant for its honors program in *Peterson's Honors Programs* (op. cit.), p. 404; Richard Moll in *The Public Ivys: A Guide to America's Best Public Undergraduate Colleges and Universities* (New York, 1985), quoted the director of the honors program at the University of North Carolina (Chapel Hill) but never gave her name, p. 97. An honors program instructor at Indiana University, Bloomington, used the wrestling metaphor in an interview, 9/10/99; he asked to speak off the record because "I don't think that it's very politic at IU to publicly criticize the regular students and the lecture system." Melinda Moore was the high school senior on a college-visiting trip to the University of Illinois, Champaign-Urbana; I happened to interview her while on campus there, 11/11/98.

The *U.S. News* cover story on student cheating (op. cit.) quoted Professor Robert Corless of the University of Western Ontario on helping the "genuine learners catch fire," 11/22/99. The University of Maryland honors program brags about its faculty on its website; see the section, "What's So Special about Honors?" The honors program professor who discussed his students doing "scut work" and the one who has his students "digging into databases for references for my projects and grant applications" spoke strictly off the record; they indicated that they were violating the terms of their research grants by using students in this way, and they had no intention of, as one said, "announcing this fact publicly."

Commonwealth College at UMass boasts of its honors research opportunities on its website; see the section "Independent Study & Research." The quote about "the opportunity [for faculty] to teach bright students" in Indiana University's honors program is in *Peterson's Honors Programs* (op. cit.), pp. 154–55; it should be noted that the entrance requirements for this honors program are much less rigid than most others, and that regular students have much greater access to its courses than at any other school where I did research for this book. Unfortunately, the IU honors program has not helped regular undergraduate education at the school, but has impacted it negatively in the ways described in the text.

The description of Clemson University's Calhoun College is in *Peterson's Honors Programs* (op. cit.), pp. 78–79; the details on "Holmes Hall" are from the *Insider's Guide* (op. cit.), 2000 edition. The quote from *Peterson's Honors Programs* (op. cit.) about "centers or lounges" is on p. 3. The honors student at the University of Texas at Austin made her comment in an on-campus interview, 11/24/98; she explained her request to speak off the record: "The director of Plan I, the program I'm in, is very sensitive about the perks we receive, and would not appreciate seeing my name in your book on this topic." The comments on the University of Iowa's "Unified Program" were in *Insider's Guide* (op. cit.), 1999 edition; the interviews with the non-honors undergraduates occurred on campus, 10/21/99; the interviews with the honors student were on campus, 5/27/99; I spoke to them after they filled out the questionnaire for this book and, because of the anonymity of the survey, I did not ask their names.

A University of Maryland honors student told Michael Hill of the *Baltimore Sun* about the studying and partying habits in her honors dorm, 2/17/99. *The College Guide for Academically Talented Students* is published in Durham, N.C.; the quotes in the text about Michigan State are from the 1997 edition, p. 47; the *Insider's Guide* comments on MSU are in the 2000 edition. David Hall and Mike Hudson of the MSU student newspaper explained the history of the Munn Field riots, 8/17/98; the AP carried stories on the major MSU riot, 5/3–4/98 (no authors given); Barbara Yost of the *Arizona Republic* compared the "Right to Party" protests to those of the 1960s in a column circulated by the *Chicago Tribune* syndicate, 5/12/98; Michelle Boorstein of the *Newark Star-Ledger* detailed the effect of the "Right to Party" movement on other campuses, 5/31/98; and Gary Trudeau's *Doonesbury* comic on the movement appeared 8/16/98. Kit Lively of the *Chronicle of Higher Education* reported that Michigan State led the nation for campus alcohol violations 3/21/97 and 5/8/98 (MSU was first for two straight years); Julie L. Nicklin of that journal reported another number-one finish for MSU in this category—although the arrest total dropped somewhat and school administrators were declaring victory, 5/28/99. The AP carried the story on the death of the MSU undergraduate from an alcohol overdose, 11/7/98; and columnist Robert Lipsyte of the *New York Times* wrote about Michigan State, 4/11/99.

In doing research for the sections of this chapter on UMass (Amherst), I e-mailed questions to administrators of the school, as well as to some faculty members with whom I am acquainted. My questions were never answered. I then asked the influential professor, Andrew Zimbalist, at nearby Smith College, to help me, and he tried. All to no avail. At that point, I turned to the public record, following the adage of the great newspaperman I. F. Stone, that everything you ever want to know is on the public record; today, computer databases greatly simplify the task of finding information. The public record on UMass is full and rich—the *Boston Globe*, among other newspapers, follows the school closely. Therefore, the quotes and facts about UMass are from the public record; I have used only the most pertinent ones for this chapter, but the interested reader can find the full record on UMass in the databases, particularly Lexis-Nexis and Dow Jones.

14: Cheap Beer: The Oxygen of the Greek System

The chapter title is from a line in an article in the *New Orleans Times Picayune*, "A Drier Rush at LSU," 8/8/98; the story did not have a byline and began, "Generations of college students have made a fetish of alcohol consumption, and cheap beer is the oxygen of the Greek system." The *Animal House* review is at http://us.imdb.com. An unsigned editorial in the *Durham Herald-Sun* termed *Animal House* "a defining moment," 9/27/96; Patrick Healy in the *Chronicle of Higher Education* quoted Minnesota governor Jesse Ventura's comments about the film, 5/4/99; Lynn Franey and Diane Carroll of the *Kansas City Star* examined the party scene in their region, 9/30/97, and Mike Hendricks of that newspaper quoted the KU internal poll, 11/13/98. The *Insider's Guide* (op. cit.), 1999 edition, described the K State "Patty Murphy" party.

Linda Temple of *USA Today* did the feature on college drinking, and quoted a Cal Poly at

San Luis Obispo student about "people drinking on the porch of the president's house," as well as the University of Mississippi student about slide shows of past parties. The *Insider's Guide* (op. cit.) had the "Party, Party, Party," section in its 1999 and 2000 edition, including the story that "husbands bring their wives." The studies on alcohol consumption by Greek organization members are cited below; all of the studies that link Greeks, binge-drinking, and big-time college sports programs are discussed in the notes to chapter 16; the main citations are to *Alcoholism and Drug Abuse Week*, 11/18/96; *Last Call*, published by the Center for Science in the Public Interest (op. cit.); and the ongoing Harvard School of Public Health College Alcohol Study. Dr. Henry Wechsler runs this study and his major and most accessible statement on it is his article, "Alcohol and the American College Campus: A Report from the Harvard School of Public Health," *Change* magazine, July/August 1996, pp. 20–26, 60–61.

Simon Bronner (op. cit.) wrote about popular drinking games, p. 123. *The Complete Book of Beer Drinking Games* was written by Andy Griscom, Ben Rand, and Scott Johnston, and published in Memphis (TN); the citation for the "beery evening" and "angry letters" are on p. 11 of the 1994 edition. Many books give the "bring out that old silver goblet" verse, but folklorist Simon Bronner (op. cit.) offers the most definitive version, p. 140. The *Houston Chronicle* ran the unsigned "SIGMA DIE" article, 8/30/97; Barb Albert, the excellent education writer on the *Indianapolis Star*, did the piece on the IU student's death, 12/16/98; Claudia Kalb and John McCormick wrote the *Newsweek* cover story on college drinking, 9/21/98.

Henry Wechsler of Harvard announced his latest research on the increase in binge drinking in March 2000; Ben Gose wrote about it in the *Chronicle of Higher Education*, 3/15/00. Raymond A. Scroth described his work in an article, "Brotherhoods of Death: College Fraternities and Binge Drinking," *America*, 10/18/97, pp. 6–10. The woman at the University of Washington wrote her long P.S. to the survey on the web for this book, 8/8/99; Ben Peled, student columnist for the *Indiana [University] Daily Student*, glimpsed the non-alcoholic future at his school, 5/29/97. *Last Call*, the Center for Science in the Public Interest booklet (op. cit.), has the "Binge drinking is not evenly distributed" quote and the statistics following it on p. 1.

The Harvard School of Public Health College Alcohol Study run by Dr. Henry Wechsler and also the Center for Science in the Public Interest study announced the over 80 percent college student alcohol consumption rate, see *Last Call* (op. cit.), p. 1; they also wrote about High Binge and Low Binge schools, and the higher rate of bingeing among Greeks than non-Greeks, and at universities with big-time intercollegiate athletics programs throughout their work. Because only a small percentage of the undergraduate population totally abstains—often for religious reasons—this cohort does not provide critical information about solving the binge-drinking problem. Arthur Levine, in *When Hope and Fear Collide* (op. cit.), also wrote about the High Binge/Low Binge distinction, and quoted an unnamed dean at the University of Colorado at Boulder, p. 107.

In 1997, various studies put the college student alcohol consumption cost at $55 million a year, including fifty-five six-packs per student; see Scott Baldauf's article on this in the *Christian Science Monitor*, 10/2/97, and Joanna Coles in the *Guardian* of London, England, 9/13/97. Extrapolating the rate of increase for the three years before 1996 (the year reported in the studies) to the year 2000, $6 billion and sixty six-packs is a very conservative estimate.

Ed Carson, in his article, "Purging Bingeing: Drinking, Alcohol, and College Students," *Reason* magazine, December 1995, quoted David Hanson. Many excellent academic schools also have a binge-drinking scene on the weekends; Rice University is a good example, and students love their weekends as well as their "Beer Bike" festival every spring—drinking at Rice is described in the *Insider's Guide*, 2000 edition. The AP reported a Michigan study comparing the binge-drinking habits of students versus non-students, 5/3/99; the unnamed author quoted William Sederberg, president of Ferris State University, about the implications of the study. Dr. Henry Wechsler published his comments on binge drinking by members of Greek organizations, and the difficulties in curtailing their drinking traditions in an op-ed article in the *Chronicle of Higher Education*, "Getting Serious about Eradicating Binge Drinking," 11/20/98; Leo Reisberg of that publication discussed the current state of fraternity houses and moving "the parties off-campus," 1/7/00. The interview with the University of Kentucky official took place in Lexington 11/15/99; the official requested anonymity, "Hey, the *Lexington Herald-Leader* is always quoting you [the interviewer] criticizing our athletic department. I don't mind talking to you, just don't tell anyone that I did."

The 1998 study on binge drinking by Greek leaders is "Alcohol Use in the Greek System: Follow the Leader?" by Jeffrey R. Cashin, Cheryl A. Presley, and Philip W. Meilman, *Journal of Studies on Alcohol*, January 1998, pp. 63–83. Ron French, Jodi S. Cohen, and Wendy Case wrote the story about the woman at Scorekeepers bar for the *Detroit News*, 1/4/99; Susan C. Thomson of the *St. Louis Post-Dispatch* quoted Henry Wechsler on the history of college female drinking, 10/20/97. Amy Ringel of Indiana University quoted Lynn Allen Steigerwold about the minimal female drinking in the 1950s and 1960s in an unpublished paper, "Indiana University in the Sixties," 11/7/94; the "co-ed" who disdained beer was Aneta Wharry, class of 1964 at the University of California, Berkeley, in an interview, 3/15/00.

Simon Bronner (op. cit.) discussed the effect of drinking games on women, p. 123; the story about the condoms in the Chinese restaurant is in Anne Matthews, *Bright College Years* (op. cit.), p. 50; Mike Rosen of the *Denver Post* began his story, "If the legendary Sweetheart of Sigma Chi," 9/29/95; and Arthur Levine, in *When Hope and Fear Collide*, discussed the sexual effects of binge drinking, p. 107. The fall 1999 college issue of *Rolling Stone* appeared 10/14/99, and Evan Wright wrote "Sister Act" about sorority life at Ohio State University, p. 99f. Ed Carson quoted David Hanson on "a get-out-of-jail-free card" in his article, *Reason* magazine, December 1995. An administrator at Ohio State University commented about "date-rape" in an interview on campus, 11/17/98; he asked to speak off the record because "this subject is the briar patch of university life; if I'm public with you about date rape as the school's cost of doing business, you can bet that some lawyer for an OSU date-rape victim will use it in a trial someday about the school's callousness."

The Center for Science in the Public Interest's *Last Call* (op. cit.) discussed "student vandalism"; quoted Henry Wechsler on "secondhand binge effects"; and "student willingness" to live in substance-free dorms on pp. 5–6. Matthew Decapua wrote about the false fire alarms in the UConn *Daily Campus*, 3/10/99; Rick Hampson of *USA Today* discussed the Seton Hall fire and the false-alarm problem in the dorm there, 1/20/00. Arthur Levine, in *When Hope and Fear Collide*, discussed the "secondhand alcohol–related" effects of binge drinking, pp. 107–8; John Milne of the *Boston Globe* reported on student tour guides at the University of Vermont referring to the alcohol-free dorm as "the place where the geeks live," and quoted UVM official Dennis McBee on student unwillingness to come out of the closet as non-drinkers, 4/2/95. Jennifer A. Galloway of the *Madison State Journal* quoted the *New England Journal of Medicine* estimate that 65 percent of UW undergraduates binged, and she discussed the substance-free housing at the school, 11/2/97; Meg Jones of the *Milwaukee Sentinel* wrote about the drunken student who wedged himself into a small garbage chute in Witte Hall, 11/3/97. Barb Albert of the *Indianapolis Star* reported on the speech by Myles Brand, president of Indiana University, to the fraternity group, 12/28/97; Eric Nave of the *Indiana Daily Student* reported on Alpha Sigma Phi's penalty for repeated alcohol violations, and quoted Jason Boumstein, the chapter's social chairman, 11/4/99.

Vicki Smith of the AP interviewed Robert Biggs, executive vice president of Phi Delta Theta, 10/11/98; Anne Matthews, in *Bright College Years* (op. cit.), gave the statistic that 85 percent of all non-freshmen students live off-campus, p. 67; the interview with the University of Michigan administrator occurred on campus in Ann Arbor, 12/14/98, and, for obvious reasons, he spoke off the record. Ever since its 1994 edition the *Princeton Review* has featured a "Stone-cold sober school" list, and Brigham Young has always been on it, usually in first or second place.

15: Drinking Off-Campus and Far Off-Campus (Spring Break)

Steven Girardi of the *Tampa Tribune* reported on the local college student drinking scene, 10/17/97; Eric Deegans of the *St. Petersburg Times* wrote about the day-to-day USF bar scene, 10/17/97. I distributed questionnaires on the University of South Florida campus, and interviewed some students after they filled them out, 5/21–22/98; because the survey indicates anonymous responses, I did not ask students for their names during the subsequent interviews.

Larry Olmstead of *Playboy* magazine wrote about the top college bars, October 1997, pp. 126–28; Scott Austin and Deborah Satter of *ESPN The Magazine* offered their college bar list, 7/27/98.

Chris Dufresne of the *Los Angeles Times* traveled around the country, 9/26/96; *U Magazine* wrote about the "most puked-upon stretch of concrete in the United States," December 1996; Plott Brice of the *Atlanta Constitution* quoted Carole Middlebrooks of the University of Georgia health service about the "52 businesses," 10/4/97; the 2000 edition of the *Insider's Guide* had the "campus mascot" as "a drunk person." The 2000 Georgia-Florida football game was held in Jacksonville, Florida, but most tailgaters at "The World's Outdoor Cocktail Party" were students and alumni of UGA and UF.

UConn student Amy J. Miller wrote the article for the *Daily Campus* about drinking at that school, 2/3/99; Jennifer Hanson wrote *The Real Freshmen Handbook* (Boston, 1996), and the section, "How to Get a Fake ID," is on p. 164. The Internet firms selling fake IDs claim that these are strictly "novelty items," similar to fake newspaper headlines involving one's brother marrying Julia Roberts, etc. This legal dodge parallels the one used by the companies selling recycled term papers—they claim that the latter are not to be submitted as one's own work, but used only as "study guides."

Benita Y. Williams of the *Kansas City Star* quoted Ashley Udden of the KU Panhellenic Association, 11/13/97; the bar manager in East Lansing, Michigan, spoke off the record for obvious reasons, 12/16/98; and the *Columbus Dispatch* published the story, "CASE AGAINST BEER VENDOR," 5/1/99, and "NO ID NEEDED," 4/27/99, no reporters given for either story. The Center for Science in the Public Interest's *Last Call* (op. cit.) provided an overview of the last decades of campus drinking and discussed "the campus drinking environment," pp. 2–4. The AP carried the Abercrombie & Fitch catalog story, 7/25/98, and Richard Berman of the *Louisville Courier-Journal* did a follow-up on the criticism of the catalog, 7/15/98. However, this was hardly an idiosyncratic corporate gaffe; subscribers to *Sports Illustrated* recently received an advertising catalog from a company called Tailgate Clothing, selling college clothing paraphernalia, including their "trademark" T-shirt, "Join the Party." Their logo closely resembles the Miller Beer Company's famous logo.

The bar manager in Iowa City, Iowa, spoke off the record on 5/28/98; I must thank Abby Sutton, the manager of Mother Bears in Bloomington, Indiana, and a former student, for explaining the college bar scene to me, 11/27/99, and I have used her insights in this section of the chapter. "Lose Those Midweek Blues" was an ad for a local nightclub in the *Indiana Daily Student*, 9/18/97; the "MIND ERASER" was an ad for a local bar in the *Auburn [University] Plainsman*, 3/7/96; and "Kilroy's on Kirkwood" advertised in the *Bloomington ADD [sic] SHEET*, 11/10/99.

Bruce Horovitz wrote about the corporate tie-in to Spring Break 1995 in *USA Today*, 3/22/95; and Jayne Clark wrote about Spring Break 1999 for that newspaper, 3/5/99; using the numbers in their stories and projecting them to 2000 prompts the numbers in the text for that year. Many *Rolling Stone* staff writers did its guide to "Spring Break 1999" section, and gave an overview of the history as well as the current scene at various popular destinations, 3/4/99, pp. 61–74.

The senior woman at Ohio State explained her Spring Break plans in an interview after she filled out the questionnaire for this book on campus, 11/17/98; the *Indiana Daily Student* published Gretel Hakanson's article about the Grateful Dead fans, and Kaylene Riemen's "Tanning Salons Work Overtime" in its "Spring Break Special Edition," 3/3/92. The Iowa State woman filled out the questionnaire and did an interview in Des Moines, Iowa, on the Drake University campus (where she was visiting), on 10/23/99; the University of Maryland honors student, a senior male, did the questionnaire and interview on campus in College Park, 2/16/99. The *Indiana Daily Student* ran Jill Prosi's article, "Start Working Out Now" in its "Spring Break Guide 1998," 1/15/98.

The *Rolling Stone* "Spring Break 1999" guide (op. cit.) quoted the Florida bartender, p. 73, and that edition also had the T-shirts from Mazatlan, p. 68. The Penn State senior male wrote his comments in the P.S. section of the web survey, 6/12/99. *USA Today* reporter Edna Gundersen covered Woodstock 1999, and quoted organizer John Scher about the scene, 7/26/99;

the next day in that newspaper, Cesar G. Soriano and Bruce Harding described the end of the festival in terms of the "Right to Party" riots at Michigan State and Ohio University.

16: Party Round the Team

James Naughton of the *Chronicle of Higher Education* covered the 1998 NCAA meeting, and quoted and paraphrased Donna Shalala's comments, 1/23/1998. The university president who criticized Donna Shalala heads a Division III school in Wisconsin and made his remarks in a phone interview, 9/13/99; he asked to speak off the record because "my school deals with her Department of Health and Human Services frequently, and I do not want to start any trouble in any way, shape, or form with them." In this article, Naughton quoted Thomas C. Hansen, commissioner of the Pac-10 conference; Naughton later described the NCAA meeting in an interview in Des Moines, Iowa, 10/23/99. The Furman Bisher article appeared in the *Atlanta Constitution*, 1/14/98.

James Naughton of the *Chronicle of Higher Education* wrote a feature article on the topic of college sports and the connections to beer advertising money for his journal, 1/9/98. In it he quoted Jeff Becker, a beer industry executive, on "the best audience"; he referred to the Baylor and Brigham Young bans; and quoted Elise Lenox, Stanford University director of alcohol abuse prevention. *USA Today* described the Superdome party scene, 1/5/00 (no author given).

Over the years, a number of NCAA officials, notably former executive director Dick Schultz, have attempted to distance college sports from alcohol beverage advertising. They had some minor successes, for example, reducing the percentage of alcohol beverage advertising in the programs and scorecards for NCAA tourneys; however, in the many years since Schultz's departure from the NCAA, his successor, Cedric Dempsey, has shown minimal interest in this policy, and has pointed out that the initiative must come as much from the conferences and schools—because they sign many TV and radio broadcast contracts—as from the NCAA. Checkmate. Stalemate. As an associate athletic director of Wake Forest University (at one time, a strict Baptist school) told Jim Naughton of the *Chronicle of Higher Education* (op. cit.), "Because the beer industry is perhaps the biggest commercial supporter of college athletics, the development of restrictions [on beer ads] is unlikely." And during the NCAA's premier event, March Madness, CBS-TV includes many beer ads.

The Indiana University administrator spoke off the record, 4/20/99; Charles Bullard of the *Des Moines Register* wrote about UI's leadership in "a national effort," 10/8/96; he quoted Mary Sue Coleman, and the statistics on national and UI binge drinking, 9/11/98. Marilyn Aguirre-Molina was the spokesperson for the Robert Wood Johnson Foundation, and mentioned "the profile of schools with drinking problems" in an article in *Alcoholism and Drug Abuse Week*, 11/18/96 (no reporter named). Henry L. Davis, the medical reporter for the *Buffalo News* summed up the research on "highest-risk campuses," 10/5/97. The *Insider's Guide* reported on drinking at Iowa in its 1999 edition but significantly toned down the comments in 2000. The *Des Moines Register* discussed UI's order for Greek units "to turn off the tap," 6/18/97 (no reporter given); and Nathan Hill of that newspaper reported on the alcohol-free tailgate parties, 9/5/99. The AP carried the story on UI's rejecting Miller Beer's offer, 7/30/99 (no reporter given); and Andrew T. Dawson of the student newspaper *Daily Iowan* examined the Stepping Up program, 4/12/00. In this article, the results of the most recent "study of nearly 1,500 UI students revealed that 71 percent meet the criteria for binge drinking," according to UI psychology professor Peter Nathan, and "There has been virtually no change in UI's binge-drinking rate." This number is somewhat higher than the almost 64 percent recorded by the Harvard School of Public Health researchers at UI, and indicates the full extent of the problem. The quotes from UI students are from the 4/12/00 article in the *Daily Iowan*, and from articles in that paper the previous and following days.

Joel Eskovitz offered his comments, 2/17/00. Jennifer Cassell of the *Des Moines Register* gave the liquor license number, 9/21/97, and Evelyn Lauer of that paper discussed the laissez-faire attitude of many residents in the surrounding communities, 4/28/98. Mary Sue Coleman acknowledged the problems with the off-campus drinking scene in an article by Jodi Wilgoren,

New York Times, 3/15/00. The interviews with the Iowa students and officials quoted in this part of the chapter took place on campus and in off-campus public places, 10/20–21/99. Shari Roan, the health writer for the *Los Angeles Times*, visited the University of Iowa and wrote about the anti–binge drinking campaign there, 10/19/98; she quoted Philip Jones, vice president for student services at UI, on the plans "to reclaim Mondays and Fridays," and sponsor cultural events and non-alcoholic parties for students. The Florida State professor explained his teaching scheduling in a phone interview, 1/10/00; he spoke off the record because, "Believe it or not, the administrators of this school are very sensitive about the number one party school image." The *Princeton Review* editorialized, "Few students are interested," in a front section, "What Did We Learn from the Survey?" in the 1995 edition; it later dropped this section but its comments are still valid.

The poll on visits by administrators and faculty to student housing began by accident, as a sort of conversational filler during interviews with college officials. When I realized that their responses gave me an important insight into contemporary university life, particularly in terms of the binge-drinking issue, I had already completed a large number of interviews with administrators and faculty, and it was too late to put the poll on any sort of regular footing. Therefore, I present my results as anecdotal evidence, but I urge other researchers to undertake a formal study of this question. I believe that their results will validate my point about the distance of university officials and faculty from undergraduate life. Finally, I want to note an exception to the above: Indiana University dean of students Richard McKaig not only frequently eats in campus housing units but sometimes stays overnight in them—not as a policeman but as a person who genuinely wants to learn about student life.

Jason Waymire of the *Atlanta Constitution* wrote about the drinking scene at Georgia Tech, 10/13/97. The *Princeton Review* 2000 commented on campus drinking policies in a front section, "About Those College Rankings"; it also discussed the law of unintended consequences and how off-campus drinking could create drunk-driving incidents. The Purdue University senior female filled out a questionnaire and did an interview on campus in West Lafayette, Ind., 6/27/99. See the preface of this book for an explanation of the methodology of the survey.

The woman at the University of Texas, Austin, did a questionnaire and interview on campus, 11/24/98; the Clemson woman also filled out a questionnaire and did an interview on campus, 4/15/99; the Oregon State sophomore woman completed a web survey form, 5/14/99; and the senior female at North Carolina State did her web form, 6/2/99. The Indiana University male senior filled out a web survey form after Jackie Tirey of the *Indiana Daily Student* discussed my work on this book, 10/1/99 (this article distributed by U-Wire prompted many respondents to the web survey). The University of Iowa males did questionnaires and interviews on campus, 10/21/99; both Ohio University males completed web surveys, 10/10/99; the Washington State senior male did his the following day; and the senior woman at the University of Illinois, Champaign-Urbana, did a questionnaire and interview on campus, 11/11/98. University of Maryland fraternity house president Rich Zeoli offered his comments on ABC-TV's *Nightline*, 5/11/98.

The Indiana University fraternity member was a former student of mine and agreed to an interview, 4/4/98; he asked to speak off the record. The Arizona State male senior filled out a web survey form, 6/17/99; I visited Arizona State University on 10/7/95 and, according to Andy Bagnato of the *Chicago Tribune*, a native son of nearby Phoenix, the athletic facilities and library have not changed in the five years since. Anne Matthews, in *Bright College Years* (op. cit.), provides a good description of Arizona State's "night campus," pp. 80–84; the *Insider's Guide* also describes the party scene there, see the late 1990s and 2000 editions. The ASU undergraduate who wrote, "Sometime in your freshmen year," filled out a web survey form, 10/1/99, and the University of Arizona in Tucson student did his, 9/21/99.

17: Rally Round the Team—As Long As It Wins and Covers the Spread

Matthew Decapua wrote his article in the UConn *Daily Campus*, 3/10/99; the Ohio State senior filled out a questionnaire and did an interview on campus, 11/17/98; the Ball State University junior filled out a web survey form, 11/12/99; I visited that university on 2/25/00, and discussions with faculty and students confirmed the validity of the BSU junior's opinion. The research of Dr. Robert Cialdini was quoted by Bob Andelman in *Why Men Watch Football*, Lafayette, La., 1993, pp. 39–40. The unhappy University of Iowa junior male filled out a web survey form, 12/13/99.

ESPN The Magazine ran the "Loser University" comment, 4/19/99, p. 26 (no author given); Nick Bakay did the mock gambling chart, 9/7/98, p. 34; the painted FSU students appeared, 12/14/98, pp. 14–15 (no author given). George David of Indiana University wrote an unpublished paper, "Indiana University Sports—Then and Now," 12/4/94; Erik Brady of *USA Today* wrote about "Fans behaving badly," 11/19/99. Tim Witosky of the *Des Moines Register*, a reporter who has covered college sports exceptionally well for many years, quoted Ted Harris, a former college athlete, on the campus betting problem; reprinted in *USA Today*, 1/13/98.

Tim Layden of *Sports Illustrated* wrote the campus gambling series, 4/3–4/10–4/17, 1995; the quote on the Juice Generation, the discussion of "23 percent of students gambled," and the betting of the Cameron Crazies came 4/3/95, pp. 70–74; former bookie William (B. J.) Jahoda commented to *SI*, 4/10/95, p. 74. The Michigan State student wrote his P.S. on the web survey form, 1/10/00; Chad Millman, a former student of mine and a contributor to the *SI* series (op. cit.), told me about the "serious betting scene" at IU in a phone conversation, 10/8/98. The University of Maryland undergraduate talked about the scene at home games after he filled out a questionnaire, 2/17/99; the ACC athletic department official spoke totally off the record, explaining, "Everyone I work with dislikes your books on college sports, and I don't want to catch flack from them for talking to you. I happen to like *College Sports Inc.* and so I'll talk to you now like I did for that book," 2/24/99. (It was easier to interview people *before* I had published a book critical of college sports, but I thank the ACC official for his time and comments.)

For a detailed history of the late-1940s and early 1950s fixes in college basketball, see *Onward to Victory* (op. cit.), part 5, "Scandal Years," pp. 285–410. I met the University of Florida student who discussed campus gambling on the University of Florida campus on 5/17/98; he filled out a questionnaire and, in the interview, he talked about betting on campus.

Robert Dorr of the *Omaha World-Herald* asked Peter Ruchman, a Las Vegas bookmaker, about the action on various college sports events, 11/15/98; this article has some of the national statistics. *USA Today* reported on the University of Michigan study, 1/12/99 (no reporter given); Tim Lowry of that paper wrote an excellent feature about on-line betting on "March Madness," 3/12/99. *Indianapolis News* sportswriter Phil Richards translated the athlete betting statistics into game situations, 5/6/99; the Big Ten athlete who predicted future college game fixes admitted that he bet on his team—"But only to win when we have a sure lock"—and requested that I not print his name, school, or the date of the interview.

Rick Morrisey wrote about Bill Saum—the single NCAA monitor of gambling activity—and quoted him on the decline of morality in America in the *Chicago Tribune*, 3/11/99. Matt O'Connor of that paper discussed the Northwestern basketball players' motives for fixing in a front-page article, 3/28/98. Robert Lipsyte of the *New York Times* commented about Northwestern University's "bet," 3/14/99; Rick Telander of the *Chicago Sun-Times* wrote many columns about the scandals, most memorably, 12/4/98 and 12/13/98; Andy Bagnato of *Chicago Tribune* wrote fewer columns on it, but his best was 3/29/98. Joanne C. Gertsner of *USA Today* visited NU in the aftermath of the scandal and wrote about its effect on the school, 12/14/98.

The unsigned editorial in the Rutgers University *Daily Targum* appeared, 3/22/99; the bookie in the Big Ten college town spoke off the record, adding, "The police know all about my operations but they sure don't want me to advertise in your book." Fredreka Schouten of *USA Today* quoted gaming industry head lobbyist Frank Fahrenkopf, 1/13/00; Gene Wojciechowski described the March Madness scene at Caesars Sports Book in *ESPN The Magazine*, 7/27/98, p. 83; and Andrew Zimbalist explained the CBS approach to the Internet in *Sports Business Journal*, 12/27/99.

Finally, if the NCAA actually managed to have gambling on college sports in Nevada made illegal and the courts upheld this legislation—two highly doubtful outcomes—the law of unintended consequences could result: illegal betting on college sports would flourish, and campus gambling would increase considerably. Dan Boykin of the State of Minnesota Tobacco, Alcohol, and Gambling Control Commission made this point in a discussion with the author on Minnesota Public Radio, 3/17/00.

18: College Sports MegaInc.

Tony Kornheiser discussed the "Six billion dollars" in *ESPN The Magazine*, 12/13/99, p. 48; Michael Hiestand wrote the *USA Today* article on the new NCAA/CBS-TV March Madness deal, 11/19/99; and Andrew Zimbalist quoted NCAA lobbyist Doris Dixon in *Unpaid Professionals* (op. cit.), p. 198. *USA Today* quoted North Carolina State athletic director Les Robinson on the ACC as a "corporate group," 1/7/00 (no reporter given); Steve Weiberg of that newspaper quoted Mike Kryzewski on the poor "marketing of our product," 2/5/99; Rudy Martzke of that paper included Jim Wheeler's comments on the BCS in a column, 12/8/99; Martzke also explained the 2000 bowl problems and he quoted TV analyst Terry Bowden on Roy Kramer's love for money, 12/31/99; and, that day, Steve Weiberg also wrote about the BCS's success. *USA Today* covers college sports more thoroughly than any other daily paper in America, and it discussed the average annual revenue of the BCS and other conferences, 12/20/99, and Michigan AD Tom Goss's admission of money lost, 11/30/99 (no reporters given on these stories); Steve Weiberg and Jack Carey did an article on the ISL's offer of a post–bowl game playoff, 1/25/00.

College Sports Inc. (op. cit.) discussed athletic department money losses in detail; see the first section, "Ol' Siwash in Red Ink," pp. 15–145, for an analysis of general and specific revenues and expenses; this book was published ten years ago and I advise current readers to multiply the numbers by ten for a sense of the contemporary scene. The exorbitant costs of women's sports programs is pure myth: even a quick glance at athletic department books reveals that spending on women's teams is far less than on men's programs; for example, frequently the women travel in university vans at minimal cost to the athletic department, whereas the men often board jets, sometimes private charters, and rack up enormous travel expenses. But the sports media rarely examines athletic department books, instead accepting the male athletic director's lame line about the "phenomenal costs of women's sports." One media exception is columnist Christine Brennan of *USA Today*; she took a shot at the myth, particularly the huge, unwarranted expenses from football, 3/9/00.

Joshua Rolnick of the *Chronicle of Higher Education* analyzed the NCAA's most recent financial report, *Revenues and Expenses of Intercollegiate Athletics Programs* (op. cit.), 10/23/98. Andrew Zimbalist (op. cit.) stated his conclusion on athletic department deficits, p. 171–72. I interviewed Howard Schein at the University of Illinois, Champaign-Urbana, 11/11/98. Wisconsin newspapers are not typical of the media coverage of college sports, and they have long listened to state auditor's concerns about waste in the UW athletic department. They never manage to end that waste but they did report on the UW Rose Bowl trip. Anthony Jewell (a former student of mine) broke the story for the AP, 10/21/99, and supplied the basic facts; the next day, he provided a breakdown of the expenses for all of the members of the traveling party; Jeff Potrykus of the *Milwaukee Journal Sentinel* got reactions from state officials on 10/22/99; and Beth A. Williams of the UW student paper, *Badger Herald*, discussed the $1.1 million deficit for 1998–99, and the projected deficit for 1999–2000. The interview with the travel manager took place in San Francisco, Calif., 12/19/99. I thank him for his time and professional expertise, and I respect his desire to stay strictly off the record; he explained, "My company does business in all parts of the country, and who knows when we'll do business with the University of Wisconsin."

The saddest bowl-game stories and the greatest losses involve schools playing in lower-tier events, far from the BCS bowls. Yet universities never refuse or complain when invited to the Obscure.com Bowl. Not only are the payouts for these games much smaller than those for the top-tier bowls, but often participating schools have to buy blocks of tickets from the bowl committees, and if they do not sell the seats, they have to swallow them, often in six-figure gulps. Of course, these schools have large traveling parties and expenses; therefore, the poor manage to become even poorer as a result of bowl-game appearances.

One small sliver of financial good news from bowl games appeared in the 1990s—but only for schools in BCS conferences. If, like Indiana University, they had mediocre football teams and rarely went to bowl games, they won the bowl game sweepstakes *by staying home*. In 1999, with Wisconsin in the Rose Bowl, and four other Big Ten teams bowling, Indiana and its losing record remained in Bloomington. But because of its conference share of the payouts from these five bowls, IU received almost $2 million, clear and free. In 2000, again staying in Bloomington, Indiana did even better, receiving almost $3 million as its share of Big Ten payouts. The bottom line is obvious: in the corrupt world of bowl-game trips, the best way to win is to spend New Year's at home.

As to the people on the gravy plane, faculty often call them, particularly professors on the Intercollegiate Athletics Committee, "jock sniffers," men and women so enchanted by the glamour of intercollegiate athletics and its coaches and athletes that they are willing to compromise their integrity, as well as the fiscal integrity of their institutions, to support big-time college sports. I wrote about this species in "Flagrant Foul," *Lingua Franca*, November-December 1993, cover article. *Academe*, the journal of the American Association of University Professors, also mocked them in an article by Richard Robinson, "Reversal of Fortune," September-October 1996, pp. 45–49. In the *Academe* piece, a "jock sniffer" brags, "As Chairman of the [Faculty] Athletic Committee, I get a parking space next to the stadium as well as free tickets for the games," and lots of other perks.

The administrator of the Sunbelt university spoke off the record; he was quoted in the introduction to this book in an interview done 7/12/97, and the comments in this chapter were in an interview, 6/18/99; I thank him again for his time and patience during these interviews. The NCAA tries to explain the association's ultra-complicated formula for distributing tournament revenue on its website; Andrew Zimbalist commented on the new CBS contract in his *Sports Business Journal* article (op. cit.); and Steve Weiberg of *USA Today* predicted "a continued migration," 11/19/99. All of the institutions that enter Division I pray for a "Cinderella" miracle—their small school going a few rounds in the tourney; the 2000 event showed the perils of this prayer: Midnight struck for almost all of the Cinderellas in the opening game when they lost and disappeared without any publicity except for a stack of athletic department bills back home as a result of joining the big-time poker game. In the text, I refer to "300-plus" schools in Division I because the number keeps moving up; as of early 2000, it is 318, but it will be higher when this book is published, and higher still in a few years.

College Sports Inc. (op. cit.), part 4, "The NCAA: The Fox in the Henhouse," pp. 309–44, explained the NCAA as a trade association for coaches and athletic directors. Ball State University is a good example of a school with problems meeting the NCAA's minimum football attendance rule: its team played so poorly in the late 1990s and drew such small crowds that the NCAA threatened to drop it from Division I-A; school officials scrambled to convince local businesses to buy blocks of seats to inflate attendance figures with "no shows"; the ludicrousness of an institution of higher education doing this is obvious. I learned the details of BSU's attendance problem during a campus visit, 2/25/00; Professor Jeff Fry was particularly helpful.

USA Today quoted University of Minnesota football coach Glen Mason, 9/24/99 (no reporter given). Andrew Zimbalist in *Unpaid Professionals* (op. cit.) discussed the recent wave of new stadiums and upgrades, pp. 133–34. Gary Mihoces of *USA Today* quoted Virginia Tech AD Jim Weaver and an unnamed former associate athletic director at Nebraska, 1/3/00. *The Kansas City Star* discovered NCAA executive director Cedric Dempsey's annual salary of $650,000, plus multiple perks, and an unsigned editorial excoriated him for it, 5/25/98.

19: *College Sports MegaInc. versus Undergraduate Education*

The college newspaper advertisement for Jimmy John's Sandwich Shops appeared in the *Indiana Daily Student*, 10/2/98; students sent in their questions and answers, and the Jimmy John company published them as the main feature in their ads. In referencing the responses to the survey questions in this chapter, I have given the dates and circumstances of answers of over a sentence in length; however, to avoid totally cluttering these notes, I have not referenced the short responses. The Clemson senior male filled out a questionnaire and articulated his "strongly agree" position in a subsequent interview on campus, 4/15/99; the University of Maryland male in the honors program filled out a questionnaire and made his comments, 2/16/99; the University of Kansas junior woman added the P.S. to her web survey form, 10/22/99; and the DePauw University student, a senior male, commented in a questionnaire and interview session on campus, 7/12/98. Reid Epstein, sports editor of the student newspaper, remarked on academics coming first at his school, 4/14/99. The freshman female at Kansas State commented on the jocks in a P.S. on her web survey, 12/22/99; and the UMass sophomore woman left her P.S. on the web survey form, 6/6/99. The cynical prediction from the FSU senior male appeared on the web survey, 12/1/99.

Gary Mihoces of *USA Today* quoted Kansas State president Jon Wefald on college sports as "the window," 1/3/00, and that article applauded K State's rise to football fame, focusing on its carrying out the formula. Welch Suggs of the *Chronicle of Higher Education* spotlighted Kansas State, 10/15/99. Kevin Allen, an alumnus of the university, commented in an e-mail, 1/22/00; he knew about the beer-and-circus thesis of this book after "reading your conclusion to *Onward to Victory* and the preview for *Beer and Circus*" in it; he subsequently gave me permission to publish his comments, and I thank him. The K State sophomore male left his comments about JUCO transfers on the web survey form, 9/12/99; the sophomore female at that school wrote about architecture on her web survey form, 1/3/00. The 2000 edition of *U.S. News* ranked K State in the third tier of national universities.

20: Who Loves the Jocks?

Edward "Moose" Krause commented on JUCO transfers in an interview, 8/9/91; for background information on this topic, see pp. 233–39 and 294–95 in *College Sports Inc.* (op. cit.). James Naughton of the *Chronicle of Higher Education* wrote about the different admissions standards for athletes and regular students at various schools, including UNC–Chapel Hill, and also supplied excellent charts to illustrate his points. The 2000 edition of *U.S. News*'s college issue put the Alabama (Tuscaloosa) acceptance rate at 94 percent. The Georgetown male junior filled out a questionnaire and did an interview on campus, 2/18/99; a Clemson senior male said, "I can't answer this question" during an interview after he filled out a questionnaire, 4/16/99.

U Magazine published the results of its survey, January/February 1997. I realize that by including Division III responses—schools without athletic scholarship athletes on campus—in my results, I weight the percentages; however, I wanted a comparison with the *U Magazine* results, and the latter included responses from students at Division III schools. Sports journalist Teri Bostian commented about the doublethink of regular undergraduates, 10/20/99. Georgetown University faculty member Ted Gup wrote about student attitudes toward a star athlete in his op-ed piece "Losses Surpass Victories, by Far, in Big-time College Sports," *Chronicle of Higher Education*, 12/18/98, A52; students at the school confirmed that they had seen Iverson with the Mercedes and the Rolex.

The Tulane female tennis player filled out a questionnaire and did an interview on campus, 6/7/98; the Boston College football player put his comments on the web survey, 8/8/99, as did the University of Texas, Austin, female distance runner, 11/14/99. The media covered Robert Smith's problems at Ohio State in detail; among the more comprehensive articles were Scott M. Reid's story in the *Atlanta Constitution*, 12/29/92, and Rock Bozich's in the *Louisville Courier-Journal*, 9/4/92. The Robert Smith case was exceptional—not many athletic scholarship winners want to be doctors or architects or anything else involving long lab or studio sessions. *Sports Illustrated* put Andy Katzenmoyer on the cover, 8/27/98, and Austin Murphy wrote about his case in detail. The *Insider's Guide* (op. cit.) said about Ohio State at this time, "If you sign up for four classes, you're lucky if you get into two of them if you don't have priority scheduling—which goes [only] to athletes and honors students," 1998 edition. Katzenmoyer told Larry Guest of the *Orlando Sentinel* that he regarded football "as a job," 8/17/98; and he explained to Tim May of the *Columbus Dispatch* how he learned the "Ohio State defensive system," 5/4/99. HBO's "Real Sports with Bryant Gumbel" took one of the few in-depth looks at the Katzenmoyer case, probing the question of athletes' vocationalism and the context of the OSU incident; the show aired 10/20/98.

Syracuse University professor David H. Bennett told Jim Naughton of the *Chronicle of Higher Education* about the "innumerable 'guts' on every campus," 7/12/96.

21: The New 3 R's

Jeffrey Turner wrote his comments in a letter to the editor of *Sports Illustrated*, 6/2/97; he worked with many schools, including Washington State University. Richard W. Moll quoted David Smith of Syracuse University in his article "The Scramble to Get the New Class: Is the Dean of Admissions Now Outside the Academy?" in *Change* magazine, March/April 1994, pp. 11–17. Anne Matthews (op. cit.) discusses "outsourcing admissions" and "bounty hunters," p. 33; Alice C. Cox wrote an excellent article on the ethics of the new college recruiting procedures, "Admission Recruiting and Selection: Some Ethical Concerns," in the anthology, *Ethics and Higher Education* (op. cit.), pp. 84–102.

U.S. *News* discussed the "pressure to win" on admissions officials in its 1994 edition. Jack Carey of *USA Today* quoted Texas Christian University athletic director Eric Hyman, 10/12/99; the *Insider's Guide* for 2000 gives the statistics on TCU's in-state percentage of undergraduates; the numbers on Rice are in U.S. *News*'s college issue for 2000. TCU was with SMU and Rice in the old Southwest Conference until that group disintegrated in the early 1990s; then the three schools joined the WAC.

The interview with the University of Kentucky professor took place on campus in Lexington, 5/14/96; he asked to speak off the record because "Administrators here get angry and vengeful toward any faculty member who speaks the truth about this place's jock school image." The NCAA has studied the dropout rate for athletes, particularly freshmen, and one of its committees actually considered making freshmen ineligible—but the idea died in the summer of 1999. Patty Pensa of the *Columbus* (Ohio) *Dispatch* wrote about this, 7/4/99; later that month, Vahe Gregorian of the *St. Louis Post-Dispatch* probed the reasons for the high freshmen athlete dropout rate and discussed "de-recruiting"—what occurs when recruited athletes encounter the reality of big-time college sports, and their problems in dealing with the "de-recruiting" process, 9/10/99. Some coaches also "fire" athletic scholarship holders, see the note in the chapter 2 notes about Tommy Tubberville, the football coach at Auburn.

The U.S. *News* college issue for 2000 discussed "Vanishing freshmen—one in four does not return for sophomore year," and how Division III schools have much higher retention rates, including for athletes, than do Big-time U's. The 1998 edition of that magazine quoted Alison Albrecht, the discus thrower at Ohio Wesleyan, about "the Division III philosophy."

College Sports Inc. (op. cit.) discussed alumni and booster donations, and the research into this topic, pp. 70–81; Andrew Zimbalist in *Unpaid Professionals* (op. cit.) updated this information, pp. 248–49. University of Notre Dame vice president Richard W. Conklin wrote his comments in his article, "The Role of Public Relations," in *The President and Fund Raising*, edited by James L. Fisher and Gary H. Quehl (New York, 1989), pp. 91–101. For a discussion of the history and role of the "Notre Dame Family" in alumni support for the university, see *Onward to Victory* (op. cit.), pp. 255–265. All the references to the "Alumni Giving" rankings in U.S. *News*' annual college issue are to the 2000 edition. The University of Minnesota (Twin Cities) alum asked to speak off the record because members of her family currently work for the university.

College Sports Inc. (op. cit.) explained "priority seating," pp. 32–34, 67–69. In the 1990s, the IRS occasionally challenged this tax scam but always backed off; the most recent challenge occurred in 1999, when it questioned a claim by an Iowa State fan to write off his luxury box in the Iowa State football stadium as a donation to higher education; see Kent Pulliam's article in the *Kansas City Star*, 5/10/99. In speaking with "development officers" at various schools while doing research for this book, I found that most complained that athletic department fundraisers competed with them for money from the same alums. But not one of these fund-raisers would go on record with complaints, explaining: "In development [fund-raising], we really stress teamwork, and we're supposed to be on the same team as the athletic department people." I believe that universities would be better served if they discussed this conflict openly. Doug Lederman of the *Chronicle of Higher Education* probed Southern Methodist University's post-scandal years, 11/25/92; the good news is that alumni donations increased significantly after university administrators convinced alums that they had control of the athletic department and the scandals would not recur.

Onward to Victory (op. cit.) discussed the Ivy League decision to pull out of big-time intercollegiate athletics, pp. 363–64, 373–74; John Thelin in *Cultivation of Ivy* (Cambridge, Mass., 1976) focused on it, pp. 30–35. John R. Gerdy in his article, "Hold That Line," in *Trusteeship* magazine warned about the coming problems in intercollegiate athletics, September/ October 1998, pp. 18–22. Incidents of trustees participating in the corruption of college sports occur regularly; *USA Today* discussed how a trustee at Dayton University had violated NCAA rules with under-the-table loans to a basketball recruit, 5/10/99 (no author given).

The president of Emory University, William M. Chace, summed up alumni giving with his comment: "Alumni donors to Emory, among the most generous in American higher education, obviously never consider our college sports program when making contributions. If anything, they are pleased that we clearly emphasize academics over athletics, and intramurals over intercollegiate athletics" (interview on campus, 4/14/99).

Conclusion: *What Should Happen versus What Probably Will Happen*

Patrick Welsh wrote his comments in *USA Today*, 1/19/99; a regular contributor to that newspaper, he also wrote a very good article on the high percentage of high school students who have limited preparation and motivation for college work, 12/18/97. Christopher Lucas in *Crisis* (op. cit.) gave the percentage of entering freshmen unprepared for college work, pp. 204–5. The Boyer Commission report, *Reinventing Undergraduate Education* (op. cit.), discussed entering freshmen unprepared for college and their need for remediation on p. 20; "Construct an Inquiry-based Freshmen Year" on that page and the previous one; "Build on the Freshmen Foundation," and "Long-term Mentorship," pp. 21–22; and "Culminate with a Capstone Experience," pp. 27–28.

Alexander Astin's comments on the GRE are in *What Matters in College?* (op. cit.), p. 199; I proposed the GRE for exiting seniors, particularly athletes, in a *New York Times* op-ed piece, 1/9/95. William Atchley's comments came in an interview (op. cit.); Gordon C. Winston wrote about *"positional good"* for *Change* magazine (op. cit.); and John Chambers, the head of Cisco Systems, offered his comments to Thomas L. Friedman of the *New York Times*, 11/17/99.

Edward "Moose" Krause commented on athletic scholarships in an interview (op. cit.); he added that at Notre Dame, "athletic scholarships have always been controlled and paid out by the Main Building . . . [specifically] by the Financial Aid Office." In *Onward to Victory* (op. cit.), see the index entry under "NCAA, athletic scholarship controversy" for the history of athletic scholarships; pp. 363–64 and pp. 373–74 for the Ivy League refusal to give them; and p. 228 for Bill Stern's quote on athletic scholarships. *USA Today* quoted NCAA official Bill Saum on "Amateurism deregulation," 3/1/00 (no reporter given); Mark Asher, one of the best reporters on college sports, wrote about Cedric Dempsey's ideas for stipends to athletes, 11/20/99; Mike McGraw, a Pulitzer Prize–winning investigative reporter, focused on the NCAA's billions and possible payments to athletes, *Kansas City Star*, 11/6/97—this article was part of that paper's brilliant series on the inner workings of the association. The *Chronicle of Higher Education* discussed the NCAA's settlement of the assistant coaches' judicial triumph, 4/30/99 (no author given). Emory University broke into *U.S. News'* Top Ten of national universities in 1998.

INDEX

ABOUT THE AUTHOR

For many years, Murray Sperber, professor of English and American Studies at Indiana University, Bloomington, has studied and written about intercollegiate athletics. With the publication of his book *College Sports Inc.: The Athletic Department vs. the University* (Henry Holt, 1990), he achieved national prominence as an expert on this topic, often discussing his work on network television and radio programs, and in major newspapers and journals such as *The New York Times* and *The Chronicle of Higher Education.*

With the 1990s publication of his two books on the history of intercollegiate athletics, *Shake Down the Thunder: The Creation of Notre Dame Football* (Henry Holt, 1993), and *Onward to Victory: The Crises That Shaped College Sports* (Henry Holt, 1998), he consolidated his reputation as a leading authority on the subject. Sperber has also worked actively for the reform of intercollegiate athletics, and currently serves as the chair of NAFCAR, the National Alliance for College Athletic Reform.

His newest book, *Beer and Circus: How Big-time College Sports Is Crippling Undergraduate Education,* extends his critique of intercollegiate athletics, and he illustrates its negative impact on all parts of the modern university, particularly on undergraduate education.

Murray Sperber has also participated in the debate on the role of college sports on his campus. His criticisms of his university's policies have attracted national attention and have propelled him into a number of major controversies. Harvey Araton of *The New York Times* recently praised Sperber for his willingness to attack "the increasingly dysfunctional college sports system" at his school and throughout the country.